Commerce and Print in the Early Reformation

The Northern World

North Europe and the Baltic c. 400–1700 AD
Peoples, Economies and Cultures

Editors

Barbara Crawford (St. Andrews)
David Kirby (London)
Jon-Vidar Sigurdsson (Oslo)
Ingvild Øye (Bergen)
Richard W. Unger (Vancouver)

VOLUME 28

Commerce and Print in the Early Reformation

By

John D. Fudge

BRILL

LEIDEN • BOSTON
2007

Cover illustration: Woodcut *'Antverpia Mercatorum Emporium'*, (1515) artist unknown. By kind permission of the Museum Plantin-Moretus/Prentenkabinet, Antwerpen: collectie prentenkabinet. © Photograph by Peter Maes

This book is printed on acid-free paper.

Library of Congress Cataloging-in-Publication Data

Fudge, John D., 1950–
    Commerce and print in the early Reformation / by John D. Fudge.
      p. cm.
    Includes bibliographical references and index.
    ISBN-13: 978-90-04-15662-3
    ISBN-10: 90-04-15662-3 (hc : alk. paper) 1. Reformation. 2. Printing—
Europe—History—16th century. 3. Christian literature—Publishing—Europe—
History—16th century. 4. Book industries and trade—Europe—History—16th
century. I. Title.

BR307.F83 2007
070.5094'09031—dc22   2006050039

ISSN 1569-1462
ISBN 978 90 04 15662 3

CONTENTS

LIST OF MAPS AND ILLUSTRATIONS

Maps

Illustrations

ABBREVIATIONS

AA	*Antwerpsche Archievenblad*
AGDB	*Archiv für Geschichte des Deutschen Buchhandels*
APM	*Altpreußische Monatsschrift*
ARG	*Archiv für Reformationsgeschichte*
BB	*Bibliotheca Bugenhagiana*, ed. G. Geisenhof
BL	British Library
CD	*Corpus Documentorum inquisitionis haereticae pravitatis Neerlandicae*, ed. P. Fredericq
CW	*The Complete Works of St. Thomas More*, ed. L.A. Schuster et al.
DCR	*Documents illustrative of the Continental Reformation*, ed. B.J. Kidd
ENT	*The First English Printed New Testament translated by William Tyndale*, ed. E. Arber
	Fox, *Acts and Monuments: The Acts and Monuments of John Fox*, ed. G. Townsend
GJB	*Gutenberg-Jahrbuch*
	Hall, *Chronicle: The Union of the Two Noble and Illustre Famelies*, ed. H. Ellis
LH	*The Letters of Sir John Hackett 1526–1534*, ed. E.F. Rogers
LP	*Letters and Papers Foreign and Domestic of the Reign of Henry VIII*, ed. J.S. Brewer and J. Gairdner
LW	*D. Martin Luthers Werke: Kritische Gesammtausgabe*
NB	*Niederdeutsche Bibliographie*, ed. C. Borchling and B. Claussen
NK	*Nederlandsche bibliographie van 1500–1540*, ed. W. Nijhoff and M.E. Kronenberg
PI	*Post-incunabula and their publishers in the Low Countries*
RB	*The Reformation and the Book*, ed. J.-F. Gilmont and K. Maag
SAA	Stadsarchief Antwerpen
SRP	*Scriptores Rerum Prussicarum*, ed. T. Hirsch et al.
STC	*A Short-Title Catalogue of Books Printed in England, Scotland, and Ireland*, second edition
TNA:PRO	The National Archives of the UK: Public Record Office
UBRG	*Urkundenbuch zur Reformationsgeschichte des Herzogthums Preußen*, ed. P. Tschackert
VD	*Verzeichnis der in deutschen Sprachbereich erscheinenen Drucke des XVI. Jahrhunderts*

PROLOGUE

The 1520s, a watershed decade of change in Christian Europe, began in many places with the condemnation and public burning of books authored by Martin Luther. By the time the decade drew to its close the schismatic consequences of the innovation that Luther initiated were irreparable. Diverse and specific criticisms of the institutional Church had evolved into doctrinal positions grounded in *sola scriptura* and *sola fide*. In turn, the elaboration of heterodox doctrines had fostered confessional novelties and divergent creeds, paving the way for the emergence of sectarian Protestantism. Whereas Luther himself continued to challenge Rome while at the same time advocating obedience to secular princely authority, others had linked their faith to a quest for radical social change. The spread of nonconformity in these early years, as well as attempts to control it were therefore crucial to all that followed.

Diffusion of Luther's views, broadly identified in Germany as the *neue Lehre* ('new learning' or 'new doctrine'), was accomplished by diverse means. Throughout Europe and the British Isles the principal modes of communication for most people were oral, ranging from animated debate or careless gossip to sermons and hymns. Beyond this, pictorial representations, in particular woodcuts, also contributed to the transmission of opinion and belief, as did the pageantry of theatre, festival, and public procession. In addition, there was the printed word. Whether perused in silence by the individual or read aloud for the benefit of attentive audiences, the substance of books and pamphlets was in turn mediated by conversation and discussion. The propagandists themselves understood this, often tailoring their work accordingly.[1]

Wide circulation of controversial ideas in general, to say nothing of religious literature in particular, ultimately depended on pre-existing networks of communication that connected diverse geographic regions. Effective diffusion further required a measure of mobility

---

[1] R.W. Scribner, "Oral Culture and the Transmission of Reformation Ideas," in *The Transmission of Ideas in the Lutheran Reformation*, ed. H. Robinson-Hammerstein (Dublin, 1989), 83–104.

for the intermediaries who would utilise these corridors: the capacity to move from place to place. The requisite channels of interregional contact—roads, coastal and deep-water shipping lanes and
inland waterways—were developed largely because of commerce.
Transcontinental trade and transport therefore provided the basic
infrastructure that permitted distribution of much more than commodities and consumer items. Recent historical scholarship draws
attention, for example, to the importance of interconnected urban
markets for the integration of material culture, particularly along the
Baltic and North Sea coasts, in regions where commercial exchange
was both vital and intensive.[2]

Notwithstanding the influence of itinerant evangelical preachers,
who made use of these channels, people with business connections
might in various ways contribute to the transmission process. Those
engaged in bilateral trade travelled and/or corresponded with associates over long distances. Like the propagandists and master printers, they were necessarily literate, often overcoming linguistic hurdles
by learning more than one language. And while merchants were
therefore generally capable of reading books, the urban settings in
which they worked offered particularly good opportunities to acquire
them. Moreover, they were practised in bringing merchandise from
producer to consumer. Books were items of trade and irrespective
of the content their production and sale were commercial enterprises.
The livelihood of printers and booksellers hinged on turning a profit,
a reality that no measure of religiosity could alter. But the propri-
etors of bookshops and printing houses were now part of an increasingly diversified mercantile economy that also included independent
publishers and non-specialists—dealers in other merchandise who
might also dabble occasionally in wholesale distribution or perhaps
invest in a printing venture. The common characteristic was that
regardless of specific function, all of these people sustained themselves through some form of business activity. They could be at once
purveyors and consumers, and potentially at least, agents of dissemination. Were they especially important in the circulation of heterodox literature? Was there collusion within and between merchant
communities and did those communities also constitute associations

[2] W. Blockmans and L. Heerma van Voss, "Urban networks and emerging states
in the North Sea and Baltic areas: a maritime culture," in *The North Sea and Culture
(1550–1800)*, ed. J. Roding and L. Heerma van Voss (Hilversum, 1996), 10–20.

of faith? And aside from the traffic in printed material, how might commercial interaction have initiated or contributed in other ways to the exchange or transmission of contentious viewpoints?

The following study investigates the spread of religious innovation and the significance of mercantile settings in that process. It begins with communication and transportation systems, and the distribution of commercial printing houses. The first chapter also examines some typical relationships between publishers, typographers, and distributors. These themes are then tied to the spread of evangelical reform within and beyond Germany, with particular attention to the production and dispersal of early polemical tracts and vernacular Scripture books. The economic and cultural integration of the Baltic and North Sea regions fostered an intellectual exchange or commerce in ideas. It also encouraged development of associations of merchants from particular places. Traders with common provenances constituted resident communities of foreigners in metropolitan centres like London, Antwerp, and Lyon. There and in other large towns, business brought individuals together in a range of settings, including trade halls. Merchants were also drawn to mercantile fairs, some of which were increasingly identified with particular items of trade, for example books at Frankfurt and Leipzig. And specialisation extended to the individual. While many professional merchants bought and sold a variety of goods, some dealt primarily or exclusively in items of one sort. Booksellers were, by definition, specialists. Investigation of inter-regional book circulation naturally raises questions about regulation. Secular and spiritual authorities resorted to various means in order to inhibit or in some instances allow dissemination of heterodoxy. They developed, utilised, and adjusted tools of censorship in response to particular concerns and circumstances. Those efforts were crucial to the overall result. There were medieval traditions of dissent and control on which to build, but the relatively new dynamic was the mass-produced book. Measures aimed at regulation were inevitable. Their implementation and, ultimately, their effectiveness would be determined according to the will of churchmen far from Rome as well as the juridical prerogatives of central, territorial, and civic governments. This, then, provides the essential context for closer examination of specific developments that in turn help explain the overall pace and direction of change.

The complexities of dissemination and control come to light in particular episodes, each a sojourn into northern Europe's merchant milieu and courts of law, both spiritual and secular. The first centres on London and the prosecution of foreigners for possession of forbidden books, drawing special attention, then, to the alleged importation of heterodoxy from Germany to England. It was a threat perceived by English authorities as both new and alien in origin. Yet it was resisted with measures designed ostensibly to contain manuscript and incunabula circulation locally or within national borders. Details of the investigation ultimately lead to an overseas trade network stretching from the English capital to ports in the eastern Baltic. Within it we encounter tides of dissent and nonconformity as well as the literature to which the accused would have been exposed: influences they were positioned to absorb and transmit. Yet as the story unfolds it becomes clear that German merchants resident in England did not subvert devotional conformity there by importing books. Nor were men from Hanse towns, where evangelical reform made early inroads, an association of faith. It is plausible that smaller sub-groups, defined in part either by their orthodoxy or preference for the *neue Lehre*, did develop within the Hanseatic fellowship. And there is little doubt that some itinerant traders, albeit more likely Englishmen than Germans, were intermediaries in the transmission of innovation from overseas. This story further suggests that very little literature by the leading continental reformers was read in England and its impact was minimal. The subtext is the degree to which change was embraced widely in Germany and the Baltic region, and the fusion there of religious dissent and social unrest.

By the later 1520s contentious books and unauthorised English New Testaments did in fact circulate illegally in England, but they were not printed there. If German merchants did not bring them into the kingdom, then who did? Where did they originate and under what circumstances? How were they distributed? Providing answers to some of these questions is another story that takes us to Europe's commercial hub, Antwerp. It focuses on the town's printing houses and international merchant community, and their links to markets outside the Low Countries. In this case the efforts of a sovereign but external authority to apprehend and prosecute expatriates illustrate a range of logistical and legal issues that came into play when one jurisdiction's interpretation of justice did not necessarily carry over to another. It therefore accentuates some of the larger concerns that shaped patterns of co-operation and international diplomacy, suggesting a principal reason why, after nearly a decade of attempts to censor subversive literature, the subsequent protracted battle to eradicate religious nonconformity could not be won. Confessional trends and interregional politics aside, the efforts to suppress propagandists and their books again bring to the fore relationships between authors, printers, and publishers. To what extent did merchant interests support dissident writers logistically or financially? What typified the relationships between propagandists and those who issued their works? The evidence does not point to authors or merchants outside the book trade financing very much of what was printed. Publishers and master printers made the important decisions and the capital investments. Book production was an entrepreneurial pursuit.

The final chapter looks at a particular book distribution network that linked the Antwerp emporium with Paris, Calais, London, Oxford, and Bristol. It draws attention to the parts played by a number of specific authors, presses, traffickers, and prosecutors. The principal context is the emergence of sectarian Protestantism on the continent and the early phases of Henry VIII's break with Rome. One of the aims is to measure the achievements of reform propagandists and their opponents towards the end of the 1520s. Another is to identify the beginning of a new phase in heresy prosecution, featuring more direct state involvement. It was a perfectly understandable shift because to this point remarkably few evangelical reformers on the continent had been silenced and the flow of suspect books into England had not been stopped. But why had suppression been ineffective? Comparisons of developments in Germany, France, England, and the Low Countries suggest some possible reasons. For England a fairly straightforward explanation emerges. Church and government authorities had relatively good intelligence about bookrunners and indeed several were caught, but the resolve to eliminate them was for various reasons not as strong as it needed to be. The network leads back to the fundamental question of whether or not merchants were greatly involved in dissembling reform propaganda. To some extent it appears they were. However, printers and publishers were still underwriting the costs and taking the financial risks. And some of them were paying authors to correct and improve texts for reprinting.

By the end of the 1520s the distribution of what may be termed major typographic centres—towns with three or more active commercial presses—had not changed appreciably. It was still very uneven and concentrated in the Low Countries, Germany, and France. Even so, with the exception of Poland and Royal Prussia, Lutheranism and its derivatives had pervaded the entire Baltic region, where presses were scarce. The new learning also affected print culture in France and Britain even though much French-language and all English-language reform literature was printed elsewhere. Authors from England and France found sanctuary and printing houses beyond their national borders. The Reformation's first decade benefited typographers and publishers in general, and especially those in Germany and the Low Countries. But precisely because the geographic distribution of continental presses remained uneven the viability of many, and ultimately the spread of reform, relied on the links provided by other sectors of mercantile commerce.

The diffusion of nonconformist literature and vernacular Scriptures is to a large degree mirrored in the records of those who would have stopped it. 'Heresy' prosecutions also illuminate numerous juridical prerogatives. But the defenders of Catholicism, and eventually of Protestantism as well, could only act in accordance with what they knew or thought they knew at any given time. Information obtained from local informants and through the interrogation of suspects was augmented with reports from agents and ambassadors operating in the shadowy world of espionage, highlighting specific concerns that ultimately shaped censorship policies. In addition to yielding the identities of dissident nonconformists, intelligence reports from England's ambassadors in the Low Countries, for example, constitute a running account of efforts to confound them.

In emphasising interrelated thematic considerations and a broad interregional context, this book is wide-ranging in a geographic sense. It is, however, confined to transalpine Europe, especially areas where German reformers had an early and lasting influence, and England. It places Britain and France together with the Low Countries in the North Sea/Atlantic region, defined not only by common seacoasts but also by centuries-old bonds of commerce and culture. It was integrated with its counterpart region to the east, one consisting of countries with Baltic shorelines: German principalities, Ducal Prussia, and territories ruled by the Teutonic Order and kings of Denmark, Sweden, and Poland. A relatively large cast of characters shares the stage. Printers and publishers, associations of merchants, and nests of authors in exile become vehicles for drawing together some of the salient strands of the northern Reformation in its formative years.

And it is through them that we glimpse some key connections between the book trade and the pervasive religious dynamic. The temporal scope has been circumscribed, though, to highlight the Reformation's pivotal first decade. It is a demarcation determined appropriately by a number of developments, among them the summoning of England's Reformation Parliament and publication of that nation's first index of prohibited books. The autumn of 1529 also marked a turning point in the Low Countries, where the latest in a long series of edicts attempted to take discretionary sentencing of heretics out of the hands of local and provincial courts. The following summer, articulation of the Augsburg Confession together with the creation of new church orders in northern towns ushered in the confessional phase of the Reformation in Germany.

The geographical range of this investigation has called for an assessment of records written in various languages. For the most part there are readily discernible modern equivalents for recurring terms, regardless of language, and their meanings have changed little or not at all over the centuries. However, one or two exceptions warrant some clarification. In sixteenth-century English usage the term 'Dutchman' could be ambiguous. A.G. Dickens observed that at least once in the York diocesan registers it is translated as *natione tutonicus*, even though most names of Dutchmen suggest Netherlanders rather than Germans. In this story also, the persons that English sources call 'Dutchmen' came from Antwerp. It may be, then, that the term was usually reserved for individuals from the Low Countries. With regard to the language of printed books, though, English speakers might use 'doch' or 'dwtch' in an almost generic sense to describe any German dialect, not necessarily Dutch or Low German (*Niederdeutsch* or *Plattdeutsch*). The simplest modern approximation would be *Deutsch* (German). Writing from Worms in 1521, the soon-to-be bishop of London, Cuthbert Tunstall, lamented the proliferation of Luther's works in the "doch tonge", by which he certainly meant German. The placard of 1529 banned New Testaments in "Frenche, Dwtche or Inglys", according to England's resident envoy in the Low Countries. His dispatches also distinguished "Dwtchland" from Holland, Zeeland, Brabant, and Flanders, thus acknowledging political rather than ethnic or linguistic boundaries.[3] Most of the Low Countries' constituent

---

[3] A.G. Dickens, *Lollards and Protestants in the Diocese of York 1509–1558* (Oxford, 1959), 17; C. Sturge, *Cuthbert Tunstal* (London, 1938), 361; *LH*, no. 36, 134.

lordships were in fact fiefs of the German or Holy Roman Empire:
the vast conglomerate of political entities that encompassed most of
German-speaking Europe. However, they were governed collectively
according to their own peculiar representative bodies and constitutional systems. The ambassador's distinction between the Habsburg
Netherlands and Germany is therefore especially relevant to this
study.

Substantial portions of the following chapters have to do with clandestine or illegal activity and attempts to enforce laws. They therefore rely to a considerable extent on evidence relating to persons
who were caught rather than those who succeeded. Hence, not every
strand of every story can lead to an obvious or satisfactory end.
Some conclusions leave little room for dispute, while others are speculative albeit plausible suggestions. By the same token, although none
is intended to be provocative for its own sake, not all interpretations
of known events are necessarily in agreement with conventional his-
toriography. The ultimate aim is to place religious controversy and
its dissemination within interregional and mercantile contexts, and
thus contribute to a better understanding of the transmission and
suppression of ideas in an age of profound religious upheaval.

Research for this study was made possible by the generous financial
support of the Social Sciences and Humanities Research Council of
Canada. The archivists and librarians at Antwerp's *Stadsarchief*, London's
Guildhall Library, the Public Record Office, and the British Library
gave expert direction regarding sources. And for helping to bring
the study to publication I thank Marcella Mulder, editor at Brill
Academic Publishers in Leiden. Several friends and colleagues
influenced and contributed to the project. Much praise and many
thanks go to Ross Nelson at Thompson Rivers University, who gra-
ciously donated his time and cartographic expertise to the creation
of the maps that accompany this narrative. I am also indebted to
Diane Purvey, who read part of the manuscript and offered valuable comments and suggestions, and to Christine Ducharme and
Brent Ducharme for technical assistance with the illustrations and
typescript. My gratitude extends as well to Richard Unger, Christopher
Friedrichs, and David Sylvester for their advice and encouragement.
Finally, thank you Jinnie Schiele and Julian Farrell. The book's completion owes much to your sensibility, genial humour, generosity,
and enduring friendship.

CHAPTER ONE

COMMERCE, BOOKS, AND DECREES

Writing from Louvain in late February 1520 northern Europe's fore-most man of letters, Desiderius Erasmus, complained at length about a recently published critique of his New Testament translation. He addressed his letter to Wolfgang Capito in Basel, several hundred kilometres away. The offending tome was authored by an Englishman, Edward Lee, and printed at the press of Gilles de Gourmont in Paris. Erasmus had anticipated its publication for some time. His brief *Apologia*, which announced a forthcoming response, likely was ready even before he had seen Lee's book. Antwerp printer Michiel Hillen van Hoochstraten issued it and the second rejoinder as well. Capito penned a supportive reply to Erasmus in mid-March. In it he identified Lee's publisher as Konrad Resch, who had commissioned the printing at his own expense and then brought some copies to Basel. Resch was a bookseller and principal Paris agent for the Basel press of Johann Froben. And Froben often printed for Erasmus. At Erasmus's request he proceeded to pair Lee's text with the responses and some related correspondence. The result was a twenty-eight-piece compilation, in print by mid-summer.[1]

Among intellectuals and theologians the feud between Erasmus and Lee attracted interest for awhile. Lee's criticisms were read in Louvain, Cologne, Basel, Wittenberg, Nürnberg, and of course in England within a few weeks of their publication. In the long run, the controversy proved little more than tangential to the fierce polemical debates of the subsequent decade. Nevertheless, the sequence of events introduces important facets of communication and the dissemination of ideas in print. A Catholic humanist and a later supporter of Luther informed each other through written correspondence.

---

[1] *The Correspondence of Erasmus*, vol. 7, trans. R.A.B. Mynors (Toronto, 1984), 215–19, 229–32, 267, 280; *The Correspondence of Wolfgang Capito*, vol. 1, ed. and trans. E. Rummel with the assistance of M. Kooistra (Toronto, 2005), 71–77, 92; *VD* E3613; *NK* 765, 782, 864. Erasmus's responses were also reprinted in Cologne and Mainz. *VD* L921, E2031.

A contentious publication precipitated a 'debate' that ultimately involved printing houses in three major typographic centres: Paris, Antwerp, and Basel. The man who initiated it was an upstart without a reputation, and yet an entrepreneur within the book trade was willing to pay for the printing. And in a short time viewpoints were exchanged and imprints disbursed over a substantial geographical area. Much of this was possible because of mercantile commerce and its transportation and communications systems, which enabled a high level of integration. Not every territory or town of commercial importance had a printing house, however interregional trade provided vital connections with those that did.

Communications and the Merchants' Domain

Although the passable roads that criss-crossed Europe's northern expanses in the early sixteenth century were relatively few in number, a web of well-travelled primary arteries sufficed to link the major urban centres. Over many decades Italian merchants in particular had organised and developed transcontinental routes, especially for cloth shipments. Maintaining agents at selected staging points, specialised firms now managed some of the commercial transport. Considerably more of it, though, was left to independent carriers. Horse-drawn wagons, many guided by drivers from Hesse and Frammersbach, trundled year round along roads connecting Antwerp and Cologne with manufacturing towns and transit hubs in upper Germany. From Basel and Augsburg they pushed onward to Lombardy and Venice by way of alpine passes.[2] Roadways in France stretched from Paris to Bordeaux in the south, east to the borders of the Empire, and north to the industrial and commercial towns of the Low Countries. The main overland route from Antwerp to Spain passed through Paris to Orleans and thence to Poitiers, Bordeaux, and Bayonne.[3] Commercial waterways were also vital, not least the

---

[2] P. Jeannin, *Merchants of the Sixteenth Century* (New York, 1972), 99; G.D. Ramsay, *The City of London in international politics at the accession of Elizabeth Tudor* (Manchester, 1975), 9–10; H. van der Wee, *The Growth of the Antwerp Market and the European Economy* (The Hague, 1963), 2: 328; *Aus Antwerpener Notariatsarchiven: Quellen zur deutschen Wirtschaftsgeschichte des 16. Jahrhunderts*, ed. J. Strieder (Berlin, 1930), xxiv–xxvii.

[3] J.A. Goris, *Étude sur les colonies marchandes méridionales à Anvers de 1488 à 1567* (New York, 1925), 137–40; E. Coornaert, *Les Français et le Commerce international à Anvers* (Paris, 1961), 2: 204ff.

Seine estuary, connecting Paris and Rouen to international maritime traffic along the Atlantic seaboard and across the Channel to England. The Channel trade was served further by England's continental foothold, the garrison and wool staple at Calais, together with French ports such as Honfleur, Dieppe, and Boulogne. There was regular traffic to the Kentish harbours of Dover, Sandwich, Faversham, and Rochester. They in turn were connected by road to London and integrated into England's busy network of coastal shipping. In favourable conditions it might take little more than a day to cross from Calais to the English coast, and from ports in the southern Low Countries only marginally longer. Shipping in the Narrow Seas was but one component of a much larger maritime network stretching the length of Europe's Atlantic shore. Biscay was nine day's sail from the Low Countries. Lisbon could be reached in as few as fifteen.[4]

In merchant circles no clear distinction was yet drawn between persons engaged exclusively in merchandising or in finance. The degree to which either one or both pursuits occupied the individual entrepreneur varied. Nevertheless, three categories delineated by Pierre Jeannin remain useful. Modest personal wealth and business enterprises that seldom involved significant collaboration distinguished members of the first cohort. Resourceful in their own right, they differed from middle-level entrepreneurs, who had more money and typically pooled their investment capital with other partners for specific or limited-term ventures. The third group constituted a veritable "business aristocracy" that combined merchandising and banking, trading in money as well as commodities. They formed multiple partnerships that were essentially companies or firms.[5]

Trade partnerships and the raising of venture capital reflect commercial diversity beyond local markets, which necessarily required communications systems. It was a longstanding practice among successful Germans and Italians to appoint agents or factors, commonly family members, to represent them in specific towns or territories—in the Low Countries, for example, or at London or Lyon. Traders living in widely separated locales also served each other as commission agents.[6] For interregional commerce, therefore, a regular

---

[4] Goris, *Étude*, 155.
[5] Jeannin, *Merchants*, 51ff.
[6] *Ibid.*, 41–44; Goris, *Étude*, 27.

exchange of correspondence was indispensable. Merchants' letters, when not entrusted to associates or servants, were routinely carried by paid couriers. Packets of correspondence were also moved from one port to another in trading ships. Service might be affected by seasonal weather and was apt to be interrupted in wartime, yet on the whole was reliable between major commercial centres. From Antwerp letters could be delivered to Amsterdam in less than a week and to Danzig in a fortnight. Between Antwerp and Cologne courier service was non-stop, according to an English agent writing in 1533, with messengers departing hourly from both towns.[7]

Riders bearing the official correspondence of governments used many of the same corridors along which merchants' goods and letters travelled. Several kingdoms, including France and Aragon had postal services, as did Italian states. Emperor Maximilian inaugurated a Habsburg system in 1490 to ensure regular communications between his Austrian seat of power and the Burgundian Low Countries. As the Habsburg territories increased so did the postal connections, under the direction of entrepreneur Jean-Baptiste de Taxis and his siblings. By the 1520s it was an imperial system providing dependable service to and from Europe's major courts: in Brussels, Paris, Innsbruck, Toledo, Granada, and Rome. Development and refinement of postal networks was not unique to western countries. Prussia's *Ämterpost*, initially established during the rule of the Teutonic Order, facilitated exchanges between state, provincial, and town officials. And the Prussian routes were linked in turn with systems in the eastern Teutonic possessions (Livonia), Germany, and Poland.[8] Interregional postal communications and the attendant dissemination of news and information relied on towns. Those that happened to be centres of national or territorial government were integral, but perhaps no more so than commercial ports and towns on inland trade routes, where business communities depended heavily on shared information. Moreover, these places typically were gateways to wider regions and more dispersed populations. The Baltic ports of Danzig and Riga

---

[7] Goris, *Étude*, 133–36; Coornaert, *Les Français*, 2: 188–95; *LP*, 6: no. 1182.

[8] *Quellen zur Geschichte des Europäischen Postwesens 1501–1806*. Thurn und Taxis-Studien 9, ed. M. Dallmeier (Kallmünz, 1977), 1: 46–65, 2: 13–33; E.-B. Körber, *Öffentlichkeiten der frühen Neuzeit: Teilnehmer, Formen, Institutionen und Entscheidungen öffentlicher Kommunikation im Herzogtum Preußen von 1525 bis 1618* (Berlin, 1998), 130–31, 137–38, 147–49, 151–52.

were two prime examples. Understandably, the content of personal letters was not limited to business and family concerns. It was apt to include information or commentary on topical issues, which recipients might choose to share willingly with others. Hence, written correspondence was *inter alia* a medium for the spread of opinions and beliefs, augmenting the transmission of ideas through print culture. In a similar sense, messages from spies and diplomatic dispatches from ambassadors were the essential means by which governments became apprised of distant political and economic developments and religious controversy. And ultimately, as theological debates began to develop it was through the exchange of letters that the main participants—traditionalists and reformers—kept each other informed.

In urban settings resident non-denizen traders typically rented houses and warehouses, and in some instances purchased them. Alternatively, they found lodging at inns, storing goods with the innkeepers. Great commercial firms, by contrast, maintained branch offices staffed by salaried employees. In Antwerp the large 'factory' operated by the Fugger merchant bankers of Augsburg consisted of a domestic residence, garden, and barns sufficient to house large inventories of goods.[9] Antwerp also provided facilities for select communities of foreigners identified by nationality or provenance. The merchants of England were given a house; one of numerous incentives aimed at attracting purveyors and buyers of English cloth. Elsewhere, though, preferential treatment of foreigners was not the norm. The protectionism enforced at nearby Bruges, formerly a magnet for international trade, confounded English cloth dealers. Baltic seaports, especially Lübeck, Danzig, and Riga also had ordinances that restricted alien traders, including peddlers. In England ancient treaties and statutes obliged the Crown to favour some non-denizen constituencies with incentives, especially lower customs rates, but municipal authorities offered no tangible concessions.

Away from the routine of artisans and small shopkeepers, much commercial activity in large towns was concentrated at sales halls. Once a defining feature of the seasonal mercantile fair, in many places they now were maintained year round. Several manufacturing towns in the Low Countries owned or leased buildings in Antwerp

---

[9] R. Ehrenberg, *Capital and Finance in the Age of the Renaissance*, trans. H.M. Lucas (London, 1928), 64–118, 133–89; Jeannin, *Merchants*, 56.

for the storage, display, and distribution of their products. To some
extent the English House at Antwerp had served the same purpose
for woollens.[10] Likewise, English wool exporters had their Staplers'
Hall in Calais. Several English ports—London, Ipswich, Boston, and
Hull—sent wool fleets to the Calais staple. By contrast, the lion's
share of textile consignments destined for the Low Countries came
via London. For manufacturers and exporters alike, the main cloth
exchange in southern England was Blackwell Hall, located in the
heart of the capital's commercial district and not far from Guildhall,
the seat of civic government. Much of England's woollen export
trade was directed to the Brabantine entrepôts of Antwerp and Bergen
op Zoom, but another important destination was Danzig in Prussia,
which in turn supplied western markets with grain and timber. There
too the affairs of large-scale interregional commerce focused on a
great hall, the *Artushof*. It fronted onto the public space of the Long
Market, principal venue for citizens' meetings and demonstrations,
and like London's Blackwell Hall, was scarcely more than a stone's
throw from the centre of municipal administration. Within the *Artushof*
several confraternities or *Banken* had evolved. One was an association of Danzig and Lübeck merchants and another brought together
men involved in the Low Countries trade. Yet another, the *Reinholdsbank*,
included numerous Danzigers and traders from Poland and other
towns in Prussia. Sometimes it admitted foreign guests as well, from
the Netherlands, England, southern Germany, and Russia. There
was also an association of shippers and ship's masters.[11] Organisations
like these were quite typical elsewhere. London had many, and the
St. George's guild in Lynn is another example. Twenty-two fraternities (*Gaffeln*) and guilds (*Zünfte*) existed in Cologne. Three *Gaffeln*,
the 'Eisenmarkt', 'Himmelreich', and 'Windek' were reserved for the
town's merchant elite. Their representation at the highest levels of
town government far surpassed that of the lesser guilds. The eastern Baltic towns of Reval, Dorpat, and Riga had brotherhoods of
bachelor merchants, the Blackheads (*Schwarzenhäupter*), whose members became eligible to enter larger trade guilds once they married.
In every case these associations performed economic and social func-

---

[10] Van der Wee, *Antwerp Market*, 2: 329.
[11] P. Simson, *Der Artushof in Danzig und seine Brüderschaften, die Banken* (Danzig, 1900),
esp. 36–44.

tions and wielded political influence in civic politics.[12] Within the greater merchant milieu they were communities in their own right, important forums not only for occupational solidarity but also for civic sociability.

Many commercial centres of interregional significance were seaports, while others were situated on navigable inland waterways. Docking facilities, whether for ocean-going ships or river craft, were of course an indispensable facet of such places. Vessels from England discharged and took on freight at Antwerp's English quay, situated towards the north of the waterfront. Numerous wharves dotted the north bank of the Thames in London. Weigh scales and cranes for loading and off-loading cargo were two common features of commercial docks, where trade stirred a range of subsidiary economic activity centred on the freighting and servicing of ships. The corollary was further extended with the transference of cargoes to inland destinations, which provided employment for porters, packers, wagon drivers, and boatmen.

The most vibrant and cosmopolitan trading centre in northern Europe was Antwerp: maritime gateway, emporium, and distribution conduit for continental commerce. Ships from many countries came directly to the town, on the Scheldt estuary. Others tied up at Arnemuiden, Vlissinge, Zierikzee, Veere, or Middelburg: out-ports in Zeeland where cargo was stockpiled or transferred to lighters for onward transport, and where large vessels could be re-freighted. The same quays served trade to and from Bergen op Zoom, forty kilometres north of Antwerp. An extensive array of goods changed hands. Italian merchants brought silks, brocades, armour, cotton, and alum. The Spanish and Portuguese offered dyes, fruits, drugs, metals, ivory from India, and spices. Goods manufactured in the Low Countries— furniture, tapestries, objects of art, and countless varieties of cloth— were available for export. Antwerp and Bergen and their out-ports were also primary transhipment points for fish, beer, metals, and forest products from Germany and Scandinavia.

Mercantile fairs or marts, each scheduled to last four weeks but typically extending to six, were held twice annually at Antwerp and

---

[12] For the Blackheads see A. Ritscher, *Reval an der Schwelle der Neuzeit: Teil 1 1510–1535* (Bonn, 1998), 207–9 and K. Deppermann, *Melchior Hoffman: Social Unrest and Apocalyptic Visions in the Age of Reformation*, trans. M. Wren and ed. B. Drewery (Edinburgh, 1987), 43.

at Bergen. Both towns were situated within the duchy of Brabant,
part of the Habsburg territorial domain. The ducal authority regulated the number and duration of fairs, but otherwise had little direct
involvement in market activity except in times of war, when food
and munitions supply was critical. Even so, the overall significance
of the fairs had waned considerably since the fifteenth century.
Virtually unrestricted trade in precious metals and specie at Antwerp
together with extensive use of bills of exchange had obviated much
of the need for ready money, giving rise to book transactions. So
while the fluid merchant populations of Bergen and Antwerp still
swelled during the seasonal marts, many foreign traders now stayed
there on a permanent or semi-permanent basis. By the early sixteenth century there were several resident colonies of them at Antwerp.
Some were formally recognised as 'nations' and accorded the freedom and protection of the town as well as other economic privileges. Italians were preponderant. Alongside their counterparts from
Portugal and Spain, the Genoese, Florentine, Lombard and Lucchese
traders each constituted a nation. The French, however, had no special status. All of the 'national' associations had administrations typically consisting of an executive hierarchy of governors and aides,
although the men of Genoa preferred to regulate themselves somewhat differently than the others, through a grand council.[13]

The English nation at Antwerp was synonymous with the Company
of Merchant Adventurers, which held a chartered monopoly of trade
to the Low Countries. All English traders doing business there, except
for wool merchants associated with the staple at Calais, were Merchant
Adventurers. Their headquarters were in Antwerp, with the English
House serving as residence for the elected governor and meeting
place for his court of assistants. It was their responsibility to ensure
compliance with Company ordinances. The Company was in essence
a cartel; its supposedly national character mitigated by the reality
that Londoners far outnumbered men from provincial towns. The
woollen cloth that the Adventurers brought across the Narrow Seas
was the most important branch of the kingdom's export trade and
an integral part of Antwerp's economy. For decades the English had

---

[13] Ehrenberg, *Capital and Finance*, 236; Goris, *Étude*, 4–6, 20–21, 71, 76; Coornaert,
Les Français, 1: 133; G. Marnef, *Antwerp in the Age of Reformation*, trans. J.C. Grayson
(Baltimore, 1998), 23–24.

benefited from economic freedoms there. Their privileges had been extended and updated, and their trade further enhanced and protected by similar formal agreements with Bergen op Zoom and Middelburg.[14] The Low Countries was now home for many Adventurers. They purchased or rented pack houses in Antwerp for storage of their merchandise. The English House itself was well on its way to becoming a commodity exchange, where transactions involving English cloth were negotiated. Payments were arranged at the monetary exchange nearby: the Bourse. Adventurers residing in the Low Countries maintained links with their suppliers in England and naturally associated with fellow expatriates and local brokers. They also came into contact with numerous German and Italian merchants, who purchased textiles for transhipment to Frankfurt and points east and south. The Germans provided the Antwerp market with raw materials and various manufactured wares. Ultimately, then, business in the Netherlands linked English overseas trade to southern and central regions of the Empire as well as ports and principalities of the north.

Also possessing 'nation' status at Antwerp were merchants of the German Hanse. Their house, known as the *Clause*, was granted initially in 1468 for use during the fairs and later expanded through purchase of adjacent property. The Hanse or 'Hanseatic League' of towns was a commercial and political alliance stretching from the lower Rhine to the distant ports of the eastern Baltic. It had come together in the thirteenth century, its membership growing subsequently to a hundred and more. Entrepreneurs from these towns controlled much of the trade, shipping, and finance of the Scandinavian kingdoms and northern German territories. They were also key contributors to the economic life of the Low Countries, a principal market for grain, fish, and bulk commodities such as flax, timber, tar, and iron. From Antwerp they sent herring, salt, dyestuffs, cloth, and sugar to northern and eastern markets. There were plenty of other Germans in Antwerp besides men of the Hanse towns. Merchants from central and southern Germany traded there too, independently or on behalf of great firms, without special privileges. As well, the

---

[14] *The Merchant Adventurers of England: Their Laws and Ordinances with Other Documents*, ed. W.E. Lingelbach (Philadelphia, 1902), 238; G. Schanz, *Englische Handelspolitik gegen Ende des Mittelalters* (Leipzig, 1881), 2: 231, 250.

Brabant emporium employed many skilled German support personnel, especially packers and freight carriers.[15]

Another cornerstone on which the Hanse's trade depended was London. Over many decades the Hanse had won and defended preferential economic freedoms in England, and from London they and their resident factors managed a lucrative import and export trade that substantially integrated the English capital into the vast European commercial network. While London bustled with economic activity of all sorts, the domain of alien merchants who came there was not nearly so open as it was at Antwerp. Protective of domestic industry and trade, Londoners were not especially welcoming to foreigners. Even so, unlike other non-denizen merchants, the Italians or Spaniards for instance, Hanse men collectively possessed their own living quarters and warehouse facilities on the Thames waterfront. For two centuries they had occupied the site known as the Steelyard, situated between Thames Street and the north bank of the river, a short distance west of London Bridge. Their proprietary right to the complex was enshrined in a treaty with the Crown. Ships from Hanse ports as well as those on the Narrow Seas routes discharged all types of imported wares at the Steelyard wharf. They were re-freighted primarily with consignments of woollen cloth destined for Hanse towns, the fairs in Brabant, and ultimately for distribution across the continent. Most of it was obtained at Blackwell Hall, where country suppliers sold directly to exporters. Notwithstanding their possession of the Steelyard, the right of access to Blackwell again made Hanse merchants uniquely privileged among non-citizens in the capital. Hundreds of Germans invested in the London trade. Hanse merchants shipped upwards of twenty thousand broadcloths each year, accounting for about one third of the port's woollen exports. From Hamburg alone some forty-two individuals had trading interests there in 1528.[16]

---

[15] C. Wehrmann, "Die Gründung des hanseatischen Hauses zu Antwerpen," *Hansische Geschichtsblätter* (1873), 77–106; D.J. Harreld, "German Merchants and their Trade in Sixteenth-Century Antwerp," in *International Trade in the Low Countries (14th–16th Centuries)*, ed. P. Stabel, B. Blondé and A. Greve (Louvain/Apeldoorn, 2000), 169–91.

[16] K. Friedland, "Hamburger Englandfahrer 1512–1557," *Zeitschrift des Vereins für Hamburgische Geschichte* 46 (1960), 1–42 and Beilage 3. For Blackwell Hall see Ramsey, *City of London*, 37–39. Cloth exports for the 1520s are listed in E.M. Carus-Wilson and O. Coleman, ed., *England's Export Trade, 1275–1547* (Oxford, 1967), 115–16.

Administration of the Steelyard was the responsibility of its secretary and elected aldermen; there were by-laws to regulate the
behaviour and business practices of its fellowship.[17] Kinship within
the merchant networks fostered trust that extended beyond simple
occupational solidarity, much as it did among the Italians. Although
they might be widely dispersed, it was not unusual for brothers and
brothers-in-law to work on behalf of common family interests. Young
sons often gained essential business experience abroad, in Antwerp
or London for example, under the guidance of one of the father's
associates before assuming responsibility for management of some
particular part of the family business. So while commercial privilege
and the Steelyard facilities combined to make Hanse men a highly
distinctive community in London, they were in every other sense
quite typical of other non-native traders.

Commercial Typography—Paris, Antwerp, and Paternoster Row

Europe's largest typographic centre north of the Alps was Paris.
Although France had several other publishing centres of regional
significance, including Poitiers, Avignon, and Toulouse, printing for
the domestic market was largely concentrated in Paris and Lyon.
The Parisian presses also printed for foreign clientele, supplying
French literature to Europe's cultured elite. They issued educational
and devotional texts as well, including the vast majority of all printed
material used by the English clergy, especially service books and breviaries. Sometimes the work was financed by English capital and
done to order for stationers in England or in partnership with them.[18]
The chief concentration of Parisian printers, binders, and vendors
was in the university quarter, in and near the rue Saint Jacques
above the Sorbonne. Simon Du Bois, Simon de Colines, Nicolas
Higman, Thielman Kerver, and Nicolas Prévost numbered among

---

[17] N. Jörn, *"With money and bloode": Der Londoner Stalhof im Spannungsfeld der englisch-
hansischen Beziehungen im 15. und 16. Jahrhundert* (Cologne, 2000), 303–89.

[18] E. Armstrong, "English purchases of printed books from the Continent
1465–1526," *English Historical Review* 94 (1979), 268–90; D. Loades, "Books and the
English Reformation prior to 1558," *RB*, 277; N. Orme, "Martin Coeffin, the First
Exeter Publisher," *The Library*, 6th series, 10 (1988), 220–30. By the beginning of
the sixteenth century about forty towns in France had established printing houses.
M. Greengrass, *The French Reformation* (Oxford, 1987), 70.

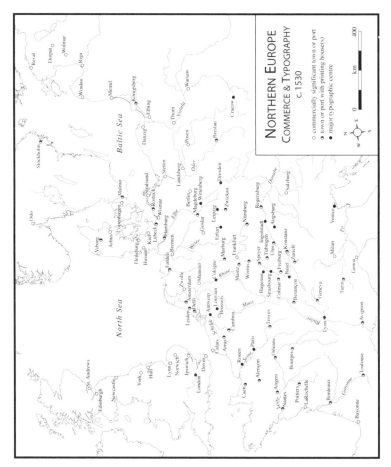

Commerce and Typography

the printers of liturgical and devotional texts. The Sorbonne had its own print works. Like other retailers, many booksellers (*libraires*) not only operated shops but also worked from stalls within or outside the Palace of Justice or on the steps of the Great Hall. Religious texts and popular literature could also be purchased in a second, smaller district associated with the trade, in the immediate vicinity of Notre Dame cathedral. Several Paris printing houses were family establishments, passing to heirs one generation after the next. It was common too for widows of booksellers and master printers to manage their husbands' businesses, whether or not sons were of age to assume the responsibility.[19] Success depended to some extent on retail sales directly to customers but increasingly on the wholesale purchase of inventory by intermediaries, some of whom commissioned print runs and were therefore publishers.

To the south, book distribution was served especially well by the printing houses and shops of Lyon, where by 1519 the sellers had formed *la Grande Compagnie des Libraires*. The town of about fifty thousand also was a banking and commercial centre of international significance, its four annual fairs integrating subsidiary markets in southern France, Spain, and especially Italy. As a result, it was home to a large community of Italian merchants and financiers. They were more numerous in Lyon than in any other place outside Italy, including Antwerp and London, to which they were connected nonetheless through trade and commercial banking. Italians owned some of Lyon's printing houses, however technical operations were left to French professionals. Commerce also linked Lyon—via Geneva—to Basel, an important university and typographic centre and a major dispersal point for trade along the Rhine. Among the most successful printing houses in Basel was Johann Froben's. Agents from the town, especially Konrad Resch and Johann Schabler (alias Wattenschnee) supplied many of the French-language imprints offered by booksellers in Lyon and Paris. Schabler himself established outlets in both centres, identified by the Basel coat of arms. A wide range of material, including controversial religious texts, could be found at the *Ecus de Bâle*.[20]

---

[19] A. Tilley, "A Paris Bookseller of the Sixteenth Century—Galliot Du Pré," *The Library*, 2nd series, 9 (1908), 36–47; A. Erdmann, *My Gracious Silence: Women in the Mirror of 16th Century Printing in Western Europe* (Luzern, 1999), 227–64.

[20] P.G. Bietenholz, *Basle and France in the Sixteenth Century* (Toronto, 1971), 25–38;

In France the early diffusion of contentious ideas in print was not accompanied by the extensive itinerant preaching that was so much a part of religious reform in Germany and Scandinavia. It relied more on the work of biblical humanists, who in turn depended on royal and episcopal patronage. Their translations of the Scriptures and their influential commentaries tended to be augmented with renditions of Lutheran works in which doctrinal essentials were articulated but specific controversies avoided.[21] The king's sister, Marguerite d'Angoulême was supportive, and some bishops—especially Briçonnet of Meaux and Sadoleto of Carpentras—worked towards diocesan reform, endeavouring to ensure regular preaching of the Gospels. Briçonnet also sponsored several humanist scholars, among them Jacques Lefèvre d'Etaples, whose scriptural commentaries were published anonymously before the hostility of Sorbonne theologians compelled him to relocate to Strasbourg.

Many printing houses served denizen consumers in the Low Countries, northern Europe's most urbanised and densely populated region. Dutch and Low German publications circulated widely there. The domestic presses catered particularly to large urban readerships. Literacy among town dwellers transcended the social hierarchy that distinguished patrician from worker. It was not uncommon for labourers and artisans to read and to acquire books. As in Germany and France printers kept some inventory for sale directly to local customers, while professional booksellers and peddlers distributed to other towns and less populated regions. Imprints brought from Italy, Paris, and the German fairs also circulated in this way. Another important factor in dissemination was the simple exchange of reading material between individuals unconnected to the commercial trade.[22]

Several Antwerp presses looked beyond the Low Countries and produced books for export, in Latin, English, French, and Danish.

Coornaert, *Les Français*, 1: 288–94. E. Droz, "Pierre de Vingle, l'imprimeur de Farel," in *Aspects de la propagande religieuse*, ed. G. Berthould et al. (Geneva, 1957), 38–78. For a survey of the printing houses of Lyon see C. Clair, *A History of European Printing* (London, 1976), 163–73.

[21] Greengrass, *French Reformation*, 9–14; F. Higman, *Lire et Découvrir: La circulation des idées au temps de la Réforme* (Geneva, 1998), 342, 534.

[22] A.G. Johnston, "Printing and the Reformation in the Low Countries, 1520–c. 1555," *RB*, 157–59, 168–75.

The Antwerp and Bergen trade fairs facilitated some of the long-distance distribution. Other conduits were the quays in Zeeland that serviced international shipping. Economic integration and book distribution also relied on road systems and inland waterways linking the southern Low Countries with the principal towns of Holland—Delft, Dordrecht, Amsterdam, and Leiden—and with German centres to the north-east.[23]

Commercial printing in the north was not insignificant. Doen Pietersoen was especially prolific in Amsterdam, issuing forty titles between 1518 and 1532. Another comparable operation was Albert Pafraet's in Deventer. Presses in Delft, Leiden, and for a time Zwolle also contributed a substantial corpus of works. However, the greatest concentration of printers was in the south. And of the eighty-two presses operating in the southern Low Countries from 1500 to 1540 sixty-six were located in Antwerp. Together they accounted for more than half of all book production in the Low Countries.[24] Antwerp's typographic industry was concentrated in the commercial heart of the town along two intersecting thoroughfares, the *Lombaerdeveste* and *Cammerstraet*. Dozens of print works, binderies, and bookshops operated within a few metres of each other. A high degree of print-related occupational continuity defined the neighbourhood. There was social cohesion as well. Skilled pressmen might work interchangeably at different houses and master printers typically began their careers as apprentices in other shops. Business relationships and personal loyalties developed among and between families involved in printing, much as they did in the rue Saint Jacques district of Paris. Individual and collective identity was reinforced through fraternal association, the St. Luke's Guild of printers and book dealers. On the one hand its members were marketplace competitors. But the demands of print culture were such that many publishing ventures were undertaken in partnership. It was also quite common for one printer simply to contract another for a specific job. Govaert van der Haeghen, who was primarily a publisher before 1530, brought work to Martin de Keyser and Christopher Ruremund. Both of them also printed for Willem Vorsterman. Antwerp printers often included

---

[23] F. Bruns and H. Weckzerka, *Hansische Handelsstrassen* (Cologne, 1967), 2: 475–518.
[24] A.A. Den Hollander, *De Nederlandse Bijbelvertalingen 1522–1545* (Nieuwkoop, 1997), 27–126.

publishing and/or retailing as part of their business. When Hendrick
Eckert van Homberch and Joannes Steels financed a work for distribution in Louvain, London, and Antwerp they chose Michiel Hillen
van Hoochstraten to print it but designated Vorsterman as the resident Antwerp retailer. Both Vorsterman and Hoochstraten issued
titles for local vendors and for publishers/booksellers in Brussels,
Gent, Zierikzee, 's-Hertogenbosch, and Amsterdam.[25]

Well over half of all books published in the Low Countries during the first four decades of the sixteenth century dealt with theology. Production of vernacular Catholic works, such as Books of
Hours, experienced a sharp decline in the 1520s, as many Antwerp
printers, including Vorsterman, Hoochstraten, Ruremund, and Martin
de Keyser, became involved in vernacular reform literature and biblical texts. They routinely appropriated German publications for translation, especially early tracts by Luther that were broadly evangelical
but non-confessional. Beginning in 1522, the attendant output of
Scripture books was extraordinary. By the mid-1540s Low Countries'
printers had issued eighty vernacular Bible editions.[26] Imperial placards and town ordinances made many translations and virtually all
reform literature unlawful. Nevertheless printers, whether motivated
by the chance of profit or commitment to evangelical reform, chose
to risk indictment. But seldom during the 1520s did they encounter
systematic enforcement of censorship laws by town regimes and
regional arms of government. Antwerp's presses emerged in the second half of the decade as vital cogs in the dissemination of contentious doctrine and Bible translations—in several vernacular languages.

There was also a typographic industry in England in the first quarter of the sixteenth century, though its development lagged behind
that of the continental printing houses. While provincial towns had
stationers and bookbinders, presses were sustained only intermittently
in York, Oxford, and Cambridge and their output was compara-
tively meagre. Most titles printed for York stationer John Gachet
came from either Rouen or Paris.[27] Many of the books read by
Oxford and Cambridge students were issued in university towns on

[25] Den Hollander, *Bijbelvertalingen*, 61–62, 68, 78, 88–89.
[26] Johnston, "Printing," 154, 170; Den Hollander, *Bijbelvertalingen*, 26–27.
[27] W.K. Sessions, *A Printer's Dozen: The First British Printing Centres to 1557* (York,
1983), 55–59; *STC* 15858–59, 16135, 16221, 16223, 16250.5, 16251.

the continent, especially Louvain and Cologne. In Cambridge John Siberch produced a modest number of educational and humanist works for the university community in the early 1520s.[28] But while his seems to have been the only press in Cambridge and short-lived at that, European university centres—Basel, Paris, Cologne, Louvain, and Leipzig—each had several. There were presses in London of course, but they were unable to satisfy growing demand across the kingdom for books of all kinds. Wynkyn de Worde, who capitalised on the commercial potential of educational material in particular, collaborated with provincial stationers to facilitate more effective marketing. The king's printer Richard Pynson, on the other hand, seems to have been content with the risk-free institutional market in London, preferring direct subventions to speculative ventures.[29] The dependence on continental presses resulted in the importation of printed material on a commercial scale. Two thirds of all books sold in England originated elsewhere. A statute dating to the reign of Richard III, intended to stimulate the book industry by attracting skilled professionals, exempted those engaged in the trade from protectionist restrictions. Until it was repealed in 1534 aliens could sell retail and English customers were not obliged to buy through the agency of a denizen vendor. Thus the sector was one in which non-denizens were significant if not dominant both as printers and purveyors. John Siberch was German by birth, as was his brother-in-law Franz Birckman, who sold books in London and Antwerp. Two more brothers-in-law, Servatius Sassen and Johann Grapheus operated printing presses in the Low Countries. Another foreigner selling books in London in the early 1520s was the Netherlander Peter Kaetz.[30]

Customs records for the late fifteenth and early sixteenth century show imports largely in the hands of professionals within the book trade sector: booksellers, binders, and printers. The noteworthy exception was the distribution of primers. Not uncommonly they were brought to London and to provincial ports by importers of other merchandise, together with consignments of inexpensive mass-produced

---

[28] O. Treptow, *John Siberch*, trans. T. Jones (Cambridge, 1970), 21–37.
[29] A.S.G. Edwards and C.M. Meale, "The Marketing of Printed Books in Late Medieval England," *The Library*, 6th series, 15 (1993), 114–24.
[30] Armstrong, "English purchases," 268–90; S.C. Roberts, *A History of the Cambridge University Press* (Cambridge, 1921), 1–14; C. Schnurmann, *Kommerz und Klüngel: Der Englandhandel Kölner Kaufleute im 16. Jahrhundert* (Göttingen, 1991), 54, 67.

wares like brushes, wool cards, combs, and shears. Merchant Adventurers, whose primary interest was in the cloth trade, seldom shipped printed books, and when they did the quantities were small. In their circles, unspecialised trade in small manufactured items and primers was considered typical of the lesser merchant.[31]

What was in effect England's national book market was situated in the metropolis of London, also the main point of entry for imports. Rented tenements in Paternoster Row served as both retail outlets and domestic residences for a substantial community of bookbinders and sellers. There and from numerous other shops and stalls clustered around St. Paul's Churchyard diverse titles were offered for sale, most in Latin and English; some originating in England, others imported from France and the Low Countries. As the focal point of ecclesiastical administration in London, St. Paul's was necessarily a centre of literacy and education. St. Paul's School and other educational institutions meant an assured market for Latin grammars printed in Antwerp and sold by Henry Pepwell and others. Kaetz and Birckman imported and sold liturgical material.[32] The professional stationers acquired stock wholesale as unbound sheets, whether printed in the capital or commissioned from foreign presses. Prior to subsequent retail distribution from their shops, they sometimes saw to the binding as well. Alternatively, they might sell bound or unbound imprints at regional fairs, thus avoiding municipal regulations that typically restricted such activity to local freemen. In London freeman status was normally required for anyone engaged in retail sales and for aliens seeking admission to the booksellers' guild, the Stationers' Company. It was a moot issue, though, in light of the immunities that the parliamentary statute extended to non-denizens, and in any event the suburbs west of Temple Bar were not within

---

[31] P. Needham, "The customs rolls as documents for the printed-book trade in England," in *The Cambridge History of the Book in England*, vol. 3, ed. L. Hellinga and J.B. Trapp (Cambridge, 1999), 159–60. Thereto: H.R. Plomer, "The Importation of Books into England in the Fifteenth and Sixteenth Centuries," *The Library*, 4th series, 4 (1923–24), 146–50.

[32] F.C. Avis, "England's Use of Antwerp printers," *GJB* (1973), 234–40; P.W.M. Blayney, *The Bookshops in Paul's Cross Churchyard* (London, 1990), 1–19; C.P. Christianson, "Paternoster Row and the Tudor Book-Trade Community," *The Library*, 6th series, 11 (1989), 352–56 and "The Rise of London's Book Trade," in *The Cambridge History of the Book in England*, vol. 3, ed. L. Hellinga and J.B. Trapp (Cambridge, 1999), 128–47.

the jurisdiction of London courts. Nor were the numerous royal and clerical liberties that existed within London's boundaries, where printers and vendors operated without worry of interference from the civic authorities.[33]

In some parts of the kingdom illegal vernacular Bibles circulated in manuscript, part of a legacy of religious nonconformity dating to John Wycliffe. Scripture-based Lollardy had long been the principal challenge to the established Church in England, but diffusion of Bibles and Lollard tracts does not appear to have been extensive, and in any event not dependent on printing presses. Early Lutheran texts imported from the continent, some incorporating doctrinal positions similar to those of Lollards, found readers in the academic communities and among the higher clergy schooled in Latin, but circulation was not widespread among the lay population. Vernacular English translations of tracts by continental reformers did not begin to appear until the later 1520s. Even then, London's presses did not print them.

Mercantile Networks and Printing—Germany and Beyond

While Anglo-French mercantile and cultural exchange depended on Channel shipping lanes and the Seine, it was via the Rhine that countless commodity items, from English and Flemish textiles to North Sea herring and Atlantic stockfish, reached consumer markets in the heartland of Germany. In turn the river brought metals, durable goods, Rhine wine, and dyestuffs to the heavily populated and urbanised Netherlands. Also among the cargoes transported downstream were books from the printing houses of Basel, Strasbourg, Mainz, and Cologne. They were produced in many languages and destined for any number of markets within and outside of Germany, including the Low Countries, Scotland, England, and Scandinavia.

Dozens of towns in Germany had commercial printing presses, though few could match the output of Paris or Antwerp. Prior to the domination of Germany's book market by religious reformers in the 1520s most tomes published there were printed in Latin. Those

---

[33] G. Pollard, "The Company of Stationers before 1557," *The Library*, 4th series, 17 (1937), 17–23 and, especially for retail distribution at fairs, "The English Market for Printed Books," *Publishing History* 4 (1976), 10–12.

offered in German consisted primarily of pharmacopoeias, saints'
lives, folk legends, or popular satires. The southern and central regions
of the Empire produced works in High German, albeit with numerous variations. Cologne printers, situated on the linguistic divide
between north and south, were moving toward High German orthog-
raphy by the end of the decade. In the north Lübeck was initially
a main source of works in Low German. Subsequently, Magdeburg
and Hamburg gained importance. Also contributing were two presses
in the university town of Rostock. Brothers of the Common Life
printed a modest catalogue of Scripture texts and works by allies of
the traditional Church. Rostock's other printing house was managed
by Ludwig Dietz with the backing of town secretary Hermann
Barckhusen.[34]

During the 1520s a quarter of the roughly four hundred books
issued in Low German were the work of the reformers Luther,
Melanchthon, and Bugenhagen.[35] Their publication went hand in
hand with evangelical preaching, which spread throughout northern
Germany and the Scandinavian kingdoms. Another key to highlighting controversies and influencing public opinion was the short
and cheaply produced pamphlet or *Flugschrift*. Known simply as a
little book (*Büchlein* or *Libellus*), for combatants on both sides of the
religious divide it became a chief means of expression. Reform propagandists also appealed to the common people by way of the vernacular dialogue pamphlet (*Dialogus* or *Gesprächbüchlein*). Often published
anonymously, it featured the defence of heterodox positions by the
simple ordinary man and was the most common type of pamphlet
produced in Germany between 1518 and 1526. The greatest number of publications came from Augsburg, followed by Strasbourg,
Erfurt, and Nürnberg. Although they circulated in German towns
farther north, none appear to have originated there. Wittenberg printers published relatively few *Dialogflugschriften*, specialising instead in

[34] W. Stieda, "Studien zur Geschichte des Buchdrucks und Buchhandels in
Mecklenburg," *AGDB* 17 (1894), 119–25; Clair, *A History*, 138.
[35] J.L. Flood, "The Book in Reformation Germany," *RB*, 33, 46–47. Three-quar-
ters of the nearly four thousand editions of Luther's works published in his lifetime
were issued in High German, less than 5% in Low German. About 16% were in
Latin. B. Moeller, "Luther in Europe: His Works in Translation 1517–46," in *Politics
and Society in Reformation Europe*, ed. E.I. Kouri and T. Scott (London, 1987), 236.

Scripture translations and first editions of Luther's works.[36] With the Bible so much the foundation of early evangelism, the demand for vernacular New Testaments was correspondingly great. Luther's German version was available in many editions. French, English, Swedish, and Danish New Testaments were in print by 1526. Another effective vehicle for the communication of evangelical views among lay readers was the published sermon, which usually included a foreword and summary of contents. Numerous biblical commentaries were also published albeit primarily for circulation among learned specialists.

Until mid-century the German book trade was the domain of printers/publishers and of professional stationers. Printers could sell from their shops or use local helpers to hawk new imprints at markets and in the streets as soon as they came off the press. Alternatively, commissions might be offered to vendors otherwise unconnected with the particular printing house. Specialist book merchants (*Buchhändler*) acquired inventory from the presses for sale in their own shops or on behalf of other established retailers in major centres. When Ingolstadt dealer Georg Krapff wanted books in 1523, for example, he placed orders with publisher/printer Simprecht Ruff of Augsburg, who sent him the requested titles, along with an itemised price list. Krapff did not have to come to Augsburg and apparently could order imprints in advance of publication: Ruff was unable to send his good friend one of the desired editions because it was not quite finished. Independent retailers could look as well to regional wholesalers. By 1529 some of Krapff's inventory came from the stockrooms of Wolf Präunlein in Augsburg. Präunlein sold in volume. Some of the more than three hundred scientific, humanist, and religious texts he provided Krapff were printed in Mainz and Paris.[37]

Professionals in the book business—wholesalers and smaller retailers alike—also bought, sold, and exchanged stock at mercantile fairs, whether in Germany or France or the Low Countries. Extensive use

---

[36] More than half of the134 different dialogue pamphlets printed in Germany between 1518 and 1526 were in the vernacular. In all there were over 300 editions, with circulation peaking just before the Peasants War. A. Zorzin, "Einige Beobachtungen zu den zwischen 1518 und 1526 im deutschen Sprachbereich veröffentlichten Dialogflugschriften," *ARG* 88 (1997), 77–117.

[37] A. Kirchhoff, "Buchhändlerische Geschäftspapiere aus den Jahren 1523 bis 1530," *AGDB* 8 (1883), 286–95.

of credit was necessary to facilitate the trade. Rivalling Frankfurt as a magnet for printers and purveyors was the Leipzig book fair. From there the network also extended north and east to the Baltic coast. Rostock dealer Lambert Hoymann had Leipzig business connections, and by 1525 so did Jacob Knop of Danzig. Hoymann also travelled to Stettin in Pomerania. Commercial traffic from Leipzig was routed to Danzig over Wittenberg, Berlin, and Landsberg or alternatively via Stettin, Köslin, and Stolp.[38] The *Buchhändler* utilised the same transportation infrastructure as other merchants. Non-specialists, though, seldom involved themselves directly in the large-scale commercial distribution of printed material.

Of paramount importance were the annual spring and autumn marts at Frankfurt, drawing dealers and printers from Germany and many other parts of Europe to the town's *Buchgasse*. Since the 1480s booksellers had rented stalls there, giving rise to Frankfurt's development as a distribution rather than printing centre. As in Leipzig, the fairs afforded the opportunity to settle outstanding accounts, collaborate on new ventures, and exhibit available stock. Among the regular visitors at the turn of the century were great entrepreneurs like Anton Koberger of Nürnberg, who maintained a resident manager in Paris and dealt extensively with the presses in Basel. He often came in person to the fairs at Frankfurt and by 1506 had a permanent shop there as well. Other vendors, from Strasbourg and Basel, were especially important because of their links to Lyon. Only large publishing houses like Koberger's could afford branch offices and factors in distant or foreign places. Consequently, much of the wholesale and retail distribution was left to the independent professionals and to itinerant non-specialists of more modest means, who went from town to town buying and selling small consignments and individual imprints.[39]

With their livelihoods reliant in the long term on retail sales, purveyors of books had a vested interest in what was issued. The clerical community was a sure market for standard Latin service books

[38] Stieda, "Studien," 129–30; A. Kirchhoff, "Ein etwas räthselhaftes Document," *AGDB* 10 (1886), 9–26; P. Jeannin, "The Sea-borne and the Overland Trade Routes of Northern Europe in the XVI and XVII Centuries," *Journal of European Economic History* 11 (1982), 28–29.

[39] J.W. Thompson, ed., *The Frankfort Book Fair* (Chicago, 1911), 20–54, 77; A. Dietz, *Frankfurter Handelsgeschichte* (Frankfurt, 1921), 3: 8–12.

however with few exceptions some risk was involved for printers or publishers who, on their own initiative, underwrote something new. Success depended in the first instance on an informed assessment of commercial potential, taking into account not only the content of the work and its intended readership but also the logistics of marketing and distribution. If he did not already have buyers for the books that Ruff printed for him, Georg Krapff undoubtedly had a very strong sense of what was saleable. These circumstances naturally resulted in the emergence of entrepreneurial publishers (*Buchführer*), who financed the printing of specific editions.[40] They took chances in doing this and to some extent also determined what became available to the reading public. Employing printing houses in various localities, it was not unusual for these publishers to work in partnership with master printers. Some, like Franz Birckman, eventually bought their own presses. Authors did not receive royalties, and in the absence of copyright protection competing publishers and presses frequently duplicated successful or potentially successful editions. In 1525 Nürnberg copies of Luther's works turned up for sale in Wittenberg, much to the detriment, so Luther claimed, of the Wittenberg houses that produced originals. He complained about it to Nürnberg, in effect accusing printer and bookseller Johann Herrgott of stealing his work.[41]

Germany and the Habsburg Low Countries were linked to wider spheres of commerce in particular by two key transit centres. Much commercial traffic originated at or was eventually channelled through the emporium at Antwerp. And on the lower Rhine trade from the Netherlands to Frankfurt and upper Germany was to a great extent in the hands of intermediaries at Cologne. Distinguished by large merchant and artisan communities, both Cologne and Antwerp were consumer markets for books. During his northern sojourn in 1520–21 the esteemed Nürnberg artist Albrecht Dürer had no difficulty purchasing inexpensive Lutheran imprints in both towns.[42] And Cologne,

[40] A. Kirchhoff, "Kurze Notizen über die Buchführer der ersten Hälfte des XVI. Jahrhunderts," in *Beiträge zur Geschichte des deutschen Buchhandels* (Leipzig, 1851), 1: 132–52.
[41] A. Kirchhoff, "Johann Herrgott, Buchführer von Nürnberg und sein tragisches Ende. 1527," *AGDB* 1 (1878), 19.
[42] Albrecht Dürer, *Diary of his Journey to the Netherlands, 1520–21*, ed. J.-A. Goris and G. Marlier (London, 1971), 71–72, 94. The prices of printed books had dropped

like Antwerp, had a substantial typographic industry. Consequently, for production as well as distribution the two towns were important in the process of publicising religious controversies.

Challenges to the status quo in northern Germany were not simply confined to matters of devotion and spirituality. Nor were they in Scandinavia. Reasons for the evangelical movement's early success there were complex, in many instances as much political as religious. In the first place, though, new ideas had to reach northward in order to be received or rejected. Evangelical tenets were transmitted and spread, both orally and in print, along routes integrating the principal market towns of the north German plain with coastal centres.[43] There were roadways, but also important for wider distribution of Wittenberg theology was yet another commercial waterway, the river Elbe, leading to Magdeburg and thence to the port of Hamburg. Hamburg's trade was extensive and international in scope. By land it reached directly into the border regions of Holstein and Schleswig and thence to Denmark.

Interregional corridors of economic and cultural exchange were particularly vital to book distribution in Scandinavia because there were few printing houses. Some itinerant German and Dutch printers had worked intermittently in Danish towns: Nyborg, Copenhagen, and Århus. But prior to 1528, when Olaf Ulriksson set up shop in Malmø and Hans Weingarten came to Viborg, the printing of Danish books, including early controversial material generally fell to foreign printing houses. German presses in Lübeck, Rostock, Magdeburg, and Cologne were the main suppliers.[44] Imported books were sold by German vendors in town markets and at regular fairs held on the Øresund shores. In the 1520s booksellers distributed Danish New Testaments commissioned by the exiled king, Christian II, and attributed to the Leipzig press of Melchior Lotter. The king's chaplain

steadily since the fifteenth century. An unbound copy of Luther's first German Bible now sold for half of what a German Bible had cost in the 1480s. Pamphlets of the sort Dürer purchased were much shorter and far less expensive than Bibles. Johnston, "Printing," 166.

[43] Bruns and Weckzerka, *Handelsstrassen*, 2: 167–225.

[44] A. Riising, "The Book and the Reformation in Denmark and Norway, 1523–40," *RB*, 433; M. Schwarz Lausten, "The Early Reformation in Denmark and Norway 1520–1559," in *The Scandinavian Reformation*, ed. O.P. Grell (Cambridge, 1995), 12–20; Clair, *A History*, 226.

Christiern Pedersen also translated and edited several texts, issuing them through Willem Vorsterman in Antwerp. When Pedersen returned to Malmø in the early 1530s to establish his own press, managed by another Antwerp printer, Jan Hillen van Hoochstraten, he likely brought copies of his already-published works for distribution.[45] Most Danish translations or adaptations of reform literature were done from German.

The attendant evangelism that came from Germany initially permeated the border duchies of Holstein and Schleswig, both held by Frederick, crowned king of Denmark in 1523. Linguistic divisions were not difficult to overcome there. Even before Frederick's election Luther's disciple Hermann Tast was preaching in German at Husum. His first patron was a prosperous merchant and town councillor, Mathias Knutzen. Schleswig, Holstein, and Denmark were consumer markets for imported wine and cloth, and transfer points for the international trade in meat and cereals. Ships and merchants from northern Germany and the Low Countries called regularly at Husum, where grain originally shipped from Riga and Danzig was transferred to vessels bound for Amsterdam. The trade's overland segment traversed the peninsula along roads linking Husum to Flensburg, the town of Schleswig, and Kiel. Overland exchange also extended into western Denmark. Dissemination of evangelical reform was an extension of the process in Schleswig. Most Jutland towns had Lutheran preachers by the mid-1520s, beneficiaries of strong support from civic authorities. For eastern Denmark there were other conduits. Across the greater Baltic region major coastal towns, including those within the Danish kingdom had resident German populations. Economically and politically the two most important were Copenhagen and Malmø, strongly bound through trade and shipping to the Hanse ports of the north German coast—Lübeck, Rostock, and Stralsund—and the eastern Baltic. Most elected civic officials in Copenhagen and Malmø were involved in trade to some extent, and their magistracies remained intact after submitting to Frederick in 1524. Aside from German pamphlets and the presence of itinerant German preachers in Denmark, Danish merchants were likely to

---

[45] *Ibid.*, and A.G. Johnston and J.-F. Gilmont, "Printing and the Reformation in Antwerp," *RB*, 193–94; *PI*, 34–35, 100. The earliest Danish translation of Luther was printed at Rostock in 1526. Moeller, "Luther," 237, 245.

encounter new ideas by virtue of their commercial relations with
German harbour towns, from distant Königsberg and Danzig to
nearby Stralsund.[46] Trade to the Danish dependencies of Norway
and Iceland afforded similar circumstances for transmission. German
ships came regularly to the Norwegian coasts and especially to Bergen,
where Hanse interests controlled the North Sea cod fishery. Hamburg
and other German ports also sent fishing and trading vessels to
Iceland.

Hence, for the broad diffusion of reform theology in northern
Europe and the early distribution of controversial works North Sea
and Baltic shipping lanes bear examination. At Helsingør, north of
Copenhagen, Danish toll collectors monitored the passage of hundreds of craft annually through the Øresund. Predominant among
German merchantmen were those from Hamburg, Lübeck, Stralsund,
and Danzig.[47] Aside from the Baltic network, into which Hamburg
was also integrated, the trade of these towns extended westward to
the British Isles and the Atlantic seaboard. Conversely, Hamburg
was a regular port of call for vessels from the Low Countries, England,
and Scotland, and each summer merchants from those countries also
sent ships to the Baltic, especially to the Prussian staple at Danzig.
The stop at Helsingør was normally brief, but elsewhere ships could
spend several weeks in port discharging and taking on cargo, re-
provisioning, or simply waiting for favourable weather. Also part of
this network were smaller ports on the Mecklenburg and Pomeranian
coasts. It was in harbour towns that ships' crews and foreign merchants, some of them resident factors employed by large consortiums,
would encounter firsthand the overt manifestations of religious change,
from evangelical preaching and the circulation of printed propaganda
to violent expressions of intolerance. In Lübeck conservatives prevailed, working hand in hand with the bishop, Hinrick Bockholt,

---

[46] O.P. Grell suggests, however, that while evangelism in Jutland was an extension
of the distinctively Lutheran movement in Schleswig and Holstein, the new doctrines that took hold in Zealand and Scania differed in content and origins. Malmø
and Copenhagen were mercantile centres with close commercial ties to southern
Germany, especially Strasbourg and Nürnberg, where radical ideas flourished. O.P.
Grell, "Scandinavia," in *The Early Reformation in Europe*, ed. A. Pettegree (Cambridge,
1992), 110.
[47] N.E. Bang, ed., *Tabeller over Skibsfart og Varetransport gennem Øresund 1497–1660*
(Copenhagen, 1906–32), 1: 2–5.

and cathedral chapter to ban provocative *Flugschriften* and restrain Lutherans. Meanwhile in Stralsund anticlericalism both within and outside the town's governing council fuelled public turmoil. Following iconoclastic agitation, Lutheran church and school orders were promulgated and opponents purged from the government in November 1525.[48] Already by then the printing presses in Hamburg had produced a significant selection of Lutheran tracts and evangelical preachers were active as far east as Riga and Reval.

The Baltic trade network also included Sweden, and especially the predominantly German population of Stockholm. Commercially, Stockholm was an exporter of iron, the basis of strongly sustained links to Hanse ports such as Danzig and Lübeck. Such popular support for evangelicals as did exist in Sweden in these early years was confined to urban centres, principally coastal ports, among which Stockholm was the largest. By 1524, within two years of their introduction by itinerant merchants, the town's German residents had accepted evangelicals and recruited a Wittenberg minister, Nicholas Stecker. Economic and cultural contacts with Germany contributed to the flow of ideas, however Swedish towns, including Stockholm, were small by German standards. Hence, popular urban reformations such as occurred in Danzig, Hamburg, and other places in Germany were unlikely. Evangelism planted some early roots in Stockholm but religious reform in Sweden was guided by the monarchy.[49]

Sweden's typographic history dates to the late 1480s, when the archbishop of Uppsala recruited a German printer to produce breviaries and missals. He worked in various locales: Stockholm and the monasteries at Vadstena and Mariefred. But this press had fallen silent by the time early Lutheran imprints from Germany began to circulate. In 1523 the bishop of Linköping, Hans Brask, sponsored a new one at Söderköping. Its master was Olaf Ulriksson. Latin and

---

[48] W. Troßbach, "Unterschiede und Gemeinsamkeiten bei der Durchsetzung der Reformation in den Hansestädten Wismar, Rostock und Stralsund," *ARG* 88 (1997), 122–42; J. Schildhauer, *Soziale, politische und religiöse Auseinandersetzungen in den Hansestädten Stralsund, Rostock und Wismar im ersten Drittel des 16. Jahrhunderts* (Weimar, 1959), 112–14, 173–93; W.-D. Hauschildt, "Die Reformation in Hamburg, Lübeck und Eutin," in *Schleswig-Holsteinische Kirchengeschichte*, ed. W. Göbell (Neumünster, 1982), 3: 202–6.

[49] E.I. Kouri, "The Early Reformation in Sweden and Finland c. 1520–1560," in *The Scandinavian Reformation*, ed. O.P. Grell (Cambridge, 1995), 44–45.

Swedish prayer books were the main priority at first but Brask also used the press to promote the glory and historical achievements of the Swedish episcopate. Thus it was not long before the Crown decided to rehabilitate the old Uppsala press for its own ends.[50]

In addition to imprints from Sweden and various German presses, book circulation in the Baltic region also included material from Poland. Beginning in the 1470s German printers worked intermittently in Poland for a quarter century until more permanent establishments emerged. Kasper Hochfelder started a printing house in Cracow in 1503 and was still there twenty years later. Hieronymous Viëtor, who learned his craft in Vienna, set up a very successful press in 1518. Cracow, centre of court and university culture, developed into Poland's typographic capital. From 1473 through 1518 eight of the twelve presses known to have existed in Poland and Royal Prussia were located there. At least three were active in the 1520s, primarily serving the clergy and the university community. Sometimes merchant capital financed the print runs. Viëtor frequently issued works for entrepreneur and statesman Ludwig Decius. Another merchant publisher, Johann Haller, was responsible for bringing Hochfelder to Poland, and eventually owned his own press. Aside from Cracow imprints in Latin, German, and Polish there was a demand for imported material. Polish clerics used liturgical books produced in France and Venice. Booksellers also offered tomes from Germany, carting them overland from the Leipzig fairs. Another important commercial link was Nürnberg. Early works by Luther were sold at Cracow's university in 1519. But trade with the Empire also ensured that the views of his opponents circulated widely too.[51] All of the presses not situated in Cracow prior to 1518 were in Royal Prussia: three at Danzig and the other at nearby Marienburg.

---

[50] K. Johannesson, *The Renaissance of the Goths in Sixteenth-century Sweden: Johannes and Olaus Magnus as Politicians and Historians*, trans. J. Larson (Berkeley, 1991), 45–46; Grell, "Scandinavia," 113; Kouri, "Sweden and Finland," 50.

[51] C. Schmidt, *Auf Felsen gesät: Die Reformation in Polen und Livland* (Göttingen, 2000), 39–44, 221–22; Clair, *A History*, 247–8; B. Bieńkowska, *Books in Poland: Past and Present* (Wiesbaden, 1990), 8–9; D. Bacewiczowa and A. Kawecka-Gryczowa, *Drukarze dawnej Polski od XV do XVIII wieku*, vol. 1(1). (Wrocław, 1983), esp. 44–62, 299–313, 325–52; R. Bartolomäus, "Justus Ludwig Decius: Ein deutscher Kaufmann und polnischer Staatsmann (1485–1545)," *APM* 35 (1898), 63, 75–76, 85; A. Swierk, "Hieronymous Vietor (Wietor): Ein Pioneer des polnischen Buchdrucks im 16. Jahrhundert," *GJB* (1976), 194–99.

Hans Weinreich printed in Danzig until 1524, when he relocated to Königsberg in what was about to become Ducal Prussia. His departure apparently left the eastern Baltic's largest town, Danzig, without a commercial printing house in the later 1520s. Königsberg had a paper mill, so Weinreich was not burdened with the costs of importing paper. For two decades he faced no competition. His was the only press east of Danzig until Hans Luft of Wittenberg opened a second Königsberg print works in the 1540s.[52]

As elsewhere, the *Buchhändler* did much of the distributing. Some of them may have been quite closely associated with bookbinding. Binders took books as payment and resold them, thus becoming entrepreneurs as well as craftsmen. Weinreich's imprints circulated outside Prussia, turning up in Posen and Gnesen in Poland.[53] Königsberg's maritime trade also meant that imprints could reach other Baltic ports, including those in the eastern Teutonic territories where there were no printing houses. Though remote from the great metropolitan centres and commercial entrepôts of the west, the Livonian lands of the Teutonic Order were connected to a wider world through trade. Hinterland towns—Dorpat, Wolmar, and others—facilitated a network along which grain, furs, flax, and forest products passed to the Hanse ports of Riga and Reval. From there consignments were shipped to western markets in exchange for manufactured wares. Riga and Reval were crucial conduits for international and intra-Baltic trade, with strong ties to Königsberg, Stockholm, Danzig, and Lübeck.

Jurisdictions and Censorship—The Empire and the Baltic region

Within the Holy Roman Empire there existed an established tradition of ecclesiastical censorship. In the 1480s the archbishop of Mainz tried to regulate texts translated from Greek or Latin, assigning

---

[52] Schmidt, *Auf Felsen gesät*, 224; M. Caliebe, "Die Literatur," in *Handbuch der Geschichte Ost-und Westpreußens: Teil 2/1*, ed. E. Opgenoorth (Lüneburg, 1994), 188; A. Bues, *Das Herzogtum Kurland und der Norden der polnisch-litauischen Adelsrepublik im 16. und 17. Jahrhundert* (Giessen, 2001), 285. There seems to have been no commercial printing in Danzig in the later 1520s but that does not preclude the possibility that equipment was available and used, perhaps, for the publication of local ordinances.
[53] Körber, *Öffentlichkeiten*, 218–23.

responsibility for their examination to university theologians at Mainz and Erfurt.[54] By 1517 one of the two appointed censors in the archdiocese was a canon of the cathedral at Frankfurt, an especially advantageous place from which to monitor circulation. However, restrictions promulgated by one archdiocesan authority did not necessarily apply to all. It was not within the power of an archbishop of Mainz or Cologne, for instance, to demand censorship at the market in Leipzig, within the see of Magdeburg.[55] Pope Innocent VIII had done his part to suppress subversive literature with an edict calling for printers to submit texts for examination and empowering episcopal authorities to destroy any they deemed heretical. It had been reissued in 1501 for the benefit of the archbishops of Cologne, Mainz, Trier, and Magdeburg, prompting complaints from Cologne's booksellers. More recently, in the wake of the Reuchlin controversy in 1515, Leo X had proclaimed the sweeping *Inter solicitudines*, which not only prohibited vernacular transcriptions from Latin but also Latin translations from Greek, Hebrew, and Arabic. It also took aim at libellous pamphlet literature. The fines and excommunication prescribed for authors and printers provided a means by which bishops and papal inquisitors could attempt to control dissemination at the diocesan level.[56] Yet however seriously individual prelates may have taken this mandate, its overall effectiveness ultimately required at least some cooperation from secular jurisdictions, especially the magistracies of the free towns where printing presses were located. Moreover, Rome's efforts to promulgate these early restrictions appear to have been less than fervid. The bull of 1515 circulated in a single printed edition while that of 1501 was not printed at all. Nevertheless, when the university theologians at Cologne and Louvain judged Luther's theses in 1519 proscription of his writings was a foregone conclusion.

---

[54] H. Pallmann, "Das Erzbischofs von Mainz ältestes Censuredict," *AGDB* 9 (1884), 238–41.

[55] F. Geß, "Spuren der Censur in Sachsen um das Jahr 1500," *AGDB* 13 (1890), 246.

[56] Clair, *A History*, 158; W. Schmitz, "Der Kölner Buchdruck," and "Daten Buchdruck," in *Chronik zur Geschichte der Stadt Köln*, ed. P. Fuchs (Cologne, 1991), 2: 32–39; *500 Jahre Buch und Zeitung in Köln: Ausstellung, vor allem aus den Beständen der Universitäts- und Stadtbibliothek, veranstaltet von der Stadt Köln* (Cologne, 1965), 33; R. Hirsch, *Printing, Selling and Reading 1450–1550* (Wiesbaden, 1967), 88–90 and "Bulla super impressione librorum, 1515," *GJB* (1973), 248–51; Thompson, *Book Fair*, 103. In Cologne the 1501 edict drew the ire of at least fourteen booksellers.

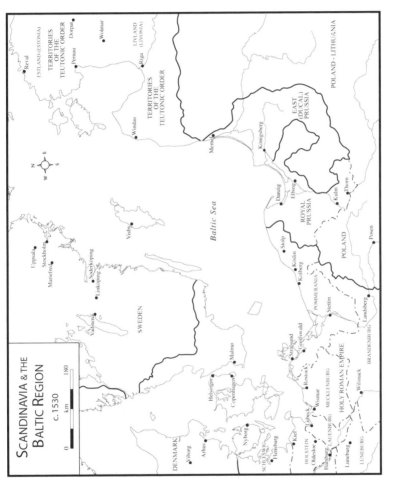

Scandinavia and the Baltic Region

In June 1520 Leo X's bull of excommunication, *Exsurge Domine*
precluded the possibility of resolution through discourse and paved
the way for Luther's subsequent condemnation by the Imperial Diet.
It remained only for his opinions and those of his followers to be
suppressed. Promulgation of *Exsurge* in Germany and the Low Countries
fell to papal nuncios Johann Eck and Girolamo Aleandro. Copies of
Luther's writings already had been destroyed at Louvain and Cologne
in autumn 1520 during the stay of Emperor-elect Charles, who at
that time was also persuaded to ban them throughout the Habsburg
Netherlands. There were more fires to come, not only in Germany
and the Low Countries but also in Paris and London. But they failed
to eliminate the controversy created by Luther. Itinerant preachers
stirred traditional concerns regarding the Church—absenteeism, lax
discipline, and clerical privilege, but more importantly articulated
Luther's increasingly doctrinaire positions regarding sacraments and
lay religiosity. This combination in turn fuelled an unprecedented
polemical campaign for which print was the principal medium.

Exsurge Domine caused much resentment north of the Alps. In some
towns, including Mainz, Aleandro and Eck encountered open public protests over their bonfires. They were also reproached in anonymous pamphlets, such as *Hochstratus ovans*, which also lampooned
Edward Lee and the Dominican inquisitor at Cologne, Jacob
Hochstraten.[57] So to shore up the position to which it was now committed the papacy lobbied hard for an imperial decree. The young
emperor was amenable, and a draft was ready by the end of 1520
for inclusion among the numerous propositions to be put before his
inaugural *Reichstag*, set to convene at Worms in January. The proceedings of that assembly are well documented, and need only be
mentioned briefly here. Neither Charles's advisors nor Aleandro could
forge a consensus. Elector Frederick of Ernestine Saxony and others refused to condemn Luther without first giving him an opportunity to defend himself. Even so, the Diet had proscribed his writings
some three weeks before he entered Worms under imperial safe conduct. His dramatically defiant speech to the Diet on 18 April was
followed the next day by the emperor's equally striking and unequiv-

---

[57] M.U. Chrisman, *Conflicting Visions of Reform: German Lay Propaganda Pamphlets,
1519–1530* (Atlantic Highlands, 1996), 54–55; *Correspondence of Wolfgang Capito*, 1: 72,
92–99, 109–10, 118.

ocal statement in which he dedicated himself to the preservation of the Catholic faith and exhorted the assembled princes to do the same. The Edict of Worms, outlawing Luther and condemning his works and any others critical of the institutional Church, bore the date 8 May 1521, yet only circulated among a sparse gathering of representatives after the Diet had formally concluded. In the weeks and months that followed it was printed in several places in Germany, as was Luther's response.[58] Whether it constituted effective law remained to be seen.

Charles soon departed Worms, entrusting governance of the Empire during his absence to his brother Ferdinand, Archduke of Austria, and a newly created Imperial Governing Council of princes. Their disparate views militated strongly against any resolution of religious affairs. Moreover, effective initiatives proved difficult to implement even within the territories of those who were staunchly Catholic. Shortly after the appearance of Luther's New Testament Duke Georg of Albertine Saxony ordered his subjects to turn in their copies for burning, but had little success coaxing or forcing compliance. His agents also monitored the Leipzig market for Wittenberg imports. Prior to the Peasants War, however, only two prosecutions, neither of which involved book dealers, resulted from his decrees. On the other hand, good relations with the duke were important to Leipzig, so few Lutheran works were printed there. When one of the local presses wanted to reissue Luther's New Testament text, without his foreword and glosses, town officials asked the diocesan authority if papal and ducal edicts still applied. Presumably the answer was yes and the edition did not go to press, since there is no extant copy. Printer Wolfgang Stöckel was right, however, when he wrote in 1524 that if Leipzig presses did not issue Luther, those in Zwickau, Jena, and Wittenberg undoubtedly would. His own business strategy was to relocate to Dresden and become one of the main printers of conformist theologians favoured by the duke, especially Cochlaeus and Hieronymous Emser.[59] Much to the chagrin of the Roman curia,

---

[58] U. Eisenhardt, *Die kaiserliche Aufsicht über Buchdruck, Buchhandel und Presse im Heiligen Römischen Reich Deutscher Nation (1496–1806)* (Karlsruhe, 1970), 24–27; *VD* D917–924, L3669.

[59] F. Geß, "Versuchter Nachdruck des Lutherischen Deutschen Neuen Testamentes durch Jacob Thanner in Leipzig, 1524," *AGDB* 12 (1889), 302–3; Kirchhoff, "Johann Herrgott," 21–25; A. Götze, *Die Hochdeutschen Drucker der Reformationszeit* (Strassburg, 1905), 19–20.

enforcement of the Worms decree in Germany was on the whole
ineffective and in some principalities and imperial towns non-exis-
tent. Duchess Katharina of Braunschweig-Lüneburg issued an order
early in 1523 specifically demanding that *Buchhändler* coming to
Hannover not sell Lutheran imprints. Her position contrasted sharply
with that of East Friesland's count, Edzard I, who encouraged evangelical preaching and allowed unrestricted circulation of Luther's
books as soon as the first German editions appeared. Similarly, the
prince-prelate of Bremen was actively anti-Lutheran, but east of his
territorial domain Duke Magnus of Saxony-Lauenburg was not. In
1524 he appealed directly to Wittenberg for an evangelical preacher.[60]
The Empire's constituent principalities could not be compelled to
enforce imperial directives on religious conformity.

Prudent civic governments weighed the mandates of territorial
princes or, in the case of free imperial towns, the emperor. They
also had authority to create their own *ad hoc* censorship regulations.
When contemplating such laws, the extent to which enforcement was
possible and practical, given available resources and the expectation
of the body politic, had to be considered. And once in place, there
remained the question of how rigorously a municipal administration
would chose to enforce them. Several important towns with established typographic industries issued censorship ordinances. Following
the *Reichtag* of 1524 Lübeck essentially reiterated the Edict of Worms.
Clerics were permitted to confiscate imprints from booksellers and
turn them over to municipal officials.[61] Cologne's law was similar.
An enumeration of printers in 1523 and a prohibition on anything
that cast spiritual or temporal authorities in a bad light was followed
within a year by a ban on printing and sale of all Lutheran material. By early 1525, amid renewed attempts to silence evangelical
preachers, no books were to be produced in Cologne without the
consent of the civic magistrates. It was not a particularly new pre-
sumption on their part. Servas Kruffter had issued an anti-Reuchlin
invective by Pfefferkorn in 1521 without permission, and was arrested
because of it. Established printers continued to flourish, though,
among them Johann Gymnich and Johann Soter, who issued clas-

---

[60] *Aus der Reformationsgeschichte Niedersachsens*, ed. P. Meyer (Hildesheim, 1952), 7,
9–12; Flood, "Reformation Germany," 92–95.
[61] W. Jannasch, *Reformationsgeschichte Lübecks* (Lübeck, 1958), 123–25, 199.

sics, humanist literature, and theological texts.[62] And as one of the
few major typographic centres in Germany where the governing elite
remained true to Roman Catholicism, Cologne became an important source of imprints supportive of the old Church. Control was
achieved through co-operation between municipal authorities and the
university faculty, especially Jacob Hochstraten. Together with this
apparently strong tradition of censorship, trade and security concerns
also helped shape a policy of general outward compliance with imperial directives. Indeed it has been suggested that preservation of
Cologne's trade demanded untroubled relations with the ruler of the
Low Countries, who by the autumn of 1521 had been crowned
emperor as well.[63] As a free *Reichstadt*, Cologne was accountable to
no other prince.

Other German towns were much less keen to emphasise discor-
dant religious views in their censorship laws, instead drawing the line
more generally at libellous material. In March 1523 Augsburg's printers were sworn to refrain from printing any insulting book, song, or
poem. All publications required prior permission from the council,
and all imprints had to identify the author and printer. The same
was soon true in Strasbourg. And there too the law simply banned
the production and sale of scandalous or blasphemous books or pictures of the sort that turned Christian neighbours against one another:
"gemeyn Christen mensch gegen seynem neben Christen menschen".[64]
There was no specific reference to Luther or his followers or to vernacular Scripture texts. Applicable equally to denizens and strangers,
Strasbourg's law left magistrates plenty of leeway to deal with non-
compliance, stating only that punishment would be appropriate
("gebürendt") to the transgression. In Augsburg, meanwhile, shortly
after swearing their oath printers seem to have been exempted from

---

[62] Schmitz, "Kölner Buchdruck," and "Daten Buchdruck," 2: 32–39; *500 Jahre
Buch und Zeitung in Köln*, 91.
[63] *Beschlüsse des Rates der Stadt Köln 1320–1550*, ed. M. Huiskes and M. Groten
(Düsseldorf, 1988–90), 1: 954, 3: 198, 209, 213; R. Scribner, "Why was there no
Reformation in Cologne?" in *Popular Culture and Popular Movements in Reformation
Germany*, ed. R. Scribner (London, 1987), 217–24.
[64] The Strasbourg ordinance: "Mandat des Raths gegen Pasquill-und Lästerschriften
1524," *AGDB* 5 (1880), 86–87. Thereto: K. Schottenloher, *Philipp Ulhart: Ein Augsburger
Winkeldrucker und Helfshelfer der 'Schwärmer' und 'Wiedertäufer' (1523–1529)* (Munich,
1921), 9–10. For Augsburg see A. Buff, "Die ältesten Augsburger Censuranordnungen,"
AGDB 6 (1881), 251–52.

its provisions. During the 1520s in Augsburg, issuers of predominantly Lutheran works co-existed with their pro-Catholic counterparts. Nürnberg, site of three assemblies of the Imperial Governing Council from 1522 through the spring of 1524, duly posted the imperial decree but beyond warning booksellers against printing or selling Lutheran material, civic officials made no attempt to prosecute Luther's supporters or destroy their books. Imprints were bought and sold quite openly there and in Strasbourg as well.[65]

In the free towns of southern Germany the evangelical movement had powerful patrons and enjoyed much popular support. Measuring this against external pressure from ecclesiastical and princely interests, some civic oligarchies shielded evangelicals and printers in order to safeguard communal peace. For a time they succeeded in striking a balance. Little was done in response to the Council's reiteration of the Worms Edict in February 1522, but a year later the Diet's decree that preachers limit themselves to the Gospels and interpretations approved by the Church of Rome brought conscious attempts to avoid trouble. A number of towns, including Strasbourg, Augsburg, Worms, and Frankfurt, issued non-partisan regulations requiring local clergy to stick to the Gospels.[66] Already, and not surprisingly, regulation of potentially controversial and provocative literature had become selective. Strasbourg authorities refused to allow printing of an anti-Lutheran invective by Frankfurt deacon Johann Cochlaeus even though the author's opening salvo in what became a very personal feud with Luther had been issued there only a few months before. Censors in Cologne, chief among them Jacob Hochstraten, had no objections, however, so Cochlaeus prevailed upon printers there to do the work.[67]

---

[65] Götze, *Die Hochdeutschen Drucker*, 1–10; G. Strauss, *Nuremberg in the Sixteenth Century* (New York, 1966), 163–65; M.U. Chrisman, "Reformation Printing in Strasbourg, 1519–60," *RB*, 219.

[66] T.A. Brady, Jr., "The Reformation of the Common Man, 1521–24," in *The German Reformation*, ed. C.S. Dixon (Oxford, 1999), 94–132.

[67] M. Spahn, *Johannes Cochläus: Ein Lebensbild aus der Zeit der Kirchenspaltung* (Berlin, 1898), 104, 341–42; R. Bäumer, *Johannes Cochlaeus (1479–1552): Leben und Werk im Dienst der katholischen Reform* (Münster, 1980), 24–25. Not long after this Sigmund Grimm of Augsburg found himself in trouble with civic authorities not for contentious reform imprints but for issuing Johann Eck's *Missa est sacrificium*. Götze, *Die Hochdeutschen Drucker*, 2–3. In 1521, before the Edict of Worms, Eck had threatened to have Augsburg's civic authorities excommunicated if they did not suppress a work by Luther's supporter Oecolampadius. *Correspondence of Wolfgang Capito*, 130.

Early in 1524 Charles unequivocally demanded enforcement of his directives. *Reichstag* delegates, wary of serious backlash among common people, were very reluctant to agree. Even then the Empire's free towns refused to endorse the closing recess, knowing full well that within their populous jurisdictions the emperor's law was plainly unenforceable. Drawn to non-confessional evangelism, not necessarily to Luther, urban delegates convened again in the summer at Speyer, adopting a policy aimed at accommodating not only those who favoured the *neue Lehre*, such as Nürnberg and Strasbourg, but more conservative centres like Cologne as well. They proposed establishing a commission to hold public hearings on religious issues, and to abide by its decisions. Charles responded with a renewed call for enforcement of the Edict of Worms. In their reply, drafted in December, the towns warned that this could not be done without provoking dangerous uprisings, bloodshed, and even more disaffection within their communes. Still careful not to advocate anything that could be construed as Lutheran doctrine, they also made clear their desire to ensure the preaching of God's word as well as their dissatisfaction with laws that appeared to discourage or forbid it. A plan of mutual protection was formulated to help those vulnerable to intimidation by bishops. The estrangement was critical. With southern Germany now drifting ever closer to rebellion, civic regimes were hamstrung in the absence of effective royal leadership.[68] Yet irrespective of the volatility of the commonalty and the foreboding of urban oligarchs it must also be remembered that there existed no practical or uniform mechanism for the implementation of imperial censorship decrees. The Nürnberg Diet's closing communiqué in 1524 clearly left protection of Catholic orthodoxy to the towns and territorial princes. But not until five years later, when the Diet met at Speyer, were the civic and territorial jurisdictions specifically required to appoint committees of experts to vet manuscripts for heretical content prior to publication.[69]

In the Nordic kingdoms the responses to Lutheran innovation had highly political overtones. In 1525 Frederick I formally invited the Franciscan house at Hamburg to extend evangelism throughout Holstein. The Friars Minor traditionally read masses for the fishermen

---

[68] Brady, "Common Man," 94–132.
[69] Eisenhardt, *Aufsicht über Buchdruck*, 28–29.

who worked the coastal waters of Friesland. Their preaching would now extend to the entire western coast of Schleswig-Holstein. Frederick also appointed Schleswig cathedral's first reform minister, Marquard Schuldorpe, in 1526. By year's end all ministers in nearby Kiel were evangelical, delivering their sermons in either Danish or German.[70] Soon more Wittenberg evangelicals arrived, encouraged by the king's son, Duke Christian, who had witnessed Luther's address to the Imperial Diet at Worms. He assumed full administrative authority over the duchies early in 1526, and within three years most towns had been won over. Notwithstanding his coronation oath to oppose religious innovation in the Danish kingdom, Frederick I overrode the bishops' jurisdictions by issuing royal letters of protection for evangelicals. Few of Denmark's bishops were trained in theology. Royal nominees to the episcopate generally lacked strong papal endorsement and Rome's supporters had little hope of consolidating an anti-evangelical front. The archbishopric of Lund saw five different appointees come and go from 1519 to 1535. Lauge Urne, bishop of the Zealand diocese, disapproved of the monarchy's position on evangelicals but overall the resistance of Denmark's Church hierarchy proved inconsequential. One outcome of Frederick's policy of tolerance was that the vernacular New Testament commissioned by Christian II failed to stir significant political sedition following its publication in 1524. Two years later the Danish parliament extended protection to Lutherans, paving the way for the nation's acceptance of evangelical reform in accordance with the wishes of the monarchy.[71]

Earlier, in 1524, books authored by Luther were proscribed in Denmark ostensibly to appease the ecclesiastical nobility during the early months of Frederick's reign. Since neither the author nor the presses were within Danish jurisdiction this was essentially a prohi-

---

[70] Grell, "Scandinavia," 94–105 and "The Emergence of Two Cities: The Reformation in Malmø and Copenhagen," in *Die dänische Reformation vor ihrem internationalen Hintergrund*, ed. L. Grane and K. Hørby (Göttingen, 1990), 129–45; H. Reincke, *Hamburg am Vorabend der Reformation* (Hamburg, 1966), 80–81, 112. For the overseas trade of Husum and other ports see B. Poulsen, "Wagons and Ships," in *Maritime Topography and the Medieval Town*, Studies in Archaeology and History 5 (Copenhagen, 1999), 203–12.

[71] Grell, "Scandinavia," 104–12; W. Göbell, "Das Vordringen der Reformation in Dänemark und in der Herzogtümern unter der Regierung Friedrichs I. 1523–33," in *Schleswig-Holsteinische Kirchengeschichte*, ed. W. Göbell (Neumünster, 1982), 3: 35–86; *DCR*, no. 100.

bition on imported literature. It was repeated periodically prior to establishment of the Danish Church on the Lutheran model in 1536, when Christian succeeded his father. However, even in these years of confessional development enforcement was next to impossible, given Denmark's location within the northern commercial network. The monarchy lacked any means to regulate what was brought into the kingdom and was more inclined in any event not to try. A Danish translation of Luther's *Betbüchlein* that circulated in manuscript in 1524 was printed two years later at Rostock, whence copies could be imported quit easily. There were no restrictions on vernacular Scripture books. Only when political sensibilities were offended did the government step in. The first Danish New Testament, awkwardly translated by Malmø's former mayor Hans Mikkelsen, contained an address to the Danes that was critical of the clergy for their part in deposing Christian II, whom Mikkelsen had followed into exile. Copies of this edition were confiscated so that the subversive message could be removed. Edited imprints, minus the letter but still containing a pair of Luther's New Testament prefaces, were permitted to circulate, although the distinctly colloquial translation apparently had limited appeal. Another translation, attributable to Pedersen and based on the Vulgate and Luther's German version, was published anonymously at Antwerp in 1529.[72]

In Sweden too, politics provided backdrop for religious upheaval. The successful rebellion against Danish rule that began in 1521 foreshadowed Christian II's demise. Within two years Gustav Vasa was Sweden's elected king. The split from Denmark also left the Swedish episcopate in disarray. The archbishop of Uppsala had fled to Denmark. Several other sees were vacant. Nominees for high ecclesiastical offices were pressured, regardless of their opinions of Luther,

---

[72] P.H. Vogel, "Erstdrucke ausländischer Bibeln von deutschen Druckern des 15. und 16. Jahrhunderts," *GJB* (1959), 93–96; N. Jørgensen, "Zu welchem Zweck haben die dänischen Reformatoren das Druckmedium benutzt?" in *Die dänische Reformation vor ihrem internationalen Hintergrund*, ed. L. Grane and K. Hørby (Göttingen, 1990), 232; Göbell, "Das Vordringen," 82; Riising, "Denmark and Norway," 438, 447; *PI*, 34. Aside from its anticlerical message Mikkelsen's letter claimed Christian was still lawful king of Denmark. Mikkelsen indicated he composed the address at Antwerp but the colophon attributes the printing to Melchior Lotter in Leipzig. For a full-text English translation see E. Henderson, *A Dissertation on Hans Mikkelsen's Translation of the New Testament* (Copenhagen, 1813), 8–13.

to acquiesce to the new king's agenda, which was driven less by spiritual concerns than by his aim to control political debate and clerical wealth. Evangelicals stirred up anticlericalism, which in turn provided some rationale for curtailing the political and economic power of the Church establishment. The bishops in any case received no direction from Rome regarding Luther's supporters. By 1524 it was clear that Gustav I would not initiate prosecutions or meaningful censorship. When Hans Brask urged a prohibition on the sale of Lutheran imprints, the royal reply was emphatic: there were no grounds for a ban because impartial judges had not yet evaluated the reformer's teachings. Furthermore, since writings by Luther's enemies were allowed to circulate, it was only reasonable that his be in the public domain also, in order for Catholic theologians to point out the errors.[73] Brask used his press at Söderköping to promote the historical privileges of Swedish bishops and increasingly to criticise Lutherans, including Gustav's newly promoted advisor Olaus Petri, who had studied at Wittenberg. But the Crown determined to take print communication away from churchmen. In 1525 the inactive Uppsala press was appropriated and its equipment moved to Stockholm. A German printer, Georg Richolff of Lübeck was put in charge. The next and final step followed within a few months when Brask was ordered to close down his Söderköping operations. His printer, Ulriksson, relocated in Malmø and began issuing evangelical material. Brask fled to Danzig, already the new home of the archbishop-elect of Uppsala, Johannes Magnus, who had gone there on diplomatic business in 1526 and not returned. Other prelates found sanctuary in Denmark. Propaganda from the Stockholm press now portrayed them as traitors.[74]

A Swedish New Testament was issued in 1526 and for the next decade and a half most other imprints from the royal press in Stockholm concerned religion. The utility of polemical works was substantially obviated by the government's efficiency in eliminating bishops and monks opposed to the creation of a national church independent of Rome; a process bound tightly to the quest for sovereignty. Printing concentrated instead on sermons and small works of religious instruction, most of them prepared by Petri. They included

[73] *DCR*, no. 74.
[74] Johannesson, *Renaissance*, 22–28, 45–46.

Swedish translations of Luther's sermons and an adaptation of his *Betbüchlein*. Petri and the king's secretary, Laurentius Andreae, worked from imported German and Latin editions of Luther and other German reformers—especially Martin Bucer, Johann Bugenhagen, and Urbanus Rhegius. The New Testament translation made use of Erasmus, Luther, the Danish translation of 1524, and versions printed in Low German.[75] While some of these may have been brought in expressly for Petri's use, it is likely that German editions were easily obtainable in Stockholm, where they circulated among the literate German-speaking inhabitants.

The Stockholm press quickly came to depend on royal sponsorship, but whether that was true from the outset is doubtful. In 1526 it issued a pair of tracts in Low German by Melchior Hoffman. Hoffman had been banished from Livonia for eschatological preaching and iconoclastic agitation. He already had a reputation for attracting violent followers. It was only a matter of months before he was expelled from Sweden for involvement in iconoclastic demonstrations in Stockholm. That a German lay evangelist was permitted to use the press indicates that initially Petri's supervision may have been less than stringent. One of Hoffman's texts was an indignant address to the Livonians, of no obvious interest to the Swedish Crown. The other was an exposition on the twelfth book of Daniel that contained millenarian commentary inconsistent with the king's deliberately measured Lutheranism. Within the widening evangelical spectrum Hoffman was fast becoming a 'radical', who ultimately rejected Luther's views on auricular confession, predestination, and a range of other doctrinal points. It is hardly plausible that the Swedish government underwrote his printing. Hoffman's biographer, Klaus Deppermann, points instead to wealthy German merchants in Stockholm, who certainly would have had sufficient resources. As for motive, it is suggested they supported Hoffman's radicalism to protest the king's "half-hearted" religious reforms.[76] If the Crown did in fact control the press, making it available to malcontents intent on

---

[75] Kouri, "Sweden and Finland," 47–52; Grell, "Scandinavia," 112–15; R. Kick, "The Book and the Reformation in the Kingdom of Sweden, 1526–71," *RB*, 449–68. Richolff returned to Hamburg and eventually Lübeck shortly after 1526. He came back to head the Stockholm press again from 1539 to 1541.

[76] Deppermann, *Melchior Hoffman*, 93–94. See also G.H. Williams, *The Radical Reformation*, 3rd ed. (Kirksville, MO, 1992), 623.

subverting the king's religious policy would make no sense. However, technical operations had only just been turned over to Georg Richolff, and during this transition phase regulation of what he printed probably was not comprehensive. Coincidentally, Richolff's tenure in Stockholm was brief. The timing of the publications coupled with the virtually simultaneous departure of the author and the master printer points to collaboration between German merchants and Richolff. The texts were not necessarily printed with the Crown's knowledge or with its whole-hearted approval. After 1526, however, attempts to manage the content and flow of information were far more deliberate and effective, with the government determining what was printed domestically. Less easily regulated or suppressed were German and Latin imprints that originated elsewhere.

Initially, Lutherans threw their support behind a 1527 *Rikstag* edict that instructed Sweden's bishops to preach the Gospels and, implicitly, to stay out of politics.[77] Once Gustav I had silenced potential opponents within the traditional Church, however, would-be reformers would have to defend their own freedom of expression. Gustav I dictated a pace and direction of religious reform that may not have completely satisfied the Germans in Stockholm. Monastic orders and clerical celibacy were retained, and the traditional Catholic liturgy was simply augmented with evangelical preaching of the Gospels. The king prudently steered clear of more radical innovations so as not to antagonise his principal constituents outside Stockholm, the conservative Swedish peasantry.

The political uncertainties in Sweden and efforts to control and exploit the print medium stand in sharp contrast to Poland, where the royal Jagiellonian dynasty was secure and national sovereignty uncontested. In July 1520, long before the Edict of Worms, Sigismund I banned the importation and sale of Luther's books. Rome's envoy had lobbied forcefully for the decree.[78] As a sovereign Christian king and ruler of Royal Prussia and the Grand Duchy of Lithuania as well, Sigismund was duty-bound to uphold the faith. He also needed to tax clerical assets in order to finance military campaigns against Muscovy, and this too may have inclined him to support Rome's

---

[77] *DCR*, no. 101.
[78] *Bibliographia Polonica XV ac XVI ss*, ed. T. Wierzbowski (Warsaw, 1889), 2: 981; Schmidt, *Auf Felsen gesät*, 35–36.

position on Luther. His decree proved inadequate. Books from Erfurt, Magdeburg, Leipzig, and the Wittenberg presses continued to reach Posen in Great Poland, whence they were taken to populous centres south and east.[79] The response was more royal proclamations in 1521 and 1523, again at the urging of the pope's ambassador. Whereas up to now transgressors were to have their property confiscated, it now became a capital offence to import or print heresies. A censorship commission made up of university rectors and theologians was empowered to proscribe any book printed locally or elsewhere. Still, only a few months later the provincial convocation in Gnesen sought stronger policing at the local level. Although the commissioners initiated several investigations, no one was burned. In all there were only about thirty heresy prosecutions in Cracow until mid-century. Scarcely more concerted or effective were measures by Poland's bishops. The bishop of Posen, Piotr Tomicki, was unable to hinder the flow of tainted literature on his own so he complained to the civic magistrates in Posen. But several of them already were estranged from the traditional Church, as were many students at the town's new gymnasium. Residents of Cracow also embraced religious innovation. Bishop Andrzei Krzycki worried that Lutheranism within the diocese was on the rise in 1525. Archdiocesan authority was compromised to some extent by boundary considerations, especially in Breslau, where Lutheran reformers also gained a foothold. Although the town was within the archbishopric of Gnesen, politically it was part of the Bohemian kingdom. The edicts of a Polish monarch did not apply there, and the archbishop, Jan Łaski, was left to his own devices to remedy the Lutheran problem.[80]

That Sigismund's edicts were not enforced vigorously is partly a reflection of humanist influences at the royal court. In 1521 the

---

[79] For the overland trade routes to Poland see Bruns and Weckzerka, *Handelsstrassen*, esp. 2: 672–92.

[80] Schmidt, *Auf Felsen gesät*, 36, 40–42, 226; P. Fox, *The Reformation in Poland* (Baltimore, 1924), 21–25; A. Musteikis, *The Reformation in Lithuania* (New York, 1988), 39; J. Tazbir, "Poland," in *The Reformation in National Context*, ed. R. Porter et al. (Cambridge, 1994), 168–70; A. Kawecka-Gryczowa and J. Tazbir, "The book and the Reformation in Poland," *RB*, 410. In the early 1520s Breslau's two commercial presses undoubtedly contributed to print circulation in Poland. Adam Dyon and Kasper Libisch issued sermons by Luther. Libisch also issued some of Zwingli's articles in 1523–24, although thereafter his press was silent for a decade. Neither printing house issued Scripture translations. *VD* L4796, L6058, L6100, L6256, L6282, L6307, L6378, L6457, L6554, L6565, L65–99, L6604, Z825–30.

bishop of Kamieniec accused Ludwig Decius of heresy. Decius was by then in the king's service. Sigismund protected him and suggested the bishop would do better to channel his energies into anti-Lutheran polemic. Krzycki, who had served in the king's secretariat, welcomed humanist scholars to his residence near Cracow. In the mid-1520s he and other Cracow clergymen published a few anti-Lutheran sermons and some polemic by Johann Eck. On the whole however, the episcopal response was mild and ineffective. Erasmian humanists within the high clergy, among them Krzycki, were not adverse to Church reform, improved clerical discipline, and consistent preaching of the Gospels. Few could be considered staunch Romanists. The same was true of a secular nobility that was not uniformly for or against evangelical innovation, although in central Poland the Duke of Mazovia remained strongly opposed to Luther. Reform was slower to take root there than in the western regions.[81]

Sigismund's response to heterodoxy and grassroots evangelism was to issue edicts. Only once did he intercede directly to counter evangelical influences. In 1525 religious controversy in Danzig combined with political and social discontent to undermine established order. Agitators ousted members of the town's patrician council and Sigismund personally saw to their restoration.[82] Danzig was in Royal Prussia, under Polish rule since the 1460s. For two centuries prior to that the territory was governed by the Teutonic Order. Its three principal towns—Danzig, Elbing, and Thorn—had substantial German populations. And in the early 1520s many within these communities, artisan families more so than landowners and merchants, were receptive to the sermons of transient Lutheran preachers. Social, political, and ethnic tensions were commonplace, although the outcomes in the three towns were not identical.[83] Thorn had the smallest German community. There was little question of Polish residents being marginalised politically or economically by a patrician class

[81] Schmidt, *Auf Felsen gesät*, 37–38, 238–39; M. Greengrass, *The European Reformation* (London, 1998), 304; *Bibliographia Polonica*, 2: nos. 1004, 1019, 3: nos. 1019, 1026, 2117.
[82] Schmidt, *Auf Felsen gesät*, 130–32; E. Cieślak and C. Biernat, *History of Gdańsk*, trans. B. Blaim and G.M. Hyde (Gdańsk, 1988), 123–28.
[83] M.G. Müller, *Zweite Reformation und städtische Autonomie im Königlichen Preußen: Danzig, Elbing und Thorn in der Epoch der Konfessionalisierung (1557–1660)* (Berlin, 1997), 29–31.

that was ostensibly German. No dramatic fusion of socio-political and religious tensions occurred, and not until the 1530s did the civic administration accept Lutheran theology. A different story unfolded in Elbing, where a pattern of social conflict developed prior to 1520, essentially pitting non-patricians against their social superiors over taxes and fiscal policy. Not surprisingly, clerical wealth and immunities became serious issues, ripe for exploitation by evangelists. By 1523 most of the town, magistrates and commoners alike, were pro-Lutheran. Though it did suffer some early setbacks, a process of social harmonisation and confessional reform was set in motion. Political and educational changes were introduced, and mendicant friars, especially Dominicans, were made unwelcome. It was enough to cause Sigismund to address a long list of anti-reform articles to Elbing in the autumn of 1526.[84] By then he already had intervened in Danzig.

Neighbouring East Prussia remained a Teutonic possession until 1525, when the Order's Grand Master, Albrecht of Hohenzollern-Ansbach, swore fealty to Sigismund, ruling thenceforth as duke. Affirming his Lutheranism, he renounced the semi-clerical vows of the Order so that he could marry. Thus Ducal Prussia became a hereditary secular fiefdom. By the time of Albrecht's metamorphosis from Catholic *Hochmeister* to Lutheran duke, the majority of his subjects were already won over to evangelicals, thanks in large measure to his bishops, Eberhard Queiß of Pomesania and Georg von Polentz of Samland. Their open and energetic support of Luther helped unify the populace and the regime. They benefited immeasurably from the fact that their dioceses were intact within the duchy's borders. However, the see of Kulm overlapped the territorial boundary and most though not all of it was territory of the Polish Crown. Emland, part of Poland since 1479, was another border diocese and one whose bishops were consistent in their opposition to Lutheranism. The border with Ducal Prussia therefore became to some degree a confessional divide between Catholics and Lutherans.[85]

Albrecht corresponded with Luther and conferred with him in Wittenberg. Luther's suggestion that the Order be secularised was

---

[84] Schmidt, *Auf Felsen gesät*, 135–37.
[85] H.-J. Karp and A. Triller, "Die Katholische Kirche," and "Humanismus und Bildung beim katholischen Bevölkerungsteil," in *Handbuch der Geschichte Ost- und Westpreußens: Teil 2/1*, ed. E. Opgenoorth (Lüneburg, 1994), 145–54, 175–82.

published in 1523. Two years later, faced with the prospect of resuming hostilities against Poland following a four-year truce, this was seized upon as a viable political alternative.[86] In the principal town, Königsberg, a press had been established under Albrecht's auspices and with the technical assistance of Danzig expatriate Hans Weinreich. It was located, according to one of Weinreich's colophons, by the castle steps in Königsberg's *Altstadt* quarter. The sermons of Johann Brießmann, dispatched to Königsberg by Luther in 1523, and of Polentz were among the earliest works printed there. In 1526 Albrecht also had book consignments sent from Wittenberg for his own library and for distribution to clerics, churches, and schools. Another of Luther's disciples, Johannes Gramann (alias Poliander) was appointed to preach in the *Altstadt* and subsequently became instrumental in establishing new schools.[87] A Lutheran church order came into effect that year. It required regular visitations and necessarily created a need for printed religious texts. From 1524 to 1527 Weinreich issued no fewer than forty-one titles, from ducal decrees to sermons and hymnbooks. Publication of reform literature was encouraged not only for the German population but also in Polish, with the result that Königsberg became an exporter to other German ports and to the Polish-speaking inhabitants of the Prussian hinterland and the Polish kingdom.

On the Baltic's eastern horizon stretched the vast territories of Livonia (*Livland / Estland*), still under the nominal and unconsolidated authority of the Teutonic knights (Livonian Order) and *Landmeister* Walther von Plettenberg. Spiritual authority rested with four bishops and the archbishop of Riga. Though towns were few they were rife with anticlerical sentiment directed especially toward the Church hierarchy and friars. There was considerable opposition to *Exsurge Domine* in Riga, Dorpat, Reval, and among the secular nobility as

---

[86] U. Arnold, "Luther und die Reformation in Preußenland," in *Martin Luther und die Reformation in Ostdeutschland und Südosteuropa*, ed. U. Hutter (Sigmaringen, 1991), 28–34; *UBRG*, 2: nos. 113–14, 176–77, 183–85, 208, 227, 249, 365, 369–71.

[87] K. Lohmeyer, "Geschichte des Buchdrucks und des Buchhandels im Herzogthum Preußen," *AGDB* 18 (1896), 34–36, 86–88; *UBRG*, 1: 91–93, 2: nos. 135, 145–46, 154, 160, 186, 188, 202, 214, 259, 516; P. Schwenke, "Hans Weinreich und die Anfänge des Buchdrucks in Königsberg," *APM* 33 (1896), 67–109; I. Gundermann, "Die evangelischen Kirchen im Herzogtum Preußen," and "Humanismus und Bildungen beim evangelischen Bevölkerungsteil," in *Handbuch der Geschichte Ost-und Westpreußens: Teil 2/1*, ed. E. Opgenoorth (Lüneburg, 1994), 155–60, 175–82. Weinreich printed "Bey der schloßtreppen der Alde stadt" (*VD* B5441).

well. While reformers did attempt to reach out to the rural peasantry in the 1520s, their early success was confined almost entirely
to the towns, where propertied German merchants dominated political affairs. Religious innovation, sometimes tinged with social criticism, became closely tied to a struggle against the prelates for urban
autonomy. By mid-decade it included the installation of evangelical
ministers and the expulsion of Dominican and Franciscan friars.
Plettenberg remained an avowed Catholic, but his acceptance of the
temporal lordship of Riga in 1525 effectively neutralised episcopal
interference, especially from the town's most formidable opponent,
the pluralist archbishop, Johann Blankenfeld.[88]

The Empire and specifically Germany was the fountain of early
Lutheran reform. Culturally and commercially Germany was tied to
and indeed part of two greater regions: the North Sea/Atlantic zone
that included France, the British Isles, and the Low Countries, and
the Baltic region encompassing the Nordic kingdoms, Poland, Prussia,
and Livonia. Wittenberg theology and its early derivatives came to
both areas in the early 1520s. It found especially fertile ground on
the Baltic perimeter because medieval German expansion had left a
lasting imprint there. Port towns, even in Denmark and Sweden,
had ethnic German communities. Their root language was part of
a culture that naturally drew upon printed vernacular literature from
Germany. These same communities had also developed an integrated
system of multilateral trade, again linking them to Germany as well
as to the North Sea/Atlantic region.

New learning was disbursed through a combination of preaching
and print. Maritime communications strengthened interregional contact and enabled direct transmission of ideas from one port constituency to another. Evangelical preachers and/or printed books
from Hamburg and Rostock, for instance, might come directly to
other German communities in the Scandinavian kingdoms, Prussia,
and Livonia. An alternative was gradual and incremental dissemination in areas where, whatever the political and diocesan boundaries, ethnic and linguistic ones were vague and fluid. Holstein
was one example and the Brandenburg-Poland frontier another. No
matter how immediate the initial contact state, civic, and religious

---

[88] W.O. Packull, "Sylvester Tegetmeier, Father of the Livonian Reformation: A
Fragment of his Diary," *Journal of Baltic Studies* 16 (1985), 343–56; Ritscher, *Reval*,
109–35.

authorities had to respond. The integration that encouraged transmission was not about to be undone; Roman Catholicism was itself universal and part of the common culture. Nor was the commercial system that greatly facilitated intellectual exchange about to alter. Once evangelical tenets were introduced and embraced at the popular level, the next phase of the process hinged on the extent to which governing bodies were prepared to repress, tolerate, or exploit them, and how far they would let heterodoxy radicalise. Gustav Vasa took advantage of religious discord, in part to advance his own political ambitions. He intimidated bishops and took the power of the printed word away from them. Sweden's only press was used to help forge a national Lutheran Church, even though initial popular enthusiasm was anything but strong outside Stockholm. The situation in Ducal Prussia was comparable in so far as there was but one press and the government determined its use. In both instances the result was an outpouring of vernacular religious texts. Regarding the motives of the two princes, it is fair to say that while Albrecht also saw political advantage in the religious reform that had begun before he became a secular duke he was more genuinely interested in theology and spiritual renewal than was his neighbour to the north. Elsewhere, royal and ducal regimes in Denmark and Schleswig-Holstein encouraged evangelicals. And in Poland and Royal Prussia a king made anti-heresy proclamations that were unenforceable. The high clergy in Scandinavia and Poland proved incapable of suppressing Lutheranism without tangible help from temporal rulers. That assistance was withheld deliberately in both Nordic Kingdoms, while in Poland and Royal Prussia it was measured and inconsistent. In Ducal Prussia meanwhile, Queiß and Polentz placed themselves at the vanguard of confessional reform. Some more slowly than others, town governments also responded to popular consensus within the body social. Adversarial relationships with Church authorities could be bound up with issues of municipal autonomy, as in Riga and Reval. Subtexts varied, and some patrician oligarchs were reluctant at first, yet most civic regimes within the Baltic region accepted or at least tolerated elements of early Lutheran evangelism. The only notable holdout was Lübeck.

Where it existed at all, censorship of printed material was reactionary and ineffective. Two presses, at Königsberg and Stockholm, had become instruments of state-supported religious reform. Cracow's printing houses might have been capable of mounting an articulate and concerted defence of Rome. They were utilised to produce some polemic and criticism but not fully exploited by the Crown or episcopate to influence the outcomes of confessional debate. Moreover Sigismund's decrees failed to prevent German imprints circulating within his dominions. Beyond the borders of Poland and Royal Prussia book circulation and evangelical preaching were not seriously hindered.

How important was the print medium? Scripture-based Lutheranism, which resonated in towns, necessarily required vernacular texts. Early Danish and Swedish New Testament translations, as well as the numerous German editions, attest to their utility for state-orchestrated reform and a demand for them among urban lay readers. On the other hand print distribution may not have been crucial in sparsely populated rural areas where literacy levels were lower and German was not the first language of most people. Esther-Beate Körber suggests that evangelism in vernacular Polish and Lithuanian depended far more on preaching than print. Few towns in Poland and Royal Prussia had more than 2,000 inhabitants. Larger ones such as Thorn, Elbing, and Warsaw would not reach 20,000 until the end of the sixteenth century. Königsberg, the largest town in Ducal Prussia, may have had about 10,000 residents. Ducal Prussia's new church order eliminated many symbolic forms of instruction and thereby placed more emphasise on preaching, though perhaps not on books until literacy rates improved.[89] The main Livonian towns were not appreciably smaller than towns in Prussia and Poland. There were fewer of them, however. Hinterland communities accepted change more slowly than towns. Even in Riga and Reval, though, reform was as much concerned with clerical wealth and urban autonomy as Scriptures. Also, resentment of the clergy contributed to popular upheaval in several Baltic towns. The presence of large numbers of mendicants and secular clergy played to the advantage of evangelical agitators.

By mid-decade Lutheran innovation faced no serious obstacles in the Baltic region and in many places it was actively encouraged. And in the easternmost regions Bible-based evangelism was radicalised by image-breakers and millenarians. Meanwhile, trade and shipping remained in the hands of Hanse merchants, who integrated

---

[89] Körber, *Öffentlichkeiten*, 176. Population estimates are taken from Schmidt, *Auf Felsen gesät*, 111, 128, and Bues, *Das Herzogtum*, 71.

commerce and thereby enabled cultural exchange with the North
Sea/Atlantic region. Resident foreigners in Antwerp and London
included traders from Riga, Danzig, Lübeck, Hamburg, and Bremen.
In essence, the northern Hanseatic domain was by 1525 well on its
way to becoming a Lutheran one too, so implications for the North
Sea/Atlantic region were inevitable. West of Germany an array of
different social and political circumstances awaited the proponents
of change. There was also a pre-existing tradition of non-conformity,
English Lollardy. Yet for centuries all of Europe had shared the
same faith. How would the people and governments of France, the
Low Countries, and England respond to the new learning?

Heresies and Institutional Response—France, the Low Countries, and England

Unlike Denmark, where a king was deposed, and Sweden, where
the struggle for sovereign independence and dynastic legitimacy had
just begun, regal authority in the French and English kingdoms was
both established and centralised. And in contrast to Royal Prussia
and Livonia, and to some extent the Empire, urban regimes were
not about to test the resolve of prelates or princes on matters religious. In the Low Countries such a challenge was not far off, however it would have to be measured and indirect, in light of the
Habsburg regent's effective albeit incomplete authority over the constituent territories.

Typographic contributions to some extent made France part of
the early northern Reformation. Equally and perhaps more important, especially in the 1520s, was the theology faculty at the University
of Paris and its tradition of scholastic philosophy. Opinions and decisions of Paris theologians carried weight internationally. Reluctance
to reconcile with humanists necessarily entangled the Sorbonne in
the new doctrinal controversies. Political ramifications were unavoid-
able. Although there was some serious debate, the Sorbonne clung
to scholastic tradition even as patronage of humanist learning became
increasingly fashionable in royal and aristocratic circles. The Valois
court at Paris embraced that culture. Although François I remained
conventionally devout he was open to new approaches and would
not countenance persecution of evangelical humanists. Not until much
later was he provoked into active prosecution of radical subversives.

Organised sectarian heresy in France had long since faded away. Waldensian heterodoxy survived only in small isolated pockets in alpine regions and rural Provence. No major or systematic persecutions had occurred within living memory. And no jurisdiction, lay or clerical, had viable mechanisms for controlling or exploiting the printed word. The domestic book market already offered more than traditional religious themes. From Italy came humanist literature and the classics and via the Rhineland the influences of 'Devotio Moderna': lay spiritual renewal based on silent prayer and contemplation. France's reading public could acquire the works of classical antiquity as well as meditative expositions such as *Imitatio Christi* by Thomas à Kempis.[90]

Papal inquisitors had minimal influence in the kingdom, especially after the Crown's Concordat with Rome in 1516. Authority to judge doctrinal questions was vested in the Sorbonne faculty. In April 1521, after two years of deliberation, they condemned 104 of Luther's propositions, but it was not their prerogative to impose any pertinent action. Diocesan courts prosecuted heresy. They were constrained, though, by appeal procedures. Also, most French prelates were royal nominees. Not necessarily churchmen thoroughly schooled in fine points of doctrine, they were poorly equipped to judge the limits of heterodoxy and would have little to do with the censoring of books. The principal arms of secular administration were the sovereign regional *parlements*, especially the *Parlement* of Paris. Though more of an appellant court than legislative body, it registered and enforced royal edicts. It consisted of royal appointees but maintained a strong sense of independence. And from time to time it questioned the king's religious policies, especially regarding beneficed appointments and the Concordat.

On the advice of the Sorbonne, François I instructed the Paris *Parlement* to forbid the printing of Luther's works as well as any others critical of the Church hierarchy in 1521. Yet there was no attendant effort to control the flow of imprints between Basel, Lyon, and Paris. The constraint on presses was largely without consequence

---

[90] Greengrass, *French Reformation*, 5–8; D. Nicholls, "France," in *The Early Reformation in Europe*, ed. A. Pettegree (Cambridge, 1992), 121; R.J. Knecht, *French Renaissance Monarchy: Francis I and Henry II* (London, 1984), 55. A French translation of Thomas à Kempis, *L'imitation de Jesus-Christ* was published in Paris in 1493.

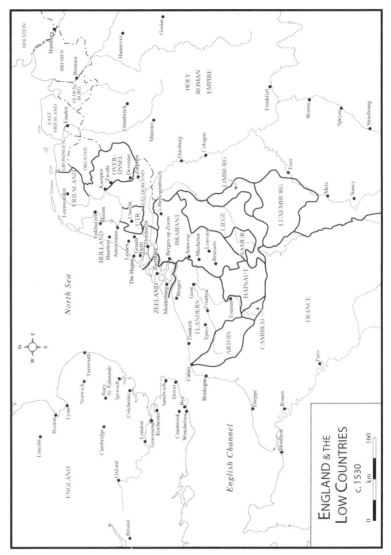

England and the Low Countries

until two years later, when the Sorbonne condemned the views of Parisian humanist Louis de Berquin and the *Parlement* began confiscating books from Paris dealers. Berquin's own library contained a substantial amount of German reform literature, some of which he had already translated into French. Moreover the theologians now presumed to debate the merits of the work of Jacques Lefèvre d'Etaples, France's pre-eminent biblical scholar, whom François had commissioned to translate the New Testament. Lefèvre was part of a humanist circle at Meaux, east of the capital, a group that also included Pierre Caroli, Guillaume Farel, and Gérard Roussel. Their main patron was the reform-minded bishop of the Meaux diocese, Guillaume Briçonnet. Another was Marguerite d'Angoulême. Royal intervention prevented any serious action against them. In 1522 the king ordered the Sorbonne not to condemn works by Lefèvre. A few months later he came to Berquin's rescue, albeit not in time to prevent the burning of his books.[91]

But the king's disastrous military defeat in Italy and subsequent captivity in Madrid opened the way for collaboration between the university and the court. During his absence the queen mother ruled as regent and acquiesced to the formation of an anti-heresy commission consisting of *parlementaires* as well as clerics. Its mandate to prosecute initially applied to the Paris diocese but soon encompassed all areas within the *Parlement*'s jurisdiction. Pope Clement VII approved, allowing the commission's judges to act independently from Church tribunals. Since the *Parlement* was the appellant court, it now had indirect control over heresy cases, and collaborated with the Sorbonne to ban books and silence the Meaux group. Several specific works by reformers were proscribed, as were Scripture texts in French. Berquin was arrested again and the *cercle de Meaux* disbursed. Lefèvre and Roussel went into temporary exile at Strasbourg. The commission then turned to works by Erasmus. The harassment stopped, however, with François' return in 1526. Exiles came back and patronage resumed. The commission was dismantled and replaced by a four-member ecclesiastical tribunal outside the *Parlement*'s control. For the next several years—until the Affair of the Placards in 1534—persecution of religious dissenters was rare, except for more attacks

---

[91] Nicholls, "France," 123–25; Greengrass, *European Reformation*, 287, 290, 297, 305, 307, 318.

on Berquin that resulted in his execution in 1529 when the *Parlement* again exploited the king's absence from the capital.[92]

The Bible-centred humanism of the Meaux circle reflected 'Devotio Moderna' spirituality. Farel and the others were not concerned with fashioning a new religion. Heightened spiritual awareness was to be gained through the Scriptures and critical editions of the early Church fathers. It was a very Erasmian approach, not incompatible with Luther's doctrine of justification through faith. Reforming bishops like Briçonnet also emphasised the Gospels. The Sorbonne's narrow definition of nonconformity, which extended to Lefèvre and Erasmus, was simply unacceptable to the king. On the other hand, François I was never persuaded to reject the sacraments. In fact he urged the *Parlement* to act against Jacques Pavanes, an outspoken sacramentarian. Ultimately, royal support extended to only a few individuals. The beneficiaries nevertheless were men of letters closely tied to a print culture that could influence much larger audiences. Ecclesiastical politics and jurisdictional rivalries also came into play. Bishops, cathedral chapters, mendicant friars, and the Sorbonne did not forge a united front against heresy. The king's sympathy for Catholic humanists, coupled with the absence of concerted intervention or book censorship, except in 1525, meant that French evangelical reform was relatively free to radicalise. Farel, for one, eventually rejected Lefèvre and Luther in favour of Zwingli.

Even prior to 1525 it is doubtful that Paris and Lyon bookshops carried especially large inventories of controversial books. Many Parisian booksellers and printers were located in or near the academic quarter. Traditionally, twenty-four of them were distinguished as officers of the university, *libraires jurés*. Four were *grands libraires*, designated to regulate prices and generally monitor the book trade.[93] While Luther's works, printed in Basel, were available in Paris as early as 1519, the direct role of French presses in generating early evangelical propaganda was not great. Luther's *De Libertate Christiana* circulated in translation, yet his strongly polemical works, such as *De Captivitate Babylonica Ecclesiae praeludium* were not rendered into

---

[92] *Inventaire de la Collection Anisson sur l'histoire de l'imprimerie et la librairie*, ed. E. Coyecque (Paris, 1900), 1: 1, 280; Hirsch, *Printing*, 94; F.M. Higman, *Censorship and the Sorbonne* (Geneva, 1979), 15–26, 73–82; Greengrass, *French Reformation*, 14–20; Nicholls, "France", 123–26.
[93] Tilley, "Paris Bookseller," 39–40.

French. Few Paris printers showed more than a token interest even before the regulations were introduced, with the possible exception of Simon de Colines, the first printer of Lefèvre's New Testament translation, and Simon Du Bois, who issued works by Farel and Lefèvre. Not much original reform literature was printed in Paris in the later 1520s. François Lambert's French version of *De Libertate* was published in 1525 at Strasbourg. Most subsequent French translations of Luther came either from there or Basel, or from the Antwerp presses of Willem Vorsterman and Parisian expatriate Martin de Keyser (alias Martin Lempereur).[94] Similarly, while some Paris presses issued French prayer books and New Testaments early on, later editions of Scriptures originated elsewhere. Lyon printer Pierre de Vingle had already begun publishing Farel in 1525, and within a year or two there was a Lyon edition of Lefèvre's New Testament. Schabler issued one at Basel as well. No more French New Testaments were legally produced in Paris until the second half of the century. Lefèvre's complete Bible was printed in 1530 by Simon de Colines— at Antwerp.[95] The nominal significance of printers in the capital was a direct consequence of the censorship in 1525, which failed to silence authors and translators but gave rise to publication of their work in other places.

While Parisian printers were disinclined to issue reform-related texts, several in the Low Countries did not hesitate. They faced anti-heresy decrees that were stern and pervasive, however they worked in a land where several legal jurisdictions appeared to overlap. Within the Habsburg Low Countries the ecclesiastical hierarchy was by the 1520s very much a branch of the state apparatus. Spiritual authorities did not rule any part of the domain, ducal favourites occupied the six episcopal sees, and there was no archbishopric. Bishops could take the initiative against heretics and so could papal inquisitors, relying on the unquestioned competence of Louvain's theology faculty with regard to doctrinal questions. The authority of diocesan inquisitors was augmented by the decrees of the temporal lord,

---

[94] F.M. Higman, *Piety and the People: Religious printing in France 1511–1551* (Aldershot, 1996), 5–6 and "French-speaking Regions, 1520–62," *RB*, 106–10. Lambert's translation of *De Libertate* (*VD* L7217) was issued by Strasbourg printers Johann Schott and Wolfgang Köpfel.

[95] Greengrass, *European Reformation*, 258; Higman, *Censorship*, 73–82; Droz, "Pierre de Vingle," 44, 78.

with the result that heresy could be and was closely equated with
treason.[96] However, since prosecutions were not the prerogative of
any particular court, towns and provinces sought to have heresy
cases, like other criminal proceedings, tried within their boundaries,
in order to safeguard their own legal privileges.

Urged on by Aleandro as he toured the Low Countries with
Charles's retinue in 1520–21, the bishops saw to the promulgation
of *Exsurge Domine*.[97] Results were mixed, in part due to contrasting
circumstances within the dioceses, especially the two largest: Liege
and Utrecht. Another contributing factor was the degree to which
the diocesan prelates engaged in the affairs of secular government.
The prince-bishop and cardinal of Liege, Erard de la Marck, was
an advisor to the regent and therefore very much a part of the
regime that ruled in the emperor's name. Liege bordered the archdiocese of Cologne in the east, and one of its principal towns was
Louvain, home to the university theologians who censored Luther.
Support of the papacy vis à vis Luther was never in doubt. The
bishop ordered anti-Lutheran sermons to be preached and books
burned, and also issued his own edict in October 1520. By comparison the bishops of Utrecht, Charles's cousin Philip of Burgundy
and his successor in 1524 Heinrich of Bavaria, were more remote
from the affairs of the central government. Like Liege, Utrecht was
a vast, sprawling diocese. Within it stood the seaports of Zeeland
and the great commercial and industrial towns of Holland: Dordrecht,
Amsterdam, Leiden, and Haarlem, distant from Louvain and the
Church province of Cologne, but with strong economic, cultural,
and linguistic ties to lower Germany. To the east of Holland, though
still in the Utrecht diocese, were other important centres—Zwolle,
Deventer, and Zutphen—in lordships not yet fully consolidated under
Habsburg political authority. Hence, although the papal bull was
published in Utrecht, enforcing compliance presented many challenges.[98] Of the four remaining sees, the largest were Cambrai between

---

[96] Greengrass, *European Reformation*, 138; J.A. Führner, *Die Kirchen- und die antireformatorische Religionspolitik Kaiser Karls V. in den siebzehn Provinzen der Niederlande 1515–1555*
(Leiden, 2004), 42–45.
[97] M.E. Kronenberg, *Verboden Boeken en Opstandige Drukkers in de Hervormingstijd*
(Amsterdam, 1948), 9–10, 20, 24.
[98] *CD*, 4: nos. 34, 5: nos. 750–53.

Utrecht and the river Scheldt and Tournai to the west of it. Titular authority in spiritual matters at the Brabantine metropolis of Antwerp, situated within the margravate of Antwerp, was vested in the Cambrai bishops. However, an agreement with the bishop in 1490 rendered the town largely free of ecclesiastical interference and in any event there were too few clerics in the town to carry out episcopal initiatives.[99] As elsewhere in the Low Countries, real power for heresy prosecutions rested with civic authorities, provincial courts, and Habsburg vicegerents. To be effective, therefore, any ecclesiastical campaign required secular co-operation and assistance at both the provincial and municipal level, as well as support from the central government.

Habsburg administration was centred at Mechelen, in the capable hands of Charles's aunt, Margaret of Austria-Savoy, and her Privy Council. Among her chief advisors were the stadholders (*stadhouders*), Charles's provincial lieutenants, who took overall responsibility for security and justice, and for the calling of provincial assemblies. The most authoritative voice was Antoine de Lalaing, Count of Hoochstraten, appointed stadholder of Holland, Zeeland, and Friesland in 1522. For the registering of edicts and the administration of justice stadholders and the government at Mechelen looked to the state councils of Holland, Brabant, and Flanders, each with a president chosen from councillors ordinary. Provincial delegates assembled every three years as the States General (*Staten Generaal*) to make collective decisions on legal and financial matters, especially taxation. Constituent courts of the provincial councils, in particular the Court of Holland, advised and monitored their local counterparts. Town administrations consisted of burgomasters, magistrates, aldermen, and treasurers, and in large centres such as Antwerp there were ward masters. Beginning in the early sixteenth century Antwerp also retained two university-trained lawyers on a permanent basis. Criminal prosecutions for capital offences involved civic authorities with the *schout*, a bailiff appointed by the territorial prince. The *schout* proclaimed and enforced decrees and arraigned offenders before the *Vierschaar*, a court of aldermen (*schepenen*) empowered to conduct trials and pass sentence. Magistracy appointments were made by the

---

[99] Goris, *Étude*, 546. Most of the town's clergy were attached to monastic houses. Marnef, *Antwerp*, 48–49.

stadholders from lists submitted by civic officials. During Margaret's regency Hoochstraten approved appointments in the main towns of Holland without consulting the central government. His counterpart in Flanders did likewise in Gent and Bruges.[100]

Upon assuming responsibility for his Burgundian dominions in 1515, Charles had undertaken the traditional processional entry— the *Blijde Incomst* or *Joyeuse Entrée*—into his provinces, pledging to uphold and protect the rights, privileges, and customs of his subjects in return for their loyalty. In 1517 he departed for Spain, entrusting governance to Margaret. She actively tried to enforce religious conformity. Although she later complained to the regional councils of Brabant and Flanders about lax compliance, one of her early initiatives was an anti-blasphemy decree. In 1520, after university theologians at Louvain and Cologne had examined and rejected Luther's writings, *Exsurge Domine* was issued. The following March, still several weeks before the Edict of Worms, the printing or mere possession of Luther's books in the Low Countries became punishable by forfeiture of property. Promulgation and enforcement of these heresy laws fell to the provincial councils and ultimately to local magistrates, whose duty it was to investigate transgressions and stage the requisite public book-burnings.[101] Whether or not Charles V should have been somewhat better able to compel observance of his edicts in his patrimonial lands than elsewhere is open to question. As the lawful ruler of each principality he could claim direct authority over his subjects, an impossibility in Germany. The Low Countries also constituted considerably less territory. On the other hand, his dependence on the States to raise the capital needed for repayment of high-interest loans made them more valuable, from a fiscal stand-

---

[100] Marnef, *Antwerp*, 14–15, 19; P. Rosenfeld, *The Provincial Governors from the Minority of Charles V to the Revolt* (Louvain, 1959), 43–44. J.D. Tracy, "Heresy Law and Centralization under Mary of Hungary: Conflict between the Council of Holland and the Central Government over the Enforcement of Charles V's Placards," *ARG* 73 (1982), 286; Fühner, *Religionspolitik*, 15–24, 33–46. Writing from Louvain in December 1520, Erasmus remarked on the popularity of evangelical reform in the Low Countries and the people's rejection of *Exsurge Domine*. *Correspondence of Wolfgang Capito*, 110.

[101] *CD*, 4: nos. 13, 22, 34, 39, 42, 47, 68, 76, 81, 82, 92, 100, 5: nos. 755, 760. Before his imperial coronation the decrees were issued in the name of Charles, King of Spain and Count of Flanders, etc. Later, he was by grace of God Roman Emperor, King of Germany, King of Castile, etc.

point, than the *Landtag*, which collected and disbursed revenues on his behalf within Germany.[102] His war chest was much more dependent on taxes from the Netherlands than from Spain or the Empire, so he could ill afford to be too antagonistic toward the provincial assemblies that voted money and the populous urban centres that generated much of it.

Until March 1524 placards issued through the regency government did not proscribe specific titles. They did, however, raise some fundamental legal and constitutional issues. In them heresy was interpreted as treason against God—*lèse majesté divine*—and therefore it could be claimed that, as with civil treason, normal legal rights and procedures were not applicable. This cut close to the enshrined judicial prerogatives of towns; powers that civic magistracies were bound to defend. The typically measured responses of municipal officials to the imperial edicts seldom had much to do with devotional preferences. They were rooted in the duty to uphold existing civic liberties. Another consideration was the general mood of the citizenry. In urban constituencies such as Amsterdam, where sixteen cloisters took up as much as one third of the land area, reformers and traditionalists alike resented clerical exemptions from excise and property taxes. So as observant friars railed publicly against Luther, heresy laws that targeted his followers were open to interpretation by the laity not only as a threat to town rights but also as implicit support for the privileges of the clerical estate.[103] At Antwerp, with by far the largest and most cosmopolitan urban population in the Low Countries, clerical privilege was not especially contentious. But that did not preclude other controversies or popular resistance to decrees that required traditional conformity. A chief concern of civic officials was simply the preservation of public order, a prerequisite for the mercantilism that allowed the entrepôt to flourish.

The circumventing of normal legal procedures to prosecute individuals allegedly sympathetic to Luther also compromised the

---

[102] J.D. Tracy, *Holland under Habsburg Rule, 1506–1566: The Formation of a Body Politic* (Los Angeles, 1990), 41. H.G. Koenigsberger outlines relations between the States and the regency administration with regard to taxes and finance in *Monarchies, States Generals and Parliaments: The Netherlands in the Fifteenth and Sixteenth Centuries* (Cambridge, 2001), esp. 113–22.

[103] A. Duke, "Salvation by Coercion," in *Reformation Principle and Practice*, ed. P.N. Brooks (London, 1980), 137–38, 146–49; Tracy, *Holland*, 60–61, 147–52 and "Heresy Law," 285–90.

authority of provincial assemblies, especially in heavily urbanised
Flanders, Brabant, and Holland. The States too had prerogatives to
defend as they strove to balance compliance with the preservation
of due process. Tensions came to the fore in the spring of 1522
when the emperor attempted to create a state inquisition. Full investigative and prosecutorial powers were bestowed on a member of
the Council of Brabant, Franz van der Hulst, who, assisted by several clerics, set up a mobile heresy tribunal in Brussels and The
Hague. It operated well outside accepted legal tradition and was at
once presumptuous and confrontational. In particular, the prosecution of two individuals—a Delft schoolmaster and a distinguished
humanist advocate of the Council of Holland, Cornelis Hoen—
drew impassioned criticism. Hoen's subsequent removal to St. Geertrui-
denberg, still within the county but well south of The Hague, was
deliberately antagonistic. The Council of Holland complained pro-
fusely to the regent, pointing to the privilege of *de non evocando* by
which, except for counterfeiting and treason *lèse majesté*, Hollanders
claimed immunity from prosecution outside provincial boundaries.
Furthermore, in neglecting to confer with the provincial body Hulst
was subverting its judicial authority, which so far as the Council was
concerned extended to heresy cases. The situation worsened when
in June 1523 Pope Adrian VI, a Netherlander and former tutor of
Charles, attempted to bring heresy prosecutions back under Church
control. Hulst was designated papal inquisitor, with authority over
all others except the bishops. The great towns of Holland dismissed
Hulst's inquisition as "contra antiquam consuetudinem, contra ius
commune" and demanded he be reined in. The situation had become
untenable, giving Margaret little choice but to order the suspension
of Hulst's investigations in Holland and ultimately to prevail upon
her nephew to revoke his commission. His papal mandate was not
renewed by Adrian's successor Clement VII.[104] Thereafter, by agreement with Rome, inquisitors in the Low Countries were to be nominated by Charles or his regent and formally appointed by the pope.
Nicholas Coppin, one of Margaret's nominees, was named inquisitor general in 1525 but had no special authority from the government.
Thus heresy cases reverted once again to more familiar jurisdictions

[104] Tracy, *Holland*, 152–55 and "Heresy Law," 285; *CD*, 4: nos. 79, 123–26, 131, 136, 149–57, 161–69, 219, 639–40; Führer, *Religionspolitik*, 219–38.

and courts. Coppin's deputies were far more active in Flanders than in the north. It was a victory of sorts for the States. Even so, the political power structures and the continuous interplay of all three tiers of government—the regency, the councils of the provinces, and the town administrations—would have much to do with both the pace and direction of Church reform. By early 1524 they had yet another imperial decree to enforce, this one prohibiting the printing of the Scriptures or religious texts anywhere in the Low Countries without the consent of Louvain's theology faculty.[105]

It was Louvain's ruling against Luther in 1520, together with the papal decree, that had prompted the first burning of his books in England. The prerogative of English Church authorities to prosecute authors of heretical works had been confirmed by parliamentary statute a century before. Diocesan consistories and provincial convocations tried heresy cases. In geographical area the episcopal jurisdictions varied considerably. The Lincoln diocese, which included Oxford, stretched north to the river Humber. Far smaller was neighbouring Ely, where Cambridge was situated. Much of East Anglia and England's second largest town, Norwich, fell within the see of Norwich. Ecclesiastical administration and heresy prosecutions in the south, where wealth and population were concentrated, fell to the bishops of London, Rochester, Winchester, Salisbury, and the archbishop of Canterbury. It was in this part of the country too, especially in the dioceses of London, Rochester, and Canterbury that pockets of nonconformity already existed. Southern bishoprics and Norwich were all the more significant with regard to heretical books because of coastal and overseas commerce. All had continental trade links.

Ecclesiastical censorship in England had for the most part proved sufficient to control homespun Lollardy and limit the diffusion of Wycliffite Bibles. Once specific material was identified and prohibited, it became the responsibility of local mayors to investigate and report. Prior to the 1520s production and sale of books was not restricted systematically on the basis of content.[106] The works of

---

[105] *AA*, 2: 314–15.
[106] Loades, "Books," 266; H.W. Winger, "Regulations relating to the Book Trade in London from 1357 to 1558," *Library Quarterly* 26 (1956), 165–66; Hirsch, *Printing*, 92. The relatively small number of presses in England and their concentration in

Luther, however, presented a new challenge in that they originated abroad. Moreover, while most Lollard tracts had circulated only in manuscript, there was now an established international traffic in mass-produced printed material. Existing regulatory measures were inadequate. New ones would need to be devised. No secular authority in England, including the chancellor, Thomas Wolsey, had clear independent authority to prosecute suspected heretics. However, in his capacity as cardinal-legate Wolsey could initiate proceedings and override the decision of any Church court. The laity's resentment of such courts complicated matters. The absence of a precise legal description resembling the statutory definition of treason meant that English bishops already interpreted heresy very broadly.[107] Secular magistrates merely carried out punishments. So while popular anti-clericalism drew attention to immunities enjoyed by churchmen, it was also an expression of dissatisfaction regarding the criminal juris-diction of diocesan courts over laypersons. The recent scandalous death of a London merchant-tailor, Richard Hunne, provided a rally-ing cry for critics. Hunne's attempt to sue the bishop of London had resulted in his arrest for heresy. He then perished in the bishop's prison before he could be brought to trial. A coroner's inquest ruled it was homicide.

Although England had few presses, imported editions of Luther's works were available as early as May 1519, circulating primarily within the academic communities at Oxford and Cambridge. Some may have been burned ceremoniously in Cambridge the following year, after their condemnation by the Louvain faculty. The papal bull of June 1520, forbidding anyone to print or own Luther's works in any language, was applicable throughout the kingdom. In another gesture of support for the pope and emperor in the aftermath of the Diet of Worms, Wolsey directed bishops to proscribe Lutheran and Lollard books in their respective dioceses. Enough were surrendered to make another fire, in the spring of 1521, at Paul's Cross in

London likely deterred would-be printers of illegal Bibles because avoiding detec-tion would have been all but impossible. A. Pettegree, "Printing and the Reformation: The English Exception," in *The Beginnings of English Protestantism*, ed. P. Marshall and A. Ryrie (Cambridge, 2002), 167.

[107] "Heresy was whatever the church defined it to be, so anyone who willfully defied church teachings could be condemned as a heretic": L.M. Higgs, *Godliness and Governance in Tudor Colchester* (Ann Arbor, 1998), 101–2.

London. By then Henry VIII, assisted perhaps by his almoner Edward Lee, Bishop John Fisher of Rochester, and Sir Thomas More, had written a defence of Catholicism, *Assertio septem sacramentorum*. Printed by Richard Pynson in July and subsequently reissued in Rome, the initiative earned Henry high praise from the pope: the dignity Defender of the Faith. No other monarch would attempt a comparable contribution to the theological debate in print. In that regard Henry was unique. Even so, his involvement in the Luther controversy did not yet extend to book censorship, which remained in the hands of England's clerical establishment.

Presses in Cologne, Mainz, Strasbourg, and Augsburg were soon producing reprints of *Assertio* as well as German translations.[108] Indeed well before English exiles began to exploit the foreign presses effectively, England's most articulate spokesmen for conformity were well served by continental printers, who published Latin rebuttals of Luther for circulation among Europe's learned. Antwerp printers, Vorsterman and Michiel Hillen van Hoochstraten, issued some of John Fisher's early polemical works and so did Peter Quentell in Cologne. Certain master printers would eventually become identified with one side or the other of the religious debate, while others recognised economic opportunity in both. Hoochstraten, for example, who printed Fisher's comprehensive *Assertionis Lutheranae Confutatio* in January 1523, had by then already offered editions both of Henry's *Assertio* and Luther's *De Captivitate*.[109] Much of the printing done for Church and government interests in London was handled by Pynson and Wynkyn de Worde, who were unlikely to risk anything potentially controversial precisely because of their reliance on royal and ecclesiastical patronage. As time would tell, regardless of where individual tracts were printed and by whom, counter-propaganda from the pens of Fisher and Thomas More could not stem the flow of Lutheran imports. Bishop Tunstall of London foresaw as much, so in October 1524 he issued a warning to London's stationers. Thenceforth no books were to be brought into the country or sold there without his permission.

---

[108] *VD* H2166–71; *Flugschriften gegen die Reformation (1518–1524)*, ed. A. Laube (Berlin, 1997), 344–61.

[109] G. Tournoy, "Humanists, Rulers and Reformers: Relationships between England and the Southern Low Countries in the First Half of the Sixteenth Century," in *Antwerp, Dissident Typographical Centre*, ed. D. Imhof, G. Tournoy and F. de Nave (Antwerp, 1994), 22–23, 90.

England's ecclesiastical hierarchy would determine what was suitable for the English people to read.

Aside from the polemical battle into which John Fisher was already drawn and More soon would be, some of the circumstances leading to this drastic measure come to light in the reports of English observers abroad. Henry's *Assertio* elicited an astonishingly crude response from Wittenberg, Luther's *Contra Henricum regum Angliae*. Late in 1522 Wolsey's agent in Rome, Thomas Hannibal, sent him a copy, along with assurances that he would see to the burning of any others he could find. In fact he was powerless to suppress circulation there or anywhere else. It was reissued frequently, in Latin and in German translation. Nor was one of the staunchest German Catholic princes, Albertine Saxony's Duke Georg, able to accomplish much. He already had urged the *Reichsregiment* at Nürnberg to suppress the imprints, when in early 1523 a complaining letter from Henry arrived. He could do little else but have the correspondence translated into German and published together with a sympathetic reply.[110]

There was no possibility of Henry VIII immediately stooping to respond to Luther's diatribe, so the task of refuting it and doling out appropriate ridicule fell to Thomas More. Thus, before the end of 1523 Pynson had issued More's first published polemical work, his pseudonymous *Responsio ad Lutherum*.[111] Throughout that year, though, diplomatic dispatches to England were far less concerned with any Lutheran challenge than with Charles V's ambitions to expand his empire at the expense of France and the papacy. The correspondence of Robert Wingfield, England's ambassador to the Habsburg court in the Low Countries, and indeed most other reports from overseas informed the home government of diplomatic manoeuvring, alliances, troop strengths, and the fall of Rhodes to the Turks. Into the autumn letters continued to emphasise military matters, with William Knight providing intelligence whilst Wingfield participated in a disastrous English expedition into France. But more firsthand

---

[110] *LP*, 3/2: no. 2714; *VD* L4244; *LW*, 2/2: 175–262; *Flugschriften gegen die Reformation*, 484–98. Emser's German translation of the letters was issued by Stöckel in Leipzig and later by Quentell in Cologne. In Strasbourg Wolfgang Köpfel printed a version by Thomas Murner.

[111] *CW*, 5/1 and 5/2; *STC* 18088.5, 18089; D. Trevor, "Thomas More's *Responsio ad Lutherum* and the Fictions of Humanist Polemic," *Sixteenth Century Journal* 32 (2001), 743–64.

news of the Lutheran heresy did come when two other envoys, Lord Morley (Henry Parker) and Edward Lee, reported from Germany. Morley's dispatch on 4 October spoke of the wide circulation of Luther's books and "abominable pictures" in upper Germany, especially at Frankfurt. They could even be found at Cologne, where town senator Sir Hermann Rinck hosted the foreign envoys.[112]

Following the report from Cologne another letter arrived from Nürnberg. Johannes Fabri, vicar general of Konstanz and advisor to Archduke Ferdinand, exhorted Henry VIII to extinguish the Lutheran heresy, against which he recently had published his *Malleus Haeresim Lutheranae*. Already stung by the insolent vitriol of *Contra Henricum*, the king required no further prompting. Letters were dispatched to Ferdinand and to Elector Frederick and his brother Johann in early January, urging suppression of Luther's Bible translation. Henry claimed to have no objection to the Scriptures in translation per se, but only to Luther's. Naturally, Ferdinand vowed to do his best, but the replies from Electoral Saxony in May 1524 made clear the dukes' intention not to intervene.[113] The impending showdown with François I now preoccupied Charles V. Henry's professed concern for the preservation of traditional orthodoxy on the continent previewed an apparent willingness to assume a more active role. Clearly the intent was to stifle any incursion of doctrinal innovation into the kingdom, although there existed another context for a position against Luther that essentially mirrored the emperor's. While Henry VIII was reluctant to commit military resources to Charles in 1524, he nevertheless wished to remain on good terms in the event of a Habsburg victory in Italy. Should that occur, he could then assist the imperial cause and advance his own territorial claims by invading northern France. Foreign policy therefore remained fluid and driven by events far from England's shores. In the end, so complete was the victory of Charles's army at Pavia in February 1525 that Henry's self-serving proposal to invade France was neither necessary nor desirable from the Habsburg point of view.

To these considerations were added one more piece of diplomatic correspondence that helped set the stage for future action by England's

---

[112] *LP*, 3/2: nos. 3390, 3391.
[113] *VD* F214; *LP*, 3/2: no. 3630; 4/1: nos. 40, 228, 301; R. Rex, "The English Campaign against Luther in the 1520s," *Transactions of the Royal Historical Society*, 5th series, 39 (1989), 99.

chancellor. It came in the spring of 1524 from Hannibal and another English envoy then in Rome, John Clerk. Lorenzo Campaggio, the papal legate for Germany, had asked that Wolsey be informed of the alarming strength of Lutheranism there. His suggested remedy, wrote Clerk, was that "other strange nations wher the nation of germanye hath entrecours or medelyng by marchandise or otherwise shold shewe themself that they ded abhorre the said nation of germanye for maynteynyng suche a detestable sect amongst thaym". To this end, therefore, cardinal Campaggio was hopeful "some demonstration myght be made in london [to] the nation of germanye".[114] The nation to which he alluded was a specific and highly privileged cohort within London's business community: merchants of the German Hanse.

[114] BL Cotton. MS Vitellius B VI fo. 58; *LP*, 4/1: no. 320.

CHAPTER TWO

BONFIRES AND THREATENING WORDS

The actual or potential involvement of merchants as intermediaries in heresy dissemination was bound to draw attention to laws intended to regulate them. And this in turn brought into focus the obligations, whether clearly defined or implied, of bilateral treaties of commercial intercourse. Political leverage was an intrinsic corollary when governments extended special status to specific foreign business coteries. A case in point was the German Hanse. In England, according to ancient charters, merchants from Hanse towns paid lower customs rates than denizens and other aliens. This extraordinary advantage and possession of residences in London, Lynn, and Boston were enshrined in the Peace of Utrecht in 1474. The privileges were reconfirmed in February 1510, during Henry VIII's first parliament.[1]

Chancellor Wolsey nevertheless could threaten to curtail or revoke liberties on almost any pretext. And he did not hesitate to do so, though usually with the aim of reducing the competitive advantage of the Steelyard men or gaining reciprocal arrangements for English merchants overseas. Repeated diplomatic discussions in the early 1520s had failed to resolve these and other trade-related issues. It was against this backdrop that controversy over Luther's alleged heresy emerged. The mobility of individuals engaged in long-distance trade meant they were especially capable of bringing informed opinions and printed books from one locale to another. Inherent, too, were opportunities to exchange ideas through interaction both within and outside the merchant milieu. Regardless of the degree to which early evangelical propaganda ultimately influenced reception of the Henrician reform, during the 1520s English government and Church authorities necessarily took measures to suppress imported heterodoxy.

---

[1] T.H. Lloyd, *England and the German Hanse, 1157–1611* (Cambridge, 1991), 212–17, 251, 254–59; J.D. Fudge, *Cargoes, Embargoes, and Emissaries: The Commercial and Political Interaction of England and the German Hanse, 1450–1510* (Toronto, 1995), 74–76.

Penance at Paul's Cross

The first proclamation outlawing possession of Lutheran books in England was issued from the pulpit at Paul's Cross, within the cathedral precincts of old St. Paul's, on 12 May 1521. Wolsey's attendance, together with that of a distinguished retinue drawn from the high clergy and nobility, served to emphasise both the grandeur of the established Church and the gravity of the issue for a large crowd of onlookers. John Fisher, bishop of Rochester, preached a lengthy sermon denouncing Luther, later printed for distribution to a wider audience by Wynkyn de Worde. A quantity of offending books was burned. Any more that had not been seized were to be surrendered to Church authorities.[2] Evidently no exhaustive searches had been conducted; certainly no cells of book smugglers exposed. In the absence of an official index of titles it was a rather predictable proscription, consistent with the tried and true approach to suppressing Lollard manuscripts. England's bishops necessarily had to revise and update formularies of articles used in heresy cases. Periodic forfeitures of books were a way of staying informed of the latest innovations and errors in circulation. On this occasion Fisher's sermon also served to advertise Henry's *Assertio*, thus foreshadowing a strategy that for the next half decade relied heavily on waging a polemical battle with Luther.[3] The ban proved less than satisfactory, and so did an attendant round of prosecutions for Lollardy orchestrated by the new bishop of Lincoln, John Longland, carried out in various dioceses, including London and Salisbury. Hence, the efforts of Cuthbert Tunstall, who succeeded Richard Fitzjames as bishop of London the following year, were much more focused on preventing the dissemination of printed heresies. Having spent several months on embassy in Germany prior to his appointment, he knew firsthand of the circulation of Luther's German imprints. His correspondence

---

[2] *LP*, 3/1: nos. 1210, 1234, 1273–74; *Ecclesiastical Memorials*, ed. J. Strype (Oxford, 1822), 1/2: 20–25; C.S. Meyer, "Henry VIII Burns Luther's Books, 12 May 1521," *Journal of Ecclesiastical History* 9 (1958), 173–87. Fisher's sermon: *The English Works of John Fisher, Bishop of Rochester*, ed. J.E.B. Mayor, Early English Text Society, extra series, 27 (1935), 311–48; *STC* 10894.

[3] J.F. Davis, *Heresy and Reformation in the south-east of England, 1520–1559* (London, 1983), 9; C.W. D'Alton, "The Suppression of Lutheran Heretics in England, 1526–1529," *Journal of Ecclesiastical History* 54 (2003), 230.

from Worms had alerted Wolsey to the great trouble that would ensue if they were translated into English, and had urged that London's printers and stationers be ordered not to bring such books into the country.[4] He was vested now with episcopal authority, and in the autumn of 1524 proceeded to issue his own warning against importing or translating. No newly imported material was to be sold without first being examined by Fisher, Wolsey, Archbishop Warham of Canterbury, or Tunstall himself. They alone could approve books for sale. This, then, marked the introduction of licensing in England, a response directed at professionals within the legal book trade. A measure of its effectiveness, perhaps, is that for the most part London's established printers and booksellers do seem to have steered clear of the clandestine traffic in imported heresies.[5] By late 1525, however, there was renewed concern. Intelligence from the continent informed of the persecution of humanist reformers in Paris but also of an unauthorised English translation of the New Testament in Germany. Disciples of Luther would soon attempt to have printed copies smuggled into England.[6] Time had come for a pre-emptive demonstration of authority. With the king's approval, Wolsey now proposed to search secretly in "diverse places" for offending literature and to require further that all Lutheran books be turned over to the bishops on pain of excommunication. Anyone who refused to comply would be prosecuted as a heretic.[7]

A few weeks later, on Shrove Sunday 1526, the Jesus Bell at St. Paul's summoned London's faithful. The cathedral environs soon overflowed with the devout and the curious. Seated with Wolsey upon the new scaffolding erected for the occasion were some three dozen abbots, priors, and bishops. In front of them knelt a learned Austin friar, Robert Barnes, and five other individuals allegedly tainted by Lutheranism. As Fisher rose to recite another homily, the fire was made ready. What followed was a solemn and precisely orchestrated exercise in counter-propaganda as much intended for the

---

[4] Sturge, *Cuthbert Tunstal*, 120–21, 360–63.
[5] Winger, "Regulations," 166–68; A.W. Reed, "The Regulation of the Book Trade before the Proclamation of 1538," *Transactions of the Bibliographical Society* 15 (1920), 162–63.
[6] *ENT*, 36–37; *LP*, 4/1: nos. 1802, 1803.
[7] *LP*, 4/1: no. 995; A.G. Chester, "Robert Barnes and the Burning of the Books," *Huntington Library Quarterly* 14 (1951), 215–16.

instruction of the audience as for the correction of the accused.
Baskets of prohibited books fuelled the bonfire. Into the flames Barnes
and four of his co-accused cast their faggots, while a sixth man bore
a taper to be offered at the rood by the north door. Each of them
publicly abjured, asking God's forgiveness and that of the Church
and the cardinal-legate. All of them received absolution and were
escorted back to the Fleet prison, their fate still entirely in Wolsey's
hands. Descending from his lofty perch with due ceremony, he also
departed. The flames burned low; the congregation dispersed. For
those who witnessed it, as well as for those who would hear of it
later, this elaborate public display reinforced important and powerful images. Erroneous teachings had been turned to ashes, bold and
misguided men humbled by the all-pervasive authority of the institutional Church.

By far the least obscure member of the group was Robert Barnes.
The circumstances surrounding his arrest, as well as his subsequent
fate, were chronicled by the Anglican martyrologist John Fox, and
have been retold many times since.[8] Doctor Barnes, prior of the
Augustinian house at Cambridge, had preached an inflammatory sermon on Christmas Eve 1525 at Trinity Hall. It included a particularly sharp harangue against Wolsey and the prelates, prompting
some of those who took issue to accuse him of heresy. Controversy
consumed the university community for several weeks before a
sergeant-at-arms was sent from London in early February. As the
chambers of his supporters were ransacked for Lutheran literature,
Barnes was taken into custody. His interrogation on points of doctrinal orthodoxy began in London on 8 February. For three days
he refuted a series of articles presented against him by a commission of bishops, before Wolsey's secretary, Stephen Gardiner, persuaded him to recant on the very eve of his ordeal at Paul's Cross.
He spent perhaps another half year in prison prior to being transferred to the house of the Austin friars in London but eventually
escaped to Germany in November 1528. During his absence from
England he lived among Lutherans in Hamburg and Wittenberg.

---

[8] Fox, *Acts and Monuments*, 5: 414–21; Robert Barnes, *The Reformation Essays of Dr.
Robert Barnes*, ed. N.S. Tjernagel (London, 1963), 7–19; Chester, "Robert Barnes,"
211–21; J.P. Lusardi, "The Career of Robert Barnes," *CW*, 8/3: 1367–1415; N.S.
Tjernagel, *Henry VIII and the Lutherans* (St. Louis, 1965), 47–55.

Three years passed before Henry VIII, in serious need of political allies, allowed him to return. Appointed the king's chaplain, Barnes liased on England's behalf with German Lutheran towns and princes. Once interest in an Anglo-Lutheran alliance waned, however, he was expendable. In the purge that followed the demise of Thomas Cromwell, Barnes was arrested once again and condemned for heresy by his old acquaintance Stephen Gardiner, by then bishop of Winchester.

In his initial brush with the ordinaries in 1526 Robert Barnes tried, so far as the circumstances permitted, to engage them in disputation. This was hardly true of the other men who were compelled to abjure along with him. These were not members of the Cambridge intelligentsia, and at first glance they would seem to have had little in common with the eloquent prior. All of them were resident foreigners, merchants by profession, and citizens of towns belonging to the German Hanse. The concentration of Hanseatic trade at the Steelyard meant that it was relatively easy to locate members of the London fellowship. The arrests in 1526 came as the result of a raid on the enclave at the end of January led by royal councillor Sir Thomas More.

Ever diligent in the cause of religious orthodoxy and already a participant in the print debate, More had good reason to be concerned in the autumn of 1525. The government was aware that the renegade English dissident William Tyndale had been translating the New Testament. The first attempt to print it at Cologne had been disrupted by the pamphleteer Johann Cochlaeus in collusion with one of the town's patrician oligarchs, Sir Hermann Rinck, both of whom were in communication with Wolsey. But Tyndale and his accomplice William Roye had escaped to continue their work elsewhere. Moreover, the summer months also had witnessed the hideously violent conclusion of the peasant rebellions in Germany, where some of Luther's views had been interpreted as a call to radical social change. Of the potent mix of sectarian heterodoxy and social radicalism in their own country Thomas More and the chancellor hardly needed reminding. Lollardy too, was equated with vernacular Bibles for the lay reader. And their consternation no doubt heightened with the publication of *Epistola Johannis Bugenhagii Pommerani ad Anglos*, an assertion of the basic tenets of Lutheranism—especially justification through faith—addressed specifically to the English nation. Its author, Johann Bugenhagen, was a member of Luther's inner circle at

Wittenberg. Cochlaeus, who published a rejoinder at Cologne and dedicated it to Rinck, speculated that Bugenhagen was attempting to rally the evangelical movement on the continent with the false notion that the English were about to join. In any event, by the end of the year *Epistola* was circulating in three Latin and three German editions.[9] To Wolsey, More, and England's Church hierarchy the virtually simultaneous publication of Bugenhagen's letter and Tyndale's New Testament seemed too opportune to be a coincidence. Surely there was a conspiracy afoot to contaminate the kingdom with pernicious doctrine and corrupt translations of the Gospels.

The London Steelyard reported More's raid to the Hanse's political leadership—Lübeck and Cologne—in early March 1526, though without reference to the resultant demonstration at St. Paul's.[10] There can be little question, however, that news of it soon reached other Hanse towns through less formal channels: merchants' correspondence and word of mouth. The difficulties of the fellowship had begun shortly before Christmas with the imprisonment in the Tower of a young merchant from Bremen. Presumably this was Hermann van Holt, mentioned in the deposition of one of the men questioned later on suspicion of heresy. The Crown confiscated his goods and those of his business associates. Although initially at least Holt was not accused of heresy but of clipping coins, his arrest nevertheless appears to have had a direct bearing on the subsequent chain of events. It certainly caused an anxious moment or two for his acquaintance, Hans Reussel, who later testified that he had burned the only Lutheran book he possessed when Holt was apprehended. A month after that arrest, on the night of 26 January, More and other Crown authorities turned up at the Steelyard, claiming to have reliable infor-

---

[9] *VD* B9299–9302, B9305–7; *BB*, 215–20; F. Manley, "Circumstances of Composition: Bugenhagen's 'Letter to the English'," *CW*, 7: xvii–xxxv. The text of the letter: *CW*, 7: 393–405. Cochlaeus's rebuttal, *Epistola Johannis Bugenhagii Pomerani ad Anglos. Responsio Johannis Cochlaei* (*VD* C4374) was issued by Peter Quentell. Spahn, *Cochläus*, 347; *BB*, 220–21. More also wrote a response to Bugenhagen, although it circulated only in manuscript.

[10] *STC* 16778; *Hanserecesse*, 3rd series, ed. D. Schäfer and F. Techen (Leipzig, 1881–1913), 9: no. 260; M.E. Kronenberg, "A Printed Letter of the London Hanse Merchants (3 March 1526)," *Oxford Bibliographical Society Publications*, new series, 1 (1947), 25–32; C.S. Meyer, "Thomas More and the Wittenberg Lutherans," *Concordia Theological Monthly* 39 (1968), 246–56; R. Pauli, "Die Stahlhofskaufleute und Luthers Schriften," *Hansische Geschichtsblätter* (1871), 155.

mation that many of the Germans there owned and continued to import prohibited reading material. Reussel and two others were taken into custody immediately, even before the facility was searched. The search, during which a few German prayer books and New Testaments were confiscated, did not occur until the following day, by which time More was armed with the names of all the members of the Hanseatic fellowship. Senior representatives were summoned to Chapter House at Westminster and ordered to bring with them Helbert Bellendorpe. Evidently implicated by one or more of the suspects taken the previous evening, Bellendorpe was duly arrested and led away. A tribunal of clerics headed by John Clerk, bishop of Bath and Wells, would interrogate those in custody. The other Hanse merchants were bound by a £2,000 surety not to leave the country for twenty days.

Whether or not chancellor Wolsey or Thomas More really expected to discover a more substantial cache of printed material or uncover an organised nucleus of book smugglers, the investigation did produce the requisite fodder for the sort of demonstration requested by Rome many months before. In doing so, it also provided a reasonably strong rationale for another ploy aimed at intimidating a much larger constituency. Campaggio had encouraged Wolsey to find occasion to "spek som thretenyng words unto the hedds of steeds and of that felawship in london concernyng the losse of ther pryvilegs they have in englond" if they did not rid their towns of Lutheranism.[11] The opportunity presented itself when the bond of the merchants was cancelled at the end of February and each was required to promise under oath not to traffic in Lutheran literature. This had been Wolsey's intention from the outset. The king himself, when informed of the strategy in early January, had been of the opinion that recognisance would be a much more effective deterrent than the threat of excommunication. But the chancellor did not leave it at that. He upbraided the Germans for abusing their trading privileges by importing goods of non-Hanseatic origin and now threatened them with drastically increased customs duties. This, of course, was the language of politics and business; an implicit warning, already punctuated by the recent imposition of a travel restriction, that so

---

[11] BL Cotton. MS Vitellius B VI fo. 58.

far as ownership of prohibited books was concerned, individual transgressions could conceivably put at risk the commercial interests of
the entire German Hanse. The chancellor's word was indeed the
king's will, and the Steelyard men knew as much. That the message
struck a responsive chord is apparent in subsequent correspondence
from Lübeck to Lüneburg, Wismar, and Danzig expressing profound
concern that possession of Lutheran books by young merchants trading to the west could seriously jeopardise the Hanse's hard-won privileges in England and in the Low Countries. Even more emphatic
was the response at Cologne, where Lutherans and their books already
had been banned for some time. Civic authorities advised merchants
trading to England, the town's *Englandfahrer*, of the latest memoran-
dum from London and ordered it printed and distributed to all member towns of the Rhine sector of the Hanse.[12]

Steelyard Merchants and their Books

What had the investigation discovered? For the German suspects
there were three principal lines of inquiry, focusing on observance
of Church statutes, recognition of papal authority, and possession of
Lutheran books. Most of the recorded testimony, however, pertains
to the third of these concerns, so the depositions of the accused are
central to the question of whether or not German Lutherans at the
London Steelyard conspired to traffic in illegal material.[13] Among
the four deponents whose testimony has survived interest in controversial religious literature appears to have varied quite markedly. All
of them, though, belonged to the parish of All Hallows the Great,
one of the hundred or so churches dotting London at the time.
Standing directly adjacent to the Steelyard, it was the place of wor-

---

[12] *STC* 16778; *Hanserecesse*, 3rd series, 9: nos. 268–69; *UBRG*, 2: no. 457; Jannasch, *Reformationsgeschichte*, 176; *Beschlüsse*, 3: 306, 308. For censorship in Cologne: *Beschlüsse*, 3: 213, 424 and Scribner, "Reformation in Cologne?" 231, 234–5. German mer- chants would have been aware of the heresy laws in force in the Low Countries. At least one of Charles's placards, issued at Antwerp, was rendered into Low German ("uth der westwerdesken sprake up unse sprake") and printed, probably by Ludwig Dietz at Rostock. *NB*, no. 803.

[13] *LP*, 4/1: no. 1962. Transcripts of the articles and the surviving testimony are printed in Pauli, "Das Verfahren wider die Stahlhofskaufleute wegen der Lutherbücher," *Hansische Geschichtsblätter* (1878), 167–72.

ship for most of the Hanse merchants. And they were its principal benefactors.[14] At the time of his arrest, Hans Ellendorpe had been in England for only about fifteen months. He was the resident London factor of an unidentified master, and it was in the chamber of a deceased colleague that he claimed to have found a book by Luther. Which tract this was we do not know. The accused denied reading it, but he had not destroyed it, because it did not belong to him. Little more about Ellendorpe is revealed in the transcript of his inter-rogation except that, having taken up his duties in London rather recently, he probably was a young man, something all the more likely because he was still doing business in London in the mid-1530s and lived until 1557.[15] The second defendant, Henry Pryknes, said that about Michaelmas 1525 a ship's purser had given him a small book by Luther in German. Identifying it for the commission, he said he had read in it a treatise on the Lord's Prayer.[16] Pryknes had resided in England for two and a half years prior to his arrest, yet professed to have been unaware of the burning or condemnation of Luther's books until early November 1525. Although this was scarcely a credible defence, the amount of proscribed material in his pos-session was quite minimal and he had acquired it only recently. Like Ellendorpe, he submitted himself to correction.

With the other defendants, however, we find many more books, and much more than a passing interest in what they contained. Helbert Bellendorpe, likely the eldest of the suspects, had first come to England in 1511 and had lived there almost continuously for the past six years. Prior to burning them shortly after Christmas, he had possessed German copies of *De Captivitate* and Luther's considerably more recent admonition of the Teutonic Order.[17] He had read parts

---

[14] Jörn, *Der Londoner Stalhof*, 462–63.

[15] Friedland, "Englandfahrer," 15.

[16] Although the books identified by the merchants were printed in German, their titles and descriptions were written in Latin in the official record. Hence, the purser had given Pryknes "unam librum in Teutonico, . . . in quo libro intitulantur opera quedam Martini Lutheri".

[17] *Von der Babylonischen gefengknuß der Kirchen* (*De Captivitate*) had been reprinted many times since 1520: *VD* L4185–96. The other book Bellendorpe burned was "de Castitate", presumably *An die herrn Deutschs Ordens das sie falsche keuscheyt meyden und zur rechten ehlichen keuscheyt greyffen Ermanung* (Exhortation to the Knights of the Teutonic Order that they lay aside False Chastity and assume the True Chastity of Wedlock). It was issued at Wittenberg and Augsburg in 1523 and a few months later at Erfurt and Strasbourg. *VD* L3779–84.

of each. The previous summer he also had brought from Germany two other books by Luther and one authored by Andreas Karlstadt, as well as a German New Testament and a Pentateuch. The biblical translations, in particular, would not have been hard to come by. Editions of Luther's New Testament had been in circulation since 1522 and his rendering of the five books of Moses since the following year. Bellendorpe was fully aware of the condemnation of the reformer's works before leaving England; he had been in London when they were burned at Paul's Cross. Yet he returned from abroad evidently laden with proscribed imprints. Moreover, he gave some of them to associates at the Steelyard. One by Karlstadt went to Georg van Telight. Other material, including a tract written by Luther against Karlstadt, he passed on to Hans Reussel.

Reussel, too, confessed he had heard of the prohibition and burning of Luther's books shortly after his arrival in London some three years before. However, he was out of the country throughout the latter half of 1524. While away in his homeland he had attended sermons critical of the pope and read a number of Lutheran tracts, including *De Libertate*. He also had seen, though claimed to have not read Luther's diatribe against England's king. Both now circulated in several German editions.[18] During the fourteen months since his return his reading had included Luther's translations of the New Testament and Pentateuch. Among various other books he admitted were his own was a Lutheran treatise on the Lord's Prayer. About a half year before his interrogation Hans Reussel had in fact borrowed and read Luther's tract against Karlstadt. He kept it for a few weeks and then burned it, he said, when Hermann van Holt was arrested and committed to the Tower. If Holt was the young fellow apprehended by More initially for fraud, it seems likely that he denounced Reussel. It is also possible, though far from certain, that his knowledge of the material in Reussel's possession was enough to make Holt the fifth of the Steelyard men to do penance at Paul's Cross.

A postscript to the punishment of these individuals brings to light an even wider circle in Danzig. Royal Prussia's largest town was

---

[18] *Antwort deutsch Mart. Luthers auff König Heinrichs von Engelland Buch (Contra Henricum)*: *VD* L4244–49; *LW*, 10/2: 223–62. *Von der freyheyt eynes Christen menchen (De Libertate)*: *VD* L7193–7211; *LW*, 7: 12–38.

ostensibly autonomous in matters of trade but subject to the ecclesiastical authority of the bishop of Leslau. In January 1525 a political coup brought down the old civic administration and a new one
charted a course for social, economic, and religious change. The
Polish Crown intervened in April 1526. Conservative councillors and
orthodox preachers were restored, thirteen instigators of the insurrection were executed, and many more imprisoned or exiled. The
king established new regulations for civic government, the "Constitu-
tiones Sigismundi". He also banished Lutherans and banned their
books.[19] But that was not all. During his three-month stay in Danzig
he also attempted to intercede on behalf of various local merchants
who had been implicated in the London Steelyard scandal. Evidently,
they had been prevented from resuming their trade in England. One
was Georg van Telight, the man to whom Bellendorpe claimed to
have lent the Karlstadt treatise. He was not in London when More's
search party descended on the Steelyard, however. Nor had any
incriminating evidence been found in his chamber there. Drafted in
May 1526 at the behest of a member of the reconstituted Danzig
council, Sigismund's petitions to both Wolsey and Henry VIII requested
that Georg van Telight be allowed to return to England and continue his business activities. Whether he was able to do so is unclear,
for within a couple of years he seems to have perished in the epidemic of sweating sickness that carried off many victims in both
London and Danzig.[20] Two similar pleas reached Westminster in the
summer of 1526 on behalf of Jacob Egerth and Hans Molenbecke.

<hr />

[19] Schmidt, *Auf Felsen gesät*, 132–33; Cieślak and Biernat, *Gdańsk*, 125–30;
P. Simson, *Geschichte der Stadt Danzig bis 1626* (Danzig, 1924), 2: 87–92; *UBRG*, 2:
nos. 478–85, 505; *SRP*, 5: 544–77, 6: 275–80. The statutes and Danzig council's
ceremonial swearing of allegiance to Sigismund were publicised in Viëtor imprints
issued later that summer. *Bibliographia Polonica*, 3: nos. 2115, 2120–21.
[20] Pauli, "Die Stahlhofskaufleute," 160–62. An extant but only partially legible
petition concerning contract litigation identifies Georg van Telight as "late mar-
chaunt of the Stilierd" and John Blome as administrator of his goods. It addresses
Wolsey as chancellor, so could not have been drafted later than October 1529. It
also refers to the "swetyng sekenys". TNA:PRO C 1/552/71. There was a devas-
tating outbreak of the illness in London in June 1528. The following year it came
to Prussia, decimating Danzig. Simson, *Geschichte*, 2: 162–63; *UBRG*, 1: 156–57.
Perhaps Blome was Hamburg *Schonenfahrer* Hans Blome. R. Postel, *Die Reformation
in Hamburg 1517–1528* (Gütersloh, 1986), 168. There was also a burgess of Danzig
by that name in 1535. *Hanserezesse*, 4th series, ed. G. Wentz and K. Friedland
(Cologne, 1970), 2: no. 102.

Egerth's stepbrother, Danzig merchant Johann Furste, and "sex viros
bone fame et virtutis" had assured Sigismund that Egerth was not
a Lutheran.[21] It does not appear that any of the three men recommended in these testimonials were arraigned in London in the winter of 1526. Georg van Telight is the only one mentioned in the
depositions of the arrested merchants, so presumably the names of
the other two came up during the interrogations.

The investigations in London had therefore resulted in accusations
against eight different individuals. Their arrests or banishment underscore the general composition of the Steelyard community, as well
as its main commercial links. At any one time there were probably
forty or more merchants at the Steelyard, exclusive of their servants
and employees. There is an unfortunate dearth of customs evidence
for the 1520s, but accounts for earlier years typically list three to
four dozen men either importing or exporting merchandise. They
ranged from agents of large firms and partners in limited ventures
to independent merchants trading on their own accounts. In addition to the consignees, there were other junior partners and factors
whose names do not appear. Litigation records reveal still more individuals involved in transactions with local mercers, drapers, and cloth
workers.[22]

The vastness of the network of towns making up the Hanse and
the resultant diversity of regionally produced goods that their trade
brought to England meant regional representation at the Steelyard.
There were bonds as well as divisions. The common thread in the
events of the winter of 1526 is that the accused Germans were so-
called *Esterlings*: men from northern ports, who traded extensively
but not exclusively to and from Hamburg, Bremen, and towns in
the Baltic, and who constituted a principal sub-group within the

---

[21] Sigismund's letters are calendared in *LP*, 4/1: nos. 2168–70, 2179. The one
supporting Molenbecke (BL Cotton. MS Nero B. II fo. 83) is printed as "Brief
Sigismunds I. von Polen an Heinrich VIII von England," ed. R. Toeppen, *APM*
33 (1896), 297–98. Those sent on behalf of Egerth and Georg van Telight are in
Pauli, "Die Stahlhofskaufleute," 158–62. Pauli also suggested Ellendorpe was Egerth's
London factor. "Das Verfahren," 161.
[22] Some London customs accounts survive for 1490–91, 1502–3, 1507–8, 1512–13,
and 1520–21. TNA:PRO E 122/78/9, 122/80/2, 122/80/5, 122/82/9, 122/83/4.
Litigation involving Steelyard merchants brought appeals to Chancery. TNA:PRO
C 1/403/28, 1/437/31, 1/497/50, 1/499/54, 1/507/41, 1/549/59, 1/600/43,
1/653/44, 1/653/44, 1/653/45.

London enclave. Egerth, Molenbecke, Pryknes, and Georg van Telight were Danzigers. Hermann van Holt was from Bremen and Ellendorpe from nearby Hamburg.[23] Reussel's birthplace was "Estlande", and he had been there for about six months in 1524.[24] Bellendorpe's testimony does not disclose his civic affiliation. It is instructive, however, that he had owned a copy of Luther's call for the secularisation of the Teutonic Order. Both the suggestion and the new realty in Prussia and Livonia would have been particularly topical for men from Königsberg, Danzig, and other eastern Baltic locales. And Bellendorpe also knew and trusted Hans Reussel and Georg van Telight well enough to lend them his Lutheran books.[25]

The suspects came from towns and territories where Lutheranism rapidly gained considerable albeit uneven acceptance in the 1520s. The other main constituency at the Steelyard comprised of merchants from Cologne, who traditionally accounted for much, though by no means all Hanseatic commercial traffic through Antwerp. Usually a third or more of the Hanse men named in London customs accounts for the late fifteenth and early sixteenth century were Cologners, and they likely were just as numerous in the 1520s. The seven surviving portraits of identified Steelyard merchants painted by Hans Holbein in the 1530s attest to the presence of a substantial and well-heeled Cologne contingent at that time. Four of the subjects were Cologners and a fifth was from nearby Duisburg.[26] What matters here is that Lutheranism was not permitted to gain an early foothold in Cologne. For two years prior to the investigation in London authorities in Cologne had sought consistently to

---

[23] Pauli, "Die Stahlhofskaufleute," 155–62. For Pryknes: *Hanserezesse*, 4th series, 2: 524. For Ellendorpe: Postel, *Die Reformation in Hamburg*, 183 and Friedland, "Englandfahrer," 19.

[24] *LP*, 4/1: no. 1962; Pauli, "Das Verfahren," 170.

[25] A copy of the initial Steelyard communiqué to Lübeck, dated 1 March, identifies Bellendorpe as a Cologner, but a second, sent to Cologne two days later, does not. Kronenberg suggested that Bellendorpe's civic affiliation was omitted from the letter sent to and later printed at Cologne because he was known there already. However, the second missive contained other textual changes, and it seems equally plausible that, regarding Bellendorpe's identity, it simply corrected the earlier one to Lübeck. Kronenberg, "A Printed Letter," esp. 29; *Hanserecesse*, 3rd series, 9: no. 260. Moreover, Lutherans were unwelcome in both towns. Authorities in Cologne would not have hesitated to identify and thereby ostracize Bellendorpe if he was in fact a Cologner.

[26] P. Ganz, *Hans Holbein: Die Gemälde* (Basel, 1950), 222–30.

silence Lutherans and outlaw circulation of their books. A brief insurrection in the spring of 1525 ensured continuation of these measures. Imprints were seized, suspected Lutherans coerced, imprisoned,
or banished, and the preaching of the Augustinians curtailed.[27] Not
surprisingly, then, despite their significance within the Steelyard, merchants clearly identifiable as Cologners did not figure among the suspects summoned by the ecclesiastical authorities.

Commercial Contacts and the Tides of Reform

The episode indicates that exposure to new doctrines, if not the
transmission of literature involved a significant element of direct contact with areas where orthodoxy was being challenged effectively.
The Hanseatic confederation as a whole did not enforce a religious
policy, nor could it. In January 1525 Lübeck tried unsuccessfully to
bring about a consensus among other towns of the Hanse's Wendish
region—Hamburg, Lüneburg, Wismar, Stralsund, and Rostock—
regarding suppression of evangelism. The resultant proclamation
against conventicles and the printing and selling of Lutheran literature had little impact. And even this position did not satisfy a full
assembly of Hanse delegates convened in the summer. It resolved
only that the member towns retain good preachers.[28] In effect, then,
it was left to individual civic administrations to reject or move forward with evangelical reform.

Most resistant to change were Lübeck and Cologne, traditionally
at the forefront of the league's political affairs. Coteries of merchants
and artisans supportive of change had emerged in Lübeck, influenced
by pamphlet literature and sermons. Emphasising personal piety, they
tended to be less overtly anticlerical than their counterparts in neighbouring Hamburg. But they were opposed nevertheless by a conservative regime that was anxious not to offend the emperor. Following
the *Reichstag* of 1524 the council reiterated the imperial ban on

---

[27] *Beschlüsse*, 3: 102, 105, 116, 144, 198, 209, 213, 242–43, 257, 259, 265 283,
291, 298; Scribner, "Reformation in Cologne?" 218–40.
[28] Schildhauer, *Auseinandersetzungen*, 111–12; W. Ehrbrecht, "Köln—Osnabrück—
Stralsund: Rat und Bürgerschaft hansischer Städte zwischen religiöser Erneuerung
und Bauernkrieg," in *Kirche und gesellschaftlicher Wandel in deutschen und niederländischen
Städten der werdenden Neuzeit*, ed. F. Petri (Cologne, 1980), 26–31.

Luther's works and co-operated with the bishop of Lübeck and the
cathedral dean to discourage conventicles and restrain the local
presses. Books were confiscated and blasphemers arrested. Censorship
of printed material culminated when books were seized from sellers
and publicly burned in September 1526, a measure of the perse-
verance not only of civic and clerical authorities but also the evangelicals they were attempting to suppress.[29] There was similar unease
in Cologne, where elements of the disaffected commons had drafted
a list of articles in 1525, primarily concerned with practical economic matters and clerical privilege. Although there was also some
carping about the quality of preaching, overall the outcry was not
the product of spiritual anxieties. Even so, while civic authorities
attempted to accommodate most of the other grievances, they refused
to agree to any innovation in the choosing of preachers. Determined
to avoid religious controversy, they endeavoured, together with the
university theologians and the archbishop, actively to discourage
Lutheranism.[30] Equally important, however, was their reluctance to
suppress vernacular Scripture texts. Elsewhere within the Hanse, especially in a number of important Baltic towns, including Stralsund,
Danzig, Riga, and Reval the reception initially was more positive
and had already contributed to significant religious and political
upheaval. The continental trade links of the accused Steelyard merchants were in this northern sector, precisely where, with the exception of Lübeck, the Lutheran movement achieved so much early
success.

Another of the keys to transmission or dissemination at this time
was the mobility of the individuals who lived in London. The era
of the itinerant merchant who regularly accompanied goods to overseas markets had long since passed. Even so, the Steelyard community was not a sedentary one. Germans who were long-time
residents of the English capital periodically travelled back to their

---

[29] Hauschildt, "Die Reformation," 3: 204–5; Jannasch, *Reformationsgeschichte*, 123–27,
175.
[30] Ehbrecht, "Köln—Osnabrück—Stralsund," 32–63; C. von Looz-Corswarem,
"Die Kölner Artikelserie von 1525: Hintergründe und Verlauf des Aufruhrs von
1525 in Köln," in *Kirche und gesellschaftlicher Wandel im deutschen und niederländischen
Städten der werdenden Neuzeit*, ed. F. Petri (Cologne, 1980), 65–153; A. Franzen, *Bischof
und Reformation: Erzbischof Hermann von Wied in Köln vor der Entscheidung zwischen Reform
und Reformation* (Münster, 1971), 30.

distant homelands. Helbert Bellendorpe, though he had lived in England for six years, had been out of the country on three occasions, each time for about ten or eleven weeks, and from his last sojourn in "Germanie" had returned laden with books. And his colleague Hans Reussel recently had spent six months in "Estlande in partibus transmarinis ubi fuit oriundus". To assess the potential for heresy dissemination within and beyond the London Steelyard it is necessary therefore to revisit the Hanse trading ports.

Half of those named in the Steelyard affair and undoubtedly several more residents of the London *comptoir* had come from Danzig. The town of perhaps 40,000 inhabitants sustained a great maritime trade within the Baltic and also with the Low Counties, France, and Britain. Danzig was one of England's principal sources of timber, cereals, and cordage and the only port in the Baltic where, as yet, a few English merchants lived year round. Of course they, like their German counterparts in London, periodically returned home. For anyone, native or foreign, who spent any length of time in Danzig during the early 1520s manifestations of turmoil and change would have been difficult to avoid. Throughout the eastern Baltic region a widely pervasive resentment of beneficed and mendicant clergy had developed. Monks and absentee priests consequently bore the brunt of extensive ridicule by storm preachers (*Sturmprediger*), who evangelised harbour towns. By 1520 imported Lutheran tomes were in circulation. Others were printed locally, at Danzig. The 1523 censorship initiatives in Poland together with warnings from the bishop of Leslau, Maciej Drzewicki, may have influenced Hans Weinrich to close his Danzig press and go to Königsberg. However, local magistrates demonstrated no serious interest in regulating print distribution. Drzewicki complained in 1523 of barrels of Lutheran books being sent from Wittenberg to St. Barbara's in Danzig. Civic authorities acknowledged that a pastor at the church, Johann Bonholt, did indeed possess some of Luther's works but refused the bishop's demand for his removal, cautioning that change was inadvisable, even though Bonholt had recently taken leave to study at Wittenberg. Between 1518 and 1525 nearly one third of the Danzig students who attended university went to Wittenberg. They came home to take positions within the civic administration and as teachers and preachers, and brought with them others imbued with Luther's views. Among the returning sons was Jacob Hegge, whose fervid proselytising against monastic orders and the sacraments consistently drew receptive

crowds.[31] There was also a precedent for publicising religious controversy in the annual Shrovetide or carnival play, a facet of popular culture that lent itself to representation of topical issues. The
1522 performance satirised the pope's response to Luther, including
the burning of his books. Here too the bishop had cause to complain and once again the town fathers set his concerns aside, reply-
ing that levity on the part of the young performers was traditional.
Similar anti-papal performances were staged in nearby Elbing and
at Stralsund, and in 1524 there was one at Königsberg.[32]

Non-religious forces were also at work in Danzig. Upheaval there
became constitutional as well as confessional, in large part because
poorer sectors of society were alienated from the highly privileged
ruling elite. Civic governance was in the hands of wealthy patricians,
who managed outlying rural estates given to the town by Sigismund.
Aspiring to noble titles, some families leased Crown land or purchased knightly estates from the king, and thus assumed rights of
feudal lordship. Patrician oligarchs also lent money for Danzig's military and naval expenditures and costly fortifications. The commonalty then bore the burden of repayment, with indirect taxes on
everyday items hurting poor people especially. Resentment and the
perceived mismanagement of town finances brought calls for fairer
taxation and broader participation in decision-making. There were
some concessions, beginning in 1519 with creation of the committee of forty-eight, which gave greater political voice to non-patricians. Still, its members were fairly wealthy citizens, not disadvantaged
people. And the eventual appointment of five committee members
to advise the council was insufficient to prevent public demonstrations against the corrupt mayor in 1522. Accompanying this political agitation were demands that evangelical preachers be installed
in one of the town's churches. Rightly wary of inflaming public opinion further, town officials acquiesced. Moderate evangelicals who did
not mix new doctrine with politics were unimpeded. But by 1524
radicals and disaffected townspeople were meeting publicly, without

---

[31] Arnold, "Luther und die Reformation," 37–42 and "Luther und Danzig,"
Zeitschrift für Ostforschung 31 (1972), 94–120; Schwenke, "Hans Weinrich," 70; *SRP*,
6: 275.
[32] Arnold, "Luther und Danzig," 107; Scribner, "Reformation Carnival and the
World turned Upside-down," in *Städtische Gesellschaft und Reformation*, ed. I. Bátori
(Stuttgart, 1980), 236–37, 245–46.

the authorities' consent, to discuss additional religious and political innovations.[33]

The political leadership's rather accommodating stance on moderate evangelicals was in one respect a perfectly reasonable response to a growing public consensus. It could also be interpreted as an assertion of civic autonomy against encroachment by the diocesan authority. In that context, shrugging off the bishop's complaints about Lutherans and implicitly claiming the prerogative to formulate church and school policy clearly served communal rather than ecclesiastical interests. On the other hand, even measured acceptance of Lutheran theologians ran contrary to the wishes of the sovereign ruler, Sigismund I. There may have been hope that compromises on the religious front would alleviate popular dissatisfaction with the entrenched political establishment. As it turned out, though, tolerance of anticlerical evangelism ultimately gave rise to a radicalised faction among the common folk. In August 1524 new ministers, Hegge among them, were selected to replace delinquent priests at five churches. Just as important, the twelve *Rentmeister* chosen at that time to administer town property were encouraged if not manipulated by radicals. In the months that followed they set about undermining the ruling council and appropriating its authority. On 15 January 1525 they introduced their *Artikelbrief*, an agenda of socio-economic and religious reform that took particular aim at the friars. Again the oligarchs gave in and prohibited the monks to preach, but within a matter of days the regulation was challenged. Tensions ran high, crowds gathered. Matters were made worse as councillors armed themselves, locked the town gates, and ordered the arrests of several citizens. Apparently urged on by Hegge and other ministers, the aggrieved commons then responded by deposing most of the old council and replacing it with one that, claiming to be guided by God's word, promised social and spiritual renewal. Convents and cloisters were soon emptied. The house of the Grey Friars became a school. The Dominican friary was converted into a hospital. Bonholt was sent on a recruiting mission to Wittenberg, and amid removal of images

---

[33] Cieślak and Biernat, *Gdańsk*, 123–28; Schmidt, *Auf Felsen gesät*, 134–35. Dual religious and political upheaval such as occurred in Danzig and Elbing, though not in Thorn, perhaps marked a fundamental stage in town development. It was central to a transformation process that paved the way for later confessional organisation. Müller, *Zweite Reformation*, 19–20.

from churches Hegge and his brethren conducted worship in German. The way was paved for new church and school orders.[34]

But the expulsion of traditionalists and the new regime's programme for change did not sit well with Sigismund. For the better part of three years his letters to Danzig had demanded the suppression of storm preachers, to no avail. Ongoing defiance would necessarily cast doubt on his regal authority. Aside from this, two specific considerations probably influenced him to take extraordinary action. First, in 1524 Bishop Drzewicki came to Danzig, fully empowered to uphold the king's laws. His arrest of an evangelical preacher, Paul Grünewald, quickly inflamed resentment within a militant faction of townspeople to such an extent that he was forced to give up the prisoner. A violent mob threatened Drzewicki and abused his servants. Even after Grünewald was freed malcontents restated their contempt by hanging dead cats and dogs over the bishop's door. The fiasco exposed the civic regime's inability to assist effectively at a critical moment. Very early on town officials sought and received assurance that Grünewald would be released unharmed, but that had not satisfied the militants. It was also clear that Drzewicki was incapable of asserting his own mandate or the king's in the face of spontaneous public backlash. A second circumstance contributing to Sigismund's decision to act was that in January 1526 a small delegation of disaffected councillors journeyed to the Polish *Sejm* and formally requested that he come to Danzig and sort out the town's troubles. He obliged in the spring, arriving with Drzewicki and an armed force of three thousand.[35] Duke Albrecht, who had to contend with a minor peasant rebellion within his own territory only a few months before, also visited Danzig briefly in the spring of 1526. It was he who prevailed on the king to spare the Lutheran preachers, although some were destined to spend several months in prison before resurfacing in Ducal Prussia.

Changes in Danzig came more slowly after this. Even so, dissatisfaction with the traditional Church had been given expression in

---

[34] Bues, *Das Herzogtum*, 246–47; Arnold, "Luther und die Reformation," 37–42 and "Luther und Danzig," 94–120; *SRP*, 5: 545–87; *UBRG*, 1: 135–143, 2: nos. 320–23, 335, 339, 351, 367.

[35] *SRP*, 5: 551–56, 568; Schmidt, *Auf Felsen gesät*, 130–32; Cieślak and Biernat, *Gdańsk*, 123–28.

many forms, from printed pamphlets to open-air sermons and theatrical satires. Because of the port's significance within the northern
economy, the audience was potentially large and particularly capable of contributing to wider dissemination. It would have included
not only denizen inhabitants but also foreign merchants, the crews
of hundreds of ships that called at Danzig each year, as well as those
of local vessels that plied Baltic waters and carried the port's trade
to markets as distant as Amsterdam, Antwerp, and London. At Danzig
they might readily avail themselves of imprints from the Weinreich
press that operated at Königsberg, not far to the east and now the
centre of a concerted state-supported campaign to evangelise Ducal
Prussia.

On the whole, Danzig's governing elite of propertied businessmen
was responsive to the commons on religious matters, but apparently
not to the deeply felt resentment of their own entrenched political
dominance. Artisans, brewers, dock workers and sailors (*Schiffsleute*)
led the insurrection of 1525, demanding an effective voice on issues
other than religion and education. The comprehensive scope of their
agenda had no special appeal to those who already had such a voice;
wealthier men of better social standing, like those possessing the
wherewithal to engage in international trade. Merchants gathered at
the *Artushof* in August 1525 and listened to the town secretary rehearse
articles that the new council would present to Sigismund, though
after some discussion they collectively declined to endorse them. That
is not to say, however, that they were merely ambivalent bystanders
with regard to spiritual concerns and religious controversy. The carnival play in 1522, which mocked the pope for banning Luther, had
been staged by young members of the *Reinholdsbank*. It was performed
inside the *Artushof*.[36]

Another of the men accused in London, Hans Reussel, claimed
to be a native of Estland. Among Scandinavians and Baltic Germans
the term had narrow geographic connotations, however contemporary English usage was notably imprecise. Much as any merchant
from a northern Hanse town was an *Esterling*, Estland might refer
to almost any German territory from Hamburg to the Gulf of Finland,
even though references to specific regional or civic entities were com-

---

[36] *SRP*, 5: 568; 65, 569, 571; Scribner, "Reformation Carnival," 244–46, 257.

mon as well.[37] It is reasonably certain, though, that Reussel's home was in the Baltic region. Perhaps he too was a Danziger, but he may in fact have come from as far off as the Livonian lands of the Teutonic Knights. Use of the Estland designation rather than Prussia or "a partibus Germanie" in the Latin transcript of his testimony suggests as much.

There were no printing presses in these eastern regions, yet Reussel likely would have had little difficulty finding copies of Luther's sermons and books there, especially in the ethnically stratified ports, where Germans constituted as much as half the population. With about 10,000 inhabitants in total, Riga was the largest town. It was also the centre of the evangelical movement, initiated in 1522 by Andreas Knopken and Sylvester Tegetmeier. Tegetmeier, a native of Hamburg and formerly chaplain of Rostock cathedral, had matriculated at Wittenberg. Knopken came from Pomerania, where he had known Bugenhagen. The Riga reformers received Wittenberg imprints from Bugenhagen, who had some of his own works printed there in German expressly for Livonian distribution. He also saw to the publication at Wittenberg of Knopken's Latin commentary on the Epistle to the Romans.[38]

Evangelical reform took a different path in Livonia than in Germany and Scandinavia partly because no territorial prince authorised or aided confessional development. Change was accomplished entirely by towns and was non-confessional. Lutheran evangelicals shaped the early stages but innovation quickly extended well beyond justification through faith. The ideas of another German reformer, Andreas Karlstadt, were especially important. The Livonian experience was also distinguished by markedly violent manifestations of anticlericalism and militant opposition to the veneration of saints and images.[39] If he was in Livonia in 1524 the Steelyard merchant Hans Reussel

---

[37] The 1497 statute of England's Merchant Adventurers, for example, distinguishes "Danske" [Danzig] from "Estlond". *Merchant Adventurers*, 204. On the other hand, a document pertaining to a venture by Norwich merchants in the 1520s speaks of a ship freighted at "Dansik in Estlond". *LP*, Addenda, 1: no. 625. England's ambassador in the Low Countries referred to "Lubeckers of Estland" in a 1533 dispatch. *LH*, no. 164.

[38] *BB*, 213–14; *VD* K1477.

[39] Packull, "Sylvester Tegetmeier," 343–56; C.A. Pater, *Karlstadt as the Father of the Baptist Movements: The Emergence of Lay Protestantism* (Toronto, 1984), 173–94; Williams, *Radical Reformation*, 619–23.

perhaps witnessed or participated in iconoclastic demonstrations. At the very least he would have heard about them. Tegetmeier orchestrated much of the furore in Riga. Drawing on Karlstadt's Wittenberg Ordinance of 1521–1522, his ministry was radically austere. Latin liturgy was completely abandoned and vestments discarded. This went hand in hand with efforts to rid the churches of images. Tegetmeier's sermons inspired his supporters within the Blackhead merchant brotherhood, who in March 1524 decided to remove the altarpiece they had donated to St. Peter's church. Not content to proceed in an orderly way, however, young guild members made a great show of forcing their way in and destroying the altar, thus setting the tone for similar demonstrations. Within a few days crowds burst into the two parish churches and smashed crosses, icons, and relics. And scarcely another week passed before Tegetmeier instigated demolition of the cathedral's altarpiece. Church treasures not plundered or destroyed were sold to fund poor relief.[40]

Religious controversy spread beyond Riga. The master of the Teutonic Knights, Plettenberg, was complaining about evangelicals in Reval early in 1524, among them Johannes Lange, who rapidly gained political influence. A new church ordinance, approved on 19 September by town and guild representatives, was largely Lange's work. From then on religious services in Reval were to be conducted only in German. Local authorities addressed education concerns by establishing a school. They also eliminated a number of feast days. Not all transitions were peaceful, though. Iconoclasts caused trouble that autumn and relations between town officials and local Dominicans remained extremely strained.[41] In the summer of 1524 Reval allied with Riga and Dorpat to defy Johann Blankenfeld. Recently elevated by papal dispensation to the archiepiscopal see of Riga, Blankenfeld had condemned evangelical reform. Riga's refusal to submit to his authority was also supported at this point by members of the Livonian nobility, who closed ranks with the towns to uphold preaching of the Gospels.

The direction provided by trained theologians like Knopken and Tegetmeier was to some extent augmented by that of aspiring lay evangelists, in particular the Swabian furrier, Melchior Hoffman, who

---

[40] Deppermann, *Melchior Hoffman*, 46–49.
[41] Ritscher, *Reval*, 110–21.

came to Wolmar in 1523. His unlicensed preaching landed him in jail for a while, but he soon turned up in Dorpat. Again without authorisation he arranged secret assemblies and preached against images. The audiences in Dorpat included many Blackheads, and it was they who defended him when Blankenfeld ordered his arrest in January 1525. A bloody melee with the local bailiff ensued, leaving four people dead and several more injured. The mob then rampaged through the cathedral and the churches of St. Mary and St. John, destroying altarpieces and images, before turning on the cloisters. In the aftermath of the violence, Dorpat denied Hoffman permission to preach until he produced references verifying his Lutheranism. So early in 1525 he collected testimonials from Tegetmeier and Knopken at Riga and then went to Wittenberg, where both Luther and Bugenhagen endorsed him as well. But Hoffman's summer in Wittenberg was a season of social unrest in many other places. By the time he returned to Livonia later in the year the nobility, citing evangelical support for peasant rebellion, no longer saw eye-to-eye with the urban regimes on religion. Tolerance of religious radicals had cost the towns valuable political allies, so they were not about to countenance more discord. Within a few months Hoffman was expelled from Dorpat. Then for a short while he cared for destitute peasants at a hospice in Reval. But the magistracy there also felt he was too dangerous, and soon he was on the move again, this time bound for Sweden. By this point Hoffman was diverging from Luther on auricular confession and Christ's presence in the Eucharist. He preached that God's final judgement of mankind was imminent, and his self-proclaimed ability to explain the spiritual meanings of Scripture texts had alienated Livonia's Lutheran theologians.[42] In Stockholm, though, he soon found both a new congregation of followers and an opportunity to express himself in print.

Reappearing time and again in the early history of the Livonian reform is the Blackhead brotherhood. The Blackheads were merchants, either unmarried local men or foreigners from Germany who wintered in Livonia. Theirs was an exclusively German association because in Riga and Reval trade itself was the preserve of Germans.

---

[42] Deppermann, *Melchior Hoffman*, 51–62, 84–88. Deppermann claims the "unlawful" attempt to apprehend Hoffman sparked the riot in Dorpat. G.H. Williams, *Radical Reformation*, 620, says Hoffman instigated it.

Mercantile activity necessarily connected them to other communities within and outside Livonia, especially Stockholm, Danzig, and Lübeck. Merchants imported religious ideas and unquestionably helped propagate them in Livonia's towns. Blackhead chapters existed in Riga and Dorpat, and also in Reval, where they possessed their own house. Their traditional religious connections included patronage of the Dominicans in Reval and Narva but in the early 1520s they were quick to welcome evangelicals. If they were not already an association of faith at the time of the iconoclastic outburst in Reval, they soon defined themselves as one. Early in 1528 Reval's Blackheads and the guilds excluded anyone loyal to the old Church. They also were authorised by the town to punish anyone found participating in the sacraments or attending traditional Catholic worship. The coercion was tangible in at least one instance: a critic of evangelicals was jailed and pilloried. But Reval's council was careful to avoid antagonising Plettenberg, and made efforts to rein in people who criticised him.[43] In Riga the Blackheads were tightly linked to evangelical reform from the beginning. When town magistrates appointed Knopken and Tegetmeier to the churches of St. Peter and St. James in the fall of 1522 the archbishop and cathedral chapter had refused to pay their stipends. The Blackheads stepped forward with endowments to supplement voluntary contributions. The reformers became chaplain vicars of the brotherhood and it, in turn, helped carry out Tegetmeier's iconoclastic programme. When in 1525 Plettenberg cautioned Tegetmeier to stop his provocative sermons, the reformer noted in his diary that the Blackheads were assembled elsewhere on that occasion. The inference was that when they were with him he had nothing to fear. Certainly they protected Tegetmeier. Hoffman's modern biographer likens them to "storm troopers".[44]

Possibly the Steelyard heretic Hans Reussel belonged to a Blackhead chapter. When questioned by the English bishops about his recent trip home, he said he had listened to sermons that disparaged the papacy and heard the criticisms repeated in conversation. If the Estland he visited was in fact Livonia, his sojourn exposed him to a host of political, social, and religious undercurrents that were transforming the region. There is no way of telling whether or not the

---

[43] Ritscher, *Reval*, 123.
[44] Deppermann, *Melchior Hoffman*, 47, 58.

tracts he read there were the very latest, but that he could get his hands on Lutheran imprints is not surprising. Luther had published an address to the people of Riga, Reval, and Dorpat in 1523, a year after Riga's town secretary informed him that his works already circulated in Livonia.[45] They were brought from ports on the north German coast, no doubt from Königsberg and Rostock, and also via the principal intermediary in maritime trade to the west, Lübeck. Missals destined for St. Peter's in Riga were printed at Lübeck in 1521. In subsequent years close monitoring of Lübeck's printing houses reflected the religious conservatism of the town's governing elite, whilst on eastern Baltic shores nonconformists made great strides. Lübeck was aware that evangelicals were active in the Livonian towns in the early 1520s and sent a letter warning of their false doctrines. Church and civic authorities found themselves in a quandary when a barrel of devotional books was intercepted in Lübeck in autumn 1525. The cache consisted not only of *Taufbüchlein* and masses in German but also polyglot versions in Livonian, Latvian, and Estonian: a special print run for the regional churches.[46] Nicholas Ramm, preacher at St. James's in Riga, likely provided the Livonian/Latvian translations and Francis Witte of St. John's in Dorpat the Estonian. Luther's *Das Taufbuchlein verdeutscht* had been printed originally at Wittenberg and reissued there for three years consecutively. It is unlikely that imprints specifically intended for German congregations in Riga or Reval were rendered in High German, although that does not rule out the possibility that they or the polyglots were printed in Saxony. Luther and Bugenhagen published vernacular German exhortations to the Livonian Christians shortly after Hoffman's visit to Wittenberg in 1525. He may have convinced them of the need for other printed material as well.[47]

---

[45] *UBRG*, 2: nos. 79, 161; *LW*, 12: 143–50; V. Pengerots, "Geschichte des Buchdrucks in Lettland bis zum Beginn des 19. Jahrhunderts," *GJB* (1935), 213.

[46] P. Johansen and H. von zur Mühlen, *Deutsch und Undeutsch in mittelalterlichen und frühneuzeitlichen Reval* (Cologne, 1973), 72–3, 345. P. Johansen, "Gedruckte deutsche und undeutsche Messen für Riga 1525," *Zeitschrift für Ostforschung* 8 (1959), 523–32; Jannasch, *Reformationsgeschichte*, 156–58, 377; Ritscher, *Reval*, 114. Luther's *Taufbuchlein*, first printed in 1523 at Wittenberg, Zwickau, Nürnberg, and Augsburg, was reissued in 1524 at Wittenberg, Zwickau, and Königsberg. The revised *Das Taufbuchlein aufs Neue zugerichtet* was printed at Wittenberg in 1526 and later that year in Low German at Rostock. *LW*, 12: 38–42 and 19: 531–32.

[47] Johansen, "Messen für Riga," 523–32; *BB*, 213–14; *LW*, 18: 412–30.

Given the background of the reform movement in eastern Baltic ports, Hans Reussel's apparent interest in the writings of Andreas Karlstadt is not surprising either. The reformers in Riga drew on Luther's work, but the early influence of his erstwhile colleague was evident as well. Sylvester Tegetmeier had studied and remained at Wittenberg, with Karlstadt, during Luther's Wartburg interlude in 1521–22. In January 1522 Karlstadt published the first significant iconoclast pamphlet of the Reformation—*Von abtuhung der Bylder*— replete with biblical references illustrating the superiority of God's word over conventional ritual.[48] Tegetmeier's formative direction clearly came from Karlstadt, whose works undoubtedly circulated in towns of the eastern Baltic. His treatise on celibacy, originally published at Erfurt in 1521, was reissued in the summer of 1524 at Königsberg.[49]

The fact that Weinreich's Königsberg press printed Karlstadt's books as well as Luther's underscores its regional influence. Aside from books, many innovations affecting the entire region now emanated from Ducal Prussia. Reforms issued by Bishop Queiß at the beginning of 1524 dissolved the monasteries there, prohibited veneration of icons, and eliminated fast days. Königsberg's literate citizens, like those in Riga, and Reval, could acquire and read controversial literature, and more still might listen to the sermons of married priests.[50] Maritime trade with these ports ensured that such innovation was well known if not yet practised in Danzig. As chief centre of printed reform propaganda and regional focal point of evangelism, Königsberg absorbed and exerted many influences. Duke Albrecht continued to foot the bill for substantial quantities of imported books. Consignments were purchased on his behalf and sent from Wittenberg and Leipzig by the artist Lucas Cranach.[51] But Königsberg itself was also a source of the literature and evangelism that promoted Bible-based Lutheran theology and gave expression to latent resentment of Rome. Weinreich's

---

[48] *VD* B6213–15; J.T. Moger, "Pamphlets, Preaching and Politics: The Image Controversy in Reformation Wittenberg, Zürich and Strassburg," *Mennonite Quarterly Review* 75 (2001), 330–32; N.R. Leroux, "*In the Christian City of Wittenberg*: Karlstadt's Tract on Images and Begging," *Sixteenth Century Journal* 34 (2003), 73–106.

[49] *Apologia pro M. Bartholomeo Preposito* (*VD* B6101–2); Pater, *Karlstadt*, 303.

[50] Musteikis, *Reformation in Lithuania*, 41–42; *UBRG*, 2: nos. 161, 170, 176, 185, 190, 208, 212, 215, 226, 295, 300, 331, 363, 376; *DCR*, no. 92.

[51] *UBRG*, 2: nos. 516, 621, 664.

imprints ranged from an anonymous lampoon of the pope to Ducal Prussia's first Lutheran hymnbook. *Esterlings* at the London Steelyard quite possibly owned prayer books from Königsberg. In 1525 Weinreich issued an edition of the Lord's Prayer by little-known Danzig preacher Matthias Bynwalth. The significance of developments in Prussia was not lost on opportunists and propagandists elsewhere. Georg von Polentz's 1523 Christmas sermon, printed at Königsberg early in the New Year, was also reissued in many editions by presses in central and southern Germany. The same was true of various sermons and pamphlets by Brießmann, who later would travel to Riga to compose a new church order for Livonia.[52]

The literature that was either seized from the German merchants in the English capital or mentioned in their testimony constituted a mixture of old and new. It included vernacular translations of the Scriptures as well as some of Luther's most important and widely available tracts. Some had been in print since before the first prohibition of 1521. However, the references to Karlstadt show that the Germans may even have been reasonably up-to-date with the most current reform controversy. The enigmatic Karlstadt, estranged from Luther and banished from Saxony in 1524, had composed a series of pamphlets on various aspects of the Lord's Supper, challenging Luther's doctrine of the real presence. They were printed at Basel in the autumn of that year, more than five thousand copies ostensibly intended for distribution in the Swiss cantons. A predictably incisive and hostile response from Wittenberg then established the polemic that would dominate Protestantism for the next half decade. Luther's denunciation of his former colleague was contained in *Wider die himmlischen Propheten*, written in response to Karlstadt's *Dialogus oder ein gesprech Büchlein* of 1524, the tract with which the Hanse men likely were familiar.[53] Admittedly, the Karlstadt work that circulated at the Steelyard could have been any one of many. He already had

---

[52] *UBRG*, 2: nos. 154, 257, 573; *VD* P3958–67, B8284–8305. *Das Vaterunser außgeleget durch Matthiam Bynwalth Prediger zu Gdantzk*: *VD* B5441.
[53] *VD* B6141, L7475; *LW*, 18: 37–215; C. Lindberg, "Karlstadt's *Dialogue* on the Lord's Supper," *Mennonite Quarterly Review* 53 (1979), 35–77. For the context of *Wider die himmlischen Propheten von den Bildern und Sacramenten* ['Against the Heavenly Prophets in the Matter of Images and Sacraments'] and Karlstadt's *Dialogus oder ein gesprech Büchlein* see M.U. Edwards, *Printing, Propaganda and Martin Luther* (Los Angeles, 1994), 131–48.

published extensively and continued to do so while avoiding the
Wittenberg censors. Presses in Basel, Augsburg, and Nürnberg issued
his pamphlets.[54] Suffice it to say, though, if the merchant Bellendorpe
and his confreres in London were in fact reading the most recent
exchanges between Luther and Karlstadt they were keeping themselves abreast of the sacramentarian debate virtually as it unfolded,
in print, during 1525. Evidently it was not particularly difficult for
them to do so, no matter how distant the printing presses. Yet they
do not appear to have been at all interested in distributing the printed
word in England beyond their London enclave.

Only Bellendorpe admitted that he comprehended some Latin;
none of the others could read or understand it. All of the accused
had possessed and/or read Lutheran works in German. Where did
they originate? Imprints in a High German dialect need not have
presented a problem for Reussel, Ellendorpe, and the Danzigers,
although the language they spoke and probably read most easily was
the Low German common to the north and to harbour towns of
the Baltic. Wittenberg and Strasbourg presses produced Lutheran
works in Low German for northern distribution, some of them
authored by Pomerania's native son, Bugenhagen. Northern printers did likewise, among them Weinreich, Dietz at Rostock and, prior
to the suppression of his Lübeck press, Georg Richolff.[55] And, although
its printing houses were closely regulated, Lübeck remained an integral junction for interregional commercial traffic, which meant that
books from other German presses came to and through the port.

The recent travels of the Steelyard *Esterlings*, their provenances,
and the pamphlets they circulated combine to illustrate that access
to the new doctrine in print was not very difficult. And merchants
who ventured to the Baltic were just as likely to encounter innovation, controversy, and religious upheaval firsthand. Their London
trade brought opportunities to transmit ideas that were current in
the Baltic seaports. However, Thomas More's search of the Steelyard
also uncovered vernacular Scripture books that quite likely were produced in places much closer to England. Their possession by Steelyard

---

[54] *VD* B6232–34; Lindberg, "Karlstadt's *Dialogue*," 39.
[55] *VD* B9264, B9291, B9398, B9411, 9426; *BB*, 228, 238–40; *UBRG*, 2: nos. 160,
172, 174, 176. In 1521 Richolff printed Luther's version of the Lord's Prayer in
Low German, *Eine korte form des Vaterunses* (*VD* L5372).

merchants points to integrated Anglo-Hanseatic commerce within the North Sea/Atlantic region. Wittenberg printing houses reissued Low German versions of Luther's New Testament translation in the mid-1520s, but so did a press that had infinitely stronger trade links to London. Peter Quentell finished an edition in Cologne in August 1524, within days of the civic ordinance outlawing production or sale of Lutheran books.[56] Town authorities do not seem to have troubled him about it. Steelyard merchants may have possessed some of these relatively new imprints, brought into England easily enough via Antwerp or the northern German ports.

If on the other hand the New Testaments confiscated at the Steelyard were not Quentell's recent work then the most probable source was Hamburg. The first Low German rendition of Luther's translation—*Nygen Testament tho dude*—was printed there in the spring of 1523.[57] This was the high watermark of a rapid surge in book printing that for a brief time made Hamburg the centre of propaganda production in lower Germany. It was partly attributable to refugees who fled persecution in the Low Countries following the Edict of Worms. They were so numerous by early 1523 that the archbishop of Bremen, under whose nominal ecclesiastical jurisdiction Hamburg fell, complained. Among them was Wilhelm Korver, whose brother, Simon, had until recently run a printing house in Zwolle. To Hamburg Wilhelm brought expertise and perhaps the press equipment as well. Jan Hillen van Hoochstraten may have been there too. Within a year Hamburg's heretic press (*Ketzerpresse*) had published no fewer than fifteen different reform tracts in Low German or Dutch, including eleven of Luther's writings.[58] That these were rendered from earlier editions of the reformer's works testifies to the availability of such material in Hamburg, while variations in grammar and word choice within the new versions point to the work of more than one translator. Recalling that prayer books were confiscated from Steelyard merchants in London, a Low German

---

[56] *VD* B4500; *Beschlüsse*, 3: 144.
[57] *VD* B4498.
[58] Postel, *Die Reformation in Hamburg*, 183–91; Reincke, *Hamburg*, 72–78; K. Beckey, *Die Reformation in Hamburg* (Hamburg, 1929), 21–22, 211–14; W. Kayser, "Hamburger Buchdruck im 16. Jahrhundert," *Zeitschrift des Vereins für Hamburgische Geschichte* 72 (1986), 1–3; Johnston, "Printing," 158; *VD* L4065, L4118, L4720, L6205, L6228, L6530, L6574, L7037, L7320, B4498, B8309; *NB*, nos. 708–74; *PI*, 100.

adaptation of Luther's *Betbüchlein* is a good example of early reform propaganda directed at a specific readership defined by language. The Hamburg edition of 1522–23 combined texts of the Creed and the Lord's Prayer, the Mass, and Confession with select quotations from Luther's earlier writings, effectively presenting the essence of his theology to that point.[59] Though non-polemical, it was intentionally subversive nevertheless.

One of the accused Steelyard men came from Hamburg. Nearby Bremen was home to another. Socially and economically the two port towns had much in common, and were similar too in their responses to religious controversy. Both attracted itinerant preachers and became havens for exiles, even though the archdiocesan authority, Duke Christoph of Braunschweig-Wolfenbüttel, despised evangelicals. He was constantly at odds with Bremen. Instinctively perhaps, civic officials defied him, and in any case by autumn 1525 were won over to reform. Church ceremonies were patterned on the Wittenberg model. Imperial decrees against Luther's followers were not enforced. Nor were they at Hamburg, although the government there was not yet committed to following Bremen's lead exactly. It issued its own decree in 1523, outlawing the printing and selling of Luther's books in the town. The *Ketzerpresse* faded away but preachers did not.[60] Luther himself was well informed of enthusiastic popular support for evangelical preaching in Hamburg, much of it coming from brewers, shippers, and merchants. Hamburg was a relatively small place, with scarcely a third as many inhabitants as Danzig and without a hall equivalent to the *Artushof*. However, the town did have five churches and a correspondingly large and conspicuous population of clerics. Pressures from within the body politic spurred incremental religious change, each step overseen and endorsed by the civic authorities. There were no insurrections or iconoclastic outbursts comparable to those experienced in Danzig and Livonia, nor did a princely authority mandate swift transition, as in Königsberg. However, support within the political leadership was far from unanimous. From the summer of 1523 until 1525 traditionalists held sway, attempting

---

[59] *VD* L4118: *Ein schone beedebock*; M. Brecht, "'Tosaginge' und 'geloven': Neue Einsichten in die frühe Lutherrezeption in Hamburg," *ARG* 85 (1994), 45–67.
[60] *Reformationsgeschichte Niedersachsens*, 12–14; Beckey, *Die Reformation in Hamburg*, 19–20, 48–49.

to prevent Hamburg scholars from studying at Wittenberg. It proved impossible, however, to regulate evangelical preaching.

Although an attempt to install Bugenhagen as minister of St. Nicholas' church in 1523 was unsuccessful, Hamburg's council subsequently moved, albeit cautiously, to sanction and implement changes, especially after the imperial Diet at Speyer in 1526 permitted individual estates to address religious questions independently. That decision effectively removed extraneous pressure on town authorities to curb innovation. The following spring they sanctioned an open disputation between evangelical ministers and Catholic clergymen.[61] Long before then, the inclinations of several members of the political establishment had been made plain enough with their attendance at the wedding of evangelical preacher Johann Meyer. Within the civic administration the earliest avowed supporter of Luther was Matthias von Emersen, a wealthy patrician, who like so many others had made his fortune in trade to and from England. Another was Emersen's brother-in-law Detlev Schuldorpe, whose house was a meeting place for the like-minded as early as 1521. By the end of the decade Schuldorpe would emerge the leader of Hamburg's *Englandfahrer* fellowship and it, in turn, as a principal source of patronage for religious reform. Meanwhile, his brother Marquard continued to preach in nearby Schleswig. It was also to the port of Hamburg that another foreign refugee, the English translator of the New Testament, William Tyndale fled in the spring of 1524. Perhaps, as James F. Mozley suggested, he stayed briefly in the Emersen household, before travelling on to Wittenberg in the company of the family's eldest son, Matthias, later secretary of the London Steelyard.[62]

The few details that are known of William Tyndale's sojourn in Hamburg come from the extant petition of London draper Humphrey Monmouth, accused in 1528 of assisting him and William Roye and helping to publish their books.[63] Monmouth was a cloth dealer of

---

[61] Hauschildt, "Die Reformation," 3: 185–201; Postel, *Die Reformation in Hamburg*, 181–93; Beckey, *Die Reformation in Hamburg*, 37–43, 57–59, 73–82.

[62] B. Lohse, "Humanismus und Reformation in norddeutschen Städten in den 20er und frühen 30er Jahren des 16. Jahrhunderts," in *Die dänische Reformation vor ihrem internationalen Hintergrund*, ed. L. Grane and K. Hørby (Göttingen, 1990), 18; O. Scheib, *Die Reformationsdiskussionen in der Hansestadt Hamburg 1522–1528* (Münster, 1976), 30, 39–40, 214; Reincke, *Hamburg*, 80–81, 113; Postel, *Die Reformation in Hamburg*, 154–55; J.F. Mozley, *William Tyndale* (London, 1937), 44–53.

[63] Mozley, *William Tyndale*, 46; *ENT*, 12–15.

some means, purveying Suffolk woollens to non-denizens and annually shipping upwards of two thousand cloths overseas on his own
account. For a half year prior to leaving England Tyndale was
Monmouth's houseguest, and it was during this time that he apparently secured some of the financing for his subsequent ventures abroad
in Germany and the Netherlands. Monmouth advanced him £10
sterling, allegedly to pray for the souls of his parents. That much
again was pledged by other unnamed men and entrusted to Monmouth
when his young friend left the country. Within a year came word
from Tyndale in Hamburg requesting his money be sent there. In
the interim he had been to Wittenberg, and if he had not done so
already was about to commence his New Testament translation. In
all, the money donated by Monmouth and his associates was hardly
a fortune, yet Johann Cochlaeus, recalling many years later his intervention in 1525, said that English merchants fully covered Tyndale's
expenses. The printers in Cologne had told him as much.[64] The first
edition that was begun but not finished there is often attributed to
Peter Quentell, although the type does not match any he had used
prior to this. Tyndale may have acquired punches, matrices, or type
in Hamburg and brought them to a type-founder in Cologne. He
owned a fount of type in 1529, the year he revisited Hamburg, perhaps surviving a shipwreck *en route* from Antwerp. By then, though,
the matrices had been passed along to his sometime associate Roye,
and then to the Strasbourg printer, Johann Schott.[65]

Since Tyndale's funding originated with Monmouth, it is not surprising that commercial channels were used to transfer the money
to Hamburg. But here the complicity extended beyond the denizen
sector. Again the integrated nature of overseas trade offered a variety of avenues not only for dissemination of printed material but
also for the financing of dissenters. North Sea shipping lanes were
busy year round. About forty Hamburg men had some trade with
London each year, with up to eight of them conducting business

[64] *ENT*, 23. D. Daniell, *William Tyndale: A Biography* (New Haven, 1994), 107–8
suggests Tyndale could have seen a copy of Luther's New Testament at the Steelyard
before leaving England. This presumes that although he had no legitimate mercantile business there, he could enter the facility and someone considered him
sufficiently trustworthy to be shown a Testament.
[65] R. Steele, "Hans Luft of Marburg: A Contribution to the Study of William
Tyndale," *The Library*, 3rd series, 6 (1911), 113–31.

directly from the Steelyard. They and the Danzigers co-ordinated and controlled much of the Hanse's transit traffic between the North Sea and the Baltic.[66] Humphrey Monmouth sent Tyndale's money to Hamburg with a Steelyard man, Hans Collenbeke. Collenbeke was an acquaintance of the younger Emersen, and aside from the trust placed in him by Monmouth, his own business in England raises the possibility of deeper involvement. He imported fish and bulk cargo into London in the early 1520s; a business that placed him squarely within the Steelyard's *Esterling* coterie, among men who shared in the freighting of vessels that operated out of Hamburg, Bremen, and the Baltic ports. In the autumn of 1523, some months after Luther's New Testament was published in Hamburg, Collenbeke was one of the consignees seeking restoration of goods from the ship *Howbarke* of Hamburg, which had foundered off Lowestoft, county Suffolk. Among the others with cargo aboard the vessel were two of the Danzigers later entangled in the investigation of Lutheran books in London, Henry Pryknes and Jacob Egerth. A few months later a similar misadventure befell another vessel bound for London with the goods of other men who were part of Hamburg's Lutheran circle.[67]

A Surreptitious Trade?

There is a time-honoured historiographical tradition regarding illegal imprints in England prior to the introduction of Tyndale's New Testament. In the early twentieth century Arthur W. Reed claimed, without reference to any document in particular, the existence of "abundant evidence of the steady infiltration of Lutheran literature into London" by the Steelyard merchants. Since then, the view that already by the mid-1520s there existed in England a significant clandestine traffic in Lutheran texts, with London's German merchant

---

[66] Friedland, "Englandfahrer," Beilage 3.

[67] TNA:PRO C 1/492/44; *LP*, 4/1: no. 339. Cargo-owners in the second ship included Frederick Ostra, one of Hamburg's leading reform advocates, and Cord Meyniche. Postel, *Die Reformation in Hamburg*, 154–55, 388; Scheib, *Die Reformationsdiskussionen*, 212. Hamburg merchants trading to England and associated with the evangelical movement are listed in H.-P. Plaß, "Bernd Beseke—Ein Radikaler der Reformationszeit?" *Zeitschrift für Hamburgische Geschichte* 67 (1981), 38–46.

community playing a prominent role, has gained considerable acceptance.[68] Presumably though, had this been the case, there would
need to have existed a substantial readership for such material, a
market lucrative enough to risk involvement in both smuggling and
heresy. It is scarcely conceivable that in England there was much
of a market at all for books of the sort found at the Steelyard.
Whether prayer books, polemical pamphlets or Scripture texts, they
were in German. No English translations of Luther's writings were
printed before 1528.[69] Tribunals in London that year accused and
convicted priests of translating from Latin. In England, then, aside
from Germans and Netherlanders who lived there, the early-pub-
lished works of Luther are likely to have been read only by clerics
and scholars.[70] Some Oxford and Cambridge academics secretly
acquired proscribed imprints it is true, yet it must also be kept in
mind that the books confiscated at the Hanseatic complex in London
were in every case the personal property of the inhabitants. The
nature and location of their trade assured relatively easy access to
new and perhaps contentious books, and there is no denying that
they brought some to London. However, the proceedings against
them offer absolutely no hint that multiple copies of Lutheran tracts
were being smuggled through the Steelyard for wider distribution.
Thomas More's surprise raid did not uncover stockpiles of imprints,
and from the entire Hanseatic coterie only eight men could be implicated. The evidence against at least half of them seems to have been
tenuous at best.

Wolsey and his commissioners could have expected no more than
this. Far too much was at stake in the legitimate Anglo-Hanseatic
trade and far too many people involved in it for the London fellowship to countenance dangerous illegal schemes. Moreover, wholesale distribution of books under any circumstances was not the typical

---

[68] Reed, "Regulation," 162; Chester, "Robert Barnes," 218: Bellendorpe was
"deeply involved in the business of smuggling Lutheran books into England". See
also S. Brigden, *London and the Reformation* (Oxford, 1991), 158–9: all of the accused
Hanse men were not only converted to Luther's views but also "importers and
propagators" of his works.

[69] W.A. Clebsch, "The Earliest Translations of Luther into English," *Harvard
Theological Review* 56 (1963), 75–86.

[70] Rex, "English Campaign," 101. Geoffrey Lome and Thomas Arthur confessed
to translating Lutheran tracts from Latin into English. Guildhall Library MS 9531/10
fos. 114–28.

business of Steelyard merchants, but rather that of printers and book-sellers, many of them foreign-born, and not one of whom was com-promised at this time. Notwithstanding the absence of a ring of smugglers, however, within the Steelyard there were devout men deeply interested in matters spiritual. They owned the New Testament translated by Luther, most likely editions printed in Cologne or Hamburg. In addition, some kept well apprised of reform currents by reading pamphlets. They were therefore already part of a dis-semination network, with the potential to extend the process. Their reading material was replenished periodically by trips to their home-land and through the overseas trade that brought cargoes and ships' crews regularly to the Steelyard quay. The Steelyard was not a clear-inghouse for texts intended for an English readership. Nor should it be imagined that its residents were a fraternity of faith. It was, how-ever, home to some well-read individuals sympathetic to Luther and perhaps influenced by the more divergent views of Andreas Karlstadt.

Steelyard men possessed a few Lutheran *Flugschriften*, however we do not know what else More found that he deemed acceptable or harmless. It was the nature of the prosecution, after all, to identify only controversial or suspicious material. Yet it seems no less prob-able that some merchants read works by Catholic apologists. Even one of John Fisher's responses to Luther was available in German translation.[71] Countless vernacular works now circulated in Germany, among them editions that paired some previously issued treatise or excerpt with a refutation, Cochlaeus's reply to Bugenhagen being but one example. The merchants acquainted themselves with much else besides Wittenberg theology. And civic affiliation did not nec-essarily determine the individual's religiosity. The men detained on suspicion of heresy were not the only *Esterlings* in London, and even among those who abjured we find varying levels of interest in doc-trine. Conservatives and nonconformists likely coexisted at the Steelyard much as they did, for example, within the governing elite of Hamburg in the early 1520s and in Danzig until 1525. Ultimately, too, some-thing essential to the outcome of the debate over religious issues was quite simply the dissemination of news—of events triggered by the expression of contentious beliefs. Mercantile networks were indis-pensable in this regard because however diverse personal opinions

---

[71] *VD* F1223, F1224.

on spiritual matters were, it was in every merchant's interest to be aware of developments at home and within the broader geographical sphere of his commercial activity. Individuals from disparate towns of the Hanse no doubt learned of doctrinal controversies and their consequences in part from each other at the London Steelyard, the *Artushof* or the trade marts in Brabant. Religious issues were topical. Within the Steelyard compound, where merchants from different towns and regions interacted on a day-to-day basis, opinions and preferences likely became known to many through simple conversation, if not fraternal debate. Bellendorpe and Reussel had read a substantial corpus of material and had exchanged books and no doubt ideas as well with some of their associates. They knew they were at risk as soon as Thomas More detained another member of the cohort, and immediately took the precaution, albeit to no avail, of destroying their personal libraries.

Individuals and associations also became informed through written correspondence. Another of the young Danzigers working at the Steelyard was Georg Giese (also Gisze), later subject of one of Hans Holbein's merchant portraits.[72] Likely a betrothal gift for Giese's fiancé in Danzig, the painting is renowned for its meticulous attention to the accoutrements and décor of the sitter's Steelyard chamber. In addition to bound books, there are several pieces of correspondence indicative of distant contact. Giese holds a letter that is at once imaginary yet symbolic of real familial bonds. It is addressed: "Dem erszamen Jergen Gisze to Lunden in engelant Mynem broder to handen". The writer of such a letter would have been Georg's older brother Tidemann: friend of Copernicus, prebendary, and future bishop of Kulm and later Ermland. Ranking among Prussia's best-educated scholars, Tidemann was a Catholic humanist in the Erasmian mould. By the time of the Steelyard scandal he was also a published author. His *Antilogikon flosculorum Lutheranorum* defended traditional Catholicism against an influential work attributed to Brießmann, *Flosculi de homine*. Viëtor issued it at Cracow. Tidemann Giese would have been acutely aware of events specific to Danzig as well as the spectrum of theological issues that sparked debate there and else-

---

[72] Ganz, *Hans Holbein*, 223–24; S. Buck, *Hans Holbein* (Cologne, 1999), 88–95. Holbein's portrait of Giese was done in 1532. Another, of Duisburg merchant Dirk Tybis, also shows the sitter holding a letter.

(1) 'Der Kaufmann Georg Gisze'
    Portrait by Hans Holbein d.J. 1532
    By kind permission of the Gemäldegalerie, Staatliche Museen zu Berlin

where. A second manuscript, *De regno Christi*, finished in 1536 but
since lost, evidently reflected the influences of both Erasmus and
Melanchthon. In his later career a relatively accommodating approach
to Lutherans set Giese apart from other bishops in Poland and Royal
Prussia.[73] His younger brother Georg was involved in trade to England
as early as 1522.[74] Certainly he knew Bellendorpe and the other
Steelyard *Esterlings*. Quite conceivably he was aware of their heresy
as well. By the same token, there is little reason to doubt that he
and his brother were exchanging letters at the time. The potential
existed, then, for Tidemann's informed interpretation of contemporary issues to reach the Steelyard by way of private correspondence.
And if Georg Giese chose to, there would have been nothing to prevent him sharing his latest news from home with others, including
the suspects eventually rounded up by Thomas More.

As a matter of course, in addition to prohibited books, the Steelyard
investigation attempted to expose other traces of nonconformity and
heresy. It is likely that the line of questioning borrowed from formularies used for routine interrogation of suspected Lollards, whose
denial of Christ's corporal presence in the Eucharist was central to
their rejection of Catholic dogma. Even so, one of the specific articles introduced against the Germans—that the Mass of the Body of
Christ had been discontinued at the church of All Hallows the
Great—is curious. The recorded testimony does not indicate the basis
of the allegation. From time to time Wolsey or Tunstall may have
received information about the Steelyard from the parish clergy.[75]
That the priests would admit serious and deliberate dereliction of
their ministry, however, is scarcely plausible. Moreover, while Steelyard
merchants and porters attended All Hallows there is nothing to suggest that great numbers of them rejected the sacrament. Perhaps
some had stopped attending mass, but it is inconceivable that they
could influence the pastors of All Hallows the Great sufficiently to

---

[73] Karp and Triller, "Die Katholische Kirche," 150 and "Humanismus," 171;
Caliebe, "Die Literatur," 185; Arnold, "Luther und Danzig," 101; Schwenke, "Hans
Weinreich," 72; G. Schramm, "Danzig, Elbing und Thorn als Beispiele städtische
Reformation (1517–1558)," in *Historia Integra: Festschrift für Erich Hassinger*, ed.
H. Fenske, W. Reinhard, E. Schulin (Berlin, 1977), 126; Simson, *Geschichte*, 1: 379,
386–87; *UBRG*, 1: 68–71, 2: no. 329. Tidemann Giese studied at Leipzig in the
1490s. He was elevated to the see of Kulm in 1538 and Ermland in 1548.

[74] *LP*, 3/2: no. 2350.

[75] Jörn, *Der Londoner Stalhof*, 464–65.

discontinue it. None of the surviving depositions contain a direct response to the article. Bellendorpe, though, confessed to doubting the real presence of Christ in the consecrated host.[76]

Anticlericalism was also probed. None of the deponents cared to dispute Wolsey's authority as papal legate, though Hans Reussel admitted that on his recent trip abroad he had heard it said that the pope was simply the equal of other bishops, a view not uncommon or particularly new in England. Each of the Germans was asked if he had broken fasts, and indeed the raid on the Steelyard had been timed to interrupt the Friday evening meal there. Once again, Bellendorpe's opinion that fasts were instituted not by Christ but by the Church of Rome seems as much Lollard as Lutheran. Contrary to canon law he had in fact eaten meat on Fridays, once with mariners at the Steelyard and again in the chamber there of someone named Gysbard. While the topics of conversation remain unknown, these social settings at the very least provided considerable opportunity for the exchange of ideas. Perhaps more can be inferred, then, from another occasion when both Bellendorpe and Reussel dined at the house of a certain Gregory. They consumed meat on the eve of a fast day "cum duobus aliis Anglis", identified as Gerard Catter and Gerard Bull.

As merchants and ships' crews shuttled cargoes back and forth between London and Hamburg or Danzig or "Estland" they fostered non-commercial contact between otherwise dispersed individuals and communities. Broader dimensions of bilateral exchange—social interaction, transmission of knowledge and news, dissemination of informed opinion and doctrine—came into play whenever they went ashore. The Steelyard investigation bears this out. Upon his return from Germany about Whitsuntide 1525, Helbert Bellendorpe told Reussel that he had news from beyond the sea. He then proceeded to lend his friend one of the books he had acquired while away. Another of the resident Danzigers was given a Lutheran prayer book, apparently in London, by a ship's purser. There were daily communal suppers at the Steelyard, occasions that also served to demonstrate unity within the privileged fellowship.[77] Yet as their testimony shows,

---

[76] "Et interrogatus de sacramento altaris credit et semper credidit, quod ibidem est forma panis et vini et non substancia": from the transcription in Pauli, "Das Verfahren," 169.

[77] Jörn, *Der Londoner Stalhof*, 440.

Esterlings at the enclave also took their meals sometimes if not frequently with mariners, presumably crewmen from Hanseatic vessels anchored in the Thames. And on other occasions the same Steelyard men dined with English friends. Business necessarily brought Englishmen to the Steelyard. It also drew Hanse merchants into greater London, where the obvious venue for initial contact was Blackwell Hall in Basinghall Street. There, from Thursday through Saturday each week they encountered not only provincial clothiers but also members of the major livery companies: grocers, ironmongers, drapers, and most particularly mercers. Whatever their trade guild affiliation, the denizen buyers who came to the cloth exchange were, like their Steelyard counterparts, exporters. Their principal market overseas was Antwerp. The vast majority of these men therefore belonged to the Merchant Adventurers' Company.[78]

Whether in private homes, guild taverns or public alehouses the sharing of meals was the most common occasion for forthright discussion, regardless of subject. And candid dialogue, together with the reading aloud of pamphlet literature, was a central element of oral dissemination. As Robert W. Scribner illustrated, personal contacts and the spoken word were in fact crucial to mediating printed text, which was but one element in the process of communicating ideas.[79] There were Steelyard statutes aimed at regulating behaviour and activity both within and outside the *comptoir*. Harlots were not to be brought in and visiting brothels was discouraged. So too was gambling. At stake was the good reputation of the fraternity, to say nothing of the individual's dignity.[80] Yet beyond the confines of their riverfront residence the merchants were quite free to consort with worthy English acquaintances. And so they did, impersonal trading activity giving way now and then or perhaps regularly to informal socialising.

Though not disseminators of literature in England, Germans of Lutheran and Karlstadtian persuasion did therefore come into contact with the king's subjects. And for some it was not simply a matter of business. But this did not necessarily place them within secretive Lollard congregations of "known" men and women. In or near

[78] Ramsay, *City of London*, 37–42.
[79] Scribner, "Oral Culture," 88.
[80] Jörn, *Der Londoner Stalhof*, 449–58.

London, though, several pockets of nonconformity existed, in the market towns of Essex, Suffolk and Buckinghamshire for instance. There was plenty of opportunity for regular communication between such communities, thanks to the commerce in wool, cloth, and agricultural produce. In London itself Bishop Fitzjames had discovered and arraigned several individuals, including some in the parish of All Hallows the Great, and there were more again in searches initiated in 1521. One of the main Lollard haunts in the later 1520s was the parish of St. Katherine Coleman in east London. Not far from the capital, in Rochester and Gravesend, John Fisher found still more. London Lollards typically came from humble artisan families but also included members of the wealthier livery companies. Most were strongly anticlerical and although not all could read, possession of English Bibles was another of their hallmarks. They treasured their illegal manuscript tomes, which literate members read aloud at conventicles. Punishment of those who were caught included public penance and destruction of the precious books.[81] That some Lollards might find Luther's views of interest is not hard to imagine, but by the same token it is also difficult to envision them acquiring and reading Lutheran polemic or his German New Testament. They welcomed publication of the Gospels in their own language, and by the early 1530s if not before an organised cell, the Christian Brethren, would be active in distributing printed reform doctrine and vernacular Scriptures. Notwithstanding the fraternising of denizens and Germans, however, prior to the arrest of merchants at the Steelyard early in 1526 Tyndale's English version was not yet available there or anywhere else.

Brokers of Ideas

The direct influence of Lutheran literature on the pre-existing Lollard tradition of dissent is unlikely to have been great.[82] Even so, transmission or reinforcement of ideas through informal channels merits

---

[81] D. Plumb, "A gathered church? Lollards and their Society," in *The World of Rural Dissenters, 1520–1725*, ed. M. Spufford (Cambridge, 1995), 132–63; Davis, *Heresy*, 40–44; Brigden, *London*, 82–128. Especially common in Lollard circles were manuscript copies of the Four Apostles, the Ten Commandments, the Epistles of St. James and St. Paul, and "Wycliffe's Wicket".

[82] Davis, *Heresy*, 65.

consideration. For this, though, we should look well beyond the banks of the Thames and encounters between *Esterlings* and Londoners. Trading ventures took Englishmen to the Low Countries and to the Hanse ports of Bremen, Hamburg, and Danzig, placing them immediately among people associated with waterfront activity: mariners and dock workers. These were the very constituencies where, in the German ports at least, the evangelical *Sturmprediger* built avid followings. Moreover, like their German counterparts in London, Englishmen were at liberty to associate with denizens. Exposure to unconventional devotional practices is perhaps best illustrated by a group of six local men who returned to Hull in the spring of 1528. Their circumstances are not altogether obvious. One, Robert Robynson, was incapable of writing his signature, so is unlikely to have been a merchant of any consequence. Yet the group also included someone's apprentice, and few apprentices except those with mercantile connections would have leave to go overseas. That the group appears to have kept together throughout their time away from England may also suggest some sort of business arrangement. Whether they were small-time entrepreneurs or ordinary mariners, they were tied to seaborne commerce just the same. Their itinerary is known from the deposition given to Lincoln diocesan officials by Henry Burnett, who lived just south of the Humber. He told them that he and his five comrades had crossed from Hull to Amsterdam aboard a merchant ship, spending six or seven weeks there before moving on to Bremen. After a five-week stay in Bremen, during which they visited various places in Friesland, they headed back to Hull aboard a ship they had freighted with wheat. Although one of the men possessed an English New Testament, officials in the Lincoln and York dioceses did not accuse them of importing heretical imprints. Burnett owned nothing by Luther. He could read English but not Latin. Of much greater concern was what he and the others said and how they behaved when they came home.[83]

The tale points to the huge potential for the spread of spiritual controversy ostensibly through trade networks. A half dozen acquaintances, at least one of them only semiliterate, were free to take pas-

[83] Dickens, *Lollards and Protestants*, 24–27; "Extracts from Lincoln Episcopal Visitations in the 15th, 16th, and 17th Centuries," ed. E. Peacock. *Archaeologia* 48 (1885), 257–58.

sage or hire themselves aboard a Dutch trading ship bound for Amsterdam, a busy transit port, especially for the movement of grain. Cereals were in short supply in England at the time, so substantial quantities needed to be imported. Perhaps the Englishmen had pooled their resources with a view to finding a cargo, and when none was to be had in Holland, boarded a vessel that would take them to Bremen, another grain-exporting port. They freighted or at least had a hand in freighting that ship or some other for the voyage back to Hull. Several weeks in Amsterdam would have been plenty of time for the visitors to encounter reform currents through routine observation and social contact. Other impressions might come by way of entertainment. Performance art shaped as well as reflected public opinion, and religious and social satire had become a fairly typical ingredient of popular theatre.

In all of the Low Countries' large towns amateur thespian societies known as chambers of rhetoric created and presented plays. Artisans and merchants were prominent within the societies and, where presses existed, so were printers and publishers. Collectively the chambers contributed to regional cultural networks. Gouda, Amsterdam, Rotterdam, Dordrecht, Haarlem, and Leiden formed the basis of a circuitry in Holland, paralleled in the southern provinces by one including Bruges, Brussels, and Antwerp. A chamber from one town might occasionally perform in another, as in 1523 for instance, when an Amsterdam entourage travelled to Leiden. Productions by societies of rhetoric were staged outdoors in public places, in front of inns and town halls. Whereas earlier plays often drew on traditional moral and religious themes such as the Seven Sorrows of the Virgin, by the early 1520s they had become vehicles for anticlericalism and heterodox dissent. The contentious views of the dramatists were of sufficient concern to Amsterdam's council in 1523 that it would not allow any new acting societies to be formed. The town's two existing chambers were not seriously hampered, though, because many civic magistrates were in fact sympathetic to the new doctrine. So in 1525 and 1526 Amsterdam audiences, which quite probably included non-denizens, attended plays that criticised Rome and ridiculed the sacraments. Theatrical performances were rich in visual effects and imagery. Conceivably, then, even foreigners unfamiliar with the language might take in ideas almost subconsciously.[84]

---

[84] Marnef, *Antwerp*, 29–30; G. Waite, *Reformers on Stage: Popular Drama and Religious*

In all, the English travellers' sojourn lasted about four months.
They were not always aboard ships or at the dockside. After the
voyage to Bremen there were excursions to Friesland. Burnett's testimony does not leave the impression that the group was in any
great hurry to get home or that they were delayed. The maritime
trade system of which they were a part afforded opportunities for
new experience and learning. In a time of transition it put them in
a position to observe evangelical innovation and absorb, perhaps,
some of its influences. Predisposition to nonconformity is not certain. Burnett denied that he went abroad to learn Lutheran ways.
Nevertheless, he and the others witnessed many innovations and ate
meat on fish days. Robynson abjured a series of rather routine articles of Lollardy, including non-observance of fasts, and performed
ritual penance assigned by the York archdiocesan court. Possibly he
was a Lollard, however no evidence survives to indicate that his travelling companions were. It would be especially useful to know why
the men ventured outside Bremen to other places where Luther's
views held sway. They need not have done so to take in evangelical sermons and hymn singing. The mass had not been heard in
Bremen's churches since 1525. Problematic for the English diocesan
officials was that the erstwhile tourists, once back in England, apparently did not keep quiet about what they had done and seen. Burnett
had temporarily continued to consume meat on prohibited days and
was under investigation very shortly after his return.

A.G. Dickens drew attention to this story several years ago as he
attempted to trace the mechanics of distribution to mobile elements
within England's middle and lower social ranks. Among his other
examples was the voyage of a merchant heretic from Suffolk to
Scarborough aboard a coasting vessel. More recently, the likely impor-

Propaganda in the Low Countries of Charles V, 1515–1556 (Toronto, 2000), 81–82, 97–98
and *David Joris and Dutch Anabaptism 1524–1543* (Waterloo, ON, 1990), 12–13. The
chambers are brought to life in a collection of recent essays: *Conformisten en Rebellen:
Rederijkerscultuur in de Nederlanden (1400–1650)*, ed. B. Ramakers (Amsterdam, 2003).
Most pertinent here are G. Waite, "On the stage and in the streets: Rhetorician
drama, social conflict and religious upheaval in Amsterdam (1520–1566)," 163–73
and G. Marnef, "Rederijkers en religieuze vernieuwing te Antwerpen in de tweede
helfte van de zestiende eeuw," 175–88. Regional contexts are explored in A.-L.
Van Bruaene, "Sociabiliteit en competitie: De sociaal-institutionele ontwikkeling van
de rederijkerskamers in de Zuidelijke Nederlanden (1400–1650)," 45–63, and
A. van Dixhoorn, "Burgers, branies en bollebozen: De sociaal-institutionele ontwikkeling van de rederijkerskamers in de Noordelijke Nederlanden (1470–1650)," 65–85.

tance of merchants and shipping has been emphasised by Margaret Spufford. Again pointing to Burnett's confession, she suggests that not only clothiers but also middlemen in the grain trade functioned as "brokers of ideas" from abroad.[85] Although we might wish for more concrete examples, there is nevertheless a very sound basis for supposing this kind of interplay occurred on a much larger scale. Northern Europe's coastal and overseas shipping were interconnected, and all of the main ports on England's east coast—Newcastle, Hull, Boston, Lynn, Yarmouth, Ipswich, and Colchester—had firm continental links. If a few individuals from Hull were exposed to innovation in Amsterdam and Bremen, the potential existed for hundreds if not thousands of similar encounters. The same year that Burnett and his friends were touring Bremen and Friesland, close to five hundred merchant ships paid the toll at Helsingør for passage through the Øresund. Two dozen of them were English, trading to Danzig. Ten times that many came from ports in the Low Countries and another hundred and thirty or so from Baltic harbours.[86]

Trading vessels did not operate exclusively out of their homeports. Newcastle carriers, for example, often were chartered for Baltic ventures that began and ended in Hull or Lynn. German and Low Countries' shipping was no different. Hamburg and Lübeck hulks brought Danzig cargoes to England. The Hamburg ship *Salvator*, robbed by pirates in the Thames, was freighted with pitch and flax at Königsberg.[87] Coastal transport carried people and goods over shorter distances. An undated early sixteenth-century record, probably from Lynn, lists destinations from London north to Newcastle. Grain was the most common outbound cargo. Incoming vessels from Newcastle discharged large quantities of coal.[88] Customs records from Lynn afford additional insight because of the port's long history of trade with Danzig. *Esterlings* once played a vital role in this sector

---

[85] Dickens, *Lollards and Protestants*, 246–47; M. Spufford, "The Importance of religion in the sixteenth and seventeenth centuries," in *The World of Rural Dissenters, 1520–1725*, ed. M. Spufford (Cambridge, 1995), 44.

[86] Bang, ed., *Tabeller*, 1: 5. Bang lists aggregate passages together with the ships' provenances. Assuming that most vessels actually navigated the Øresund once in each direction, her totals have been halved to arrive at the approximate number of ships.

[87] J.D. Fudge, "Home Ports and Destinations: English Shipping in the Baltic Trade, 1536–1547," *The Northern Mariner* 9 (1999), 13–24; TNA:PRO C 1/586/52.

[88] TNA:PRO E 122/99/18.

and they still maintained a warehouse at Lynn, but by the end of
the 1520s Englishmen were the principal players. Up to sixteen of
them were involved directly, sometimes using Prussian carriers but
typically sending two or more of their own vessels each summer to
Danzig, where they had a resident English factor. Some were Lynn
men; others were based in Norwich. Presumably, ships' crews were
recruited from Lynn and other harbour communities in East Anglia.
A seaman might serve on one vessel for a particular voyage and
then switch to another. This was certainly true of ships' masters and
pilots. And ships could be used for voyages to various destinations
within a seasonal cycle, bringing crewmen to several different ports
within a period of months.[89]

While ideas and impressions, much like merchandise, could pass
from port to port it stands to reason that they might also reach
inland as far as transportation networks could take them, as was the
case in Denmark and the eastern Baltic territories. Many possibilities existed in England, well away from London. Henry Burnett's
home was Barrow, across the river from Hull, on the road to Lincoln.
Much of the cloth that was exported overseas from Hull was manufactured at York and Beverley. Norwich, East Anglia's largest market town, channelled overseas trade through Yarmouth. Two weekly
markets and a pair of annual fairs generated economic activity at
Lynn, whence barges on the river Ouse and its tributaries carried
commercial traffic to and from at least six counties. Especially important was the annual Sturbridge Fair near Cambridge. It was a market for regionally produced woollens, though much else changed
hands there too: coal from northern England, Bordeaux wine, Icelandic
stock fish, manufactured wares from the Low Countries and bulk
commodities from the eastern Baltic.[90] It thus provided an environment of contact and exchange that necessarily helped make possible the brokering of ideas.

Movement of heterodox doctrine or devotional practices to England
through trade networks ultimately depended on the English them-

---

[89] Fudge, "Home Ports," 17.
[90] J.D. Fudge, "Maintaining a presence: Baltic Enterprise and the merchants of
Lynn during the reign of Henry VIII," in *Britain and the Baltic: Studies in Commercial,
Political and Cultural Relations 1500–2000*, ed. P. Salmon and T. Barrow (Sunderland,
2003), 3–19.

selves, not Germans. And until Tyndale's New Testament was published it had very little to do with books. Crews of trading ships and merchants accompanying them to distant ports could observe manifestations of religious controversy firsthand. Conceivably, the impressions they returned with bolstered Lollard nonconformity in some communities. And soon, though not yet, English-language imprints would be available to smuggle into the kingdom. Sailors and traders from Germany and the Low Countries were not traffickers in contentious books, once again because there was nothing much for them to bring to an English readership and no incentive to do so from a business perspective. This is not to say, however, that visitors from Amsterdam or Hamburg or Danzig did not on occasion enjoy a measure of ale or share a meal and conversation with English hosts.

The *Esterlings* of the London Steelyard were not any more likely to have imported contraband books than their cousins who did business at Hull, Newcastle, and Lynn. Yet the London fellowship was singled out for investigation from the outset in 1526. The seriousness of Wolsey's intention to search other locations is debatable. When Longland broached the proposal with the king in early January, places to be investigated apparently were named. They were supposed to be searched "att oon tyme"; the intended targets were "merchands and stationers".[91] Robert Barnes, neither merchant nor stationer, was arrested well after the Steelyard men. His colleagues at Cambridge were alerted in time to conceal their books, and evidently nothing of importance was uncovered there. Yet thorough investigations in London, the kingdom's largest and busiest port, might well have netted more than a handful of obscure foreigners, had they occurred simultaneously and had there existed an organised and significant smuggling network. To be sure, plenty of denizens were rounded up in subsequent crackdowns, once copies of Tyndale's New Testament began to circulate. But among the penitents in February 1526 we find no London stationers or any of the innumerable denizen merchants who traded overseas.

Aside from Barnes, then, none of those arraigned at this time were Englishmen; an indication, perhaps, of how small the traffic in illicit books actually was, and of how little the bishops and the Crown really knew about what was being brought into the country and by

---

[91] Chester, "Robert Barnes," 215–16.

whom. But the absence of English suspects may also be an indication of Wolsey's reluctance to risk antagonising the citizenry of
London. His dominance of the central government, coupled with his
own ostentation and the perceived arrogance of the high clergy,
evoked fierce resentment in many Londoners. Spiritual controversies
aside, he was also widely blamed for the demise of the Duke of
Buckingham, a popular hero to some, sent to the scaffold for treason in 1521. In England's capital widespread anguish over the fate
of the supposed traitor had found expression in spontaneous and
unrestrained public lamentation, while libellous bills gave vent to
pervasive dislike of the king's first minister. And there was no question that Londoners were capable of violent disorder. It had been
less than a decade since the Evil May Day riot of 1517, when poor
apprentices went on a rampage against foreigners. The riot had esca-
lated to xenophobic frenzy, necessitating the arrest of nearly three
hundred persons.[92] Wolsey could not have been anxious to test the
volatility of the populace again. The need to control the spread of
heterodoxy and his desire to indulge the papacy had to be weighed
against the possibility of provoking sedition.

The solution was a somewhat contrived indictment of aliens who
were unlikely to elicit much public sympathy and whose homeland
was, after all, the source of the new Lutheran heresy. The chancellor himself had no compunction about abasing the Steelyard merchants. His contempt for them was not new. In the early 1520s they
were accused of colouring the merchandise of other foreigners and
were also prosecuted and fined heavily for allegedly exporting unfinished
cloth. Hanseatic and English representatives, among them Thomas
More, had failed to resolve these and other outstanding issues through
negotiation.[93] But whereas earlier attempts at intimidation were in
part designed to undermine entrenched Hanseatic franchises and thus
to pacify malcontents within the denizen business community, the
purpose now was different. It had become necessary to demonstrate
that non-observance of the ban on controversial literature would not
be tolerated, even within the *comptoir*, where the resident merchants
usually enjoyed considerable autonomy. Beyond this, the ritual of
public penance was a pointed warning to anyone else in the mer-

---

[92] Brigden, *London*, 129–31, 151–57; Hall, *Chronicle*, 588–90.
[93] Lloyd, *England and the German Hanse*, 253–59.

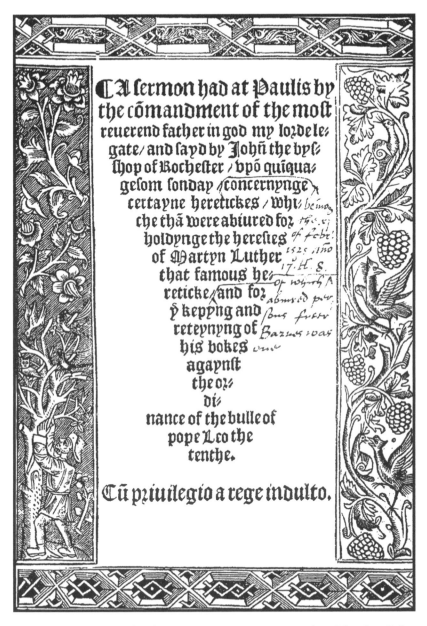

(2) *A sermon had at Paulis . . . concernynge certayne heretickes* by John Fisher. Thomas Berthelet, London [1526] (*STC* 10892) By kind permission of the Bristish Library

cantile sector that might be tempted to import heretical books. There
was an immediate practical utility as well. In order to carry out a
policy of censorship more effectively, England's government and episcopate needed to be aware of what was in print. Although he knew
of Tyndale's New Testament translation and of the proliferation of
Lutheran publications in Germany, to this point information supplied from abroad by Wolsey's agents was insufficient. The sweep
of the Steelyard uncovered no semblance of a trade in prohibited
books, but it did produce a number of specific tracts to which the
general prohibition could be applied and to which Fisher or perhaps More might respond in print. It also provided penitents for a
public spectacle that would ingratiate the prelate-chancellor with
Rome. The inclusion of Robert Barnes in that ceremony was not
predetermined. The outspoken Augustinian found himself the focus
of scandal just as the initiative was being implemented. As a result,
he became a late but not unwelcome addition to the cast of repentant heretics who could be paraded before the throng at St. Paul's.

The king himself had recommended John Fisher preach the sermon on this occasion. Characteristically sincere, and with a clear
sense of duty in his resistance to Luther, England's most accomplished polemicist strove to reach an audience larger than the one
gathered in the Churchyard. Thomas Berthelet, whose printing house
stood in Fleet Street, issued the text, prefaced with an epistle to the
reader. In it the bishop explained: "I have put forth this sermon to
be redde, which for the great noyse of the people within the churche
of Paules, when it was sayde, myght not be herde". Undoubtedly,
it was no less intended to publicise the event for its maximum propaganda value, although the number of copies and how they were
distributed remains unknown. On the whole somewhat disjointed
and rambling, the sermon was nevertheless laden with metaphorical
imagery suitable for popular consumption. Luther's heresies were
likened to weeds and Wolsey lauded for his efforts to extirpate them.
The cardinal-legate had "endeuered hymselfe for these men here
present, and other, whiche were out of the waye, to reduce them
in to the wayes of the churche". "The heretickes contende, that it
shal nat be lefull thus to do", Fisher went on, "but they wold haue
euery man lefte vnto their libertie". Twice during it and again at
the speech's conclusion he directly addressed Barnes and the Germans,
blending tempered reproach and pastoral advice. Though warning
them not to relapse, he did not specify their individual transgres-

sions or mention the one that had precipitated the arrests at the Steelyard: possession of prohibited literature. The means by which the accused had acquired their heretical opinions was only inferred in the extended title of Berthelet's imprint, which informed that they had retained Luther's books in contravention of Leo X's papal bull. Thus, persons who did not attend the burning of those books were made aware of them only in a general sense.[94] The sermon itself concentrated on refuting Luther's challenges to orthodoxy and on pointing out discord among the German reformers. Bishop Fisher did not desire his congregation and readers to know anything more specific, perhaps for fear of publicising the objectionable books and their authors, even though the *Flugschriften* taken at the Steelyard were not available in the English language. Also, since much of the confiscated material actually consisted of prayer books and New Testaments, further elaboration would have required of him some credible explanation of the danger posed by vernacular Scriptures. For Robert Barnes there was another incongruity. He was in trouble ostensibly because of his imprudent tirade against the clerical establishment. The bishops themselves had dictated his revocation. Yet Fisher's admonition gave the impression that Barnes had been convicted as a disciple of Luther.[95] Recent research of this and later prosecutions suggests that the sermon also introduced a tactical shift by Wolsey and his bishops. From this point on they would focus specifically on educated suspects. And, rather than draw attention to heresy by thrusting scholars into the limelight of trials, every discrete attempt would be made to persuade them to renounce their errors.[96]

The spectacle witnessed on that dreary February morning brought down the curtain on the initial phase of Wolsey's strategy to turn back an apparently rising tide of religious dissent and nonconformity. Thus far confined to England itself, the campaign to suppress heretical literature combined standard ecclesiastical weapons—penitential discipline and the burning of books—with a threat of economic

---

[94] *English Works of John Fisher*, 429–76; *STC* 10892: *A sermon had at Paulis... concernynge certayne heretickes... for holdynge the heresies of Martyn Luther... and for the kepyng and reteynyng of his bokes agaynst the ordinance of the bulle of pope Leo the tenthe.* The other men "out of the waye" were, presumably, the *Esterlings* from Danzig who had been denounced but not apprehended.

[95] Barnes, *Reformation Essays*, 101.

[96] D'Alton, "Suppression," 236–40.

penalties for certain foreigners. These could be used *ad hoc* within
the kingdom, taking into account possible wider political and economic considerations as well as limited alternatives. Since the London
Steelyard was not in fact a distribution point for heretical imprints,
the question of deterrence there is an open one. Other German merchants may have been spectators at St. Paul's. It is possible that the
humiliation of a handful of individuals and the prospect of financial
consequences for the entire fellowship caused some to be more judi-
cious about what they read or kept in their chambers. Yet for all
his threatening words, Wolsey knew that anything more severe, especially collective punishment in the form of tough economic sanctions
against the Hanse would bring about a diplomatic breach with potentially grave domestic repercussions. Not only did Hanse ships bring
essential grain consignments to England in times of dearth; German
merchants were also the kingdom's largest foreign customers for
woollen cloth, the lifeblood of the export economy. As recently as
the spring of 1525 attempts to finance war against France by extort-
ing an "amicable grant" from the king's subjects had sparked unlawful assemblies by impoverished cloth workers in Suffolk. Any disruption
of overseas trade raised the prospect of more trouble; textile workers idle, hungry, and threatening the public peace. Indeed this is
exactly what happened when a series of diplomatic blunders caused
interruption of commercial traffic to the Low Countries early in
1528.[97]

Heresy was not yet construed as treason in England. Prosecutions
remained the responsibility of traditional spiritual courts, especially
Court of Audience sessions, and investigative tribunals, backed by
episcopal proclamations. And so the ordinaries continued to investigate, interrogate, and prescribe penance. In April another alien,
Adrian Dolevyn, was abjured. His transgressions included reading
Luther's books "in the Dutch tongue".[98] Tunstall, having cowed
London's printers once already, would issue another warning in the
autumn, followed by a sermon at St. Paul's. London aldermen, meanwhile, dutifully toured their wards, questioning residents about printed

---

[97] *LP*, 4/2: nos. 4044, 4145, 4239, 4276, 4310; Hall, *Chronicle*, 744–47. Resistance
to the amicable grant is assessed in G.W. Bernard, *War, Taxation and Rebellion in
Early Tudor England* (New York, 1986), 110–48.
[98] *LP*, 4/1: no. 2073; Davis, "Heresy," 44.

heresies. But confronting the problem of imported books would now entail looking beyond decrees and diocesan commissions. The bishops and the government were well aware that more trouble was looming across the Narrow Seas. The events that ushered in 1526 therefore constituted only part of a larger and more comprehensive effort that anticipated a more serious threat. Within a matter of weeks, by late March, the first copies of Tyndale's English translation of the New Testament did indeed reach England's shores. Soon the cardinal-chancellor and his minions would be forced to redouble their efforts at home. And, they would begin more vigorously to attack the contagion at its source, on the continent.

CHAPTER THREE

DIPLOMACY AND ESPIONAGE

A fortnight after the Steelyard men abjured at St. Paul's another sombre penitential procession took place, this one through the streets of Antwerp. The scene was reminiscent of the recent spectacle in England: civic and princely dignitaries were out in force, the penitents carried lighted candles, and with appropriate ceremony their books were burned. They were alleged to be Loists, followers of the radial 'libertine' Eloy Pruystinck. Already by the mid-1520s nonconformity in the Netherlands was giving rise to sectarianism.[1]

Situated at the convergence of Narrow Seas' trade and shipping lanes that stretched from Lisbon to Livonia, Antwerp was in essence a free trade zone. Entrepreneurs of almost any provenance might purchase *poorter* status and acquire the attendant rights of citizenship. Yet direct merchant involvement in governance was not significant. Guilds and wards were represented on a Great Council, but it met irregularly and had little influence. The upper echelons of administration were reserved for the propertied gentry. A closed college of peers nominated burgomasters and magistrates, who along with senators made up the ruling oligarchy—aptly dubbed in English parlance the Lords of Antwerp. They governed 50,000 permanent inhabitants, a metropolis by northern European standards. The Church of Our Lady, largest in the Low Countries, dominated spiritual life albeit there were but five houses of worship in all. Antwerp's international importance exposed residents to many external influences—social, cultural, and religious. The theology of German reformers arrived early. Controversy and violence were not far behind.

Commerce with England was vital to the Low Countries, and therefore susceptible to manipulation for political ends. Henry VII resorted to embargoes on several occasions. The last, in response to the alleged harbouring of political fugitives, ended in 1506 with an

---

[1] *CD*, 5: nos. 502, 503; "Chronycke van Nederland," 92–93. Pruystinck had many sympathisers in Antwerp and continued to live there after his recantation. Waite, *Reformers on Stage*, 66–68.

accord that reopened trade and secured the extradition of the last
pretender to Henry's crown, Edmund de la Pole. The treaty's economic provisions earned it the label *Intercursus Malus* among Netherlanders, and by withholding ratification the regency government
rendered its legality uncertain. A new agreement in 1520 superseded
the contentious articles. Even so, a precedent for giving up English
rebels on demand had been established long before Henry VIII con-
cocted royal supremacy and eliminated any distinction between sedition and heresy. As his chancellor strove to curb circulation of New
Testaments and polemic, dialogue with jurisdictions abroad was
inevitable. And so too, perhaps, disagreement over expatriate
dissenters.

A Town Marvellously Corrupt

It was in Antwerp in October 1520 that the emperor-elect had issued
his decree calling for the burning of Luther's books throughout the
Low Countries, where already they circulated in several languages.
Following the Edict of Worms many imprints were indeed destroyed
at Antwerp; Aleandro reported with considerable satisfaction that
four hundred books were put to flame there in July 1521, three
fourths of them confiscated from shops within the town.[2] By year's
end inquisitors had summoned the outspoken prior of Antwerp's
Augustinian house, Jacob Praepositus, to Brussels and compelled him
to abjure his evangelism. When the following spring another visit to
Antwerp by Emperor Charles occasioned more book fires, the town's
secretary Cornelis Grapheus was also silenced. The eloquent defender
of the laity's right to read the Bible was forced to recant, dismissed
from office, and eventually deprived of his property: a reminder that,
unlike Germany, within the Habsburg Low Countries there were no
patrons powerful enough to protect outspoken evangelicals or humanists. Early on, this campaign of intimidation was fairly effective; many
fled. But the Antwerp Augustinians, several of them recently matriculated at Wittenberg, were a lingering source of concern. They likely
helped translate the six works of Luther that were printed in Dutch

---

[2] *CD*, 5: nos. 749, 758–59.

in the winter of 1521. Moreover, Jacob Praepositus slipped away, first to Nürnberg and eventually to Luther at Wittenberg.[3]

Praepositus' successor, Hendrick van Zutphen was arrested at Michaelmas 1522 on instructions from the regent. He too was accused of Lutheran preaching. But before he could be sent to The Hague for interrogation an agitated mob came to his rescue and returned him to his own priory. Although Lady Margaret demanded swift punishment of the instigators, no arrests were made until Antwerp's Great Council convened, something traditionally done only "uppon a greett cawse". Duly assembled, it agreed that the offenders should be held accountable, so a handful of the mostly women rioters were detained for a brief time. By then, however, the prior had fled, leaving the magistrates with little choice but to endorse the regency government's closure of the Augustinian house. The friars were harassed out of Antwerp in early October; sixteen of them spending an uncomfortable winter incarcerated at the castle of Vilvoorde north of Brussels. Two perished at the stake in Brussels the following July. Other monastic orders now faced a moratorium on preaching in Antwerp. As more books were consigned to the flames in the fall of 1522 the *schout* of Antwerp also prosecuted Lutheran agitators who were not clerics. Among them was a local printer, Adriaen van Berghen, who, after public shaming in the pillory "van synen mesdaden ende luteryen" spent three months in prison. Undeterred, however, he would print the first Dutch version of Luther's New Testament later in 1523.[4] Not the least for the sake of their own credibility abroad Lady Margaret and her council endeavoured to appear in firm control of the situation. Her envoy in England, Jean de la Sauch, was instructed to make only passing mention of the troubles to England's chancellor. But Wolsey was in any case informed in considerable detail by his own ambassador, Robert Wingfield.[5] And of course diplomats

---

[3] *CD*, 4: nos. 23, 34, 42, 47–54, 61, 64–65, 69, 82–85; A. Duke, "The Netherlands," in *The Early Reformation in Europe*, ed. A. Pettegree (Cambridge, 1992), 142–45.

[4] "Chronycke van Nederland, besonderlyck der stadt Antwerpen, sedert den jaere 1097 tot den jaere 1565, door N. de Weert," in *Chroniques de Brabant et de Flandre*, ed. C. Piot (Brussels, 1879), 88–89; *AA*, 2: 309–10; *CD*, 4: nos. 97–100, 109–10, 118. Adriaen van Berghen's 1523 New Testament was the first of at least five issued by him. An imperial decree banned his editions specifically in 1529. *PI*, 26; Den Hollander, *Bijbelvertalingen*, 42–46.

[5] *Calendar of State Papers—Spain. Further Supplement*, ed. G. Mattingly (London, 1940), 154; BL Cotton. MS Galba B VII fos. 357–60, 362–63; *LP*, 3/2: nos. 2586, 2593, 2595.

were not the only foreigners to observe or hear of the events in
Antwerp. Although the emporium was alive with commerce year
round, the uproar over the Augustinians began during the closing
days of the autumn fair, which usually attracted many more non-
resident foreigners.

It was not long before Antwerp's Austin priory was demolished,
but the religious tension lingered on, to be ignited once again in
1525 in the aftermath of the peasant rebellions in Germany and
upheavals in several north German ports with which the entrepôt
had strong ties. Much of the dissonance was overtly religious. The
Venetian envoy Gasparo Spinelli observed that Margaret enforced
heresy law severely in Brabant and Flanders, and therefore few nonconformists dared to declare themselves openly. But in their own
homes many of Antwerp's residents were drawn to the new doctrine
and at least twenty thousand of them, Spinelli's sources told him,
were now Lutheran.[6] Controversy spawned antipathy between conformists and iconoclasts. When it turned violent and spilled into the
streets the magistracy, wary of upheaval as any responsible civic
administration of the time, reacted accordingly. Inevitably, while pope
and emperor might presume to dictate doctrine and compliance, it
fell to local officials to enforce norms of behaviour within the municipal precincts. The melee had claimed two lives, and in its aftermath three instigators were beheaded and another banished. A bounty
of one hundred *gulden* was offered for the apprehension of evangelists, one an Augustinian who persistently defied the imperial ban on
Lutheran preaching—eventually from a boat in the Scheldt. But his
capture and execution only prolonged the ferment.[7] A fire was prepared, as if for some public spectacle, but instead the man was uncer-
emoniously drowned in the river, in an absurdly misguided attempt
to avoid inciting his numerous followers. Robert Wingfield, reporting on 5 August, though not directly from Antwerp, was unsure
whether the bedlam that ensued was spontaneous or orchestrated by
radical elements. At any rate, militia had to be summoned to restore
order. Serpentines were brought into the market place and the town
gates were shut until a street by street search was completed, result-
ing in several arrests. "What shall folow is harde to telle", wrote

---

[6] *Calendar of State Papers—Venice*, ed. R. Brown (London, 1864–73), 3: no. 1007.
[7] "Chronycke van Nederland," 91–92; *CD*, 4: nos. 341–44; *AA*, 2: 316–18.

Wingfield, "for it is thought that the sayde town is mervelusly corupte".[8]

Responses to this riot and the one in 1522 bear comparison with the treatment of alleged heretics in later years. Authorities in the marvellously corrupt town continually gauged the mood and will of the citizenry and balanced normative views with directives from the political hierarchy. At the same time, they strove to safeguard Antwerp's liberties from encroachment by the inquisitors and other levels of government. Rewards for the arrest of iconoclasts continued to be posted and there were fines for attending evangelical sermons. Persistent blasphemy or criticisms of civic officials over the drowning of the Austin friar were punished with severed tongues and banishments. In other northern towns the approach was not markedly different: preachers were scrutinised in Delft and blasphemers were pilloried in Amsterdam.[9] Clerical inquisitors, for their part, now concentrated primarily on rooting out delinquent nuns and monks. Abjurations were preferred, of course, because condemnation ran the risk of creating martyrs. One married priest, Jan van Woerden, nevertheless desired such an end and was accommodated. Opinionated and defiant to the last, he was bound over to the Court of Holland and burned at The Hague on 15 September 1525. Lady Margaret and the bishop of Utrecht attended. With the *auto-da-fé* came another proclamation forbidding anyone to even speak of Luther, let alone read his books.[10]

To wrest inquisitorial control from Hulst the provincial courts necessarily had to demonstrate a commitment to the enforcement of heresy laws in cases involving laypersons. In the fall of 1523 the Court of Holland took the lead in the north, dispatching deputies to call suspects to The Hague. Investigations in Delft, Monnickendam, Schiedam, Haarlem, Amsterdam, and Leiden continued throughout 1524. They were partly the consequence of a new imperial directive that targeted Bible translations not based on the Vulgate. Also of concern were two anonymous publications, the Gospel of Mathew and a compendium of scriptural interpretations called *Summa der godliker scrifturen*. *Summa* achieved international notoriety due to various

---

[8] BL Cotton. MS Galba B VIII fos. 219–20; *LP*, 4 (i): no. 1549.

[9] *AA*, 2: 317–19; *CD*, 4: nos. 341, 350, 366–67, 372, 375.

[10] B.S. Gregory, *Salvation at Stake: Christian Martyrdom in Early Modern Europe* (Cambridge, MA, 1999), 104, 143–44; *CD*, 4: nos. 361, 378–84, 389.

translations, including a later English rendition printed in Antwerp. Doen Pietersoen issued the first Dutch version of Mathew's Gospel in 1522, based on Erasmus's New Testament of 1519 and glossed with his annotations. The translator may have been Johann Pelt, an Amsterdam Franciscan who later fled to Bremen. The new law applied to biblical translations by Luther and attempted to close a loophole by which it might be claimed that possession of books not attributable to Luther himself was not a contravention of the Edict of Worms. His name or that of any other known heretic no longer needed to appear on the frontispiece for an imprint to be proscribed. Enquiries regarding *Summa* eventually led to the house of Leiden printer Jan Seversz. He ignored several summonses from the Court of Holland and was sentenced in absentia to lifelong banishment.[11]

Once again, though, the examination of suspected Lutherans—beguines, printers, schoolmasters, and married priests—raised concerns about juridical prerogatives and protocol. So far as the magistrates of Haarlem were concerned it made no difference that imperial placards were now enforced by the Court of Holland rather than Hulst; the principle of *non evocando* guaranteed the citizens of each town the right to be tried only before their own courts. Monnickendam and Delft also objected, and when citizens of Leiden were brought to The Hague the town sent an observer to assist them and to ensure that their legal rights were respected.[12] A degree of co-operation was possible so long as the municipal jurisdictions retained a semblance of autonomy, but even then nothing was certain. It was up to the individual towns to deal with secret conventicles, for example. With the suppression of lay preaching and printed propaganda, increasing numbers of people now met in private homes to read vernacular translations of the New Testament. Haarlem refused to prosecute them or to permit commissioners from the provincial court to intervene. Antwerp was equally lenient. In Amsterdam the magistrates

---

[11] *CD*, 4: nos. 180, 181, 183, 193–95, 199, 201, 203, 205, 207, 212–13, 224, 234; Johnston, "Printing," 179; L. Knappert, *De Opkomst van het Protestantisme in eene Noord-Nederlandsche Stad: Geschiedenis van de Hervorming binnen Leiden* (Leiden, 1908), 74–77; Den Hollander, *Bijbelvertalingen*, 40, 83–86, 307–8, 513. The supposed compiler/translator of the Dutch *Summa* was Hendrick van Bommel, whose Latin version was not printed until 1527.
[12] *LP*, 4/1: no. 1632; *CD*, 4: no. 371, 5: nos. 398, 399, 401; Tracy, *Holland*, 155–57; Knappert, *De Opkomst*, 80–99.

had prohibited conventicles as early as November 1523, however the discretionary punishments they prescribed—fines, temporary incarceration or pilgrimage—were indicative of an unwillingness to go beyond those traditionally meted out for blasphemy.[13]

Amid the momentous and concurrent events of 1525, diplomatic exchanges between English and Habsburg officials in the Low Countries understandably focused on the emperor's dynastic ambitions, in the wake of the triumph of his forces at Pavia. They also included, however, what may have seemed by comparison a rather unremarkable request pertaining to the investigation of a premeditated homicide in Antwerp. It was a contract killing, and the Spaniard who paid for it had made his getaway to Calais. He was detained there, and the regency government wanted him turned over to imperial authorities. As Wolsey supposedly took up the matter with the king, Spanish merchants resident in London lobbied Queen Katherine to intercede, alleging the right of asylum for foreigners taking refuge in the kingdom, or in this case in a town subject to English authority.[14] Jean de la Sauch's report to the regent, recounting his interview with England's chancellor and the treasurer of Calais, under whose jurisdiction the case fell, is of interest in light of the *Intercursus Malus* and subsequent developments involving English fugitives. It was the English government's view, advised Wolsey, that "we are not bound by treaty to surrender any prisoner or any malefactor of your land who has taken refuge in ours, since our sovereignty in our realm is equal to yours in yours". Evidently taken aback, Sauch replied "I presented this request not as a matter of treaty obligation but merely as a favour, which the king may do the emperor and Madame by delivering this person to justice, and the which they offer to reciprocate when occasion arises". It was the treasurer's opinion, however, that even if the emperor wished to reciprocate in a similar case, his towns would not let him, but would assert their privileges instead. Wolsey was not interested in assurances to the contrary. The ambassador was told that there would be a hearing in Calais and the king duly advised. So ended the interview. The Spaniard was never brought to justice. Some years later, amid complaints from Henry that English dissidents still lived quietly in Antwerp, despite treaties requiring their

---

[13] *CD*, 4: nos. 195, 215, 217, 226, 353–54; *AA*, 2: 312–14.
[14] *LP*, 4/1: no. 1455; 4/3: appendix 46.

extradition, Sauch would revive the story as an example set by England. And the king, for his part, would claim not to have heard of the case before.[15]

In the spring of 1526 Robert Wingfield was appointed Deputy of Calais. His replacement as England's ambassador to the regency court was John Hackett, an Irishman who had resided many years in the Netherlands, earning his living through commerce. His diplomatic dispatches bring to light various efforts to silence English heretics on foreign soil as well as a multitude of attendant issues and problems. Not the least of these was the extradition of suspects. His versions of events are those of a dedicated Crown servant toeing a line drawn for him and then very often blurred by his political masters. Inevitably, though, his ambassador's eye for detail brings us closer to some of the individual players and to their part in shaping or reflecting the course of confessional debate in the 1520s.

In mid-summer, within a few weeks of Hackett's appointment, came yet another sweeping ordinance, decreed in Charles's name by the Council of Flanders.[16] Schoolmasters were warned not to teach Lutheran heresy or to use heretical texts. Imprints were to be destroyed and there was a schedule of fines and short-term banishments for their owners. Lifelong exile was prescribed for third-time offenders. No books were to be printed, bound, sold, or purchased without the permission of the Council. Printers, binders, and sellers of banned books were to be exiled permanently and one third of their worldly goods forfeited. The censorship applied to books authored by Luther, Karlstadt, Bugenhagen, Melanchthon, Oecolampadius, Lambert, and their followers, as well as vernacular Scripture books with Lutheran prologues or glosses. There had been a proliferation of Dutch Bible editions in 1525–26, to varying degrees reliant on Luther's translations. The placard's apparent comprehensiveness was matched initially by the Council of Flanders' zeal to enforce it. Within a month two Gent bookbinders were sentenced to fifty years banishment, albeit one of them was back in town and selling imprints again by the early 1530s. To what degree the law was publicised and enforced elsewhere, in Holland for example, is much less clear. In August the

---

[15] *LP*, 5: no. 564; *Calendar of State Papers—Spain*, ed. Pascual de Gayangos (London, 1873–82), 4/2: no. 1188 and *Further Supplement*, 441.
[16] *CD*, 5: no. 529.

magistrates of Hoorn banned someone for six years for persistent blasphemy and possession of a scandalous pamphlet, however their recorded decision did not mention the emperor's law. There was direct reference to it in October, though, when the Court of Holland exiled a man who had brought a pamphlet to Gouda and sold it there.[17] Soon after this, authorities in Antwerp also took action. Possibly the regent's council had reason to be dissatisfied regarding enforcement of the edict, and was pressuring other levels of government. This would happen not infrequently later on.

For a considerable period after the penance of the Loists in winter 1526 Antwerp's magistrates seem not to have been particularly vexed by heresy-related issues. Then, at the end of October, fifteen weeks after the imperial placard in Flanders, they announced a ban on printing, selling, and possessing "boecken suspect vander Lutheraenscher ketteryen". It called for the immediate handing in of tomes with erroneous prologues or any other Lutheran content ("valsche prologen oft anderssins suspect vander voers. Ketteryen").[18] Non-compliance would be dealt with according to the emperor's (now) published law. As recorded in the town's *Gebodboek*, this order was noticeably different from the emperor's. Its wording preserved the discretionary authority of the civic courts, implying subtly that it was their prerogative to apply his law as they saw fit. It also did not mention specific authors or refer to Scripture texts. The following day sentence was passed on two itinerant sellers of heretical books, one from Bergen op Zoom and the other from Brussels (Hendrik Henricxsens and Tanneken Zwolfs). They were sent on pilgrimages to Boulogne and Paris respectively. Similar punishment awaited Hans Ruremund, one of several local printers who had issued biblical texts in Dutch. Some editions were conflagrations that to some extent used Erasmus's *Novum Testamentum*, and therefore had a tenuous connection to original Greek texts. Others were not. In 1525 Hans Ruremund printed parts of a vernacular Old Testament in small volumes and then issued an annotated New Testament that clearly relied on Luther's German translation. Although the publication was by no means the only one of its type and others had appeared in the interim, Antwerp's magistrates now required Ruremund

---

[17] *CD*, 5: nos. 530, 531, 537, 538; Kronenberg, *Verboden Boeken*, 45.
[18] *CD*, 5: no. 541.

to make himself scarce for awhile by visiting the shrine of the Sacred Blood at Wilsnack in Brandenburg.[19] This was a far cry from the long-term exile and loss of property demanded by the latest imperial mandate. It was, on the other hand, entirely consistent with penalties for blasphemy, contempt for town ordinances, or persistent contravention of societal norms. Pilgrimage or temporary banishment on pain of mutilation for non-compliance was typical punishment for first offenders.

Ruremund and the booksellers had printed and disbursed questionable books but they had not incited unrest or directly challenged public order. The restraint demonstrated by Antwerp's magistracy effectively counter-balanced the diligence of the *schout*, margrave Claes van Liere, whose duty it was to ensure that imperial decrees were not flouted. How closely he and his deputy-bailiff (*onderschout*) Gielise van Bouchout monitored the local book market is underscored by the case of one of Antwerp's best-known dealers. Early in the New Year Franz Birckman was cited for selling the work of an "auteur reprouvé", the Basel reformer Johannes Oecolampadius. Oecolampadius's own books were indeed proscribed but the one in question was his translation of a text by the fourth-century moralist John Chrysostom. Basel printing houses had issued several Latin versions of Chrysostom's works by this point. Johann Froben offered some translations by Erasmus, while Andreas Cratander looked to Wolfgang Capito and Oecolampadius. Birckman definitely had a part in the publications. Writing from the Frankfurt fair in September 1521, Cratander informed Capito that he would soon issue more Chrysostom, having arranged joint financing with three partners: Birckman, Vienna bookseller Lucas Alantee, and Johann Koberger, now director of the Koberger firm. Oecolampadius's allegedly flawed translations were scorned by some Catholic humanists, but they circulated nonetheless at the universities in Cologne, Louvain, Paris, and Cambridge.[20]

---

[19] *CD*, 5: nos. 542, 543; *PI*, 68, Den Hollander, *Bijbelvertalingen*, 66–68, 283–320.
[20] A. Kirchhoff, "Franz Birckmann, Buchhändler in Cöln und Antwerpen 1510–1530, und seine Familie," in *Beiträge zur Geschichte des deutschen Buchhandels*, vol. 1 (Leipzig, 1851), 112–15; A. Rouzet, *Dictionnaire des imprimeurs, libraires et éditeurs des XVᵉ et XVIᵉ siècles dans les limites géographiques de la Belgique actuelle* (Nieuwkoop, 1975), 19; *Correspondence of Wolfgang Capito*, 9, 46, 170. Cratander and Froben had been printing Chrysostom since 1517. *VD* J396–98. Presses in Augsburg issued some German versions in 1520–21. *VD* J453, J464. For the reception of Oecolampadius's translations in Paris see G. Rupp, *Patterns of Reformation* (London, 1969), 18, 34. In

When confronted by Claes van Liere, Birckman appealed to the regent and her council, who, after consultation with the dean of Louvain, decided that he had not subverted the emperor's law. An obvious pitfall of blanket suppression had been made plain but the case also indicates there was still some room to interpret the law's intent. That latitude eroded as subsequent placards became even more sweeping. It would not be long before publications that criticised Luther and in the process spelled out his supposed errors would have to be censored as well.

Whether or not they satisfied the regency government, the decisions of Antwerp and the Court of Holland in the autumn of 1526 ran little risk of inciting anyone. The man arrested by the *schout* of Gouda and subsequently banned from Holland had strayed rather far from his home province of Hainaut. So his exile, from a state to which he did not belong anyway, was unlikely to create much of a stir there. The lords of Antwerp, for their part, had shown they were not about to chance another riot by meting out inflexible Draconian sentences to denizen printers or to outsiders. This apparent sensitivity, especially with regard to individuals who printed or sold Bibles, would prove portentous. It also became a source of great frustration for Hackett, as he sought to stop the printing of new heresies in English. The eventual fate of printers like Hans Ruremund, who would shortly spend time in a London prison for trafficking in English New Testaments, is only part of the story. Ultimately, any English attempt to halt the transmission of heresy from abroad would hinge on the ability to prosecute. The efforts of England's ambassador were crucial, then, and so too the legal and logistical problems that would determine his relative success or failure.

Vernacular Scriptures and Scurrilous Propaganda

William Tyndale's New Testament translation was profoundly worrisome for England's ecclesiastical establishment in no small measure because of the country's peculiar tradition of heterodoxy. The nonconformity of English Lollards was in part defined by their reading

---

1526 a future Antwerp exile, George Joye, aroused suspicions at Cambridge for reading Oecolampadius's version of Chrysostom's commentary on Genesis. C.C. Butterworth and A.G. Chester, *George Joye* (Philadelphia, 1962), 30.

of vernacular Bibles. Not unreasonably, therefore, scriptural translations were equated with both heresy and socio-political radicalism.
Luther's *sola scriptura* theology, perceived from distant England as one
of the root causes of the religious chasm in Germany, was all the
more reason to deny unauthorised Scripture books to the English
reader.[21]

One of John Hackett's duties in November 1526 was to inform
the Merchant Adventurers' governor of the king's mind regarding
printed Testaments. A general assembly of the fellowship would be
apprised fully at the upcoming Bergen mart; individuals, in the meantime, were to be instructed to destroy any and all new English
imprints. In Antwerp Hackett made his own inquiries into where
the English translations were printed and sold, discovering two men
who did the work. At his request the regent then directed the margrave to see to a remedy. Along with his dispatches to Wolsey,
Hackett sent five English imprints, apparently confident that no more
would be produced or sold.[22] His troubles had just begun. Having
interrogated the printers, the lords of Antwerp were not prepared
to "iuge apon the example of anothyr Iuge ys iugement wythowt
thei hawe perfytt knowlege apon the fowndment and rayson that
thei may do hytt". They soon appeared before the regent, asking
that the supposedly heretical texts be translated into a language with
which they were more familiar, "Lattyn or Duche". It was a non-
sensical proposition, as Hackett well knew. He proposed instead to
ask Wolsey to send examples of imprints now outlawed and burned
in England, together with verification of their status. Along with the
relevant dispatch to London he included, for good measure, another
imprint from Antwerp, a town that was in his estimation a veritable fountain of heresy.[23]

The desired samples of proscribed books, their heretical content
attested by Tunstall, were in Hackett's hands by early January, and
he easily secured letters from the regent directing Claes van Liere
and the council of Antwerp to take appropriate action. Within a few
days a printer was arrested. He was Christopher Ruremund (alias
Christoffel van Eindhoven), believed to be the brother of Hans.

---

[21] C.R. Trueman, *Luther's Legacy: Salvation and English Reformers, 1525–1556* (Oxford,
1994), 12.
[22] *LH*, nos. 23, 24, 27.
[23] *LH*, no. 29.

Christopher's publications already included two Dutch New Testament editions based on Luther, for which he had not been prosecuted. Hackett was unqualified to debate the alleged heresy of Ruremund's English imprints so he presumed instead to interpret Habsburg censorship law for the magistrates of Antwerp: by issuing the Scriptures in translation the printer had defied the emperor, and therefore should be banished and his property confiscated. But that placard, as it was first promulgated in Flanders at least, applied specifically to scriptural translations with Lutheran prologues, glosses, and doctrinal errors (unspecified "erreuren of doctrine"). And Antwerp's recent declaration did not mention Scripture books. The compelling, not to say predictable argument from Ruremund's attorney was that a subject of the emperor should indeed be judged by the emperor's laws. And that meant "iuges off thys contres ought nott to gywe no blynd sentence to banyshe, dishonor or confysky eny man hys goodes with owt that they knew ryght well them selfs the very fowndment and cawse". The question was plain enough: should it be assumed that these anonymously published books, printed in a tongue that they claimed they could not read, were heretical simply because the bishop of London said so? Unless specific errors could be demonstrated, what evidence was there that a law had been broken? Further deliberation would be required *in camera*; the ambassador informed of a decision in due course. Returning to Mechelen, Hackett bemoaned this apparent miscarriage of justice, complaining further that his unnamed second suspect was deemed not to have printed English books. But another audience with Lady Margaret brought reassurances, and eventually his persistence and patience were rewarded. The lords of Antwerp were not about to condemn Ruremund, however on 16 January 1527, evidently pressured by the regent, they extended book censorship to include possession of English New Testaments printed there: "inder stadt in Engelsscher talen gedruct".[24]

Several weeks had now passed since the directive about books had been publicised to the Merchant Adventurers. Hackett had also spoken with Jean de Berghes, Bergen's temporal lord, requesting action

---

[24] *LH*, nos. 30, 31; *CD*, 5: no. 567; Den Hollander, *Bijbelvertalingen*, 70, 311–13. Hans and Christopher Ruremund published from the same address and are assumed to have been brothers. Hans was exiled from Antwerp on 30 October 1526 and not readmitted until late March. Rouzet, *Dictionnaire*, 193–95. Hackett's second suspect may have been one of the pressmen.

with respect to the distribution of English New Testaments. It was his intention to go to Bergen once he had a decision from Antwerp.[25] By the third week of February he had indeed been there, to Zeeland as well, and also had made his own enquiries at Gent, Bruges, Brussels, and Louvain. His dispatches to England informed that all imprints found at Antwerp and Bergen op Zoom had been destroyed and he was optimistic that copies of any other examples sent to him with Tunstall's signature could also be burned. Nevertheless, many books had also been bought and placed aboard Scottish vessels in Zeeland for shipment to Edinburgh and St. Andrews. The Scottish parliament had legislated against the importation of Luther's books in 1525.[26] Hackett, apparently presuming some authority to obstruct both Scots and Englishmen, now endeavoured to intervene. But his effort to seize the books and "make as good a fyer off them as there has bene of the remanaunt in Brabant" came a day too late, after the ships had already set sail. Moreover, while the destruction of confiscated copies constituted a partial success, thus far the suppression evidently had not achieved anything more than that. Both Jean de Berghes and the margrave of Antwerp implored the English ambassador to obtain from his masters particular articles of heresy in the books. Without such proof they could not hope to prosecute and punish individuals or seize their property.[27]

Tunstall and Wolsey never furnished Hackett with the required specifics. Recent dispatches remained unanswered in early May. Now alarmed at the influence of German Lutherans in the Low Countries, his warnings became increasingly dire.[28] There was still no word from England twenty days later, when he hastened back to Bergen to stop the sale of yet more Antwerp imprints, perhaps the remainder of the Testaments printed by Ruremund. Two dozen had been taken from one man alone. They could be burned, but as Claes van Liere and Lord de Berghes continued to point out, meaningful legal action against the printers still hinged on certification of particular articles of heresy in the texts. Word had also reached the ambas-

    [25] *LH*, no. 31.
    [26] J.E. McGoldrick, "Patrick Hamilton, Luther's Scottish Disciple," *Sixteenth Century Journal* 17 (1987), 82.
    [27] *LH*, nos. 33, 34.
    [28] *LH*, no. 36.

sador that two thousand New Testaments printed in English had been available at the last fair in Frankfurt, and that Englishmen in Germany were now preparing a translation of the entire Bible. It seemed to him that already in the Netherlands two of every three men who spoke their minds adhered to the views of Luther. Moreover, he had been given to understand there were many such people in England as well, although they dared not declare themselves so openly.[29]

There is a gap in the ambassador's extant correspondence until July, when Wolsey came to Calais. Hackett conferred with him there. Rumours of the separation of Henry and Queen Katherine already had reached the emperor and Lady Margaret. Concerns relating to this now superseded the trepidation about New Testaments and dominated Hackett's subsequent correspondence until the end of the year. Nevertheless, efforts to contain the diffusion of vernacular Scriptures continued.

William Tyndale's initial attempt to print his New Testament translation at Cologne was aborted in the fall of 1525. There were many presses there. All the same, in light of the town's censorship decrees the decision to go to Cologne was daring if not odd. In February the municipal authorities had ordained that nothing at all was to be printed without their permission. Cochlaeus surmised that Tyndale went to Cologne rather than Wittenberg because it was much more of a commercial centre and better situated for the conveyance of printed works to England. When he stumbled upon Tyndale's scheme Cochlaeus had been in Cologne for some time, having left Frankfurt in April. In addition to composing another attack on Luther, he now applied his editorial skills to Ruprecht of Deutz, a twelfth-century abbot whose biblical commentaries had stirred interest among Lutherans at Nürnberg. Cochlaeus set himself the task of pre-empting any Lutheran editions, which in his view would be sure to contain impious prefaces and glosses. To that end he had approached at least two of Cologne's master printers. One was Arnold Birckman, brother and business partner of Franz. The other was Peter Quentell. Following up on a careless remark by a pressman, Cochlaeus plied others with drink and discovered the plan to produce three thousand copies of

---

[29] *LH*, no. 37.

Tyndale's translation. Immediately he went to Rinck, who invoked his senatorial authority to have the printing stopped.[30] Tyndale and Roye left hurriedly, later completing their work at Worms. Despite Rinck's warning that ports should be monitored, first edition imprints of Tyndale's translation reached England the following spring, soon to be followed by a pirate printing. Thus the way was paved for the introduction of English-language polemic. The task of silencing the continental presses would prove formidable.

Among the various ambassadors, spies, and informants in Wolsey's intelligence network Sir Hermann Rinck was for a brief time a figure of some significance. Once a leading merchant at the London Steelyard, he also had been in the diplomatic service of emperors and English kings for many years. By August 1528 Wolsey was directing his man in Cologne to track down Tyndale and Roye, who had long since parted ways, and to buy up their books. Rinck took his cue from Hackett. Increasingly desperate to secure the extradition of English expatriates implicated in the illicit book trade at Antwerp, Hackett was denouncing them not only as heretics, but as rebels and traitors as well. If the regent could be convinced of this they might be extradited, as Edmund de la Pole had been twenty years before, in accordance with the *Intercursus Malus*.[31] Rinck, who had been an imperial envoy to England when the old treaty was negotiated, also reasoned that such terms applied to propagandists like Roye and Tyndale—they were rebels. The bearer of his instructions was another of Wolsey's agents, John West, an observant Franciscan from Greenwich. Travelling via Antwerp, West consulted there with Franz Birckman, who showed him copies of Roye's works and those of Tyndale. The bookseller added that many more such imprints, published by Johann Schott of Strasbourg, could be found in Frankfurt. According to West, Birckman offered to entrap the authors by purchasing the lot and arranging for payment to be made in Cologne, where Rinck could have the fugitives apprehended.[32] But the friar had no mandate for such a scheme when he departed thence and in any case Hermann Rinck already knew about the cache at Frankfurt.

---

[30] *ENT*, 18–24; R. Rex, "English Campaign," 103.
[31] *The Reign of Henry VII from Contemporary Sources*, ed. A.F. Pollard (London, 1913–14), 2: 322–23; *Letters and Papers illustrative of the reigns of Richard III and Henry VII*, ed. J. Gairdner (London, 1861–63), 2: 155–64.
[32] *LH*, nos. 78, 81.

Intending to intercept the authors as well as their books at the fall mart, he had gone there on his own initiative three weeks before West reached Cologne.

The imprints in question were *A Brefe Dialoge bitwene a Christen Father and his stobborne Sonne*, Roye's 1527 English translation of Wolfgang Capito's Strasbourg catechism, and the defamatory verse satire *Rede Me and Be Nott Wrothe*, co-authored by Roye and Jerome Barlowe, both formerly attached to the Greenwich Franciscan house. The two Englishmen were not in Frankfurt in September 1528, however Rinck did find their printer. Johann Schott had not been paid for his work, so had brought the English books—print runs of one thousand of each—to Frankfurt and pawned them to Jews, intending to redeem them to the highest bidder.[33] Rinck now did his best to prevent their distribution, prevailing on civic officials to outlaw the printing of any more such tracts in Frankfurt. It was a rather hollow gesture, since Schott's press was in Strasbourg. Equally unavailing was Schott's own promise to turn over the authors' original manuscripts. In the end, Rinck had to be satisfied with purchasing all the offending texts he could find, to be taken back to Cologne and disposed of at Wolsey's command. Otherwise, as he later pointed out, they would have been disguised in plain paper covers, packed into bundles and smuggled to England and Scotland, and there sold without suspicion as blank paper. Noteworthy in light of the senator's thoroughness is that his report identified no person in particular who might be part of such an operation. His reimbursement from England, though, totalled £73 4s sterling, indicative of a very sizeable haul of printed material.[34] But by the time the payment reached Cologne in the spring of 1529 Wolsey was preoccupied with efforts to solve the king's marital problems. Subsequent diplomatic correspondence seldom mentions Sir Hermann. His usefulness to the chancellor apparently had passed.

By 1528 the elusive William Tyndale was publishing in Antwerp. *The Parable of the Wicked Mammon* appeared in May. It was his rendering

---

[33] Jerome Barlowe and William Roye, *Rede Me and Be Nott Wrothe*, ed. D.H. Parker (Toronto, 1992), 29–38. A. Hume, "William Roye's *Brefe Dialoge* (1527): An English Version of a Strassburg Catechism," *Harvard Theological Review* 60 (1967), 307–21.

[34] *ENT*, 27–36; J. Giesen, "Ein Brief des Kölner Ratsherrn Hermann Rinck an Kardinal Wolsey," *Jahrbuch des Kölnischen Geschichtsvereins* 19 (1937), 370–76; *LH*, no. 109.

of Luther's sermon on justification through faith, first issued in German six years earlier. Du Bois had also printed a Latin edition at Paris. In the autumn came Tyndale's *The Obedience of a Christian Man*, combining a defence of Lutheran doctrines with denunciation of the English Church. He was not the only exile now using the Antwerp presses. Early in 1529 a pamphlet against the doctrine of purgatory, *A Supplicacyon for the Beggers*, was issued there, prompting an immediate response from Thomas More: *The supplycacyon of soulys*.[35] Its anonymous author was Simon Fish, a young lawyer from Gray's Inn. As well, Antwerp was the source of Ruremund's edition of Tyndale's New Testament. Already in May 1527 Hackett had been gathering up copies at Bergen. He also alluded to two thousand "sych lyke Inglys bockys" available only a few months before at "the last Frank[fort] markett".[36] These could only have been Tyndale's Worms edition or his translation of Luther's introduction to the Epistle to the Romans, both printed by Peter Schöfer in 1526. The third published work by an English exile, Roye's *A Brefe Dialoge*, was not issued until late August 1527.

A substantial stock of English Testaments printed in the Low Countries was unlikely to turn up in Frankfurt, so far to the east of Antwerp and farther still from the intended readership. But Hermann Rinck found plenty of copies of Roye's work there in the fall of 1528. They were Strasbourg imprints and their fate sheds some light on the dissemination process. Capito's catechism was intended for a wide readership. Strasbourg's presses produced Latin and German editions in 1527.[37] Although more anti-clerical in tone than the Latin original, Roye's colloquial translation presented a combination of doctrines, including modified sacramentalism, that would find appeal among many later English reformers. *Rede Me and Be Nott Wrothe*, on the other hand, was a scurrilous attack on the traditional Church and more specifically an indictment of England's prelate-chancellor. These were highly speculative publishing ventures, all the more so

---

[35] J. Scattergood, "Simon Fish's *Supplication for the Beggars* and Protestant Polemics," in *Antwerp, Dissident Typographical Centre*, ed. D. Imhof, G. Tournoy and F. de Nave (Antwerp, 1994), 67–73.

[36] *LH*, no. 37.

[37] *VD* C833–37; Hume, "William Roye's *Brefe Dialoge*," 307–21. The German edition came from the printing house of Capito's nephew Wolfgang Köpfel, who issued many tracts by Strasbourg reformers. Chrisman, "Reformation printing," 217.

in this case because the target audience clearly was such a distant one. While Tyndale now placed himself close to the maritime commercial corridor that facilitated transmission of his work to England, Barlowe and Roye laboured away in relative safety at Strasbourg, by now an international centre for production of reform propaganda. Their inability to pay for the printing and the fact that Rinck did not implicate anyone else in the enterprise casts doubt on whether the authors themselves had a strategy for distribution.

William Roye had joined Tyndale sometime in 1525, helping compare texts for the New Testament translation. When it was finished the two parted company at Worms, according to Tyndale's preface to *Wicked Mammon*.[38] Roye then "gate hym new frendes whiche thinge to doo he passeth all that ever I yet knewe. And there when he had stored him of money he got him to Argentine [Strasbourg] where he professeth wonderful faculties and maketh bost of no small thinges". Unlike Antwerp, neither Worms nor Strasbourg had a resident community of English merchants capable of providing on-going covert assistance. It is by no means certain that Tyndale knew who his former colleague's new acquaintances and benefactors were. And even if he did he would not have identified them, regardless of his poor opinion of Roye. Instead we have only an unflattering sketch of a persuasive yet pretentious character, who relied on Tyndale when short of money, but who "became lyke him selfe agayne" when he had some. A year later Jerome Barlowe came to Strasbourg and was soon under Roye's influence, composing *Rede Me* whilst Roye translated *A Brefe Dialoge*. The subsequent history of the two tracts suggests no coherent plan to get the books to England. And, obviously, the generosity of Roye's new friends had its limits. Otherwise, Schott would not have needed to pawn the imprints at Frankfurt.

Johann Schott had issued works by Luther, Karlstadt, and various Strasbourg reformers throughout the early 1520s, primarily in German. He was not timid about printing for religious radicals, though at no time limited himself to their work. However, in 1526 he turned away from reform polemic, concentrating instead on medical texts and biographies of biblical figures by Strasbourg pedagogue Otto Brunfels. Two of the town's other printing offices made similar shifts, an indication that the market was too small for any press to

---

[38] *The Parable of the Wicked Mammon* (Antwerp, 1528). The preface begins "William Tyndale otherwise called hychins to the reader".

rely solely on the polemicists.[39] By decade's end Schott would be ostensibly a printer of medical and technical books but in 1528 that transition was not quite completed. He offered a variety of works that year, including surgical manuals and several tracts by Brunfels.[40] They were augmented with the only two English-language titles he is known to have issued. *Rede Me* and *A Brefe Dialoge* quite possibly constituted an experiment at a time when he was seeking to establish some sort of specialised market niche. He was an experienced professional, unlikely to have been hoodwinked by a smooth-talker like Roye. And, mindful of recovering his costs, it is difficult to see him undertaking the printing without a good idea of how to disseminate the books. In Strasbourg, as in other typographic centres, local customers bought directly from the shops and printing houses. Wider diffusion was accomplished by way of the fairs in Leipzig and Frankfurt and through the agency of established booksellers in other large towns. Schott's best prospects for disposing of his English imprints were indeed at Frankfurt, where they might attract a professional vendor familiar with the market in England; someone like Franz Birckman, for example. In addition to his Antwerp shop Birckman operated another in St. Paul's Churchyard. Recently he had also acquired a press in Cologne. His business connections ranged from London to Paris and Basel, and as a high-profile dealer he was in regular contact with the Frankfurt market, where he could avail himself of the latest publications from Strasbourg, Basel, and Venice.[41] His livelihood, like Schott's, was the printed word, and like Schott he had been plying his trade for a quarter-century. It is not inconceivable that their paths had crossed.

Franz Birckman had at least one sample copy of *Rede Me* in Antwerp and knew that the better part of the thousand that Schott had printed were still available in Frankfurt. That he chose not to purchase them is understandable. England's diligent, not to say intrusive, ambassador already had caused printers to be called to account.

---

[39] Chrisman, "Reformation printing," 218–19 and "Printing and the Evolution of Lay Culture in Strasbourg 1480–1599," in *The German People and the Reformation*, ed. R. Po-chia Hsia (Ithaca, 1988), 87–88; F. Ritter, *Histoire de l'imprimerie Alsacienne aux XVᵉ et XVIᵉ siècles* (Strasbourg, 1955), 170–86.

[40] *VD* B8470–71, B8508, B8510, B8514, B8518, B8522, B8530, B8532, B8542, B8549, B8553, B8556, G1619–24.

[41] Schnurmann, *Kommerz*, 53–68; Armstrong, "English purchases," 289; Rouzet, *Dictionnare*, 19–20.

That very summer Hackett, once again accommodated by the regent, managed to have a prominent English merchant arrested, in part for trafficking in New Testaments. At a glance Birckman knew how contentious Roye's attack on Wolsey was bound to be. He would be courting serious trouble if he attempted to distribute it, perhaps to the point of jeopardising his lucrative business in England. Since he was well enough informed of the whereabouts of the books, Birckman probably knew also that the printer had borne the costs. The suggestion, if the bookseller ever made it, that Roye and Barlowe might be lured to Cologne to collect payment for the imprints was little more than a bit of devilment at the expense of a credulous friar. The completion of a commercial transaction such as this would not be left to amateurs, especially since it was not the Englishmen but Johann Schott who was out of pocket. The books belonged to him, not to the authors. So West was shown a copy of *Rede Me* and pointed towards Cologne, along a trail that Birckman knew would lead eventually to Frankfurt. And whoever might seek censorship in Frankfurt, where the buying and selling of printed material contributed so much to the local economy, would be unlikely indeed to persuade town authorities simply to destroy books. They would have to be purchased first. One way or another, then, the printer from Strasbourg would have his payment.

Hermann Rinck believed very few copies reached circulation prior to his intervention, and he may have been right, since scarcely a handful of first edition imprints have survived. However, *Rede Me and Be Nott Wrothe* was available in Antwerp shortly after its publication early in 1528 because Tyndale made oblique reference to it in the prologue to *Wicked Mammon*, attacking Roye and the rhymes he had set Barlowe to writing. John West was shown a copy in early September and from what Rinck later said of his instructions from England, Wolsey had seen it as well. Rinck, the former Steelyard merchant, knew how such books might be disguised and brought into England; his warning provides a useful glimpse of this aspect of smuggling. However, in West's account of his conversation with Birckman there is nothing to suggest that bringing the books to Cologne or Antwerp would have necessitated a covert operation. The authors were unknown foreigners after all, and the language of their imprints equally unfamiliar outside merchant circles, so moving them from one town to another need not have presented unusual difficulty or great risk.

According to Birckman there existed at Frankfurt "a nother holle pyppe" of books. This was in all likelihood not merely a figurative description. It was usual for multiple copies to be shipped uncut and unbound, and packed tightly into bales or barrels. Legally imported books came to England in containers variously described in customs records as casks, barrels, vats, and pipes.[42] Consignments were thus relatively easy to handle, and took up a minimum of cargo space. Binding of individual copies, often done to order, was left to retailers. The plain paper covers mentioned by Rinck would have been a relatively simple fallacious precaution. Consignments disguised in this way would be the less likely to arouse suspicion because both Strasbourg and Frankfurt were transit points for northward distribution of good quality paper manufactured in Alsace and south-west Germany.[43] Finally, had Birckman or anyone else been prepared to pay for and move the books before Rinck got to Frankfurt, there is no reason to suppose they would not have been sent along established channels, entrusted to the professional carriers on whom routine day-to-day commercial traffic depended. It was in the Netherlands that distribution of any controversial English publication was now fraught with uncertainties. Onward shipment to England was potentially more dangerous still, requiring not only caution but also the secrecy and deception to which Hermann Rinck alluded.

Fugitives and Entrepreneurs

Chicanery in the production and dissemination of literature was not new or confined to disguising book consignments. Like countless other tracts, the first edition of *Rede Me* was issued anonymously and revealed neither the place of publication nor the printer's name. Anonymity afforded a measure of protection from the censors.[44] The great proliferation of polemic and commentary, however, brought corresponding attempts to strengthen the prohibitions. Already by the winter of 1525 Antwerp required all books printed or sold there to identify author, printer, and provenance. Within three years the

---

[42] Plomer, "Importation," 146–50.
[43] F.H. Meyer, "Papierfabrikation und Papierhandel: Beiträge zu ihrer Geschichte, besonders in Sachsen," *AGDB* 11 (1888), 283–357.
[44] Of the nearly two hundred German printings of Luther's various works up to 1523 fewer than 12% gave the printer's name. Hirsch, *Printing*, 99.

imperial placards applied not only to works by a substantial list of individuals and all glossed vernacular editions of the Scriptures, but also to any publication in the previous decade that omitted its place of origin or the names of the author and printer.[45] Nothing so specific was enforced in Germany, where policing of the presses was selective and inconsistent anyway. Again Cologne, where the Edict of Worms was enforced, and Strasbourg, where it was not, provide an instructive contrast. Nineteen printers are known to have been active in Strasbourg during the 1520s, and that many as well in Cologne— more than in any other German centre. Each town had its own regulations. Long before *Rede Me* appeared, all new books in Strasbourg were supposed to be approved by the town magistrates before going to press. Furthermore, each was to include the name of the printer. Yet Schott was not taken to task even when the senator from Cologne complained about him.[46]

In the Netherlands the early placards drove some printers underground, others into temporary exile at Hamburg. Even when they re-emerged after 1525 to print Lutheran pamphlets in translation, they were somewhat vulnerable compared to those in Strasbourg or Wittenberg. Accordingly, some attempted to distract and mislead by counterfeiting the addresses of publications. For printers of controversial material in the Low Countries the primary intent of the false colophon was to draw attention to some genuine place outside the jurisdiction of the local and regional authorities. Naturally, addresses in Germany were favoured, with the names of famous centres of the *neue Lehre* possibly having the residual benefit of spurring interest among potential readers.[47] Among Antwerp's most accomplished dissemblers were Martin de Keyser and Johann Grapheus, to whom many English books with bogus addresses are attributed, including Tyndale's 1528 editions of *Wicked Mammon* and *The Obedience of a Christian Man*. According to the colophons, they were issued at Marburg by Hans Luft. Other popular foreign addresses were Basel, Wittenberg, and Strasbourg.[48]

[45] Johnston, "Printing," 179; *AA*, 2: 314–15.
[46] Chrisman, "Reformation printing," 219–22; Ritter, *Histoire*, 183–84.
[47] Johnston, "Printing," 159–61.
[48] Kronenberg's contention that Tyndale's 1528 "Hans Luft" imprints were the work of Jan Hillen van Hoochstraten is challenged persuasively in P. Valkema

(3) *Sacri sacerdotii defensio contra Lutherum* by John Fisher
Peter Quentell, Cologne, June 1525 (*VD* F1240)
By kind permission of the British Library

It is not known for certain which of the Cologne presses began printing Tyndale's translation in 1525. On the basis of Cochlaeus's tale that he chanced upon the scheme in conversation with loose-tongued pressmen, it is most often attributed to the office of Peter Quentell. Cochlaeus was particularly well acquainted with this establishment at the time. Some of his Latin tracts and two German versions of his response to Luther's infamous harangue against rebellious peasants were issued by Quentell in 1525 and 1526. So was his critique of Bugenhagen's *Epistola*.[49] The press was also busy with new material by John Fisher, including a defence of the priesthood, *Sacri sacerdotii*, dedicated to Tunstall and issued both in quarto and octavo.[50] Cochlaeus greatly admired Fisher and the two corresponded. That the former would want the issuer of Fisher's works to print his own seems only natural. He also knew the proof-reader at the press, Ortwin Gratius. Hence, we may imagine frequent contact between Cochlaeus and the employees there, and when he cast about for someone to underwrite the publication of Ruprecht of Deutz an obvious choice was Peter Quentell. Inevitably this meant connection with the Birckmans. Franz Birckman frequently brought work to Quentell and was involved in the publication of *Sacri sacerdotii*. Their long and apparently profitable relationship continued for the remainder of the bookseller's life.[51]

It is likely that Franz Birckman travelled to England in 1525. Perhaps he had not yet returned when Cochlaeus hit upon the idea of the Ruprecht manuscripts. So instead Quentell and Franz's brother Arnold were approached about a joint publication. There would have been nothing untoward about such a suggestion, collaborative ventures being commonplace enough. Initially both printers had

Blouw, "Early Protestant publications in Antwerp, 1526–30: The pseudonyms Adam Anonymous in Bazel and Hans Luft in Marlborow," *Quærendo* 26 (1996), 94–110. Thereto: Kronenberg, "Forged Addresses in Low Country Books in the Period of the Reformation," *The Library*, 5th series, 2 (1947), 81–94. Martin de Keyser came to Antwerp in 1525. Grapheus settled there in 1527.

[49] *VD* C4338–40, C4353, C4374; *NB*, no. 817; Spahn, *Cochläus*, 345–48.
[50] *VD* F1238, F1239, F1240.
[51] BL Cotton. MS Vitellius B. XXI. fo. 11; E. Surtz, *The Works and Days of John Fisher* (Cambridge, MA, 1967), 329–38, 410. Quentell issued Fisher's tract on the corporal presence of Christ in the Eucharist in February 1527. Its epistle, written by Gratius, acknowledged Birckman once again as the intermediary who, having received it from the hands of the bishop himself, brought the original manuscript from England. *VD* O333; Surtz, *Works and Days*, 413.

doubts about the project's commercial viability, however reissues of the first volume point to early commercial success. Other volumes followed in the later 1520s. To whom the task of printing actually fell is of relatively little importance. Perhaps it was done by Quentell or at the new Birckman press. It may just as well have been contracted out to any number of houses in Cologne, perhaps to Hero Fuchs, with whom Peter Quentell had collaborated in 1524 to produce a German New Testament. More significant with regard to the entrepreneurial dimensions of book production and distribution is the identity of the publisher. With a keen eye for potential marketability, it was Franz Birckman who ultimately put up the money.[52]

Cochlaeus's exploits in Cologne and the publication history of the Ruprecht manuscripts thus underscore again the function of the professional bookseller/publisher in bringing material to the reading public. Quentell and the Birckman brothers were first and foremost businessmen—entrepreneurs for whom the reform controversy presented opportunities. Their religious sensibilities were secondary and in any case remain obscure, regardless of what they published. Because of the impressive array of works he printed for Catholic apologists, Quentell is often closely identified with them; his possible involvement with Tyndale and Roye passed over as a curious and unexplainable anomaly. By the time they turned up in Cologne he had also issued Henry VIII's *Assertio* as well as several Latin editions of Fisher's *Assertionis*. And his reputation was not in question after the foreign fugitives departed. His later edition of letters exchanged by Luther and Henry VIII in 1525 was dedicated to Rinck, with Cochlaeus providing the critical commentary.[53] But this does not preclude the possibility that Peter Quentell initially accommodated the religious exiles from England as well. Vernacular German Testaments were in his repertoire and he reprinted, in tandem, works by Wittenberg reformers and their critics. Other titles ascribed to him

---

[52] Spahn, *Cochläus*, 348–51. A comparison of letters in the Cologne fragment of Tyndale's New Testament and books attributed to the Quentell press persuaded Mozley, *William Tyndale*, 61, that Quentell was Tyndale's printer, albeit the single specific example is a woodcut in Ruprecht's commentary on St. Mathew. The printing of the Ruprecht editions is commonly assigned to Quentell but he did not underwrite the costs. The first and subsequent volumes bear Franz Birckman's name, identifying him as the publisher: "Impensis . . . Francisci Birkman". *VD* R3782–84, R3793, R3796, R3801, R3805.

[53] *VD* F1215, F1216–17, F1219, F1226–27, F1238–40, H2169, H217678.

in 1525 include a pair of Lutheran prayer books in Low German, initially published by Hamburg's heretic press two years before.[54] In this sense he is hardly distinguishable from several of Cologne's other master printers—Hero Fuchs, Johann Soter, Arnd van Aich, and Gottfried Hittorp—who chose not to confine themselves to Bibles, classics, or humanist authors.

Tyndale's circumstances and Quentell's publishing record suggest an arrangement between the two men was plausible. No doubt at least some of Fisher's texts were familiar to the Englishman and from the colophons he would know who issued them. The bishop's intended audience was international, but Tyndale could quite rightly presume that the Quentell press had regular business communications with England. And as Cochlaeus later observed, Cologne was a convenient commercial hub. Keeping in mind Tyndale's determination to translate the New Testament, the year or so since his arrival in Hamburg afforded him ample time and opportunity to see the 1524 Low German edition of Luther's version. It was issued "durch Heronem Fuschs mit kosth vnde expenß Petri Quentell".[55] Fuchs had done the printing and Quentell had paid for it. This colophon is central to an explanation of why Tyndale went to Cologne. The town's typographic and commercial significance and its proximity to England had to be considered. But before he ever set foot in Cologne, Tyndale also would have known that Peter Quentell had financed the printing of vernacular Lutheran New Testaments. Still, he had limited means, and Quentell was not known to print books in English. If in fact Quentell did take on Tyndale's translation, it was the only English-language project he ever attempted, albeit that is more than can be said for all but a small handful of German printers. Although their share of England's print market was large, continental presses were not yet greatly occupied with supplying books in the English language. Antwerp houses and their French counterparts produced devotional, liturgical, and educational texts for export. In Germany, Quentell and others issued Latin treatises by English authors,

---

[54] *VD* L 4065, 4066, 4118, 4120, L4624–25, L6658, L5500–01, L6657, L7485, L7501–2, L7506, B9303–4; *NB*, nos. 808, 821, 826.

[55] *VD* B4500. Another New Testament printed by Fuchs in 1525 was a Dutch version identical to one issued by Martin de Keyser in Antwerp. *VD* B4576. Fuchs printed many Bible editions in the 1520s, including Emser's German translation. Den Hollander, *Bijbelvertalingen*, 59, 295–97.

particularly John Fisher. The half-decade since *Exsurge Domine* had seen the European typographic industry capitalise on religious discord. Fisher and even the king himself had been drawn into the Latin print debate among learned scholars. But Tyndale's project now raised the possibility of tapping another large consumer market. The obvious precedents were Luther's hugely successful Scripture translations. Reissues, critiques, rejoinders, and related polemical texts had been a boon for the printing houses. Should Tyndale's work be half as influential with English readers, then publishers and typographers might anticipate similar results. Peter Quentell and Hero Fuchs did not need to be told this. Their recent *Plattdeutsch* edition of Luther's New Testament had been a worthwhile undertaking, and apparently brought them no serious grief from the local censors. The Quentell press issued it again in 1528.[56] So until Rinck stepped in to halt production, it is quite conceivable that Quentell was willing to invest in the English translation. An important milestone for England's lay readership was achieved with the project's eventual completion at Worms. The sojourn in Cologne and then Worms, and Roye's in Strasbourg, also began a new chapter of European typography and English-language printing. Ultimately, however, it would not be German printers but rather those in Antwerp who took full advantage of their opportunity.

Supporting the view that Quentell was Tyndale's choice in Cologne, James Mozley suggested that religious views would not have coloured the printer's decision, nor would he refuse a paying customer. Within certain limitations this probably is true. However, it is just as likely that the printer himself, rather than Tyndale, bore the costs. Again Cochlaeus's experience says a great deal. Like Tyndale, he simply wanted his translations published, so he took them to people who might be interested. He would not expect payment or royalties. By the same token compensation for the publishers and printers, if they agreed to the project, was not immediate. However, they owned the finished imprints. Costs would be recovered and profits realised through wholesale and retail distribution. Cochlaeus did not and probably could not pay for the Ruprecht editions. It was left to the printing houses to decide whether or not the venture would be

---

[56] *VD* B4511. Quentell also had issued a German translation of the papal bull against Luther in 1521, at a time when other Cologne printers apparently refused to print it. *Flugschriften gegen die Reformation*, 110–26.

profitable. Although Franz Birckman was persuaded to join this particular enterprise, it was the sort that Quentell might have undertaken just as well on his own.[57] In any case, the professionals determined commercial viability and assumed financial risks. The same holds true for Roye and Barlowe in Strasbourg, where ultimately it was Johann Schott who made the decision to issue *Rede Me*. Are there reasonable grounds for believing that Tyndale's relationship with Quentell was somehow different? The merchants that supposedly paid Tyndale's expenses in Cologne are silent phantoms in this story. He had begun his continental travels with modest sums donated by Monmouth and his London friends. But well over a year had passed. Furthermore, Tyndale claimed that his associate William Roye depended on him for money. That there was enough left to pay someone in Cologne to begin the printing, or Peter Schöfer in Worms to finish it, is doubtful. Cochlaeus was led to believe there were anonymous backers who would also convey the imprints secretly to England, yet many copies of the Worms edition seem to have remained a long time in Frankfurt. It is equally conceivable that in Worms too the printer of the work assumed some or all of the expenses, with a view to turning a profit once it was completed. Of the financing William Tyndale may have had at Cologne or for that matter at Worms, we know only what Cochlaeus claimed he was told: unidentified English merchants took care of the printing expenses. The pressmen in Cologne may have said as much, not wishing to draw undue attention to their employer, whoever he was. And it would have seemed at the time a plausible enough explanation to Cochlaeus, himself well aware that an author without a subvention

---

[57] Mozley, *William Tyndale*, 61. The relevant passages of Cochlaeus's third-person narrative are published in English translation and the original Latin in *ENT*, 22–24: "Cochlæus earnestly entreated Peter Quentel and Arnold Byrckman that they should at their joint expense and profit undertake their [ie., the books of Ruprecht] publication" and "having thus become more intimate and familiar with the Cologne printers, he sometimes heard them confidently boast". R. Rex, "The English Campaign," 103, discounts Quentell as Tyndale's printer, supposing that, in attempting to track down the press, the Cologne authorities merely succeeded in driving it from the town. Cochlaeus says only that Rinck "went to the Senate and so brought it about that the printer was interdicted from proceeding farther in that work". The authorities did not have to look for the printing house; Cochlaeus identified it for Rinck, who sent someone there to verify the story before he took action. Mozley's English translation of Cochlaeus, *William Tyndale*, 58–60, does not differ appreciably from Arber's.

really had only one recourse—to professionals within the printing industry.

Those professionals saw to distribution of their own editions, whether they were controversial or not. Non-specialists—buyers and purveyors of other merchandise—seldom were greatly involved. In all likelihood it was Johann Schott's intention from the outset to bring his new English imprints to Frankfurt, along with other stock he had ready for the autumn fair. If indeed he pawned the English books, as Rinck claimed, it would have been an unremarkable expedient to secure operating capital. In the Low Countries, meanwhile, John Hackett complained of Antwerp printers, likely the Ruremunds, bringing New Testaments over to Bergen op Zoom in the spring of 1528. They too were in the business of selling what they printed, and at the time Bergen was where the potential customers were. The Easter mart was winding down and English and Scottish traders were loading vessels at the Zeeland quays.

Cochlaeus's story of his search for a publisher in Cologne implies that the Birckman press, managed by Arnold, was operational before the end of 1525, although no imprint can be positively attributed to it at such an early date. In any case, Peter Quentell continued to issue material for Franz Birckman, an astute entrepreneur of the sort that might naturally be called upon to finance the Ruprecht editions. Might such a man, so well established in the commercial book trade and with especially strong ties to the English market, also have had a hand in producing the English New Testament, if not the original then perhaps later pirate editions? If the printing at Cologne had not been interrupted, who better than Franz Birckman would have known how to get the imprints to Antwerp and thence to England? It is at least plausible, especially in light of later allegations that he directly financed Antwerp reprints. In February 1530 his Cologne office would draw special scrutiny from censors on the lookout for new Lutheran material.[58]

An early and well-documented disagreement between Erasmus and Birckman persuaded Maria Kronenberg to doubt the latter's business integrity, but others have not shared this view.[59] Erasmus was

---

[58] Mozley, *William Tyndale*, 348; *Beschlüsse*, 3: 681.
[59] Kronenberg, "Notes on English printing in the Low Countries (Early Sixteenth Century)," *Transactions of the Bibliographical Society* 9 (1928), 144–47; Schnurmann, *Kommerz*, 68.

Processionale ad vsum in-
signis ac preclare ecclesie Sarū / nouiter ac rur-
sus castigatū/per excellentissimū ac vigilātissi-
mum et reuerendissimum in Christo patrem
dominū nostrū dominū episcopū de Wyn-
tofi. feliciter incipit Anwerpie imprez-
sum/per Christophorū endouiefi.
impensis honesti viri Francisci byzckman ciuis Colo
niensis.Anno domini
1523.Die vero.16.
Martij.

C Uenundantur Londonij apud Franciscum byzck-
man/ incimiterio sancti Pauli.

(4) *Processionale ad usum insignis ac preclare ecclesie Sarum*
Christopher Eindhoven (Ruremund), Antwerp, 16 March
1523 (*STC* 16236) By kind permission of the British Library

unhappy initially because Birckman had one of his works issued by the Froben press rather than at Paris, yet he subsequently relocated to Basel and often published with Froben. Cologne merchant Andreas Imhof trusted Franz Birckman enough to make him one of his proctors in England, responsible for settling a cloth purchase account. Another of Imhof's factors was a Steelyard man, Casper Westfelinck, who sometimes carried dispatches to Wolsey.[60] Fisher and Cochlaeus expressed no qualms. Whatever Franz's reputation among humanist scholars, two things are certain. Throughout the 1520s he continued to publish books specifically for sale in England, especially devotional works. And, by mid-decade almost all of them were being printed in Antwerp by Christopher Ruremund. That the Ruremunds also issued pirate editions of Tyndale's New Testament and took substantial quantities to England is indisputable too, since both of them were arrested there for trafficking. Hans was offering copies in London by Christmas 1527. Their association with Birckman raises the possibility that he funded or at least subsidised the printing of illegal material.

Franz Birckman had acquired in England, over the course of two decades, a substantial share of the constant, risk-free, and presumably lucrative market in breviaries, hymnals, Psalters, missals, and Books of Hours. They were offered for sale at St. Paul's Churchyard. He could hardly have brought them any nearer to his principal clientele; the cathedral and its environs were home to a large clerical community. Year after year he had books reissued, always by printers in Paris: Thielman Kerver, Wolfgang Hopyl or, less frequently, Nicolas Higman.[61] Then, rather abruptly in 1523 he commissioned presses in Antwerp, and continued to use them extensively for the next three years. During this period all but one of the devotional books Birckman published at Antwerp for sale in England came from the Ruremund press. There were no reissues from March 1526 to the summer of 1527, however, and after that he again looked to Paris.[62] A crossing to London probably was made sometime in 1525.

[60] *Aus Antwerpener Notariatsarchiven*, 12–13. Imhof's other representatives were Everard van Hagen of Cologne and a Londoner, John Smith.

[61] *STC* 15790, 15790a, 15810, 15812, 15816, 15861.7, 15912, 15916, 15918, 15920–21, 15923–25, 15930–31, 16129, 16137, 16141.5, 16181, 16188, 16193, 16195, 16200, 16235, 16258.7, 16259–60, 16260.5.

[62] *STC* 13828.2, 15818–19, 15822, 15864, 15939, 15953, 15953.5, 15956, 16131, 16146, 16206–7, 16236, 17111.

Unless such a journey was intended, Birckman's designation as Imhof's factor would have been pointless. Yet it is unlikely that he went there very often. He was a busy man, whose publishing ventures employed many printing houses—in Antwerp, Cologne, Paris, Basel, and Hagenau—and whose days of regularly accompanying large consignments overseas were long since behind him. We know of no sign at Birckman's shop in London, and he is not listed in the 1523 lay subsidy assessment for the parish of St. Faith the Virgin, which included most of Paternoster Row and the area around St. Paul's. Nor was he among the thirty-one individuals present when Tunstall cautioned London's booksellers in October 1526. Other persons, therefore, took delivery of shipments from abroad and paid the required customs, brought the imprints up to St. Paul's, and managed their binding and retail distribution.

The identity of these agents is not easily determined. Direct evidence is sparse, but the 1523 subsidy enumeration and the record of the bishop's warning do suggest a possibility. Both list Henry Harman, who in another subsidy assessment in 1541 appears as the "factour" of Arnold Birckman, "keping shopp and stock" in Paul's Churchyard. He had in his service by then a certain John Rowe. According to Fox, a bookbinder by that name was abjured in 1531 for procuring, binding, and selling prohibited books. His penitential atonement included casting them into a fire. Among them were English New Testaments obtained from Christopher Ruremund, likewise seized for being the supplier.[63] How well and for how long the two had been acquainted is unclear, nor is it known for certain that Rowe was associated with Harman as early as 1531. In any event, when Rowe and Ruremund were arrested they were no longer connected to Franz Birckman. He had died the previous spring.

The Ruremund brothers, both of whom issued Dutch New Testaments based extensively on Luther's version, have left some other clues about the earlier period. Although Hans was exiled from Antwerp briefly in October 1526, the press "int huys van

[63] Reed, "Regulation," 170; Fox, *Acts and Monuments*, 5: 37; E.G. Duff, "Notes on Stationers from the Lay Subsidy Rolls of 1523–24," *The Library*, 2nd series, 9 (1908), 257–66 and *A Century of the English Book Trade* (London, 1948), 66, 139–41; *Returns of Aliens dwelling in the City and Suburbs of London from the Reign of Henry VIII to that of James I*, ed. R.E.G. Kirk and E.F. Kirk (Aberdeen, 1900), 1: 67.

Vvachtendonck" in the *Lombaerdeveste* was not closed.[64] Within a few weeks John Hackett discovered English New Testaments being printed there by Christopher. Most of the non-controversial material issued by the press during the next four years bore Christopher's name, although it seems certain that Hans was involved behind the scenes. Christopher does not appear to have produced devotional books for sale in England before he began working for Franz Birckman. By 1530, however, he was printing and publishing them independently, reissuing a Book of Hours and selling it, according to the colophon, in Paul's Churchyard by the sign of St. Augustine.[65] Early on, from 1523 to 1525, he printed such material for only one other client besides Birckman: Peter Kaetz. Kaetz also peddled books in London for awhile. All of the editions with which he is identified came from the Ruremund press, including some of the same titles issued for its other principal patron. A processional issued in 1523, for example, available at St. Paul's from Birckman or his servants—"vel a suis servitoribus"—is identical to one printed for Kaetz.[66] Looking to advance his own modest enterprise in London, Kaetz evidently financed a portion of the print run. During the three years that the Ruremund press produced the bulk of all material Franz Birckman sent to England it seems likely that Peter Kaetz was one of his London agents.

An undated letter from Kaetz to Cambridge printer John Siberch, informing of a temporary shortage of "novum testamentum parvo" and offering advice on printing, shows he was not completely independent. The writer speaks of waiting in London for his "master", whose arrival will determine when he can "cross over"—presumably to the Low Countries.[67] Siberch was a brother-in-law of Birckman. He had closed his press and shop and returned to Germany by 1524. Until then, however, he may have been a provincial agent,

---

[64] *NK* 380.

[65] *STC* 15962, 15966, 15969. Kronenberg, "Notes," 144, speculated that the sign of St. Augustine was Birckman's address.

[66] Duff, *A Century*, 82–83; *STC* 16236, 16236.3. The rest of the Kaetz catalogue: *STC* 15818.5, 15935, 15938, 15938.5, 16130, 16145, 16236.3, 16261.

[67] Treptow, *John Siberch*, 34–37, suggested Ruremund was Kaetz's master, Mozley, *William Tyndale*, 351–52, that it was Birckman. Although Kaetz's letter refers to two persons—Johann Geylkyrch and Peter Rinck—known to have been in England in the winter of 1528–29, it seems improbable that it was written so late. Siberch had long since left England and Geylkyrch had been Sir Hermann Rinck's factor there since at least 1518. TNA:PRO C 1/410/59.

with Kaetz and perhaps Henry Harman managing retail affairs in London. It may be that Peter Kaetz continued in this capacity a bit longer, although he too would soon go home. He had opened a bookshop in Antwerp by March 1525, where he sold Dutch Old Testaments printed for him by Hans Ruremund.[68] After Kaetz's departure it is not inconceivable that Hans Ruremund had a direct hand in Birckman's London business, whilst his brother Christopher managed the press in Antwerp.

Birckman, Kaetz, and the Ruremunds were by no means the only foreign suppliers of Latin-rite liturgies for England. Many were also issued by the Parisian *libraire* François Regnault. He and Birckman co-published a Salisbury breviary in 1519 and thereafter issued numerous editions of the same books independently. Nicolas Prévost, Thielman Kerver and his widow, and Nicolas Higman did much of the printing. Prévost, in particular, also worked for other stationers in London, including Wynkyn de Worde, and John Reynes.[69] Perhaps from time to time their inventories included Birckman publications as well. Reynes, another expatriate Netherlander, who did business at the sign of St. George in Paul's Churchyard, was also acquainted with the Ruremunds. In addition to the breviaries that he intended to sell in London in 1530, Christopher printed a Psalter for Reynes. The relationship with the press did not come to an end when the printer was arrested a few months later. Christopher's widow Catharyn issued a Salisbury processional for Reynes in 1544.[70] She also printed a Latin/English primer for London bookseller John Gough. Well before Christopher Ruremund's demise Gough was questioned in England on suspicion of dealing in heretical books. Eventually, in 1541, he was jailed for it.[71]

Franz Birckman's decision to switch from the Parisian presses to Antwerp was likely precipitated initially by the death in 1522 of both Thielman Kerver and Wolfgang Hopyl, whom he had relied on for many years. While legal and family matters were being sorted out in Paris, he made use of printers closer to home: Christopher Ruremund and, to a much lesser extent, Simon Cock. The volume of work Birckman chose to have done in Paris apparently remained

---

[68] *NK* 380, 381; Rouzet, *Dictionnare*, 106–7, 195; Kronenberg, "Notes," 144, and *Verboden Boeken*, 99; Den Hollander, *Bijbelvertalingen*, 71–74, 314–17.

[69] *STC* 15816, 15863–65.

[70] Duff, *A Century*, 135–36; *STC* 2825, 2827, 16242, 16263a.

[71] Duff, *A Century*, 58; *STC* 15992.

limited for some time, however. Perhaps a consideration was the Sorbonne's proscription initiative in 1525 and the uneasiness it precipitated. There were many competent printers in Antwerp to choose from, although not all would have been capable of producing breviaries and processionals. The use of multiple fonts and initials, musical staves, coloured inks, and the integration of text and music demanded a very high degree of technical sophistication and efficiency. Few other printing houses could have matched the quality of the Ruremund imprints.[72] But the old Parisian connections were not completely severed. The Hopyl press was taken over by his son-in-law Prévost. Kerver's printing house passed to his widow, Yolande Bonhomme, who did limited work for Birckman in 1524 and 1525. His subsequent brief hiatus from publishing service books for English clientele may be no more than a reflection of market conditions at the time. Reprints were issued *ad hoc*; perhaps sufficient inventory was at hand. Coincidentally, Birckman went back to the presses in Paris at the very time when his Antwerp printers got into legal trouble. Hackett's investigations drew attention to the Ruremund press and eventually resulted in the regulation against issuing English Testaments. Perhaps another contributing factor was Birckman's own run-in with the margrave for selling Oecolampadius's translation of Chrysostom. Whether or not he had a hand in their illicit enterprises, he could not have relished any more suspicion being drawn to himself through his association with the Ruremunds. Combined circumstances dictated caution and a discretionary return to the printing houses in the rue Saint Jacques, where he could depend on both Yolande Bonhomme and Nicolas Prévost.[73]

Ambassador Hackett and the Lords of Antwerp

"But the Burghemaster and the lawe of the town hawe don more delygens to sawe a cockatrice heretyk, then to plesse a noble prince".[74]

---

[72] Avis, "England's use," 239.

[73] Yolande Bonhomme's father, Pasquier, had founded one of the most successful printing firms in Paris. She published independently for many years after Kerver's death. *Documents sur les imprimeurs, etc.*, ed. Ph. Renouard (Paris, 1901), 141–42, 224. Duff, *A Century*, 16, 76, 85, 125. Simon Cock, who did some work for Birckman in 1523 and 1524, also printed Tyndale's *An answere unto sir Thomas Mores dialoge* in 1531. *STC* 13828.2, 24437.

[74] *LH*, no. 114.

The words are those of an embittered John Hackett, reflecting on a year of frustration and disappointment. His noble prince was of course England's king. The law to which he referred was that of Antwerp, and the heretic one of that town's resident English merchants, Richard Harman. In June 1528 Wolsey had instructed Hackett to see to the extradition of three persons suspected of heresy. Persuading the regent and her council to order the arrests presented no difficulty. Finding the suspects, however, was not so easy. By 12 July only Harman had been apprehended, albeit the margrave also arrested his disputatious wife as well as an apostate English priest, Richard Akerston. But summary extradition of Harman, without benefit of examination by qualified inquisitors in the Low Countries, again resurrected sensitive questions of due process and sovereign jurisdiction. While Hackett was welcome to have one or two learned clerics sent over from England to assist in the interrogations, the prisoners would only be returned to their homeland or punished in the Netherlands if and when guilt was determined. Richard Harman presented a further complication because he was a burgess of Antwerp, and had been for many years.[75] As such, he was a subject of the emperor.

In the ensuing stand-off there is the unmistakable echo of Jean de la Sauch's audience with Wolsey and the treasurer of Calais precisely three years before, itself reminiscent of an earlier occasion. Amid negotiations on trade issues between the Merchant Adventurers and Bergen op Zoom in 1519 Wolsey had asked Jean de Berghes to extradite one of Henry's purveyors. Lord de Berghes replied that he would prosecute the individual according to any evidence sent to him, but he could not simply hand over someone who was willing to come to trial in his town. The commercial agreement that was reached in May of that year reconfirmed several mutually beneficial trading privileges. The town also consented to assist the Company's governor in bringing to justice any English merchants who might rebel and come there.[76] As John Hackett was about to discover, the lords of Antwerp felt no such obligation.

Hackett's allegations against Richard Harman were numerous. They were also unsupported by evidence or witnesses. Legal proceedings were in the hands of Antwerp's magistrates. The regency

---

[75] Harman had been a *poorter* (freeman) of the town since 1512–13. SAA LZ29 V Poortersboek 1464–1538.
[76] *LP*, 3/1: nos. 21, 44, 232, 498.

council was in no position to deliver the prisoner and in any case made it clear that he would not be surrendered simply on the basis of accusation. Consequently, Hackett urged Wolsey to provide some proof of treason. In accordance with the old *Intercursus Malus* he supposed a traitor could not be pardoned.[77] Otherwise, the legal grounds for holding Harman were dubious. That he had sold New Testaments to unnamed English merchants he did not deny, but claimed they had been sent to him from Germany rather than printed in Antwerp. As a citizen he insisted on the prompt and fair hearing to which he was entitled according to the emperor's *Blijde Incomst*. He also petitioned the emperor himself, through the regency council, asking that he and his wife be released in order to recover debts and satisfy creditors. His accuser was given eighteen days to substantiate the charges, beyond which time Harman could not be denied his day in court according to the laws of Antwerp and the Low Countries.[78]

By the third week of August Hackett could produce only a royal "pattent requesitoire" sufficient to gain another postponement but not to secure delivery of Harman, since it did not specify why he was a heretic or how he had committed treason. Nor was the regent moved by the suggestion that the accused should be turned over "by vertu of the old amyte and intercours that is betwix prince and prince".[79] Co-operation based on old princely amity had hardly been the hallmark of Anglo-Habsburg relations in the months leading up to the present dilemma. Henry had now allied himself with François I, and the sack of Rome by imperial troops had given him a timely opportunity to pose as Pope Clement's friend as well—with the desired dissolution of the royal marriage still hanging in the balance. Although military action was never seriously contemplated, there had been a declaration of war against Charles in January, and a fortnight later the emperor's ambassador in England was arrested. This calculated political manoeuvring did nothing to further the king's cause at Rome. However, the uncertainty it created led to a brief disruption of commerce with the Low Countries, which in turn exac-

---

[77] *LH*, nos. 67, 68, 75.
[78] BL Cotton. MS Galba B. IX fos. 148–49; *LH*, nos. 70, 71, 72; Hackett's letters regarding the case are balanced by the official recorded summary of the court's deliberations and decisions: *AA*, 7: 164–78.
[79] *LH*, no. 74.

erbated poverty and dissatisfaction among English cloth workers.[80] Negotiations with the regency government brought about a resumption of commercial traffic; it had taken until late June to ratify a formal peace accord.

Again Hackett implored Wolsey to furnish evidence or send some able person to help him. Meanwhile, at least in part reacting to public pressure, civic authorities hindered him the best they could. The ambassador gathered they were much less concerned about Akerston, and probably would give him up at the emperor's pleasure. Wolsey's response was to dispatch John West with letters addressed to the margrave and to John Style, governor of the Merchant Adventurers. Style's instructions—to search Harman's Antwerp house—could not have encouraged Hackett. They were tantamount to an admission of the government's failure to turn up the requisite incriminating evidence in England. The premises had been sealed, so the margrave ordered his deputy, Bouchout, to obtain the keys from the civic authorities. They, in turn, claimed to be too preoccupied with other weighty matters to make themselves available, thereby causing a three-day postponement of the search. When Style and Bouchout finally did come to the house on 1 September they were greeted not by a *schepen* but by a commissary and half a dozen ordinary townsmen, including merchant Arte van Vellycke, who had the keys. The door had already been opened. Amid taunts that "yt was a grete shame for th'Emperor and for the towne of Andwerpe that the commyssaries of the Kyng off Yngland should vesit any marchantes hows or writeynges", Style and the deputy-bailiff began sifting through a large bag of correspondence that had been left on the counter.[81]

Bouchout's examination of papers not written in English turned up nothing of interest. Among the English letters, however, there were four that caught Style's attention. A message from London draper John Saddler, written in September 1526, had informed that English New Testaments were proscribed and burned in England. Potentially much more damning was one from ironmonger Richard Halle, a Londoner who had requested two English New Testaments,

---

[80] *LP*, 4/2: nos. 3879, 3928, 3930–31, 3956, 3958, 3959, 3988, 4012, 4018, 4043–44, 4085, 4231, 4280, 4377, 4378, 4415.

[81] This search and its results are described in the reports of West and Style: *LH*, nos. 78–79.

since the ones he had before were now gone. Thomas Davy and
John Andrews, both of Cranbrook in Kent, had also written concerning New Testaments in England, Andrews as recently as February
1527. Unquestionably, then, Richard Harman was involved in the
illegal distribution of vernacular Testaments. But he had friends in
Antwerp. Vellycke and his company made sure that none of the correspondence was transcribed or removed from the house; the four
incriminating documents were sealed by the commissary and left
with the others. Style relayed such details as he could remember to
John West. He found no books; any that may have been kept at
the house were removed by the margrave when he detained Harman.
What became of the letters remains a mystery. Understandably,
Hackett was anxious to have them, but was refused by the regency
council. They seem not to have been introduced as evidence in the
court proceedings. At the time of the arrests the talk in Antwerp,
according to Hackett, was that Harman and his wife were the root
of much mischief. Evidently, though, she was no longer in custody,
having joined in the ridicule of Style when he searched the house.
As head of the English merchant fellowship, John Style may have
known Richard Harman already, although we do not know his opinion of him. What he thought of Harman's spouse, however, rated
mention to Wolsey. "Ye maye be ensured", wrote the maligned governor, "that Harmans wiffe ys a myscheves woman of hir tonge and
of lyke as yll of dedes".[82] Formidable she may have been, however
the lady was of no interest to the chancellor. Neither was Akerston.

By the second week of September West was about to leave for
Cologne, to look for the two fugitives Hackett had not been able to
find, Roye and Tyndale.[83] Apparently, they were still presumed to
be working together, even though their parting had been described
in the preface to *Wicked Mammon*. That left Hackett to finesse another
delay in the proceedings against Harman and to hope again for some

---

[82] *LH*, no. 79.
[83] Wolsey's letter naming the wanted persons is not extant. Notwithstanding the
three arrests in Antwerp, Hackett says two of the suspects could not be found. So
informed, Wolsey addressed correspondence to Rinck on 5 August, instructing him
to find Tyndale and Roye. West's report confirms this impression. Once in Antwerp,
he recommended the arrest of another fugitive priest, George Constantine, but had
not brought a formal supplication for the regent. He also mentioned Jerome Barlowe.
LH, nos. 67, 68, 78; *ENT*, 32.

direction from England. In Antwerp the public outcry over Harman's plight grew louder. The magistracy lobbied the regent's advisors to allow his case to go forward expeditiously according to established statutes, and now intimated that they would contest the handing over of anyone else Hackett accused, including Akerston. A month later the ambassador still had no letters from Wolsey, and his own could then be entrusted to West, already on his way back to England.[84] Harman, after thirteen weeks in jail, was released in early October on a pledge not to leave town. Arte van Vellycke posted the bond of two thousand *gulden*. And in December, over the objections of the margrave, Harman was allowed to go to the Bergen mart to put his business affairs in order.

Whilst in England West kept in touch with Hackett, who reflected wearily at year's end. "I extymyth this mather of more importaunce than me thynke we sett by it ther at home markyng that in fowre monyths and more that I haue had no maner of answer of any lettres that I haue wrytton thetherward touching this byssenys and others".[85] Under these circumstances he could only gain temporary suspensions of the hearings. He was absolutely right, of course, about the home government's priorities. They were dominated now, and had been for some time, by the issues of annulment and dispensation, and no longer included the merchant heretic in Antwerp.

The charges, which Hackett was required to specify at Harman's October court appearance, warrant close examination.[86] It was alleged that he helped sustain English 'Lutherans' in Antwerp, and sent heretical books to England. Harman did not deny selling some New Testaments to English merchants. Sensing from the start that a conviction for heresy was unlikely, and that even if prosecution were successful the punishment would be light, the ambassador also brought accusations of treason. Richard Harman was not simply a smuggler of books, but part of a great conspiracy of English traitors. He was the author and distributor of subversive libels, which had stirred rebellion against England's king and nobility.

Was any of this true? The summer of 1528 was difficult for many in England. Sickness and grain shortages exacerbated the suffering

---

[84] *LH*, no. 94.
[85] *LH*, no. 95. Letters to West were intercepted and read by Wolsey. *LH*, no. 93.
[86] *AA*, 7: 169.

of unemployed textile workers and their families. Much frustration and anger was indeed directed at the country's governing elite. In Kent, Richard Harman's friend John Andrews was among those arrested in connection with a rumoured conspiracy of idle clothiers. It was also an anxious time for English merchants in Antwerp, hurt by recent uncertainty over shipping. In August Style informed Wolsey that the market there remained very slack, with great quantities of woollens still unsold.[87] And throughout these troubled times England's prelates busied themselves with heresy tribunals. Caught in their net was a distributor of New Testaments in East Anglia, Robert Necton, who named Harman as a supplier. More book traffickers were discovered among scholars at Oxford, where the bishop of Lincoln also took note of libellous broadsides that were set at night on church doors. England's ambassador in the Low Countries would not have been surprised to learn this; libels circulated there as well, among the Merchant Adventurers. Hackett had sent samples to Wolsey, although he had heard that thousands of people in England probably had seen them already.[88] His dispatch on that occasion was the one telling of the hearsay that Harman was a troublesome instigator. So, thirteen weeks and at least two adjournments later, having received little direction and certainly no evidence from Wolsey, he decided to cast Harman as the mastermind of sedition. It is unlikely that the complete truth about Richard Harman will ever be known; libels were printed anonymously. Nevertheless Hackett argued on, likely knowing full well that unless he got something tangible from England nothing short of a printer's confession would convince the regent and the Antwerp court.

Biographers of Tyndale and historians of the book trade and the early English Reformation have long been aware of Harman's case, yet its pivotal feature—the charge of sedition—has elicited markedly little comment.[89] Rather, much like the Steelyard men, Harman tends to be seen as representative of direct and close merchant involvement

---

[87] *LH*, no. 63; *LP*, 4/2: no. 4638.
[88] *LP*, 4/2: no. 4044; *LH*, no. 68.
[89] Mozley, *William Tyndale*, 129, mentioned the accusation of stirring rebellion but chose not to elaborate. For Brigden, Harman was someone from whom Simon Fish commissioned New Testaments, and in Dowling's estimation he was simply an industrious vendor of such material. Brigden, *London*, 118 and M. Dowling, "Anne Boleyn and Reform," *Journal of Ecclesiastical History* 35 (1984), 43.

in clandestine book distribution. That he sent New Testaments to England is easily enough ascertained from Fox or the documented confession of Necton. The trial that unfolded in Antwerp says considerably more. It dragged on for months, not because Harman sold a few books or perhaps many, but because Hackett attempted to have him bound over for treason. The case's outcome therefore became a matter of life or death, virtually ensuring that proceedings would be protracted. Records of the attempt to prosecute Harman illustrate the logistical and legal considerations that largely determined the extent to which interregional distribution could be contained. In a way he was a test case. Thereafter, the English authorities did not attempt to pursue expatriate merchants in the courts of the Low Countries—for heresy or treason.

Summoned before the magistrates on several different occasions from October through January, Richard Harman played to an audience that was not necessarily unsympathetic, insisting all along that the repeated deferments violated not only his rights but also Antwerp's. Time and again he effectively placed the onus on Hackett and the margrave. What was heretical or seditious about the books he was supposed to have sent to England? How had he conspired against the king and what specific proof was there that he harboured fugitives? Time and again the resident envoy had no answer. The delays rested on assurances that evidence from England was forthcoming. At the outset, the regency government had extended a modicum of diplomatic courtesy to Henry VIII and accommodated his ambassador by initiating Harman's arrest. But regardless of the prospect of further disaffection in Antwerp, Henry's ongoing schemes to end his marriage to Katherine had by now so impugned Habsburg dignity that any political inclination the regent and her council may have had to prolong the case was lost. In the absence of corroborating evidence, an ambassador's hyperbole that the word of his king ought to be enough to secure the extradition of an alleged traitor would not suffice. On the first Friday in February 1529 the burgomasters and magistrates of Antwerp ruled in favour of Richard Harman and he was free to go.[90]

A measure of retribution would come two months later, when Hackett ventured back to Antwerp. Harman managed to have him

---

[90] *AA*, 7: 177–78.

arrested, ostensibly in the hope of recovering costs incurred during
his lengthy confinement. The ambassador of course claimed diplomatic immunity. As the accredited representative of a sovereign
prince, in whose name he had pursued Harman, he was not answerable to the Antwerp authorities. After some deliberation, they con-
curred, and he was released within a day. Though Richard Harman
was not awarded any monetary compensation for the defamation
and financial losses he had suffered this brief personal humiliation
of England's ranking diplomat nevertheless constituted a symbolic
and quite public assertion of the rights and privileges of Antwerp
and all its citizenry. It was also a poignant reminder of the tension
Harman's arrest had precipitated vis-à-vis the regency government.
Lady Margaret and her councillors were not amused. Immediately
the lords of Antwerp were summoned to the regent's court at Brussels,
rebuked for the affront to England, and instructed to apologise. To
the Antwerp men this was perhaps a small enough price to pay for
the satisfaction of having taken Hackett down a peg, even if only
for one day. Hackett, to his credit, rose dutifully to his diplomatic
station, forgiving his antagonists on the king's behalf.[91] How much
it galled him to do so may only be imagined.

Timely Intelligence and Doubtful Resolve

When Richard Harman walked away from his accuser a free man
it had been almost three years to the day since the Steelyard merchants had done public penance in London. Unlike Harman's prosecution, theirs had been largely symbolic, although the overall
compliance of London's printers, none of whom had yet become
active reform publicists, is perhaps some testimony to a more tangible result. In any event it constituted at the time a very traditional
response to the circulation of heresy, one that employed measures
developed ostensibly for domestic control. But much had changed
in the interim. No longer could the problem be viewed as a foreign
aberration and addressed with customary expedients. Such was the
impact of Tyndale and other expatiates, and the continental presses.
In addition to vernacular Scriptures, the English exiles fashioned

---

[91] *LH*, no. 111.

their own criticisms of the institutional Church, articulated them in their native tongue, and did so beyond the reach of English bishops. Silencing fugitives abroad quickly came to depend on networks of ambassadors, spies, and informers to locate and apprehend individuals or somehow prevent printed material from reaching the intended readers. Imprints were seized and some suspects too, but they were agents within the exchange labyrinth rather than authors. All of the main propagandists avoided their pursuers. On foreign soil one disseminator of their work had been caught, however attempts to prosecute him did not succeed. They failed in part because a wider campaign against nonconformity relied on co-operation between jurisdictions for the prosecution of individual malefactors—proponents, printers, or agents. And this, in turn, presupposed a singleness of purpose that proved as illusive as it was crucial.

From the outset, Strasbourg, Frankfurt, Hamburg, and many towns in northern Germany, whence merchants carried Lutheran tracts to ports in Scandinavia and to the Hanse enclave in London had demonstrated little or no inclination to impose systematic censorship on printers. In the Netherlands, by mid-decade the discretionary prerogatives of municipal authorities effectively offset the severest provisions of the imperial decrees. At the very least towns there had struck a responsible balance that did not include suppression of the printing houses. Important publishers of English reform propaganda—Martin de Keyser and Johann Grapheus—were not indicted, either for contravention of placards or to appease the English government. Grapheus and De Keyser printed Tyndale's work in 1528. Simon Fish's *Supplicacyon* and the English version of *Summa der godliker scrifturen*, which is also attributed to him both came from the Grapheus press.[92] The addresses in the colophons were falsified. This is not to say that all presses with connections to England opted for religious content or deception. Nearly one quarter of the English titles produced at Antwerp between 1500 and 1540 were the work of Jan van Doesborch. He printed school texts, topical non-fiction, and popular fiction in English and Dutch, but closed his shop and moved

---

[92] Valkema Blouw, "Early Protestant publications," 94–110. *The summe of the holye scripture*: STC 3036; *CW*, 8/2: 1072. Prior to 1545 fifteen persons in all, including nine publishers or printers, were prosecuted in Antwerp for printing or distributing heresy. Three were acquitted. Marnef, *Antwerp*, 37–40.

to Utrecht in 1530, as production of English books at Antwerp concentrated increasingly on religious material.[93]

Artful colophons helped some printers dodge censorship regulations, while still others appear to have been none the worse for prosecution. His prescribed pilgrimage completed and notarised, Hans Ruremund was readmitted to Antwerp in March 1527. Jan Seversz., the printer of the Dutch edition of *Summa*, who went to Antwerp, rather than face the Court of Holland, came home as well. His moveable assets, including the printing equipment, had been earmarked for confiscation but turned out to be worth less than what he owed his creditors, so for a fee his wife was able to retain them. Eventually her husband returned to Leiden and resumed his work, producing small pious Catholic books and school texts for sale at the fairs in Brabant and Flanders. His other vocation, that of parchment maker, further involved him in regular commercial activity in Delft and at Antwerp, where he may have collaborated with Willem Vorsterman to produce imprints for the seasonal fairs. Among his acquaintances in Leiden were some of the town's chief investors in the English wool trade at Calais.[94] Seversz. and the Antwerp publishing houses present an instructive example. Presses were not shut down; vital commercial links between printers and distributors remained intact as well.

With regulation of the continental presses so haphazard, thwarting expatriate authors or those who initiated distribution from beyond their own national boundaries was now doubly important. In the Richard Harman affair and the efforts to stifle Tyndale, Roye, and Barlowe we find a range of tools and tactics that give a general sense of what a sovereign authority might hope to accomplish through a combination of espionage and diplomacy. In the first place, the gathering of information on which to base tactical decisions meant maintenance of an efficient diplomatic service. Ambassadors to various princely courts—the likes of Wingfield and Hackett—served their

---

[93] P.J.A. Franssen, "Jan van Doesborch (?-1536), printer of English texts," *Quærendo* 16 (1986), 259–80; Armstrong, "English purchases," 288.

[94] J.D. Bangs, "Reconsidering Lutheran book trade: the so-called 'Winkelkasboek' of Pieter Claesz. van Balen," *Quærendo* 9 (1979), 227–60, and "Further adventures of Jan Zevertsz., bookprinter and parchmentmaker of Leiden," *Quærendo* 7 (1977), 128–43. Leiden sent wool buyers to Calais and also maintained a warehouse at Antwerp, where Leiden cloth was sold.

political masters in many ways, not least by providing intelligence. The merchant milieu often was useful to them, since the requisite movement of goods and persons naturally facilitated the gathering and communication of news. Because politics could affect so many facets of trade, especially finance, market conditions, and trans-portation, merchants had every reason to keep well apprised. News travelled relatively quickly in these circles. Scarcely a fortnight after the decisive Turkish victory over Hungarian forces at Mohács, on 29 August 1526, Hackett was informed of it in Antwerp by an agent of the Augsburg Fuggers. Men with commercial backgrounds also received ambassadorial appointments. During Henry VII's reign England's principal agents at the French and Habsburg courts were Italian merchant bankers. Factors of the king of Portugal at Antwerp were diplomatic as well as economic agents.[95] John Hackett was also a businessman albeit, it seems, not an especially successful one. In addition to the resident representatives, itinerant envoys were dis-patched on particular diplomatic missions. Jean de la Sauch and Jean Hesdin, who frequently came to the English court on Lady Margaret's behalf, and their counterparts—Parker, Knight, and Sir John Wallop—carried specific instructions, but were always expected to observe and report anything of interest. They were not alone. Also lurking in Antwerp's booksellers' quarter in the spring of 1528, for example, was an agent of the emperor, Cornelis Scepperus, osten-sibly *en route* to the royal court in Poland.[96]

Beyond the deployment of accredited diplomats, effective intelli-gence also benefited from friends or political allies, informed and resourceful, independent from the regime yet motivated by a strong sense of loyalty to it or to an attendant cause. Johann Cochlaeus, the committed propagandist and friend of John Fisher, did his best to defend—and help England's king defend—the established Church. But the government was even more fortunate to have a Cologne senator at its service. Sir Hermann Rinck had received a royal annu-ity in 1504 for transferring large sums from the English treasury to the coffers of Charles's grandfather, Maximilian I, and since then

---

[95] I. Arthurson, "Espionage and Intelligence from the Wars of the Roses to the Reformation," *Nottingham Medieval Studies* 35 (1991), 134–54; Goris, *Étude*, 215–38; *LH*, no. 13.
[96] *LP*, 4/2: no. 3879; *Calendar of State Papers—Spain*, 3: nos. 323–26, 431.

had remained "redye and diligent to the furtheraunce of any of the [English] Kinges cawses".[97] It was Rinck who commissioned the only surviving contemporary portrait of Henry VII, a gift from the widowed monarch to Margaret of Savoy. Many years had passed; the old king's second son now ruled England, Lady Margaret was governess of the Low Countries, and the erstwhile merchant patrician, having proven himself a competent diplomat, had become a man of noble standing and political influence in Cologne.[98] He briefed England's envoy to Germany, John Wallop, and saw to the onward conveyance of "packetts of Luthers matters" addressed to Georg of Saxony and the archbishop of Mainz. To England he forwarded letters and books from Cochlaeus, while his own correspondence kept the chancellor informed of many developments, ranging from Habsburg intervention in Italy to the execution of Anabaptists in Salzburg.[99] He was a crucial contact for English agents in Germany, and to judge from the varied content of his reports to Wolsey, he must have had his own stable of trusted informers.

Rinck was a man of rank with a long record of distinguished diplomatic service and many important contacts. John West, on the other hand, was a temporary operative, engaged in a modicum of investigative work, but essentially sent to provide liaison between Wolsey, Hackett, and Rinck. There was nothing veiled about his purpose in 1528. He was a paid agent, the likes of which were inexpensive and interchangeable, and ultimately expendable. He was also a courier, bringing correspondence to and from the decision-makers. Others trusted with this task were drawn from the mercantile sector. Casper Westfelinck carried letters from Cologne to London for Wallop in 1526. Hermann Rinck sent news regularly to his son at the Steelyard, sometimes with his factor Johann Geylkyrch. Geylkyrch took one of Wallop's "packetts" to the archbishop of Mainz; Rinck's secretary, Gerard van Campen delivered the other to Duke Georg. Some of Hackett's correspondence also moved in this way, with merchants travelling to London or Cologne over Antwerp. He also employed his own servant messenger, John Sowhyer, although reg-

---

[97] *LH*, no. 26.
[98] *Calendar of Patent Rolls 1495–1509* (London, 1916), 282, 300; *LP*, 3/1: nos. 274, 300, 509; 4/2: nos. 2530, 2563.
[99] *LP*, 4/2: nos. 2668, 2718, 2776, 2932, 2933, 3605, 3697, 3898; *LH*, nos. 21, 24, 26, 37.

ular reports were more often sent via Calais, using several different couriers, including merchants of the Staple.[100]

Dynastic security concerns required Tudor monarchs to fund espionage abroad on an ongoing basis. The "King's spy" in France received an annual stipend, and the deputy of Calais had a budget for paying others. Covert aspects of intelligence gathering are by definition, though, not easily determined. Speculation with regard to English heretics and their books rests here on a few circumstances and John Hackett's letters and on what they do not contain. Aware that he had to "hyre and se and dyssymyll a monges this pepyll" Hackett came to count on the eyes and ears of others to help him. He had his own network of informants. "But for a general secrett", he told Wolsey, "I hawe my wech men [watchmen] that I dare trust suyrly".[101] This is, however, as close as he comes to revealing his sources, whose palms, we may assume, needed to be greased from time to time. What is even more notably absent from his correspondence is any hint at all of a reliable informer within the Company of Merchant Adventurers. Without infiltration of this circle the chancellor's intelligence apparatus would have been far from complete.

Unlike England's resident diplomat, John West could not rely on mysterious watchmen. With little experience as a spy and none in diplomacy, he must have been directed to his contacts in Antwerp. So, of all the booksellers there with English connections, it was not by chance that he conferred with Franz Birckman. Franz was in touch with printers and vendors across Europe; able to tell John West not only where *Rede Me* had been printed and by whom, but also who the authors were. And he had business contacts beyond the book trade. From his Antwerp office he was ideally positioned to know what was coming off the presses, especially what was being printed for the English market. Perhaps he passed along information, when asked, on more than one occasion. Hackett probably knew him, having begun his search for printers of English New Testaments by sending "prively to all places" in Antwerp. It was a process of enquiry that at some point likely brought him to Birckman's doorstep, "iuxta portam Camere" at the sign of the Fat Hen.[102]

---

[100] *LP*, 4/2: nos. 2563, 2718; *LH*, nos. 12, 43, 49, 54, 57, 68, 77, 88.
[101] *LH*, nos. 12, 49.
[102] *NK* 2565.

There would seem to be no obvious incentive for Birckman to provide ongoing assistance, though. Perhaps, as an astute entrepreneur
with a profitable niche in the English market, he simply deemed it
prudent to co-operate occasionally to some degree. And if, as some
evidence suggests, he was involved in publishing English New
Testaments, how better to divert attention away from himself? The
Birckman firm seems never to have run afoul of English authorities.
Whatever the service, it was discrete and minimal. Information of
the kind given to West did not put any retailers or printers at risk.
Nor did it take the friar any closer to the outlaws he was looking
for. Tyndale's *Wicked Mammon* and *Obedience* were printed at Antwerp
in 1528. Regardless of the false colophons, it is inconceivable that
a dealer of Birckman's expertise and vast international experience
would not know who did the work. At the time of his conversation
with West he may also have had a reasonably good idea of the
whereabouts of Tyndale.

Such information as could be obtained through diplomacy and
espionage helped determine strategy and tactics at higher levels. For
governments professing commitment to the defence of orthodoxy,
however, creating and carrying through a coherent strategy was a
question not only of resources but also of resolve. The English and
Habsburg responses offer some parallels. It has long been accepted
that during much of the 1520s Charles's military adventures and his
brother's defence of the Empire's eastern frontier against the Turks,
together with dependence on tax revenues from Germany pre-empted
a concerted campaign to stamp out religious nonconformity. These
factors in turn contributed significantly to uneven enforcement of the
Edict of Worms and consequently to the success of the evangelical
movement.[103] In the Low Countries, given the significance of popular support for Church reform in prosperous urban centres, enforcing edicts to the letter was equally unrealistic. Once again militating
against a heavy-handed approach was the need for money to finance
the emperor's wars. His taxation policies and the economic hardship they caused had already provoked rebellion and civil strife in
Castile. There was discontent over increasingly burdensome taxes in

---

[103] W. Blockmans has recently emphasised that the imperial court also underes-
timated both the popular impulse for religious reform and the impact of the printed
book. W. Blockmans, *Emperor Charles V 1500–1558* (New York, 2002), 41–42.

the Netherlands as well, and rioting as recently as 1525 in Bois-le-Duc. Understandably, given the spectre of unrest, the regent was reluctant to add to the potential grievances that would have to be discussed by the States General as a prelude to the voting of money. Municipal administrations in the Low Countries were quite capable of holding up approval of financial requests. Regardless of the uncompromising language of the placards, further alienation was to be avoided.

If the regency council was in tune with public sentiment in the towns, still more acutely aware were the urban governments themselves. This was certainly so in Antwerp, where civic authorities embraced an ideology and rhetoric of commerce that considered domestic peace vital to economic wellbeing.[104] In order to conduct the trade from which all of Antwerp benefited merchants required a secure environment, and it was largely up to the local magistrates to provide it. They abhorred public instability not entirely because of attendant political or religious implications, but because it might cause merchants to avoid Antwerp. Should that happen, the resultant unemployment and diminished property values would impoverish the entire community: artisans, labourers, and *rentiers* alike. By the time of the iconoclastic riots of the 1560s civic officials were fully imbued with the sense that mercantile activity was the great engine of prosperity and that Antwerp would be ruined if trade were jeopardised.

While this notion may have taken several decades to mature, it was beginning to take shape within the civic administration already in the 1520s, discernible in the measured approach to religious innovation in general and to the printing and distribution of reform literature in particular. Antwerp's printing houses flourished by responding to consumer demand. They provided work and generated wealth, and as the market had become international their success went hand in hand with the development of a viable trade in what they produced; booksellers and their clientele, both in Antwerp and without,

---

[104] A. Kint, "The Ideology of Commerce: Antwerp in the Sixteenth Century," in *International trade in the Low Countries (14th–16th Centuries)*, ed. P. Stabel, B. Blondé and A. Greve (Louvain/Apeldoorn, 2000), 213–22. Because the permanent presence of foreign merchants was so vital Antwerp had little choice but to grant them "the widest possible freedom and toleration in matters of religion". Marnef, *Antwerp*, 20.

also contributed to the town's fortune. So long as the publications themselves did not incite behaviour detrimental to the business environment, there were no reasonable grounds for restricting them. Sectarians did public penance in the later 1520s, blasphemers were sent on pilgrimages, and a handful of people faced prosecution for selling books or pamphlets.[105] But aside from Hans Ruremund's penance, no printers had yet been cast out of the town, even though many Lutheran books were issued there.

Antwerp's response to the accusations against Richard Harman, aside from the obligatory defence of a citizen's rights also bears consideration in this light. From what we know of his book smuggling, Harman hardly constituted a threat to public peace. Hence, the lords of Antwerp had no cause to pursue him on their own account. And they may have had at least one disincentive. Because the 'nations' of foreigners directly or indirectly created so much wealth it was in no one's interest to provoke or alienate any particular coterie. A rigorous prosecution of Harman risked interpretation as an intrusion into the spiritual affairs of the Company of Merchant Adventurers. His case was an internal matter best resolved by the Company rather than the civic magistracy. The Company's governor and court of assistants could take authoritative action against individuals. Richard Harman was indeed expelled from the English House: a threat not to life but to livelihood.

In England a variety of circumstances had to be weighed, though there was no groundswell of religious nonconformity to be balanced against tax policies and the prospect of animated dissent. To some extent Wolsey's reluctance to direct and properly fund Hackett or to broaden his mandate were questions of priority. One consideration outweighed all others. By the autumn of 1528 his foreign policy had been totally overtaken by the royal divorce scandal. Anglo-Habsburg diplomatic relations were in tatters. In this context the pursuit of English heretics in Germany or their prosecution in Antwerp had come to matter less and less. He was further compromised by the situation at court, where political enemies intrigued against him and where, much to Campaggio's dismay, Lutheran books now circulated. Anne Boleyn openly favoured distribution of an English Bible and had introduced the king to works challenging clerical authority,

---

[105] *AA*, 7: 164–66, 178–9; *CD*, 5: nos. 688, 693, 735.

Fish's *Supplicacyon* and Tyndale's *Obedience*. In 1528 she also interceded, along with Wolsey himself, on behalf of Thomas Garrett,
caught up in a book distribution scheme at Oxford. Years later, as
queen, she would advocate Richard Harman's reinstatement in the
house of the English merchants at Antwerp.[106] As his ability to
influence and manage political events slipped steadily from Wolsey's
grasp in the winter of 1529 the situation with regard to the pursuit
of heretics beyond England's shores became increasingly hopeless.
So far as possible the papacy still had to be indulged in order to
keep alive the slim chance of an annulment. To that end a certain
amount of posturing against heterodoxy was to be expected. On the
other hand the chancellor desperately needed the favour of his king,
whose influential mistress was sympathetic to evangelicals.

It was very much a consequence of this situation that England's
ambassador in the Low Countries was left to soldier on without adequate direction or money, and ultimately to be frustrated by Richard
Harman and the lords of Antwerp. Perhaps, after all, they had done
more to help a heretic than to please a prince. Yet for all his loathing
and blaming of the Antwerp judiciary, John Hackett was just as
much let down by his own political master, who in turn found himself increasingly constrained by other political expediencies. So he
rooted out printers, sent numerous samples of what was circulating
to Wolsey and Tunstall, and suppressed as best he could the distribution of contentious material. His nemesis, Harman, was not the
only English 'Lutheran' on that side of the Narrow Seas. Already
in 1526 there was no doubt in Hackett's mind that many within the
Merchant Adventurers' Company would be seduced by Lutheran
opinions, were it not for the king's directive regarding vernacular
Testaments. And someone had to be watching over William Tyndale.
Hackett eventually accused Harman, but he could not have been
harbouring a heretic during his own lengthy confinement nor is he
likely to have been so brazen whilst still under investigation. Tyndale's
exact whereabouts are unknown, but nothing points to him being
anywhere but the Low Countries until late 1528. Still, Hackett's
extant letters are remarkably free of accusations against specific individuals, aside from those who were identified for him. Knowledge
of the merchant communities in the Netherlands was not an issue;

---

[106] Dowling, "Anne Boleyn," 43; *ENT*, 38.

for a long time prior to his royal appointment he had resided in
Middelburg, investing in wool and serving as the designated lieu-
tenant of the Company's governor.[107] Had England's chancellor
wished him to expand his investigations, with a view to exposing
additional collaborators within the merchant sector, John Hackett
undoubtedly knew that world well enough to do so.

In the end, with all his impassioned devotion to his faith and duty,
he adhered closely to the letter of his instructions from England: to
inform Merchant Adventurers of the king's wishes, to suppress English
imprints, and to press for the extradition of individuals accused by
the home government. If he felt conflicted because of his merchant
standing, it is equally conceivable that a climate of mistrust and
secrecy dampened the candour of some of his acquaintances. To be
circumspect was to be prudent in the presence of the king's representative, regardless of how much one knew about the traffic in
heretical literature. Even so, no one else operating within Wolsey's
web of spies, including the efficacious Cologne senator, identified
any suspects either.

The intrigue surrounding continental presses and English reformers in the 1520s affords a glimpse of how difficult it was to find
expatriates and to have them extradited or brought to justice on foreign soil. Antwerp had indeed become the principal northern centre for the production and distribution of reform propaganda and
the entrepôt continued to integrate mercantile networks that were
essential for interregional dissemination. With the apparent exception of Akerston, laws that civic officials were duty-bound to uphold
effectively protected expatriate nonconformists. Insulated by municipal authorities in the interest of communal harmony, much as their
German counterparts were in many imperial towns, and drawing
popular support from within their adopted communities, they were
elusive, almost untouchable. At various levels, from negotiations
regarding the fate of accused prisoners to the implementation of placards within the Low Countries, political considerations and jurisdictional concerns ultimately took precedence over enforcement of
spiritual conformity.

---

[107] *LH*, xi–xii and no. 23; *Bronnen tot de Geschiedenis van den Handel met England,
Schotland en Ierland*, ed. H.J. Smit (The Hague, 1928–50), 2/1: no. 429.

CHAPTER FOUR

SUBVERSION AND PROSECUTION

John Hackett's dogged efforts to prosecute Richard Harman were not exhausted until early 1528. Investigations elsewhere place his diligence in a wider and comparative context. The previous year Nürnberg printer Johann Hergott had distributed an agrarian communist brochure critical of the Church and Albertine Saxony's territorial bureaucracy. Duke Georg's officers apprehended him. He was sentenced to death and beheaded at Leipzig in May. Also in the spring of 1527 someone previously expelled from Dordrecht for his dangerous opinions was back in town handing out leaflets that he had had printed in Antwerp. He was arrested by Dordrecht's *schout* and jailed. In England investigations of Lollards that began in 1527 and extended well into 1528 led eventually to a clandestine network of book distributors stretching from the capital to East Anglia and Bristol. Several traffickers were detained. All were eventually released.[1]

By the end of 1528 a coterie of exiles abided in Antwerp, poised to follow up Tyndale's New Testament with a stream of commentary, polemic, and anticlerical propaganda. To that point attempts at suppression had produced mixed results. Subversive English imprints had been bought up at Frankfurt, so few if any copies reached the lay reader. Yet the attempt to extradite a known trafficker from Antwerp failed completely. Diplomats and spies made no breakthroughs in detecting or subverting the agents. Names of suspects were forwarded from England, where tribunals exposed closely connected strands of smuggling and distribution. These investigations precipitated searches in Germany and the Low Countries, which soon would extend to Paris and Calais. In the Netherlands, meanwhile, there was no obvious need for large-scale cross-border smuggling. Although virtually all of the polemical works reprinted there originated in Germany, pirate editions quickly appeared once willing

---

[1] Kirchhoff, "Johann Hergott," 15–55; *CD*, V: nos. 581, 583; *Ecclesiastical Memorials*, 1/1: 113–34.

printers got hold of potentially profitable texts. Records of prosecutions in both England and the Low Countries provide some insight
into regional book distribution and the religiosity and doctrinal inclinations of the readership. Measures to suppress and punish also
reflect the priorities of temporal and spiritual authorities, and the
constraints and distractions they faced. Secular courts in the Low
Countries were supposed to implement legislation that was not of
their making and increasingly at odds with established juridical norms.
Responsibility for spiritual conformity in England still rested with
ecclesiastical officials, whose remedies were, by contrast, thoroughly
traditional. At hand, then, was a critical test of both the means and
will to stifle dissemination.

Contraband, Scholars, and Christian Brethren

Notwithstanding the "crafty delays" encountered by the Merchant
Adventurers' governor when he wanted to search Richard Harman's
house in Antwerp, the letters found there would not alone suggest
that Harman was a key figure in the mass distribution of illegal literature. Presumably he could conceal some books occasionally with
unaccompanied goods that were handled for him in England.[2]
Attempting to hide or disguise entire bales of contraband would
require considerably more guile, to say nothing of the logistics of
having someone take delivery. It was Hans Ruremund who came to
London with several hundred at one time. Perhaps he was personally committed to spreading the printed Gospels, but he also needed
to recoup printing costs. The Ruremunds are not known to have
dealt in other merchandise. In these circumstances they risked bringing a big consignment of New Testaments to England's busiest port,
perhaps hidden amongst service books to be sold by agents at Paul's
Churchyard. Harman, by contrast, had a stake in the English trade
at Antwerp. Acquiring imprints and sending them, a few at a time,
to people he knew in the south of England was a sideline, a facet
of distribution not driven by prospects of significant financial gain.
But as Wolsey already knew by the summer of 1528, Richard Harman

---

[2] Merchant Adventurers typically sent textiles: fustian, satin, damask, tulle, cotton, and taffeta. Needham, "Customs rolls," 161.

had other connections. He also shipped books to London, where Simon Fish sold them to people associated with the Christian Brethren.

Harman's Kentish links remain noteworthy, though, in terms of how and where some illegal books may have entered the country. Lollardy had strong roots in the textile-producing villages of the Kentish Weald—particularly Cranbrook, Tenterden, Benenden and Rolvenden.[3] Harman himself, according to West, was from Cranbrook. So too were his friends Davy and Andrews. The imprints he sent to them could have been smuggled through various small harbours in Kent or Sussex. The Cranbrook connection comes to light in the records of the collector of the king's customs at Sandwich, responsible for ports between Gravesend and Dover. His accounts for 1525–26 and 1530–31 survive.[4] The first of these shows Davy and Andrews placing modest cloth consignments in vessels at Rochester. The ships they hired—two with English masters and the other a hoy from Bergen op Zoom—are unlikely to have been large; each of them carried no other cargo. Regrettably, their arrival in Rochester harbour is not recorded, so the cover under which books may have been smuggled is impossible to tell. Wine, fish, manufactured wares, and much Normandy canvas was off-loaded from other craft. In any case, since some of Harman's acquaintances shipped woollens from Rochester, it is not unreasonable to imagine that the port was also the conduit through which occasional parcels of illicit books came their way. John Andrews was again exporting overseas in the autumn of 1530, despite his arrest in the meantime in connection with sedition among Kentish textile workers. Twenty-five broadcloths owned by him were the only freight aboard the vessel *Anne* of Antwerp, when it left Rochester on 30 October. These same customs particulars also yield a third name associated with the investigation of Richard Harman: Richard Hall. Whether he was the London ironmonger Richard Halle, who asked Harman to send him some New

---

[3] P. Collinson, "Cranbrook and the Fletchers: Popular and Unpopular Religion in the Kentish Weald," in *Reformation Principle and Practice*, ed. P.N. Brooks (London, 1980), esp. 176–77; N. Tanner, "Penances imposed on Kentish Lollards by Archbishop Warham 1511–12," in *Lollardy and Gentry in the later Middle Ages*, ed. M. Aston and C. Richmond (New York, 1997), 229–30; R. Lutton, "Connections between Lollards, Townsfolk and Gentry in Tenterden in the Late Fifteenth and Early Sixteenth Centuries," *ibid.*, 199–228.

[4] TNA:PRO E 122/208/2, 122/208/3.

Testaments is not certain, but nevertheless possible. He too shipped cloth from Rochester in the summer of 1526 and again in April 1531.

Rochester was the port of choice for some Cranbrook men, and on more than one occasion in the 1520s John Fisher discovered heretics there. They abjured a mixture of Lollard and Lutheran articles.[5] While illegal books quite likely were smuggled through Rochester, it is also probable that some came to England through Channel harbours: Dover, Rye, and Winchelsea. Rye was the closest to Cranbrook and to several other villages associated with Lollardy. They were linked to the port through regional trade, in part facilitated by barge transport on the Rotcher. Heresy was not confined to inland communities. At least twenty Rye and Winchelsea men were accused in 1536.[6]

There were of course other conduits for the book-traffickers. This much is certain from the deposition of Richard Bayfield, an old acquaintance of Robert Barnes, who was burned in 1531. Abjured initially in 1528, he fled England, but on three subsequent occasions had returned with consignments of illegal books, landing them at a different place each time: London, Colchester, and somewhere in Norfolk. From Essex and Norfolk some of the books were then taken to the capital and sold there, others in Colchester. Bayfield was a former monk and chamberlain of the Benedictine abbey at Bury St. Edmunds, so it is to be expected that he brought his contraband to East Anglia, familiar territory where he knew people he could trust. He was associated with the Christian Brethren and admitted reading to Lollard audiences. The books, New Testaments and works by Tyndale, must have originated in Antwerp. Perhaps Bayfield arranged shipping from there, however they may have been sent via Boulogne or Calais, for Fox says that he sold books in France as well as England.[7]

By the time Richard Bayfield began delivering English Testaments to East Anglia, many people there had attended or heard about the sermons of Thomas Bilney and Thomas Arthur. The two influential

---

[5] Davis, *Heresy*, 42–43.
[6] *LP*, 9: no. 1424.
[7] Fox, *Acts and Monuments*, 4: 681–85; Davis, *Heresy*, 54–55; C. Haigh, *English Reformations* (Oxford, 1993), 66.

Cambridge reformers had embarked on an evangelical preaching tour of that part of the country in May 1527. Following a long investigation they were brought before an ecclesiastical tribunal in November, and subsequently examined on a full gamut of Lollard, Lutheran, and Erasmian views. Bilney eventually abjured seven modified articles, mainly Lollard ones relating to saints and images. He was kept in the Tower for another year after his penance at St. Paul's, and did not return to Cambridge until sometime in 1529. Thomas Arthur also abjured the Lollard articles and was freed.[8] These prosecutions aimed to curb contentious preaching and were at the forefront of what turned out to be the most concerted attempt in the 1520s to root out and contain nonconformity. A wider net had been cast across London and East Anglia. Within it the bishops discovered secret circles of Lollards and Christian Brethren, and among them Bayfield. About the harvest of confessions much has been written already.[9] A brief summary serves here to highlight a particular dimension: circulation of the printed word.

Inquiries were initiated by Tunstall's vicar general, Jeffrey Wharton in the summer of 1527, with examinations and abjurations continuing well into the following spring.[10] The diocese encompassed metropolitan London as well as Middlesex, Essex, and part of Hertfordshire. By March all the bishop's prisons were full. In large measure this was due to the confession of John Hacker, a Lollard from London's Coleman Street, who disclosed secret conventicles there and at Colchester. The groups were interconnected and involved dozens of individuals, some coming to Colchester from the nearby villages of Braintree, Horkesley, Steeple Bumpstead, and Witham. Some journeyed to London for books or to Ipswich to hear Bilney. A fundamental aspect of their private gatherings was Bible reading. All were commoners, yet collectively they scarcely fit even the broadest occupational profile. Alongside cloth workers and their wives there were founders, blacksmiths and bricklayers, a baker and a fishmonger, chandlers, herdsmen, servants, and widows: a rather predicable array, consistent with the legacy of English Lollardy. All the more striking, then, is the view of Richard Nix, bishop of the adjacent see of

---

[8] Davis, *Heresy*, 45–54; Haigh, *English Reformations*, 61–63, 67.
[9] Davis, *Heresy*, 54–64; Haigh, *English Reformations*, 63–71; Higgs, *Godliness*, 106–7; Brigden, *London*, 103–6, 187–98.
[10] *Ecclesiastical Memorials*, 1/1: 113–34.

Norwich, who wrote in May 1530 that neither the gentry nor the
commonalty of his diocese were greatly infected with heresy. He
pointed instead to merchants and others living on the seacoast.[11] It
is hard to imagine Nix was poorly informed or that he made any
meaningful distinction between Lollard and Lutheran heterodoxy.
And given the experiences of seafaring adventurers from Hull in
1528, his generalisation appears reasonable enough. Yet from the
so-called *magna abjurata* that same year an altogether different picture emerges. Among the people implicated there was a smattering
of merchants, but in no sense do they appear preponderant. And a
principal distributor of books in East Anglia, Robert Necton, sold
Testaments at inland market towns within Nix's diocese—Norwich,
Stowmarket, and Bury St. Edmunds—yet was unable to find a buyer
in the harbour town of Lynn.

Robert Necton attended meetings of the Colchester conventicle.
His deposition is also that of a distributor of prohibited literature,
travelling town-to-town until somebody complained about him to
authorities in Norwich.[12] Geoffrey Lome and Simon Fish, dwelling
at Whitefriars, London, provided him with English New Testaments
and other books. Where Lome got them is uncertain, but Necton
knew that Fish's supplier was Richard Harman. Encouragement to
obtain books from Fish came from George Constantine, who also
bought and sold them. In all, the quantities appear to have been
modest. When, around Christmas 1527, the "Duche man, beyng
now in the Flete" offered him three hundred Testaments at only
nine pence each Necton hesitated, directing him instead to Simon
Fish. Fox speaks of the abjuration in 1528 of a Netherlander, John
Raimund (Hans Ruremund), for printing English Testaments at
Antwerp and bringing five hundred to England. It is widely accepted
that Ruremund and the "Duche man" are one in the same, though
we do not know if Fish took any of his books.[13] Robert Necton sold
Testaments, including a couple to Bayfield, in London, others at various places in Norfolk and Suffolk. He also peddled a few Latin
titles, among them a version of *Summa der godliker scrifturen* called

[11] *LP*, 4/3: no. 6385.
[12] *LP*, 4/2: no. 4030; L.A. Schuster, "Thomas More's Polemical Career, 1523–1533,"
CW, 8/3: 1166; *Ecclesiastical Memorials*, 1/2: 63–65.
[13] Kronenberg, *Verboden Boeken*, 102; Schuster, "Thomas More's Career," 1163.

Oeconomica Christiana, and a volume of patristic excerpts, *Unio Dissidentium*. First published at Cologne in 1522, *Unio Dissidentium* already circulated among the English clergy and from 1527 on was reissued frequently by presses in Antwerp.[14]

As members of the London and Essex conventicles recanted in early 1528 another scandal was about to break in Oxford. Thomas Garrett, curate of All Hallows Honey Lane had come back to the university sometime before Christmas and persuaded several young scholars to buy and read forbidden books. He also sold as many as sixty to the Benedictine prior at nearby Reading. Arrested by the commissary of Oxford in late February, Garrett escaped briefly but soon was recaptured. Wardens and deans at the university handled the investigations there, reporting to Longland, who in turn apprised Wolsey. Accomplices were disclosed as well as a number of other people allegedly influenced by Garrett. Ultimately, though, the network led back to London and the rector of All Hallows Honey Lane, Robert Forman, former president of Queen's College, Cambridge. One of Forman's servants was Geoffrey Lome, later implicated by Necton. Another was John Goodale, now accused of bringing books to Garrett at Oxford. Several members of the Oxford reading circle were locked up, including John Frith, whom Wolsey had recruited from Cambridge for Cardinal's College. He spent six months in the college's fish cellar before Wolsey ordered him released. He was fortunate; three other students died there.[15] The colporteurs themselves did not fare badly. Wolsey, the university's greatest patron, was understandably displeased that some of his humanist proteges had brought disgrace upon themselves. He intervened along with Anne Boleyn for at least one of the ringleaders, assigning Forman a secret penance.[16] Both Lome and Garrett, who admitted reading, distributing, and translating Luther's works, were also abjured and later

---

[14] Haigh, *English Reformations*, 65; Davis, *Heresy*, 64–65. Lome admitted that he "despersed a brode" (therefore outside London) many books by Luther and his followers. *Guildhall Library*, MS 9531/101 fos. 121v–122.

[15] *LP*, 4/2: nos. 3962, 3968, 4004, 4017, Schuster, "Thomas More's Career," 1195. One of Garrett's friends also said he bought *Farragines Lamberti* (Lambert's *Farrango Omnium Fere Rerum Theologicarum*) from a bookseller at St. Paul's named Nicholas. There is no extant record of an investigation of anyone by that name. The only stationer so named and acknowledged to have kept shop at the Churchyard in this period was Nicholas Sutton.

[16] *Ecclesiastical Memorials*, 1/1: 124; Brigden, *London*, 161.

freed. Many books were seized and destroyed. Aside from English New Testaments, most of them were Latin compendiums of scriptural excepts or commentaries by the likes of Bugenhagen, Lambert, and Luther. The target readership had been an educated and scholarly one. A wider range of material circulated among the university men than within the conventicles in Colchester and London. Even so, the scholars' confessions reflect a similar Bible-based piety rather than doctrinaire Lutheranism.

When Tunstall questioned them, Forman and Goodale insisted they were completely innocent.[17] Goodale claimed to be unaware of the contents of two heavy fardels that Garrett had sent to Oxford. Forman had not sent books, but admitted owning some, so as to be acquainted with Lutheran opinions and thus prepared to discredit them. Garrett's student friends also named London bookseller John Gough as a supplier of the texts though he too denied it, apparently convincing the bishop that he had been mistaken for someone else, a certain "Theodoryke".[18] John Gough is not known to have had a printing press. His early inventories included titles issued for him by Wynkyn de Worde, and his attendance at Tunstall's monition to stationers in October 1526 places him among independent dealers. Following de Worde's death in 1535 James Nicholson did most of his printing, and then from 1539 until 1543 John Mayler.[19] Although both can be linked to controversial publications, their association with Gough does not necessarily mean they were involved earlier in the distribution of illegal books.[20] However, eventually Gough himself spent some time in prison. The Privy Council sen-

---

[17] *LP*, 4/2: no. 4073.

[18] *LP*, 4/1: no. 2063. Tunstall may have known about "Theodoryke" already. Shortly after the *Esterlings* did their penance in 1526 Netherlander Adrian Dolevyn was abjured for reading Luther in Dutch. Wolsey's commissioners had cited him even earlier, in 1522. His alias was "Dyrck", the common variant of Theodoric. In 1526 Dolevyn also confessed to writing a book outlining his Scripture-based views. Davis, *Heresy*, 44; Brigden, *London*, 203–4.

[19] *STC* 656, 1713, 1717, 1739, 4350, 5098, 5892, 16999, 18849, 18878, 20840.5, 25587.5.

[20] Mayler was fined and jailed briefly in 1543 for issuing material contrary to royal edict. Duff, *A Century*, 102. From his press in Southwark, Nicholson reissued Tyndale's *Wicked Mammon* and perhaps Bugenhagen's epistle to the English in 1536. He later published many titles on his own, especially English Bibles and commentaries by German reformers, likely translated by Coverdale—the same sort of material he printed for Gough. *STC* 2064, 2816, 2838, 4021, 17262.5, 24219.5, 24443, 24455, 2752.5.

tenced him in January 1541, following circulation of seditious invectives and Melanchthon's criticism of the Six Articles. Even prior to this he was implicated in smuggling, and was in touch with the Ruremund press, commissioning a Salisbury primer from Christopher's widow.[21] The central consideration here, however, is that in 1528 he avoided indictment.

With Necton's confession and the evidence gathered at Oxford, the ecclesiastical authorities in England may have come very close to unravelling most of the book-running network. Necton, especially, put the key agents at risk, giving the bishops Constantine, Fish, Harman, Lome, Bayfield and perhaps the "Duche man".[22] Bayfield and Lome were apprehended. Hackett was instructed to secure Richard Harman's extradition. Constantine, however, was not to be found. Agents had already looked for him in France. In September friar West may have recognised him in Antwerp, but had no warrant for his arrest. Simon Fish was equally elusive, though there was little question of his whereabouts by the end of the year, when his *Supplicacyon* was published at Antwerp. In any case, in the early summer of 1528 Wolsey's men could not locate him or Constantine, nor did they have any inkling of what obstacles lay ahead with respect to Richard Harman. Just as important, though, all of the principals they did manage to round up in England were subsequently absolved and let go. They included not just the university men to whom Wolsey and Anne Boleyn were sympathetic but also Bayfield and Necton. The two of them, along with Constantine, had been primarily responsible for the day-to-day physical distribution of prohibited texts beyond London and the university communities. At liberty again, they resumed precisely what they had been doing

---

[21] *STC* 15992; *Proceedings and Ordinances of the Privy Council*, ed. H. Nicolas (London, 1837), 7: 98–110. Brigden, *London*, 407–8, says Gough was "From the beginning . . . one of London's most zealous reformers." Perhaps his emergence as an independent bookseller at the time Peter Kaetz left England was not simply a coincidence. Gough's London printer, Nicholson, according to both Duff and Avis, did business with Hans Ruremund. Duff, *A Century*, 58–59, 110–11; F.C. Avis, "Book Smuggling into England during the Sixteenth Century," *GJB* (1972), 183.

[22] It is possible too that John Andrews informed about Richard Harman. He was taken and bound over to the chancellor in May 1528 by the warden of the Cinque Ports, Sir Edward Guildford, who was attempting to quell the sedition in Kent. There were several arrests. Andrews was sent up to London, while other depositions were heard at Cranbrook and Goudhurst. *LP*, 4/2: nos. 4287, 4301, 4310.

before. And for another three years they continued, before reaping the consequences.

The abjurations in 1528 also put Robert Barnes in danger, and precipitated his eventual flight. One of the Essex Lollards, John Tyball, said he had sought out the friar at London's Augustinian house, specifically to buy an English Testament. In some circles, then, Barnes was known to be a purveyor. And he did not disappoint his visitor. How often such sales were repeated we do not know, since Tyball's visit took place many months before he confessed. In any case, his revelation in April 1528 triggered the removal of Barnes to the Augustinian priory at Northampton. Fearful the relocation might be permanent or worse still that he was about to be burned, Barnes determined to escape, and by year's end had crossed the sea to Germany.[23]

Various aspects of illegal book distribution in East Anglia and London come to light in the *magna abjurata*. Not surprisingly, forbidden books, especially English New Testaments were distributed in areas strongly associated with Lollardy: St. Katherine's in northeast London, Coleman Street, where some of the conventicles gathered, and Essex. They were also taken to towns and villages in Norfolk. The agents—Necton and Bayfield—worked regions they were familiar with, often among or near people they knew. Nothing suggests their motivation was entrepreneurial. Not book dealers by profession, they were quite simply meeting the demand for a particular type of material and catering to a limited constituency to which they also belonged. Such specialised distribution did not fall to independent strangers. There is no sense that transient peddlers or travelling merchants, denizen or foreign, were hawking prohibited books. The single recorded exception, perhaps, was when one of the deponents, a Colchester baker, "bowght in Colchestre, of a Lumbard of London, a New Testament in English", paying four shillings for it.[24] In this instance, however, the ambiguous term "Lumbard" may just as well be an attempt to obscure the true iden-

---

[23] Fox, *Acts and Monuments*, 4: 681–85; Lusardi, "Robert Barnes," 1384–85.
[24] *Ecclesiastical Memorials*, 1/1: 121. Italians from Lombardy acquired reputations as moneylenders in Antwerp in the fifteenth century. By the early sixteenth, the term "Lombard" had become equated with usurer, applying not merely to Lombards but to anyone who traded in money. The application is therefore generic rather than geographic. Goris, *Étude*, 72.

tity of the vendor, perhaps Necton or one of the other known distributors. The volume of material they sold can not be measured. If the depositions are any indication, the ratio of books to persons involved in the conventicles was quite low. However, it must be taken into account that not all participants could read. And within these circles books typically passed from one individual to another by exchange and loan.

Collectively the abjurations suggest that almost a decade after Luther's emergence as the principal voice of change in Germany his appeal to the English lay reader remained limited. As yet few works by him or other foreign exponents could be had in translation, and outside university and clerical circles the number of persons capable of reading Latin was quite small. A market for Tyndale's New Testament existed, however the array of other printed material circulating among the accused was far from extensive. Moreover, some of their English "books", especially Lollard standards like *The Bayly*, probably were copied by hand: relics of the pre-existing tradition of dissent rather than coherent doctrinal statements strongly influenced by Luther. In the London and Essex heretics we find people to some extent acquainted with Lutheran views, though little affected by them.[25] There were no martyrs here. Some required more time in jail than others to be persuaded, but all chose to recant. They were assigned penance and dismissed.

Within the overall distribution scheme, Robert Forman's role is ambiguous. There are no other clues aside from the enquiry in 1528, and he died later that year. His apparent involvement, however, raises the possibility of collusion within a merchant guild. Traders and tradesmen alike entrusted the management of spiritual bequests—obits, chantries, and churches—to their guild officers. In 1525 wardens of the Grocers' Company had nominated Forman as rector of All Hallows Honey Lane, one of two London parishes then within the guild's purview. He and by extension his assistant Thomas Garrett were guild clergymen therefore, drawing stipends from the Company. The choice of Forman possibly reflected the religious views of rank and file members, perhaps not. John Petit, a former warden, was later accused by More of involvement in the printing of heresies. It

---

[25] Davis, *Heresy*, 64.

may be that at the time of Forman's nomination not all of the wardens or their assistants were fully aware of his questionable orthodoxy or that traditionalists were simply outvoted. Garrett eventually became Honey Lane's parson in 1536 but in the interim following Forman's death a conservative, John Coke, held the post.[26]

If illicit dissemination of books did not depend on the collective patronage of merchant fraternities, it is nevertheless certain that within the livery companies cells of Christian Brethren existed. According to mercer Thomas Kelye there was organised collection and allocation of money to finance book distribution, activities necessarily kept secret from conformist guild fellows. Perhaps significant numbers were involved. At least six mercers are among those likely to have been part of this support system. One of them, Thomas Mekins, along with Thomas Power of the Grocers' Company, posted a £100 bond to secure Robert Necton's release in September 1528. It has been suggested that the Brethren may have funded publication of William Roye's *A Brefe Dialoge*.[27] Not all of the Brethren and their associates were merchants, however. The background of several besides Garrett, Constantine, and Bayfield was clerical.

As Tunstall prosecuted, and Wolsey's spies abroad scrambled to apprehend suspects and destroy books, the propaganda campaign for the loyalty of the English lay reader entered a new phase. John Fisher continued at the vanguard of the Latin polemic battle with Luther, however the expatriates in Antwerp were printing in English. So in March 1528 Tunstall recruited Thomas More to spearhead an English-language counter-attack. Furnished with confiscated imprints, More was authorised to read and refute anything he chose. In total he authored and published seven English works, all of them issued in London. He thus became fully engaged in a pamphlet war against the exiles, most of all Tyndale. More's published works touch frequently on the pursuit of book agents after his appointment as chancellor in 1529. Our knowledge of the covert support network at the end of the decade and in the early 1530s relies heavily on his

---

[26] J.P. Ward, "Religious Diversity and Guild Unity in Early Modern London," in *Religion and the English People 1500–1640*, ed. E.J. Carlson (Kirksville, MO, 1998), 77–97, esp. 80–83. When John Frith and Andrew Hewet went to the stake in 1534 Doctor Coke of Honey Lane "willed the people to pray no more for them than they would pray for dogges": Hall, *Chronicle*, 815–16.

[27] Brigden, *London*, 121–24.

recollections.[28] Not unlike Nix, he was convinced that heresy flourished within the English business community, the logical extension being merchant support for the fugitives beyond the sea. Thus the chronicler Edward Hall was able to conjure up More's eventual interrogation of George Constantine about the heretics in Antwerp: "I know thei cannot live without helpe, some sendeth theim money and succoureth theim . . . I pray thee who be thei that thus helpe them?"[29] By then, though, the better part of three years had passed since the trials of the Oxford book-runners and the London and Essex conventiclers.

In those earlier proceedings More's involvement was only indirect; he was not yet chancellor. He did, however, investigate Humphrey Monmouth in 1528 and search his house, by order of the king's council.[30] Very few books were discovered. There were accusations, nevertheless, of helping Tyndale and Roye go to Germany and of possessing and importing heretical literature, specifically vernacular Testaments. But Monmouth insisted there was nothing extraordinary or extravagant about his largesse. It extended to other worthy individuals, whose opinions were not necessarily controversial. Moreover, after hearing Tunstall's sermon at St. Paul's in the fall of 1526, he burned all the letters and literature that Tyndale had sent him from Hamburg. The investigation was an initiative of the Crown rather than Church authorities, and very much an indication of things to come, following Wolsey's demise and Tunstall's removal to Durham. In November 1530 four men—three London merchants and a merchant tailor's apprentice—were publicly shamed for allegedly distributing in the capital *The practyse of Prelates*, a newly issued rant by Tyndale against Wolsey and the king's divorce. Adorned with confiscated copies of it and signs proclaiming "Pecasse contra mandata Regis", they were paraded on horseback through the streets of London.[31] During Wolsey's regime such a case would have been left

[28] Especially informative are More's *The confutacyon of Tyndales answere* (*STC* 18079) and *The apologye of syr T. More knyght* (*STC* 18078). See *CW*, 8 and *CW*, 9. Of the distribution of More's works nothing is known. Presumably they could be had from London shops and regional distributors.

[29] Hall, *Chronicle*, 763.

[30] *LP*, 4/2: nos. 4262, 4282. How Monmouth's involvement with Tyndale came to the government's attention is unclear.

[31] S. Brigden, "Thomas Cromwell and the 'brethren'," in *Law and Government under the Tudors*, ed. C. Cross, D. Loades, J.J. Scarisbrick (Cambridge, 1988), 33.

to diocesan courts or episcopal commissions. Abjurations recorded and penance assigned, there would be a sermon and a bonfire, but contrite book traffickers might reasonably expect to be absolved and released. It was different under More. At least one of the penitents in 1530, fishmonger Thomas Somer was returned to the Tower and died there. So did his neighbour John Petit, another More accused of having a hand in heretical printing. The same dreadful fate awaited several others.

Of the merchants prosecuted eventually by More and London's new bishop, John Stokesley, some had previously come to the attention of Wolsey and Tunstall. One who admitted receiving Testaments and other English books and distributing them in London was John Tyndale, whose story draws us again to a commercial setting and to an exchange of views there between a London merchant and an Essex craftsman.[32] Colchester cloth worker John Boswell, questioned during the roundup of the Essex Lollards, recalled speaking with Tyndale at Blackwell Hall in 1528. When the conversation turned to economic troubles that had recently befallen England's clothiers, Tyndale allegedly said he could see no remedy "excepte we coode cause the commons to arise and complayne to the kynges grace and schewe hym how the peple be not halff set awourke."[33] Foolish words indeed were these, especially at a time of heightened dissatisfaction with the central government. Inciting disorder was not heresy but given the context of Boswell's interrogation—a heresy investigation—and Lollard propensity for dissent, John Tyndale's comments were open to very broad interpretation. Two years on, he was one of the men shamed for distributing *The practyse of Prelates*.

Thomas More was right, of course, that some English merchants gave sustenance to agitators. Monmouth helped William Tyndale in London and merchant connections are believed to have done the same in Hamburg. There is no question they did so in Antwerp. When betrayed and arrested there several years later he was the guest of mercer Thomas Pointz. Other English refugees at Antwerp—Joye, Fish, perhaps Roye, and then later Coverdale—likely were dependent to some extent also. Some Christian Brethren were merchants. Commercial networks facilitated communication among them,

---

[32] *Ibid.*, 36.
[33] *LP*, 4/2: no. 4145.

as well as the conveyance of forbidden books from Antwerp. Their involvement is much less apparent, though, once the imprints reached London. They do not seem to have organised distribution outside the capital. If the Brethren were a widespread organisation earlier than 1528, then for several years they had precious few English books to distribute. Whether they at any time in the 1520s commissioned works by the English exiles or managed their production and sale is debatable.[34]

Young Men of Virtue and Good Letters

When Wolsey's agent, John West, came to Antwerp in September 1528 the fugitives he sought were Tyndale and Roye. He also made mention of another the king would be pleased to see arrested, although he brought no written supplication to the margrave or regent. The man in question was George Constantine, vicar of Sodgley, denounced some months before by Necton. Although Constantine quite possibly was in Antwerp at the time, agents had been searching for him elsewhere too. Bishop Clerk and the Master of the Rolls, John Taylor, were in Paris in the spring, ostensibly to broker entente between France and the Empire. They also looked for Constantine, before determining early in June that he probably had returned to England. However, they were able to apprehend a young English scholar, Francis Denham, who admitted staying for some time at Constantine's house. Denham was acquainted with Bilney and Fish, on whose suggestion he had done some translating of Lambert and Bugenhagen. Examination of his possessions then turned up a piece of correspondence from someone in Taylor's own retinue, John Corbett. Corbett had been introduced by his father at Sittingbourne, near Rochester, on the day of Taylor's departure from England, and taken on because of his "virtue and good letters". He now admitted Lutheran sympathies, and between them the two scholars divulged a third individual, the Staplers' chaplain at Calais, Philip Smyth, alias Fabry.

---

[34] For a different view see Schuster, "Thomas More's Career," 1158–59: When Tyndale left England the Brethren were "headed by an undercover ring of London merchants, who expressed their affiliations with continental Protestantism by subsidizing scholars, ordering translations and managing the production, distribution, and sale of books written by overseas reformers."

Immediately Clerk dispatched a letter to Calais, instructing Wingfield to arrest the priest, whose chamber at the Staple Hall was indeed found to be well stocked with at least a dozen Lutheran books.[35]

Denham and Corbett probably had known each other for at least two years. Both of them were admitted to the Inns of Court, where they likely made Simon Fish's acquaintance, in 1524.[36] Soon, if Clerk had his way, they would be back in England. They were delivered to Calais on 18 June, along with instructions that all three prisoners and their books should be sent across. In Wingfield's view this was essentially a spiritual matter, and he would have preferred to hand them over to the commissary of Calais, Sir John Butler. The confessions of Denham and Smyth were recorded, but three weeks passed and they were still in Calais when Denham, who impressed Wingfield with his Latin and Greek, died of the sweating sickness. Why had they not been put on the first ship bound for England? Clerk had no qualms about sending them home for further interrogation. There is, though, a tone of sympathy, not altogether guarded, in the correspondence of Wingfield and Taylor. The prisoners were young and impressionable—Denham was not yet nineteen—but bright, articulate, and well mannered. They deported themselves not as renegade traitors or firebrand evangelists but as persons "of goodly fashion". Taylor thought Denham a very proper young man and was also willing to give Corbett the benefit of the doubt, convinced that he had no experience in worldly matters and could do nothing but study.[37] The whole business was repugnant to Wingfield, a reluctant custodian at best, who seems to have been genuinely affected by Denham's unfortunate death. Writing to Wolsey and the Master of the Posts, Brian Tuke, immediately upon the arrival of the two young suspects, he informed that it would be four or five days before a ship would be ready to take the prisoners to England. Apparently unwilling to act on Clerk's orders alone and without much expectation of a answer from England before the first available transport was ready, Wingfield evidently determined to wait until he had the chancellor's reply. But the English capital was ravaged by the sweating

[35] *LP*, 4/2: nos. 4326–28, 4330, 4338; TNA:PRO SP 1/48 fos. 96–97, 123, 167–167v.
[36] Brigden, *London*, 116.
[37] *LP*, 4/2: nos. 4328, 4374, 4394–96, 4407, 4493; TNA:PRO SP 1/49 fos. 99–100.

sickness. Tuke attended the king, who now avoided London. With his household laid low by illness, Wolsey was at his Hampton Court residence pondering his next move to secure the royal divorce. After months of haggling, Stephen Gardiner had wrung a decretal commission from Clement VII, empowering a legatine court—Wolsey and Campaggio—to try the case in England.

Three months after taking delivery of the young scholars and arresting the Staplers' chaplain, Wingfield was still asking that his two remaining charges be bound over to Butler or, alternatively, conveyed to England with Clerk and Campaggio, who had by then reached Calais. The entourage tarried for several days because of foul weather, finally crossing on 29 September. Did Wingfield get his wish? Three weeks later he bundled up Smyth's books, papers, and written confession, and sent them to Butler at Dover.[38] Clerk had had plenty else to worry about while in Calais, not least the comfort of the ailing cardinal and the provision of horses for the journey from Dover up to London. It seems only reasonable, though, that had he taken Smyth and Corbett across, he would have thought to bring as well the evidence against them. Corbett's fate is not known but perhaps it was no worse than that of Philip Smyth. The Staplers' chaplain was absolved. His undated letter of thanks to Wolsey speaks of his confession to Campaggio—whether at Calais or in England he does not say—and the latter's intercession on his behalf.[39]

The letter also reveals more about Denham. He had come to Calais two or three years earlier, bringing several Lutheran imprints that Smyth had not seen before. Since then the two had corresponded, sometimes about Luther, and sent books to each other. An exchange developed, not only of letters but also of reading material, between Calais and Paris. Denham acquired books in the French capital and also forwarded some by Melanchthon and Luther that he purchased in Antwerp. Smyth resold these, evidently in Calais. Although Smyth's confession does not identify the titles he sent to Denham, the scholar made a list of the ones he purchased in Paris.[40] Except for an English New Testament and a French pamphlet against

---

[38] *LP*, 4/2: nos. 4761, 4769, 4789, 4861.
[39] *LP*, 4/2: nos. 4407, 5094.
[40] *LP*, 4/2: nos. 4396, 4407. TNA:PRO SP 1/48 fos. 185–85v, 195–98.

Paris theologian Noël Béda, they were Latin editions, ranging from Luther's *De Captivitate* and François Lambert's *Commentarii de Prophetia* to something by the controversial spiritualist Casper Schwenckfeld. On the whole, Denham's Latin tomes and the books taken from the Calais chaplain were consistent with what circulated within university communities and among clerics. Smyth said he was unaware of any prohibition on them. He read for his own edification and claimed never to have openly disputed or defended Luther's opinions. Old Wycliffite tracts, material typical among Lollards, found no place in his collection or Denham's. They read commentaries on the Gospels authored by Oecolampadius, Lambert, Luther, Melanchthon, and Bugenhagen, but were also drawn to and no doubt influenced by Erasmian humanism. In addition to Erasmus's New Testament translation, Smyth owned his *De Libero Arbitrio* and parts of his *Hyperaspistes* against Luther.[41] The little book critical of Noël Béda, which Denham kept, is therefore not out of place. No friend of humanists, Béda organised the Sorbonne's criticism of Erasmus in 1528 and orchestrated the campaign that resulted in Berquin's execution for heresy the following April.

There is no description of where Denham resided in Paris. He confessed to staying at Constantine's house, which might simply mean that he cohabited with Augustinians. He lingered in the French capital not merely for a few days, but for several months. Quite conceivably, then, the address was a conduit and alternate safe house for the English book-runners. George Constantine kept one step ahead of his pursuers for a long time. Sometimes he was in Antwerp, but for him and others involved in clandestine distribution, it would have been especially useful to have more than one hideout. Denham's itinerary included Antwerp as well as Calais and Paris. And Fox, it will be recalled, says that Richard Bayfield's illicit business also brought him to France. Paris was easily reached from Calais and Antwerp. Postal communications were reliable and there was regular commercial traffic.[42] Moreover, as Denham's collection demon-

---

[41] Several German presses had issued *De Libero Arbitrio* in 1524. *VD* E3145–53. *Hyperaspistes Diatribae adversus Serum Arbitrium Martini Lutheri* was printed at Basel, Cologne, and Nürnberg in 1527. The following year Melchior Lotter printed Hieronymous Emser's German translation at Leipzig and Johann Balhorn a Low German version at Lübeck. *VD* E3029–36.

[42] Coornaert, *Les Français*, 1: 203–4, 230–35, 2: 188–95.

strates, the French capital was also a good place to buy books. If these were not Antwerp reprints, they likely came directly from the places where many were first published, Strasbourg and Basel.

The circumstances of Corbett's arrest suggest he joined Taylor's entourage in order to make contact with Francis Denham in Paris. It was his misfortune that Clerk got to Denham first. With Constantine nowhere to be found, Taylor's letters informed Wolsey that there were no more English heretics in the French capital.[43] He hoped the chancellor would show some compassion towards Corbett, who apparently made a point of saying he "hade nether frynde nor place to go". He also promised not to attempt escape, and then with remarkable ease slipped away in the dark of night and disappeared for a couple of days.[44] His intent, presumably, was to alert someone that he and Denham were taken. Equally striking was an apparent lack of concern on the part of John Taylor, who rightly surmised that Corbett would turn up again. Taylor was a kindly guardian, to be sure, and Robert Wingfield another. Nevertheless, the arrest and subsequent death of Denham was perhaps the end of the Paris connection. Béda's renewed efforts to intimidate French reformers possibly had some effect too. Following Richard Harman's acquittal in Antwerp, George Constantine became a *poorter* there. Paris was not so important now, at least so far as his own safety was concerned. Legally, English agents could not touch him in Antwerp.

If the Paris link ceased to be vital, the same can not be said of Calais, embarkation point for the shortest crossing to England. Calais facilitated many aspects of exchange, not least because of its unique status as a garrison town and the staple for English wool. The port was a busy one, the destination of wool fleets from Hull, Ipswich, and London and a steady stream of craft from many other English harbours. They delivered essential grain and foodstuffs and returned to England laden with Normandy canvas and regionally manufactured goods. Equally important, then, were commercial connections to inland markets and industrial towns. Flemish wool buyers came to Calais, as did others from Holland, Germany, and Italy. The marts at Antwerp and Bergen op Zoom brought Calais merchants to Brabant, as did the Antwerp Bourse. The coalescence of mercantile

---

[43] *LP*, 4/2: no. 4328; TNA:PRO SP 1/48 fo. 93.
[44] *LP*, 4/2: nos. 4326, 4327, 4338; TNA:PRO SP 1/48 fos. 92, 143.

interests there and at Calais necessarily made both towns important
for the transference and exchange of information. And as the only
English jurisdiction on the continent, Calais was a conduit for communications, with merchant ships regularly bringing postal dispatches
to and from Dover.

Residents or people who frequently came to Calais were therefore ideally situated for a leading logistical part in book smuggling.
A sketch of their role before Henry VIII's break with Rome relies
on a patchwork of largely episodic and circumstantial evidence. A
chief consideration has to be the regular contact Philip Smyth maintained with the book-runner Denham, who in turn was associated
with Simon Fish and George Constantine. Smyth admitted selling
books in Calais; he may well have been responsible for others reaching England. The second chief consideration is the emergence of
Calais in the 1530s as the haven of sacramentarian heretics, some
of them known to and encouraged by Thomas Cromwell. It has also
been claimed that already in the mid-1520s Calais had become the
overseas "headquarters" of the Christian Brethren.[45] Perhaps this was
so. There is no reason to doubt that many banned books passed
through the town. One renegade English author somewhat recklessly
saluted its residents: "To the Right noble Estates and to all wother
of the toune of Cales Wiliam Roye desyreth grace and peace". So
begins *A Brefe Dialoge*, issued at Strasbourg on the last day of August
1527.[46]

The tribunals in England, together with the prosecution of Harman
and Hackett's investigation of the Antwerp printing houses, imply
two strands of illegal book distribution. One involved an organised
and integrated network of denizens, reliant to some degree on logistical and financial support from individual merchants or small cells
of Christian Brethren. Until the summer of 1528 their principal
undertaking was the supply of English New Testaments. Shipments
reached London through the agency of the pivotal Antwerp contact,
Richard Harman. Fish and Lome sold books in the capital and
Garrett took some to Oxford. The itinerant distributors—Necton,
Bayfield, and Constantine—operated both within and outside greater
London. Possibly Harman also helped Bayfield with his shipments

---

[45] Brigden, *London*, 116, 302–5 and "Thomas Cromwell," 46.
[46] *CW*, 7/2: 1069.

to Colchester and Norfolk. Vernacular Testaments were augmented with Latin texts authored by continental evangelists. Beginning in 1528 some anticlerical material and translations of Lutheran polemic were available in English as well.[47] Contraband originating in Antwerp moved along commercial transportation corridors, crossing the sea either directly from the Low Countries or from Calais. Calais also served as the conduit for books forwarded by other collaborators in Paris.

The second strand is distinguished by non-English involvement. The Ruremund press at Antwerp, perhaps with help from Franz Birckman, was responsible for the only pirate editions of Tyndale's New Testament known to have been printed prior to his own revised version. In at least one instance, Hans Ruremund brought a very large consignment to London. His mischance in the winter of 1527–28 suggests he operated parallel to but outside the network of Christian Brethren that channelled books to provincial communities. Sale was not pre-arranged and evidently he had no scheme for distribution beyond offering them, two or three hundred at a time, to anyone who would pay. Immediately plain too is the non-involvement of English colporteurs. And yet by midsummer 1534 the press had gone through pirate printings totalling several thousand copies. While co-ordination and collusion among nonconformists are obvious within the English network, the Ruremund approach seems more akin to an independent entrepreneurial initiative meant to capitalise on an anticipated demand for Testaments in the aftermath of the Worms printing. But the Christian Brethren and the Ruremund press were not so unconnected as they might at first appear. Cochlaeus claimed three thousand copies of Tyndale's translation were to have been issued in quarto at Cologne—an extraordinarily large print-run. It is highly doubtful that the octavo printing at Worms exceeded this. If to this number is added an equally liberal estimate for the first pirate issue, perhaps six thousand printed English Testaments were available for distribution prior to the second pirate edition in 1529–30.[48]

---

[47] Tyndale's *Wicked Mammon* and two English-language publications from 1529, *The Revelation of Antichrist*, attributed to John Frith, and *An Exhortation to the diligent studye of scripture*, attributed to William Roye, were wholly or partly translations of Luther. Clebsch, "Earliest Translations," 75–86.

[48] *ENT*, 19–20, 23; Johnston, "Printing," 166: For most publications "print-runs of 1500 and 1000 were nearer to the norm". According to George Joye, who was

Some of the signatures completed at Cologne and evacuated by the translators—Tyndale's prologue and Gospels of Matthew and Mark—also reached England.[49] However, when Necton confessed to selling the "biggest" as well as the smaller books, he presumably was talking about complete Testaments: the Worms octavo and the sextodecimo Ruremund copies. From this it is fair to conclude that Harman's shipments were not exclusively Worms imprints and that he therefore was in touch, at least indirectly, with the Ruremund press.

The "Duche man", Hans Ruremund, got out of jail and so did the other book traffickers; all of them were absolved at one time or another in 1528 and released. Whereas in the Netherlands local and provincial courts were supposed to implement the emperor's heresy laws, English prelates still administered their own regulations. Bishops presided over trials and, unfettered by formal guidelines or influenced by the papal inquisition, had considerable latitude in sentencing. They attempted to deter as well as punish and were obliged to absolve the penitent. Only obstinate or relapsed heretics were turned over to secular authorities. Church courts could not be directly involved in the taking of a life, nor with corporal mutilation. Repentant individuals received penances meant to fit their offences in a qualitative way. Most were very public and highly symbolic, such as those of Robert Barnes and the Steelyard merchants. Archbishop Warham's examination of Lollards in 1511 is also illustrative. Sentences ranged from simply attending a divine service to carrying a faggot or offering a candle. Warham also required some sacramentarians to receive the Eucharist and confess to a priest. Most, upon completion of their sentences were released into the community, however potential troublemakers could be removed and dispersed. Lifelong confinement was prescribed for some, usually in religious houses. This was a fairly drastic measure but it could be dispensed with or commuted at any future time. The same held true for the wearing of the heretic's badge.[50]

asked by the Ruremund press to correct the third pirate printing in 1534, the two previous issues amounted to about five thousand copies. Subsequent editions had print-runs of two thousand each. *An Apology made by George Joy, to satisfy, if it be, W. Tindale*, ed. E. Arber (Birmingham, 1882), 20.

[49] Daniell, *William Tyndale*, 110; *Ecclesiastical Memorials*, 1/2: 63–65. Testaments "of the little volume" were also seized in the investigation of Forman and Gough. *LP*, 4/2: nos. 4030, 4073.

[50] Tanner, "Penances," 229–49; *CW*, 9: 377.

Tunstall and Wharton assigned sundry penances in 1528. Those that are known again reflect discretionary authority and a range of choices. Fishmonger Thomas Mathew was required to distribute alms—herrings and bread—to prisoners at Colchester castle and to the town's poor. The penance of John Hig, who had expounded his false opinions in alehouses, was itself public. He was placed at the head of the Palm Sunday procession at St. Paul's and the Easter procession at the parish church of Cheshunt. Others who had spoken out against images and pilgrimages performed similar acts of submission at churches in Colchester. Less humiliating requirements included reciting Paternosters and Ave Marias. Sentences leading to social stigmatisation and economic hardship were also possible. But they could be mitigated. John Hig for instance, was to wear for the rest of his life the heretic's sign—a silken faggot embroidered on his sleeve—unless he received dispensation not to. Immediately he appealed on grounds that the badge would make him unemployable and force him to beg. Wharton granted the dispensation.[51]

Prosecution and correction of heretics in England remained in the hands of the ecclesiastics, but they had not prevented Tyndale and other exiles from initiating a printed debate in English. The issue of the king's divorce and his poor relationship with Rome did nothing, meanwhile, to enhance traditional Church authority. Thomas More's enlistment to refute Tyndale and Luther showed that the clerical hierarchy alone was not up to the task. Nor was the imposition of penance enough to stifle domestic distribution of contentious books printed abroad. By the winter of 1529 John Hackett's efforts in the Low Countries had demonstrated the futility of trying to prosecute English book traffickers there. This combination of forces clearly signalled the need for more decisive state intervention in the suppression of books, though not yet in issues of doctrinal heresy. The first sign that more involvement was imminent was a proclamation ordering observance and enforcement of the existing statutes. It instructed local and provincial justices to investigate heresies. Suspects were to be bound over to the bishops or their commissaries within ten days of arrest, whereupon they might be held indefinitely until they abjured.

---

[51] *LP*, 4/2: nos. 4029, 4038, 4242, 4545. The wealthiest Colchester suspect was Thomas Mathew, who had served as a town alderman and would do so again. Higgs, *Godliness*, 110.

Relapsed heretics were to be returned to the secular jurisdiction after sentencing. Erroneous books were to be turned in to diocesan authorities. However, no reference was made to specific authors or titles. Nor, remarkably, to vernacular New Testaments. It was forbidden to import, sell, or possess "any book or work printed or written, which is made or hereafter shall be made" against the Catholic faith and the laws and ordinances of the Holy Church. The same applied to works that reproached or slandered the king or his lords spiritual and temporal.[52]

Law, Judgement, and Punishment

Though novel for England, princely censorship decrees were commonplace in the Low Countries. From 1521 to October 1529 numerous placards were published there in the emperor's name. Municipal magistrates and provincial officers investigated people suspected or accused of transgression. Serious doctrinal deviance and all cases involving impenitent and relapsed heretics necessarily brought consultation with the inquisitor general at Louvain, Nicholas Coppin, or his deputies. Delinquent clerics were left to them as well. The regent's advisors frequently reminded the Court of Holland to enforce the edicts and the provincial body, in turn, looked to town governments. It was in the interest of local officials to show some initiative, partly to demonstrate the validity of their own juridical privileges and also to safeguard the rights of their constituents. Appearing diligent obviated need for intervention by other authorities. There were many investigations, and substantial sums were spent on incarcerating and transporting suspects.

Occasionally, when immediate or specific concerns arose, the imperial decrees and related directives from the Court of Holland were

---

[52] Precisely when the decree was issued is uncertain. *A proclamation for resysting . . . heresyes* (*STC* 7772) is attributed to the press of Richard Pynson, who received payment on 6 March 1529 for printing papers against heresies and for the reformation of engrossing of farms. *LP*, 5: 311. At that early date, however, there were few works in English that might be considered "in reproach, rebuke, or slander of the King, his honorable council, or his lords". Appended to the copy of the proclamation printed in *Tudor Royal Proclamations*, ed. P.L. Hughes and J.F. Larkin (New Haven, 1964), 1: 181–86, a list of "Books Prohibited" includes Tyndale's *The practyse of Prelates* and several other titles not published before summer 1529. Thereto Tunstall's register: Guildhall Library MS 9531/10 fos. 128–128v.

supplemented and reinforced.[53] An all-encompassing placard issued by the prince-bishop of Liege in January 1526 repeated the blanket restrictions. Friesland's governor ordered authorities in Leeuwarden to collect and burn books by Luther and his followers, upon hearing that many people possessed and read such material in their houses. This ostensibly reiterated the emperor's ban in one of his more recent territorial acquisitions, where no printing house existed. Some civic jurisdictions interceded as well. Kampen, in Overijssel, called for Lutheran works and annotated New Testaments to be turned in. Again the concern was not with vendors or presses, but with persons who already owned and kept prohibited texts "in Duyssche ende in Latijn" at home. Since these books originated elsewhere, bringing imprints into Kampen was forbidden also. The magistrates' express consent was now required to print anything there. Amsterdam's similar stipulation was in place by the summer of 1528, some months after Margaret's councillors complained about lax enforcement of the decrees. Antwerp also had issued restrictions and later outlawed the printing of English New Testaments.[54] In 1528 there was a move to counteract the proliferation of vernacular Bibles by licensing an officially sanctioned version. Coppin at Louvain authorised a text compiled by Vorsterman, who was given the exclusive right to print it for the next three years. Though supposedly taken from the Vulgate, in fact it borrowed extensively from Luther. Reprints in 1530 advertised explicitly that that it was published with the emperor's approval: "Met gracien en Priuilegien des Keysers". Several other printers of Dutch Bibles in the early 1530s also did so "cum Gratia et privilegio".[55]

The regency council sought implementation of all the constraints set out in the placards. Not every prosecution concerned illegal books. Nor did cases dealing with books always involve master printers or professional distributors. Transgressions ranged from simply reading proscribed material to printing and selling, and incriminated all sorts of men and women, a cross-section of artisan households. Confiscated imprints were destroyed, typically as part of a penitential display, whether or not possession was the principal offence. Surviving records

[53] *CD*, 5: xliv–xlviii.
[54] *CD*, 5: nos. 445, 487, 551, 567, 578, 682, 725; *AA*, 7: 314–20.
[55] Den Hollander, *Bijbelvertalingen*, 91, 350–60, 367–74, 402–3, 408–13, 420–21.

from the later 1520s seldom mention separate ceremonial book fires.[56] Except for the handful of examples where people were punished for trying to sell them, imprints most often turned up in investigations of private reading circles or instances of public blasphemy, much as in England. It was not unusual for possession to be just one charge of several, for example in Hoorn, where a man who expounded his views publicly and sang irreverent songs at home and in the streets also owned a scandalous book.[57]

Imperial decrees prescribed serious penalties. Prosecuting courts mitigated them at their discretion. Such leeway was conventional. Discretionary sentences remained the accepted prerogative of local and provincial authorities until the autumn of 1529.[58] Yet not all expressions of dissent or nonconformity necessarily contravened Habsburg edicts. And even some that did could be addressed just as readily with standard municipal regulations against irreverent behaviour and incitement. Magistrates could hedge against challenges to their decisions by creating and enforcing their own laws and by not convicting people specifically for disobeying the emperor's. In many judgements, including the one against the songster in Hoorn, failure to mention the edicts was not likely a simple oversight.

On the whole, book-related prosecutions suggest selective enforcement of local regulations and incomplete applications of the placards. And, even in towns with printing presses censorship was more reactionary than pre-emptory, as much concerned with possession as production. Relatively few printers and vendors were arraigned, and there is no clear pattern in their sentences. Penance assigned Antwerp bookseller Hendrik Peters—pilgrimage to the shrine of the Three Kings in Cologne—contrasts strikingly with another judgement handed down on the same day in February 1525. Jan Berkmans, a "scheemaker", was exiled for six years, on pain of death, also for selling heretical books. Perhaps he was deemed to have transgressed not simply in the course of earning his living, but rather with delib-

---

[56] Printed material was burned in 's-Hertogenbosch when heretics did penance there, and at Bruges under the same circumstances. *CD*, 5: nos. 535, 726.

[57] *CD*, 5: no. 530. A Briel locksmith was abjured for reading, but he also had attended conventicles, contrary to the placards. In Ypres and Courtrai people were punished for merely possessing or reading Lutheran imprints. *CD*, 5: nos. 482, 602, 667, 690.

[58] Tracy, *Holland*, 157.

erate intent to dissemble subversive heresy. Among the penitent Loists at Antwerp in 1526 were a bookbinder and his servant. The magistrates later sent two distributors of heretical songbooks on pilgrimage. And Hans Ruremund's treatment was no worse. Yet two years later another Antwerp denizen, Cornelis vander Plassen, was banished briefly for selling libellous and heretical materials without titles or places of publication.[59] Again the record is silent about whose laws— Antwerp's or the emperor's—had been broken. But certainly the accused had contravened a municipal ordinance. Elsewhere it was much the same story. Two Gent bookbinders were exiled in 1526 for having a quantity of illegal imprints in their houses and for consorting with Lutherans. The penance of a seller of heretical books at Dunkirk, Jan Corbel, was supplemented with a fine and brief banishment. Whether he was a professional vendor is not clear. But not all investigations ended this way. An officer of the Court of Holland visited Amsterdam in November 1525 to oversee the burning of copies of Paul's Epistle to Romans, issued by Doen Pietersoen, although the printer does not seem to have been prosecuted. Primarily an issuer of devotional works, he had offered translations of the Gospels before the placards outlawed them, and a complete New Testament based on Luther's.[60]

Penitential atonement featured prominently in the punishments doled out by municipal judges. It combined abjuration with a ceremonial act of submission, the most usual form being a solemn candlelight procession. Variations reflected specific circumstances. In Amsterdam, for example, a cooper who ridiculed the sacraments at an inn had to lead a procession of the crucifix to the Old Church and then, with lighted candle still in hand, go back to the tavern and seek the forgiveness of its scandalised patrons.[61] Since powerful imagery and large audiences were all-important it was not uncommon for penitents to be added to a "processie generale" in which regalia and relics were displayed. The penance of the Antwerp Loists was true to type. Clad in linen smocks, they walked barefoot and carried candles, following the holy sacrament through the central

---

[59] *CD*, 5: nos. 502, 542–43, 735; *AA*, 7: 139–40.
[60] *CD*, 5: nos. 438, 531, 641; *PI*, 14. Den Hollander, *Bijbelvertalingen*, 38–39. The Court also investigated a Delft bookbinder and his servant. *CD*, 5: no. 638.
[61] *CD*, 5: no. 607.

market, into the Church of Our Lady and then back to the Town
Hall. Civic militia lined the route to ensure order. General processions were staged in the first instance to invoke God's favour and
mercy. The Habsburg regime also used them to induce and rein-
force loyalty. At Charles's request Antwerp ordained a procession in
early December 1527 that included prayers for him and his brother
Ferdinand, and for the extirpation of heresy. Less than a month later
Lady Margaret wanted another one to celebrate the recent libera-
tion of the pope.[62]

Beyond the penitential procession, correction of individual agitators, blasphemers, and conventicle participants could require travel
to a holy shrine. Pilgrimage was a traditional prescription for sin-
ners, but local magistrates also assigned it routinely for petty crimes
and misdemeanours unrelated to heresy. One of the Antwerp rioters in 1522, Margriete Boonams, whose objections had been a bit
too boisterous when town officials entered the Augustinian house,
was required to go to Cyprus. A couple of years earlier a blasphemer had been sent to Rome. However, in heresy-related cases many
other destinations, such as Cologne, Boulogne, Paris, and Wilsnack,
did not entail particularly long journeys.[63] The same was true of
those determined by the Amsterdam authorities. Some—Hoorn, Rijsel,
and Amersfoort—were quite close by. And yet a pilgrimage to Naples
was also ordered, for non-observance of a fast day: contempt of
Church law, though not necessarily connected directly to any placard.[64]

Since prosecution of laypersons ultimately fell within the criminal
justice purview of secular courts, there existed a range of additional
penalties.[65] Chastisements, like the burning of books, were public.
On more than one occasion, it was the Court of Holland's stated
intent not only to correct transgressors but also to make examples
of them. The grimmest of corporal punishments were reserved for
repeat offenders and for provocateurs who blatantly incited discord.
The Court ordered a particularly outspoken Amsterdam sacramentarian flogged severely and his tongue bored through with an iron
nail. Likewise, a tailor who fastened libels to the door of St. Peter's

---

[62] *CD*, 5: nos. 502, 659; *AA*, 2: 320–22. Public processions were intended to be
occasions of civic solidarity. Marnef, *Antwerp*, 28–29.
[63] *CD*, 4: nos. 24, 206; *AA*, 7: 126, 129–33.
[64] *CD*, 5: nos. 423, 546, 689, 691, 696.
[65] *CD*, 5: nos. 350, 532, 568–69, 621, 693, 700, 716, 723, 734, 736, 742.

in Leiden and threw some into the pulpit was beaten before being exiled.[66] Criticising the sacraments, especially Christ's presence in the Eucharist, had by now equalled if not superseded anticlericalism as the most common ingredient of overt dissent, especially in the north. Depending on the ruling of local judges, sacramentarians and blasphemers might be fined, whipped, jailed, exiled, or prescribed something akin to penance. In summer 1528, though, the Court of Holland decided a number of vociferous individuals should have their tongues mutilated, in at least one instance overruling a municipal court. An iconoclastic harangue by a member of the Delft conventicle, David Joris, earned him public penance and house arrest. The provincial body ordered flogging, the piercing of his tongue and exile for three years.[67] Perhaps such measures helped allay the concerns of Margaret and the inquisitor general. Even so, urban governments clung to their discretionary prerogatives and, when challenged by the provincial body, ostensibly tried to negotiate sentences for the accused.

This crucial interplay of civic and provincial courts was peculiar to the Netherlands but it did not mean that punishment of heterodoxy there differed appreciably from the norm in Germany, specifically in towns answerable only to imperial authority. Again Cologne, where university theologians investigated (and condemned) scholars and clerics while the town prosecuted laypersons, is an indicator. Municipal placards against Lutherans and their books brought plenty of arrests, and bookshops were searched periodically. However, decisions on individual cases do not suggest frequent banishment of denizens or much ceremonial penance. While a blasphemer in Antwerp might end up in a procession or on pilgrimage, someone arraigned in Cologne was more likely to spend some time in jail on a diet of bread and water.[68] In choosing to incarcerate people rather than maim or humiliate them, Cologne punished subversion no more severely than Antwerp or Amsterdam, towns that on the whole were less diligent in defending conformity.

Aside from jurisdictional issues, enforcement of heresy law in the Low Countries was problematic in other ways. That much is plain

---

[66] *CD*, 5: nos. 701–2, 723.
[67] *CD*, 5: nos. 721–22; Waite, *David Joris*, 34, 53–55. The leniency of the Delft authorities was perhaps in part due to public support for Joris.
[68] *Beschlüsse*, 3: 105, 382, 596, 607, 652, 653.

from the banishment of the outspoken layman from Dordrecht,
Cornelis Woutersz. Not only were his views contentious, he had also
had a psalm-book printed. He set off alone for Germany sometime
in 1526, abjuring and depositing his books into a fire before he left.
But his own doubts haunted him still, so much so that by the following April he had returned. Following his arrest by the *schout*,
Woutersz. told his story to a commissary of the Court of Holland,
who duly recorded it.[69] He came home, having composed a pair of
letters: statements addressed to the municipal council and citizenry
of Dordrecht. In them he reaffirmed his old heretical beliefs and
expressed regret at having accepted penance. These explications too
had been printed. Returning from his exile via Antwerp, he had
gone with his letters and a bit of money to one of the printing houses
there and simply enquired of its matron if she would make a few
copies: "of zij eenen penninc winnen wilde ende drucken eenen brieff
off twee". She agreed. Exactly when Woutersz. parted with the meagre payment we do not know, but by his account the bargain was
uncomplicated. It enabled him to bring many copies of his letters
to Dordrecht—enough, he imagined, that they would still be found
a hundred years after his own earthy life was finished. He had already
begun handing them out when the *schout* caught up with him. With
no plans to take or send them anywhere else, he was certain nonetheless that they would circulate beyond the town.

   Cornelis Woutersz. was neither peddler nor *Buchführer*. He was a
self-reliant cobbler. He could read and write, however. And although
not seeking to benefit materially, he knew how to go about publicising his opinions with printed text. His example shows that
Netherlanders otherwise unconnected with book production and marketing could and did contribute directly to the expanding range of
controversial leaflets intended for local and regional dissemination.
David Joris, a glass painter by trade, was another who distributed
and apparently authored such material, and there were plenty more
like him. In both the Netherlands and Germany hundreds of short
pamphlets by laypersons circulated, typically expressing Scripture-
based piety. Often they were the work of artisans, among them

---

[69] *CD*, 5: 387 and nos. 581, 583, 589, 591, 603, 684, 740. Thereto Kronenberg,
Verboden Boeken, 51–53 and *NK* 01256–01257. Johnston, "Printing," 182, suggests the
psalms may have been Woutersz.'s own rendering rather than Luther's.

another shoemaker-turned-poet, Hans Sachs. They offer a window into the diffusion of print culture at the popular level: the commentaries and rebuttals they contain necessarily imply possession of other printed works.[70] And not far removed from these and circular letters like Woutersz.'s was another genre, the defamatory libel. Composition of short, slanderous broadsheets also required no more than basic linguistic competence. The anonymous authors were not necessarily highly educated. The ease with which a simple shoemaker had his letters printed brings to mind the alleged mischief of Richard Harman and his wife at Antwerp, and libels that circulated there among Merchant Adventurers.

Potentially influential material could be generated in Germany and the Low Countries by unlikely sources, cheaply and without much difficulty. Woutersz.'s arrest is also of interest because he returned to Dordrecht a relapsed and impenitent heretic. What were the authorities to do with him? Recalling the public commotion that Jan van Woerden's execution had caused in 1525 and aware that dissenters could turn such spectacles to their advantage, the Court of Holland was reluctant to burn him.[71] Troublesome individuals could be expelled, however for any number of reasons an exile might risk returning. And for Woutersz., literate and able-bodied, the deterrent value had already proved negligible. Cast out of Dordrecht, he went to Amsterdam and thence to Bremen, where he stayed for half a year. Then he moved on to Goslar, which suited him even better, apparently, for it was his intention to live there once affairs in Holland were satisfactorily concluded. That was not just a matter of distributing a few provocative leaflets. He returned for his wife. When his letters could not convince her to meet him in Antwerp, he dared to come all the way back to Dordrecht, there to be jailed indefinitely on orders from the Court of Holland.

Woutersz.'s return to Dordrecht presented a dilemma for the Court of Holland. In at least one instance so did laws requiring book censorship. Restricting public exposure to innovation led to questions

---

[70] Chrisman, *Conflicting Visions*, 159–70.
[71] *CD*, 5: no. 603; Tracy, *Holland*, 156, 158–9 and "Heresy law," 287; Gregory, *Salvation*, 143. Pamphlets recounting the persecution and death of evangelicals were popular. The tale of Jan van Woerden's martyrdom was one of several that circulated in print. By the end of 1523, the year the two Augustinians were burned at Brussels, German presses had chronicled their ordeal in sixteen published editions.

about counter-propaganda. Already by 1527 the reality that books were a medium not only for subversion but also for reasoned polemical debate had underscored a principal shortcoming of blanket censorship. A Dutch translation of a tract by Johann Eck came to the Court's attention. It was printed at Delft and sold in Amsterdam. In it Eck refuted the essential errors of Luther and his followers, but perforce articulated them as well, and as a consequence the imprint fell under the most recent ban. Yet some of the Amsterdam clergy felt it was highly worthwhile reading. The irony was not lost on the Court, accustomed as it was to reminders about placard enforcement. Its call for guidance in this instance effectively shifted responsibility for the decision to the regent and her advisors. Sophisticated rejoinders to Luther were crucial to the overall defence of the Church and Eck's was a leading voice, so presumably the wider ramifications of the decision were carefully considered beforehand. It was ruled, following consultation with the inquisitor general, that copies of the book should indeed be seized and destroyed. So directed, the Court forbade anyone to buy, sell, or possess it. Unintentionally, then, edicts designed to silence Lutherans had resulted in the censoring of a work by one of their most prolific and capable opponents.[72]

Even so, there were more decrees to come, and in autumn 1529 came the severest of all. In addition to banning the works of many reform theologians, it proscribed New Testaments issued by Antwerp printers Adriaen van Berghen, Joannes Zel (alias Jan van Ghelen), and Christopher Ruremund.[73] Why these three were singled out can be surmised. Vorsterman's licence to issue a vernacular Dutch Bible implied that his was the only acceptable version. Ruremund had offered a different and therefore unauthorised edition in 1528 and so had Zel. Adriaen van Bergen was responsible for the first Dutch printing several years earlier. The new placard required all Testaments in English, French, and German to be turned in. No more heretical books were to be written, copied, printed, bought, sold, read, or

---

[72] *CD*, 5: nos. 603, 611, 673; Kronenberg, *Verboden Boeken*, 21–22. The book was *Declaracie tegen zommighe articulen der lutheranen*, translated from the Latin. Apparently the Court did not take action against the printer, Cornelis Henricsz. Lettersnijder. *NK* 752; *PI*, 114. Henricsz. Lettersnijder was responsible for two Dutch Bible editions in 1522 and 1524. He also issued devotional texts and commentaries by Erasmus. Den Hollander, *Bijbelvertalingen*, 51–58.
[73] Johnston, "Printing," 179; Kronenberg, *Verboden Boeken*, 19, 89; Den Hollander, *Bijbelvertalingen*, 70–71.

kept. All transgressions were capital offences. Relapsed heretics were to be burned without delay. The edict also attempted to deny the discretionary prerogatives of the municipal and provincial courts by stipulating that they impose the prescribed punishments. As if to add emphasis, Willem van Zwolle, a member of Christian II's retinue was then burned at Mechelen. The Louvain inquisitors had examined him following complaints from Lady Margaret. The *auto-da-fé* did not rate mention in John Hackett's dispatches, but he wrote approvingly of the placard's many "good artycles", proclaimed so far as he knew throughout Brabant on 22 October.[74]

The October edict in the Netherlands signalled a harder line against heresy. In England too, changes were in the offing, as the Crown became more actively involved. Thus far, what had been accomplished with respect to heretical books? When the Antwerp Loists and merchants of the London Steelyard performed their penance in February 1526 they were essentially puppets in set pieces staged primarily for the benefit of denizen onlookers. The scene was repeated periodically: later that year, for instance, there was another procession of penitents and book fire in 's-Hertogenbosch.[75] The persuasive power of such spectacles may only be guessed. English Church authorities and civic and provincial officers in the Low Countries could scarcely hope to curtail circulation of tainted imprints simply by destroying any and all they could get their hands on. Nor could magistrates elsewhere, in Lübeck or Cologne. The evocative value of the ceremonial bonfire may have diminished the more they tried. Though still powerful, this was old imagery. Book fires and heretics bearing faggots had become familiar sights. And in London so had the pompous pageantry of the prelate-chancellor. The solemn grandiosity witnessed at the fires in Paul's Churchyard may have instilled as much resentment as awe, given the contempt with which many people viewed him. Perhaps too, the onlookers' growing familiarity with penitential ritual fostered a degree of complacency. As Susan Brigden has noted, elaborately staged book-burnings, replete with sermons and ceremonial penance, publicised Luther to many people who might otherwise have been much less aware of him, in effect facilitating

---

[74] *LH*, no. 135; *CD*, 5: no. 705; Gregory, *Salvation*, 143. Tracy, "Heresy Law," 288–89, suggests the edict may not have been published in Holland.
[75] *CD*, 5: no. 535.

rather than slowing dissemination of his views.[76] Moreover, the destruction of New Testaments may have been incomprehensible to many
devout Catholics, leaving them vulnerable to exploitation by those
who would argue that criticism of institutional inventions was based
on Bible reading.[77]

Until Thomas More became chancellor action by the Crown with
regard to print distribution consisted of little more than warnings
and threats, coupled with failed attempts to extradite fugitive provocateurs. The ecclesiastical establishment, for its part, tried proscription and bonfires. It also investigated and abjured people, and
occasionally burned Lollards. A penitent would not suffer a heretic's
death merely for possessing or reading books or for distributing them.
The same held true in France, where Berquin's execution for heresy
was the first in half a decade, and in the provincial and local courts
of the Netherlands. In the period leading up to Charles's placard of
1529 the Council of Holland ordered the death of only two accused
heretics: Jan van Woerden and an obdurate widow from Monnickendam, burned in November 1527. Neither was involved in book
distribution and both were turned over to the secular arm after
examination by ecclesiastical authorities. Wendelmoet Claesdochter's
condemnation, as recorded by the Court, did not mention the
emperor's edicts. She had ridiculed the sacraments and ten months
in jail failed to change her mind. The southern provinces saw three
heretics burned in 1528: one each in Bruges, Tournai, and Liege.
Three dozen books belonging to the man who died at Bruges were
incinerated along with him. He had made hats for a living; the other
martyrs were clerics. Northern Germany offers a similar picture. The
two men apprehended and condemned in the archbishopric of Bremen
in the 1520s were not book agents but transient priests: Hendrik
Bornemacher and the former Antwerp Augustinian Hendrik van
Zutphen.[78]

Would harsher treatment of the propagators of contentious literature have stemmed the proliferation in the 1520s? In the 1530s secular courts across much of Europe assumed more and more

---

[76] Brigden, *London*, 156.
[77] Schuster, "Thomas More's Career," 1162–3.
[78] R. Hari, "Les placards de 1534," in *Aspects de la propagande religieuse*, ed.
G. Berthoud et al. (Geneva, 1957), 97–98; *Aus der Reformationsgeschichte Niedersachsens*,
10, 21–22; *CD*, 5: nos. 649–55, 695, 706–12, 727.

responsibility for heresy prosecutions, and regularly imposed the death penalty. Some printers were among those condemned. Until then, in William Monter's view, religious innovators and dissenters were not frightened by "old-fashioned ecclesiastical institutions" and ecclesiastical justice did not adequately punish accused heretics.[79] The dilemma was as old as the medieval Church itself; a fundamental priority of traditional ecclesiastical institutions was correction and guidance of the wayward back to the Catholic fold. It was not their purpose, nor was it that of secular magistrates to exterminate people. Above all, the institutional Church desired conformity, beginning with its own rank and file. Not surprisingly, then, most executions prior to 1530 were of apostate clerics.[80] Several seem to have courted this fate. In the popular imagination of dissenters they succeeded in becoming martyrs. The attendant publicity seldom worked in the Church's favour. The execution of the Scottish reformer Patrick Hamilton at St. Andrews in 1528, for instance, fed a curiosity that drew many others into rather than away from the evangelical movement.[81] Yet the vast majority of accused lay persons chose not to burn but to recant, much to the relief of the secular courts one would imagine. Finally, in the decades that followed, the sheer number of death sentences meted out for heresy leaves their deterrent value open to question. It is not unreasonable to suppose that for many a committed sectarian this penalty was no more deterrence than traditional penance.

Before 1529 few persons who were Lutheran in a confessional sense were martyred anywhere in Europe. Thereafter heresy executions occurred much more frequently. And in England two hundred persons were put to death for *lesè majesté* during Henry VIII's reign, after implementation of royal supremacy purposely blurred any distinction between heresy and treason. Many hundreds more perished in the Swiss cantons, the Low Countries, and the Empire, in areas that did not remain true to Rome as well as those that did. Sometimes, usurping the legal authority of religious institutions was part of the

---

[79] W. Monter, "Heresy executions in Reformation Europe, 1520–1565," in *Tolerance and Intolerance in the European Reformation*, ed. O.P. Grell and B. Scribner (Cambridge, 1996), 49–55.

[80] Gregory, *Salvation*, esp. 78–79.

[81] McGoldrick, "Patrick Hamilton," 86.

on-going process of modern state building, which required subordi-
nation of clerical prerogatives to the interests of temporal rulers. But
the impetus for more secular control and the increased severity of
punishments is not found in political vision alone. A prime consideration must be the sectarian nature of the dissent. Two thirds of
the heretics put to death in Europe between 1520 and 1565 were
Anabaptists. Their nonconformity was multidimensional, not strictly
confined to religion.

The determining factor in the fate of so many martyrs, and not
just Anabaptists, was the real or imagined threat they posed to order
and to traditional forms of secular control. In France, only after the
infamous Affair of the Placards, which directly challenged the monarchy did François I begin to use the Paris *Parlement* to prosecute religious subversives. A twelve-member commission was created for the
purpose in December 1534. The source of the libels (placards) was
Neuchâtel, far from the French capital; sedition travelled via Lyon,
within regional networks of communication and commerce. In the
scandal's immediate aftermath at least twenty persons were burned.
The condemned included a couple of printers and a bookseller, as
well as artisans and merchants. Dozens of other persons were
denounced at a great procession in January 1535, among them Simon
Du Bois. By the end of the decade a royal edict formally transferred
full jurisdiction in heresy cases to the secular courts.[82]

Outside France, there were numerous earlier instances of religious
and non-religious dissent converging to trigger action by temporal
authorities. While it is true that religious nonconformity was a cat-
alyst for insurrection in Danzig in 1525, Sigismund intervened as
much to restore the socio-political equilibrium as to defend the old
faith. The chronicles of Danzig speak of the imprisonment and exile
of many people, but not the burning of heretics. Polish bishops
accompanied the king and dutifully investigated monks, nuns, and
priests who had not already fled. In the end, however, condemnation was reserved for individuals who had undermined and ultimately
usurped political authority.

Elsewhere, three persons were beheaded for their part in Antwerp's
iconoclastic riot in 1525. Municipal authorities there also authorised
the drowning of the provocative monk who refused to abide by a

---

[82] Monter, "Heresy executions," 53–54; Hari, "Les placards," 98–104.

general ban on evangelical preaching. Whether he knew it or not, he died not so much for the substance of his proselytising but because he would not desist. It was a heresy execution in the broadest sense perhaps, but not an ecclesiastical initiative. The lords of Antwerp took action ostensibly because public defiance of their authority posed a danger to public order. In such volatile circumstances otherwise patient town regimes were sure to step in. Augsburg artisans had been rounded up in 1520 when they protested the expulsion of a Franciscan, and two were executed. And there were banishments and more death sentences following similar upheaval in Nürnberg a few years later.[83]

For an example of intervention more closely linked to the dissemination of literature we have the demise of the bookseller/printer Johann Herrgott. He rarely issued original material, but his catalogue for 1524 included a text by the millenarian Thomas Müntzer, later leader of peasant rebels in Thuringia and Saxony. The Müntzer connection clouded Herrgott's reputation. So did Luther's earlier complaint to the Nürnberg magistrates about his unauthorised reprints. The town had no interest in extricating him from more trouble of his own making in 1527, when copies of his *Von der newen wandlung* appeared at the New Years mart in Leipzig. The anonymous first-person narrative criticised the cloisters and also took exception to the imposition of Roman law in Saxony. Although the pope and the sacraments were not disparaged particularly, the grumbling was all too reminiscent of the recently extinguished peasant rebellions. Duke Georg therefore had a personal interest in tracking down its source. Probably apprehended at Zwickau, Herrgott died on a scaffold at Leipzig. Nürnberg authorities evidently made no effort to save him. Yet the duke spared two Leipzig students implicated in the pamphlet's distribution, apparently to avoid confrontation with the town and its university. Johann Herrgott thus became a kind of sacrificial quid pro quo.[84] But Georg's initial response was essentially what might be expected from any responsible temporal power that perceived its authority to be threatened. Had the Dordrecht shoemaker

---

[83] *CD*, 4: nos. 341–44; Chrisman, *Conflicting Visions*, 56–57.

[84] Kirchhoff, "Johann Herrgott," 15–55; *Flugschriften aus der Bauernkriegszeit*, ed. A. Laube and H.W. Seiffert (Berlin, 1975), 545–57. For an English translation of the pamphlet see *The Radical Reformation*, ed. M.G. Baylor (Cambridge, 1991), 210–25.

Cornelis Woutersz. attempted to distribute anything comparable to Herrgott's pamphlets we may safely imagine that there would have been considerably less dithering by the Court of Holland or the town magistrates over what to do with him.

Circles of Diffusion

The surviving evidence from heresy cases in the Low Countries says little about how people came to possess books, so delineation of a covert distribution web such as the one in England is impossible. Of large consignments seized by vigilant authorities no extant record survives. Regionally, Dutch-language books and pamphlets, whether or not they were controversial, likely were distributed through traditional channels for the most part. Typographers and their agents were not entirely preoccupied with religious texts. Educational tomes and others unconcerned with spiritual issues continued to be published and disbursed. The monitoring of shops and printing houses by town officials meant that some outlawed material might be traced, although false colophons undoubtedly hampered such efforts. Books were sold from shops in the locales where they were printed, in Antwerp, Leiden, Delft, Deventer, and Amsterdam.

Prosecution records also point to a significant role for itinerant peddlers. Certainly east of the Netherlands authorities in Cologne were on the lookout for such persons.[85] Their activity must have been less secretive than the regional dissemination in England. English carriers presumably tried to blend in with other traffic and remain inconspicuous as they travelled from one town to the next. If peddlers and urban dealers saw to most of the retail distribution in the Low Countries and Germany, we must also acknowledge the simple proponents of evangelism, who had opportunity to carry books from one place to another. And, as in England, another mechanism for local circulation was the secret conventicle, usually held in a domestic setting.[86] Some books probably changed hands at locales far less private too, for example at inns. The tavern, regardless of country or location, was in any case a primary venue for topical

---

[85] *Beschlüsse*, 3: 213.
[86] Plumb, "Gathered Church," 136; Johnston, "Printing," 169–70.

dialogue—and monologue. In such surroundings people fortified with drink might find an exchange of religious views entertaining, even edifying. But by the same token there was always the possibility of trouble. Otherwise light-hearted banter at an Antwerp inn turned sour on one occasion in 1528, after a priest called some of the patrons Lutherans. Tempers flared and an argument ensued outside. It ended with a fatal stabbing.[87]

In the later 1520s imprints that circulated in the northernmost principalities of Overijssel and Friesland were not printed there. Dutch and Latin editions came from southern presses via Amsterdam. They were augmented with vernacular publications from northern Germany. A mixture of vernacular translations could be read in coastal and border regions, where the imprecision of linguistic boundaries helped determine a common culture. Although they were separate languages, Dutch, Frisian, Danish and German had common roots. Travellers along the North Sea and Baltic shores communicated effectively using variants of Low German.[88]

When the magistrates of Kampen attributed printed heresies to non-indigenous sources they did so with justification. Before it closed in the early 1520s the Korver press in nearby Zwolle may have accounted for quite a lot of the contentious literature that circulated at Kampen. With or without Korver, though, ideas and books came across the Ijsselmeer from Amsterdam. Moreover, Ijsselmeer towns—Hoorn, Enkhuizen, and Kampen—had commercial shipping links to Bremen, Hamburg, and other harbours in Germany and Denmark. Amsterdam was particularly important. Maritime trade brought ships and crews from Atlantic ports and the Baltic, and Amsterdam vessels carried much of the German grain upon which the Netherlands now depended. Moreover, while few Dutch towns experienced economic and demographic growth in the 1520s, Amsterdam was a notable exception. As it acquired a larger share of Holland's commerce, attendant employment opportunity attracted substantial numbers of immigrants. Though few seem to have come from Brabant or Flanders, poor urban artisans and their families arrived from

---

[87] *CD*, 5: no. 730.
[88] Blockmans and Heerma van Voss, "Urban networks," 15; L. Heerma van Voss, "North Sea Culture, 1500–1800," in *The North Sea and Culture (1550–1800)*, ed. J. Roding and L. Heerma van Voss (Hilversum, 1996), 26.

Leiden, Delft, and Haarlem, others from Groningen. Among them were religious nonconformists seeking both prosperity and a measure of tolerance. Undoubtedly some brought books. By decade's end artisans inclined towards Anabaptism would be at the forefront of radical nonconformity in Amsterdam, their New Jerusalem.[89] Long before then, advisors at Margaret's court complained that the town was soft on heretics, especially foreigners. But in meetings with Lord Hoochstraten representatives deflected the accusations, hastening to point out that they had pilloried a man from Bremen for insulting a couple of Franciscans. If in truth they were relatively patient with non-denizens, there were after all other considerations. Amsterdam's spokesmen dared not say as much, but in a thriving transit port that owed so much to international trade and shipping, to antagonise foreigners systematically or unnecessarily was to risk economic consequences. In this sense their situation was not unlike the one in Antwerp. In 1528 Amsterdam sought and received reassurance from the Court of Holland that legal rights of its citizens would not be violated in heresy prosecutions.[90]

Much as trade networks between Amsterdam and northern Germany were key to the circulation of books, they also facilitated the movement of human traffic, especially of exiles and disenchanted religious refugees. Many of the émigrés in Hamburg and Bremen were Netherlanders. Johann Pelt, who perhaps translated *Evangelie van Matthaeus* in 1522 and later escaped from Amsterdam, became a minister in Bremen and lived there until 1562. Hendrick van Zutphen's flight from Antwerp took him to Amsterdam and Enkhuizen and thence to Bremen.[91] Cornelis Woutersz.'s route was via Leiden, Amsterdam, and Kampen. He would not name anyone who gave him shelter along the way but by now the path to and through Holland was well worn. If displaced persons from the southern Low Countries were a common sight in the north, doubtless there was a network of sympathisers prepared to help them. And beyond Holland's northern frontier a traveller looking for temporary sanctuary among Lutherans would have been hard pressed not to find it. Of his excursions in Bremen and "dyuerse places of ffrice lande" the English adventurer Henry Burnett recalled that "thrugh all the contraye"

---

[89] Waite, *David Joris*, 33–37.
[90] *CD*, 5: nos. 586, 694, 714–15.
[91] *CD*, 4: nos. 110, 150; 5: no. 697; Den Hollander, *Bijbelvertalingen*, 40.

people ordered themselves according to Luther's opinions.[92] Transport corridors linking Holland with Friesland and Overijssel offered numerous travel possibilities. The short crossing from Enkhuizen to Stavoren placed travellers on the road to Leeuwarden and points east. Similarly, those who reached Kampen, whether by land or sea, also might continue overland the rest of the way. As well, from Holland or Brabant, northern Germany could be reached entirely by road, especially via Deventer and Osnabrück. Another alternative was travel by sea aboard a trading vessel. Conceivably, on their voyage from Amsterdam to Bremen, Burnett and his associates shared deck space with émigrés. From Amsterdam or an Ijsselmeer harbour passage to Hamburg or East Friesland was another possibility. Whether they came to East Friesland over water or land, refugees disinclined to chance onward travel through the archbishop of Bremen's territory made the short coastal voyage from Emden. Edzard I's tolerance made Emden in particular a sanctuary not only for the persecuted but for militants too. East Friesland's population now swelled with new arrivals, many of them attracted to iconoclastic radicalism. Circumstances favoured sectarian growth. Melchior Hoffman had already been to Emden in 1528, the year of the count's death. By March of 1530 Anabaptist congregations flourished alongside Lutheran. It would not be long before Hoffman's disciples—Melchiorites—were taking their message to Holland.[93]

The international distribution of contentious books printed in the Netherlands was not limited to scattering imprints in northern border regions and smuggling English-language consignments overseas. There were other vernacular markets for polemic and propaganda and for biblical texts, most especially Denmark and France. Antwerp's printing houses produced Danish-language imprints, and books from Germany found readers in Denmark as well. In border regions, where Low German was read and spoken, translations of the German reformers were unnecessary. The same held true for Scandinavian towns with German-speaking populations. This was a readership well served by the presses in Rostock, Hamburg, and Königsberg. A

---

[92] "Extracts from Lincoln Episcopal Visitations," 258.

[93] *Aus der Reformationsgeschichte Niedersachsens*, 23–24; Tracy, "Heresy Law," 290ff.; Waite, *David Joris*, 25, 55–59. For transportation routes see Bruns and Weckzerka, *Handelsstrassen*, 2: 367–91, 477–85, 510–12.

Danish New Testament was essential, though. The translation thought to be Pedersen's was printed at Antwerp in 1530. A wider range of evangelical literature followed. Vorsterman printed six Danish translations of Luther in 1531.[94] Antwerp imprints destined for Denmark could be carried by vessels bound for Husum or Hamburg, or placed in ships that would be obliged to stop at Helsingør *en route* to the Baltic. Importing books from German presses was likewise not difficult thanks to trade between Denmark and the Hanse ports.

An even larger market for Antwerp's printers was France. They issued a considerable quantity of evangelical material in French, especially in the later 1520s. Martin de Keyser had produced a French edition of Luther's *Betbüchlein*, while still in Paris. Within five years of his move to Antwerp in 1525 he printed at least six other Lutheran translations and many editions of French Bibles by Lefèvre.[95] These would reach France along the established trade arteries. Links between the Antwerp printers and the *libraires* of Paris were strong, whatever the state of Franco-Habsburg political relations, and France's capital remained vital to the diffusion network. The English scholar Robert Denham could buy books there that prelates in his own country would have proscribed as heretical. As everywhere else, print censorship in France was unsystematic. Yet compared to placards in the Low Countries the Sorbonne initiatives in 1525 were remarkably narrow. They applied to specific titles. Most condemnations stemmed from particular legal proceedings and emphasised new material produced in Paris. Clashes over Berquin and Lefèvre accentuated tension between the university theologians and the king, and led to some jurisdictional wrangling with the Paris *Parlement*. In all, however, the university and the *Parlement* did not ban a great corpus of French-language texts. The proscriptions were not reinforced strongly with royal decrees and trade corridors were not policed, so there was little need to smuggle or sell unlisted books covertly. Although much of it originated elsewhere, evangelical literature was available in Paris. Simon Du Bois, one of the few *libraires* to issue potentially controversial books, stuck mainly to spiritual rather than polemical works. Eventually even he moved on, setting up shop in 1529 at Alençon, within a duchy held by Marguerite, his royal

[94] Moeller, "Luther," 238.
[95] Higman, *Lire et Découvrir*, 108, 201.

patroness. Many of the key authors and translators immigrated too, primarily to eastern locales, functioning in Basel and Strasbourg much as their English counterparts did in Antwerp.[96]

Whilst numerous presses in the Low Countries and Germany accommodated dissenters and reformers, the market for devotional books and works by the supporters of orthodoxy remained substantial. Simply closing down the printing houses was therefore never a viable option for censors, regardless of their secular or ecclesiastical jurisdictions. This was especially true once doctrinal debates began to supersede anticlericalism. Doctrinaire positions of all kinds were necessarily articulated, advanced, attacked and defended in print. Opportunity beckoned the entrepreneur. The Ingolstadt bookseller Georg Krapff would soon become a publisher too, financing several German and Latin editions of Eck's works in the 1530s. Most of his printing was done in Augsburg.[97] And presses in other conformist strongholds continued to do well: Stöckel in Dresden and Quentell in Cologne. Booksellers brought Cologne imprints into northern Germany along the established Hanse trade routes. Others were distributed by way of the marts at Leipzig and Frankfurt. The Netherlands absorbed some as well, Latin editions in particular finding readers in Louvain and among the literate inhabitants of other urban centres. Latin texts, regardless of their origin and content, were reprinted frequently throughout the decade, indicating a broad international readership. While vernacular translations targeted the lay reader in a limited region, the obvious advantage of Latin was that it transcended ethno-linguistic boundaries. It was the language that carried all facets of religious debate across Europe, in a sense preparing the way for the introduction and regional distribution of vernacular books that challenged the old order.

Coercion and Betrayal

At the outset of the Richard Harman affair, John Hackett had cautioned "I percewe that the solicitasson of this trayttors and heretycks

---

[96] Higman, *Lire et Découvrir*, 107–24; A. Tricard, "La propagande évangélique en France: L'imprimeur Simon Du Bois (1525–1534)," in *Aspects de la propagande religieuse*, ed. G. Berthoud et al. (Geneva, 1957), 1–5; Greengrass, *French Reformation*, 12.

[97] *VD* E283, E289, E294, E304, E389, E390, E394, E396.

may not welbe don with owt spendyng large monne."[98] But the energies and resources of the English government had been consumed
by other concerns. As Wolsey grew increasingly desperate to achieve
it, the royal divorce superseded all other matters of foreign policy.
John Hackett and Richard Harman and Richard Akerston were players in a much smaller drama, scarcely visible against the backdrop
of the divorce scandal and the international political intrigue that
accompanied it. Convinced in his own mind of the grave threat
posed by the likes of Harman, England's ambassador laboured prodi-
giously without adequate resources or direction. He was hamstrung
by a policy that may have been half-hearted from the beginning,
became increasingly inconsistent, and was at times even incoherent.

Hackett despaired in the spring of 1529. Recently widowed, bank-
rupt, and deeply humiliated by his dealings with Antwerp and the
regency council, he offered to resign his ambassadorship. And while
he brooded, the lowly priest Richard Akerston, detained the previous summer at his request, languished in an Antwerp jail. He might
have been released long before, had not Hackett assumed responsibility for the costs of his confinement. Town authorities had no real
interest in him and the margrave was ready, even anxious to deliver
him upon receipt of the expenses. But Hackett was not compensated
regularly for his own expenditures, and despite repeated requests
many more months would pass before he received funds for Akerston's
keep. Already, though, the situation was taking its toll on the good-
will of his allies. Liere and Bouchout were unhappy because for all
their trouble they had not received so much as a token of appreci-
ation. England's ambassador had none to give. They would be "the
wours wyllynge to do us assistens a nother tyme" he predicted.[99] The
appeals for money and instructions continued but eleven months
after his arrest Akerston was still in custody.[100]

In April Hackett had gone to Antwerp with a royal writ com-
manding the return to England of William Cley. It was the consequence of a petition by another mercer, who alleged that Cley and
Calais Staple merchant Richard Dawnssy had made off with a large

---

[98] *LH*, no.75.
[99] *LH*, no. 114. Thereto: nos. 95, 103.
[100] *LH*, nos. 118, 125. Akerston's ultimate fate is uncertain, albeit eventually, in
July 1530, Hackett was reimbursed £22 8s for keeping him alive. *LP*, 5: 321.

quantity of expensive cloths from his London home. Friar John West, now pestering Wolsey for authorisation to resume the hunt for subversives in Antwerp, knew this story. He also claimed that Cley kept company with Richard Harman and was a Lutheran heretic. Whatever the truth on that count, Cley had recently become a *poorter*, thus acquiring, like Harman, the protection of the town.[101] But he was not uncooperative. By the 25th he was prepared to depart for England, leaving his business affairs in disarray in order to comply with the king's summons. Hackett put in a good word for him, adding that the Merchant Adventurers considered this imposition on one of their fellows to be a contravention of privilege. Cley himself carried the dispatch to England.[102] It was on this Antwerp visit that Hackett's unpleasant run-in with Harman occurred. He took no solace that otherwise his mission was successful. To salvage his honour and continue to follow the regency court he urgently required money. Later that summer, in August, the Ladies' Peace was concluded at Cambrai, ending hostilities between France and the Empire. Tunstall and More were there, representing England, and so was ambassador Hackett, grateful that the bishop was kind enough to lend him £20.[103]

Disheartened as Hackett was, Wolsey's predicament was by comparison far worse. He had no allies at court, where support for Scripture-based piety and sympathy for critics of the English clergy were on the rise, not least because of Anne Boleyn's influence. It may have been she who showed the king a copy of Simon Fish's relentlessly anticlerical *Supplicacyon*, published earlier that year. The arrogance and avarice of England's clergy undermined his authority and impoverished his subjects the pamphlet railed. So impressed was Henry that he extended royal protection to its author, even though More had penned a rebuttal. Fish, the erstwhile fugitive, already had returned to London. He came out of hiding and was reconciled with his king, though not with More, when he fell ill and died sometime the following year.[104]

---

[101] O. de Smedt, *De Engelse Natie te Antwerpen in de 16e Eeuw* (Antwerp, 1950), 2: 612.

[102] *LH*, nos. 109, 111, 113, 114. The suit against Cley dated to 1526. John Powel alleged that Cley and others removed £2,400 worth of goods from his London house and shop while he was abroad, because of a debt he supposedly owed to one Thomas Hynde. *LP*, Addenda, 1: no. 497.

[103] *LH*, no. 133.

[104] S.W. Haas, "Simon Fish, William Tyndale, and Thomas More's 'Lutheran

The legatine court did not solve Henry's marital dilemma. Campaggio recessed it for the summer in late July; it never reconvened. Wolsey's dismissal from political office came little more than two months later. On 3 November a new Lord Chancellor, Sir Thomas More, opened the first session of what has since come to be known as the Reformation Parliament. Following his attainder Wolsey was restored to the archbishopric of York. By spring following Tunstall had been translated north to Durham, replaced in London by Wolsey's former almoner, John Stokesley. With this veritable changing of the guard, the conservative bishops Stokesley and Nix asserted themselves in the prosecution of heretics. And they could count on More's full support. To try or condemn suspects was not his legal prerogative, but he was obliged by statute to assist the churchmen. He was far more diligent and thorough than his predecessor was when it came to initiating investigations, issuing writs for arrests, and interrogating suspects. His elevation, coincidental with related developments, thus marks a departure from the status quo of the 1520s: the end of a distinctive phase, the beginning of another.

Amplifying the transition was a royal proclamation in the summer of 1530 specifically against owning and distributing books of heresy. More undoubtedly helped draft it. England now had its first index of prohibited books, all of them "worthy to be damned and put in perpetual oblivion".[105] *Obedience, Wicked Mammon*, Fish's *Supplicacyon* and John Frith's *Revelation of Antichrist* were proscribed together with "divers other books made in the English tongue, and imprinted beyond the sea". So too was all material issued abroad in French and German from which derived the errors. The king acknowledged that many among the common people wanted the Bible in their own tongue, but the prelates had told him this was unnecessary. Nevertheless, if his loyal subjects rejected the heresies and seditious opinions in the versions currently circulating he would permit an authorised translation. In the meantime, all illegal English Bibles were to be handed over to diocesan officials.

Conspiracy'," *Journal of Ecclesiastical History* 23 (1972), 125–36. Simon Fish, *A Supplicacyon for the Beggers*, ed. F.J. Furnivall, Early English Text Society, extra series, 13 (1871), v–xiv, 1–18.

[105] *Tudor Royal Proclamations*, 1: 193–97; *STC* 7775; *LP*, 4/3: no. 6487; Hall, *Chronicle*, 771. In October Richard Berthelet received payment for printing 1,600 papers and books of proclamation regarding vagabonds, beggars and "dampnyng of books containing certain errors". His rate was a penny per page. *LP*, 5: 322.

In *The confutacyon of Tyndales answere*, published in 1532 shortly after he resigned the chancellorship, More speaks of enforcing the decree.[106] He personally interviewed suspected book agents and was very proficient at getting them to talk. The arrests and abjurations, most during 1531, point not only to a reconstituted network of book-runners but also to a branch extending west of the capital. More claimed various heretics informed him about Richard Webb of Bristol, who distributed prohibited material there. Were contraband books entering England though this port as well, perhaps? Its maritime trade was not insignificant. When Thomas Garrett fled Oxford in 1528 he headed for Bristol, not London, and very nearly made it that far before he was recaptured. Conceivably, Bristol was home to sympathetic Brethren already then. Honest townsmen said that heretical books were sometimes scattered in the streets there or left at night on doorsteps: poison not sold was simply given away, as More put it. Of Webb's finances nothing is known, however this peculiar approach to dissemination raises the possibility that other persons besides him were behind it and prepared to absorb the costs. Regardless, when he was not giving away banned books he was buying and selling them, proof positive that the distribution now stretched not only to East Anglia, Kent, and London, but also to the West Country.

When his arrest warrant reached Bristol, Webb posted bond. Perhaps deluding himself that he could bluff his way through an interview with More, he came to London on his own, though not directly to the chancellor. His first call was on Robert Necton. It was a visit likely tinged with considerable anxiety about how much More might already know and whether Necton had divulged anything. Or, as More mused, Webb wanted to ensure that his friend would corroborate his testimony. Immediately after they had conferred, though, Necton for some reason grew uneasy and feared betrayal. He panicked, immediately sending word of the meeting to More. And so, unaware of this, the trafficker from Bristol was easily trapped in a tangle of denials and lies when questioned the following day. But he was also at pains to explain why he had been in London six weeks before, meeting with a priest called Nicholas

---

[106] *CW*, 8/2: 814–16.

and allegedly trying to sell him books. Possibly someone else had betrayed the cleric; perhaps the chancellor's spies had shadowed him. More says only that he knew about the rendezvous. And he had already interrogated bookbinder Michael Lobley, who handed over a cache of prohibited imprints that he claimed came from Webb. Lobley brought books from Antwerp as well. He was one of two binders apprehended and abjured in 1531, the other being John Rowe. The arrests do not appear to have resulted from targeted or even random searches. Lobley worked for the stationer Henry Pepwell, who co-operated with Stokesley. In at least some cases the chancellor and the bishop acted on leads from informants in the stationers' quarter. In addition, certain individual suspects may have been under surveillance. More knew, for example, that the priest Nicholas had met Webb in Holborne, and that Necton lived in St. Katherine's. It is also possible that in addition to the chancellor's henchmen local authorities aided the investigations. Whereas the earlier proclamation required justices to take suspects to bishops, the new one instructed mayors, sheriffs, and bailiffs to bring them before the Privy Council, there to be "corrected and punished for their contempt and disobedience, to the terrible example of other like transgressors".[107] The next step for many was examination by the spiritual authorities for doctrinal heterodoxy.

With the resources of the central government at his disposal, Thomas More created and managed something similar to an inquisition. People were detained and questioned. Nervous and frightened prisoners divulged the names of acquaintances and accomplices. Arrest writs were issued. Subsequent interrogations brought more denunciations. Probably in this way John Rowe, Christopher Ruremund, and George Constantine were detected. With his previous record as a book trafficker and participant in secret conventicles, Necton could hardly hope to be spared if denounced again. His betrayal of Webb was a desperate move to ingratiate himself with the chancellor and deflect suspicion. Ultimately, though, it was not Richard Webb who sealed Necton's fate. That dubious distinction fell to George Constantine.

Constantine was now a *poorter* of Antwerp. So long as he stayed there and behaved himself, he was beyond the reach of English

---

[107] *Tudor Royal Proclamations*, 1: 195.

authorities. Moreover, he had even secured a royal pardon. But that did not deter him from buying and selling books. Nor did he remain in the Low Countries. By October 1531 he too had fallen into More's clutches. Quite rightly he feared for his life, and was prepared to expose his accomplices in hopes of saving it. One was pitiable Necton, "by Constantynes deteccyon taken and commytted to Newgate where except he happe to dye byfore in pryson, he standeth in grete paryll to be ere it be long, for hys fallynge agayne to Tindales heresyes burned".[108] Constantine knew that to name Necton was to condemn him. How much coaxing he required can only be speculated. More emphatically denied that he ever mistreated prisoners.[109] Nevertheless some of them, to use his turn of phrase, happened to die while in custody. Constantine was restrained in stocks yet somehow escaped, though not before putting others at risk. He "studyed and deuysed how those deuelysshe bokes whyche hym selfe and other of hys felowes hadde brought and shypped, myghte come to the bysshoppes handes to be burned. And therefore he shewed me the shypmannes name that had them, and the markes of the ferdellys, by whych I haue synnys hys escape receyued them".[110] So at least one consignment never reached the Brethren. Still more books were seized when Richard Bayfield was taken. Like Constantine, apparently, he had sued for remission and was pardoned by the king for his earlier mistake, yet continued to bring printed heresies into England.[111] Stokesley and Gardiner examined him in November 1531 and at some point so did More, still looking to ensnare other collaborators. He must have enquired about William Roye and was told that he had been burned in Portugal, a story that has never been verified.[112] Bayfield was sent to the stake in early December. Several others besides

---

[108] *CW*, 8/1: 18. Whilst in custody, Constantine wrote to Necton advising him to turn in his stock of books. Necton apparently conferred with John Byrte alias Adrian alias John the bookbinder—one of Garrett's old cohorts from Oxford. They decided against the idea, agreeing to say instead that the books were already sold. Byrte replied to Constantine on Necton's behalf but of course More intercepted his letter. Unsure how far Constantine had gone with his confession, Byrte tried to persuade him to retract "yf ye haue not spoken so farre in the mater that it maye be none preiudyall or hurte vnto you". *Ibid.*, 19. The earlier episode involving Necton and Webb must have occurred prior to this, perhaps in the summer of 1531.

[109] *CW*, 9: 118–19.
[110] *CW*, 8/1: 20.
[111] *CW*, 8/1: 17.
[112] *CW*, 8/1: 8.

Necton died in gaol: Petit, Somer, and a Dutchman of Antwerp named Christopher.

The intent of the proclamation in 1530 was comparable to that of the emperor's earlier placards in the Low Countries. And on the face of it, rigorous enforcement brought results. Colporteurs were removed from the network, some permanently. Books were seized and destroyed. Why was ecclesiastical censorship not backed up much earlier with a royal directive? A book ban enforced as both Church law and the law of the land presumably would have circumvented the usual complaints of ecclesiastical courts trampling the rights of the laity. Yet not until 1529 was book censorship included in a royal proclamation. And even then, it was markedly unspecific and lumped together with a general call for observance of anti-heresy statutes. What prevented Wolsey from prevailing upon the king to regulate importation and possession, and thus curb the likes of Necton, Lome, and Bayfield? Unlike the man who replaced him, Wolsey rarely invoked the prerogative of Star Chamber—the king's council—to become involved in heresy cases. More did not hesitate to do so systematically while enforcing the proclamation against book-running, at the same time defending *ex officio* proceedings by the churchmen. Officers in his charge arrested suspects, and when he was finished with them they were turned over to the ordinaries.[113] He was a steadfast defender of conformity, committed to the eradication of its enemies. Wolsey was, quite simply, much less interested. His concerns about heretics evidently not extending much beyond their potential to subvert social order, he for the most part left the prosecuting to Fisher, Tunstall, and Warham. That Oxford and Cambridge students read the Scriptures in English apparently did not distress him much, only that some of them were indiscreet enough to be caught. So until the exiles began attacking the English clergy in print it was enough that a few Steelyard merchants performed symbolic penance and England's ambassador did his best to destroy English Testaments in the Low Countries.

The hunt for Tyndale, Roye and Richard Harman came on the heels of the *magna abjurata*, but also in the wake of *Rede Me*, Roye

---

[113] *CW*, 9: 11, 129–35. This continued after More resigned. John Frith was arrested in July 1532 and brought to the Tower by Crown officers at the commandment of the king and his council. More did not doubt that eventually he would be "delyvered vnto the ordynary". *Ibid.*, 89.

and Barlowe's scathing vilification of Wolsey and his bishops. Up to this point Wolsey's approach brought uneven and sometimes superficial results, but was sufficient to keep Lollards in check and indulge the papacy while he concentrated on grander foreign policy schemes and patronage of the universities. It was not enough, though, to silence the exiles on the continent or stop distribution of their books in England. Thomas More would endeavour to change that, but by the time he assumed the responsibilities of chancellor the odds for success were already long indeed.

Exiles

Within the cluster of English exiles now in Antwerp was George Joye, once part of the Cambridge circle that included Bilney, Arthur, Frith, Coverdale, and Barnes. Longland was informed that Joye's opinions might be questionable, and so in November 1527 he was summoned to London in connection with the trials of Bilney and Arthur. Mulling over options while awaiting his interview, Joye decided to leave the country. Possibly he went to Strasbourg before settling in Antwerp and trying his hand at translating. An English primer that was on the proscription index in the spring of 1530 was likely his work. No copy survives, but Martin de Keyser printed a revised edition later that summer titled *Hortulus Animae*, its calendar omitting errors that the bishops had criticised. Obviously aware that he was reaching readers, Joye also was mindful of their response. Some months prior to this, De Keyser had also printed an English Psalter ascribed to Joye, who used the pseudonym "Francis Foxe" in his preface. The colophon was also falsified. Next came a translation of the prophet Isaiah, issued in May 1531.[114]

While Joye created his niche in Antwerp as a translator of Scriptures and devotional books, Tyndale was now occupied primarily with translations of Luther. Despite his professed intention to do so, eight years passed before he published a corrected version of his New Testament translation. Martin de Keyser issued it in November 1534. However, by then four pirate editions had been produced, the last one altered by Joye. Tyndale's attempt to distance himself from the

---

[114] Butterworth and Chester, *George Joye*, 40–69.

changes came in an indignant blast in the prologue of his revised edition. Joye then responded in kind, publishing *An Apologye made by George Joye to satisfye, if it maye be, W. Tindale.* This clash of egos occurred some years after the period under discussion here. *An Apologye* is illuminating, nevertheless, because in it Joye speaks in some detail of the earlier printings.[115]

By early summer 1534 the Ruremund press had sold or otherwise parted with all five thousand English Testaments it had issued to that point. Another printing was in preparation. Many errors had crept in already, not least because the second edition, thought to have been printed in 1529 or 1530, required a completely new set-up; it was printed "in a greatter letter and volume" than the first.[116] The intention now was to return to the smaller format. Yet the press still had no Englishman to correct the setting. Tyndale was approached but would not commit to the task, so the printers turned to Joye. Apparently believing that Tyndale would soon get around to it, he too declined. He also warned that once Tyndale's corrected rendering became available there would be no market for imperfect printings. The Ruremunds printed them anyway, evidently chock-a-block with typographic errors. Error-ridden or not, there was a market for English New Testaments; all two thousand copies were quickly sold. Joye claimed he was in the dark about Tyndale's intentions when approached again to proof-read and correct the typography for yet another press run. But he could see that the printers intended to go ahead in any event, unconcerned about selling faulty copies even if Tyndale issued his own amended version. Should he print two thousand "and we as many" they said, "what is so litle a noumber for all englond? And we wil sel ours beter cheape and therfore we doubt not of the sale".[117] Given the alternative of more flawed copies reaching English readers, Joye decided to correct the typography and while he was at it to take liberties with Tyndale's translation.

The episode is noteworthy for a number of reasons. First of all, the printing house approached and offered to pay the translator/cor-

---

[115] *An Apology made by George Joy*, ed. E. Arber, 20–23; *STC* 14820.

[116] *Ibid.*, 20; Kronenberg, *Verboden Boeken*, 103; *NK* 0172.

[117] *An Apology*, 21. That Joye did not know Tyndale had in fact begun revisions is scarcely possible, since Martin de Keyser printed for both of them. In the prologue to his revised edition, Tyndale says he was informed that Joye was correcting at the same time he was, although he did not deign to look at a sample of Joye's work. *Ibid.*, ix.

rector. This was another business venture. Over and above the cost of materials and labour, the Ruremund press was prepared to invest in improving the copy. Joye negotiated his rate before starting and eventually took the equivalent of nine pence for every two sheets containing sixteen leaves. He therefore found absurd Tyndale's accusation that he was covetous, pointing to payment totalling only a few shillings, and hearsay that Tyndale's fee for his revised edition was £10. Regardless of the sums that may have changed hands, what is absent here is any mention of a third party contributing to publication costs. Both Catharyn Ruremund and Martin de Keyser were printing for profit; payments to Joye and Tyndale were simply factored into production expenses.

Presumably, had Tyndale been as concerned about misprints in the pirate editions as he later was about Joye's vocabulary, he would have acted on the printer's request to correct them. Possibly he had been asked to do this before the earlier, larger-format edition went to press. He did not consider revisions to be a matter of urgency either, content that eight years on his remained the definitive English translation. Tyndale had left his homeland determined to give its people the Scriptures in their own language. Yet he is not known to have expressed any opinion about the number of English Testaments subsequently printed for circulation or to have taken any proactive step to increase it. Perhaps he chose not to be informed about dissemination and sundry circumstances on which it hinged. Antwerp's printers, by contrast, were closely connected to the marketplace. They also monitored the winds of political change. Thomas More had succeeded in eliminating some of the book-runners, but his time had passed. In Joye's words, "for now was ther geuen . . . a lytel space to breath and reste vnto christis chirche aftir so longe and greuouse persecucion for reading the bokes".[118] In More's resignation and the king's ever-widening rift with Rome, the Ruremunds sensed an opportunity and seized it. Their reassessment of potential consumer demand for English Testaments was right. The market for pirate editions did not vanish with the publication in November 1534 of Tyndale's revised and corrected translation. Only two months later the Ruremund press again reissued the one altered by Joye.[119]

---

[118] *An Apology*, 21.
[119] From Joye's address to the reader in the January 1535 edition (*NK* 2490) we

(5) *Processionale ad usum Sarum*
    Christopher Ruremund (Eindhoven), Antwerp, 1528
    (*STC* 16237) By kind permission of the British Library

The Ruremunds were astute business people who, after experimenting with the larger setting, reverted to a sextodecimo format for all subsequent printings of English Testaments. There had to be a sound basis for this strategy too. Obviously, costs were taken into account. If these books were going to be inexpensive to buy then they had to be cheap to print. Consumer preference may have been a factor as well. Also, the Ruremunds had a great deal of experience printing Dutch translations in this size. Most of the twenty-three Dutch New Testament editions printed up to 1529 were indeed octavo but the three offered by Christopher Ruremund were not. Nor was the Old Testament that Hans Ruremund printed for Peter Kaetz. Small Ruremund tomes could be carried without much difficulty on one's person and were easier to conceal than larger books, if need arose, or to smuggle. The quick sale of all copies from the two English New Testament printings in 1534 suggests the format was both popular and economical. It also raises the possibility that print runs were actually commissioned by English distributors, ready to take delivery. But if there were anonymous sponsors, they were remarkably undiscerning about the typographical errors. Their assistance did not extend to providing a proof-reader.[120]

Four or five years had elapsed since the second pirate edition. During this interval the range of possibilities had grown for Antwerp printers interested in issuing English books. There was a corpus of

---

know that in the aftermath of the August printing (*NK* 2485) the two translators discussed their differences. Joye says they agreed to collaborate on an introduction to Tyndale's new version so as to alleviate controversy over Joye's "englisshyng" of the text. But instead Tyndale prefaced his November edition (*NK* 2487) with a caustic critique of Joye and his altered translation.

[120] Tyndale's prologue does not acknowledge the first of the pirate printings in 1534, which neither he nor Joye corrected. Regarding the timing of subsequent publications he is inconsistent: the printing of his revised translation was "almost fynesshed" when Joye's appeared, yet the latter's corrected text "was prynted in great nombre yer myne beganne". *An Apology*, ix. Although Tyndale's original translation was itself unauthorised and published anonymously at Worms, he was greatly offended that Joye did not affix his own name to the adulterated version and thereby take responsibility for it. This indignation seems to be shared by his most recent biographer, Daniell, *William Tyndale*, 316–25, who finds Joye's apology "self-justifying" and "tendentious and intemperate", and also scorns the Ruremund imprints as "inhibitingly chunky, even clumsy". We do not know if Tyndale or anyone else found them so. Joye's biographers judge the one surviving copy, now in the British Library, to be "a handsome sextodecimo". Butterworth and Chester, *George Joye*, 153.

polemic and propaganda by Tyndale, Fish, and Frith, largely based on translations of Luther. For the time being perhaps, the vernacular Testament was not the best choice for quick commercial success. Moreover, contentious material or English books in particular did not preoccupy Antwerp's printing houses. They issued diverse other titles as well, in Latin, French, and Dutch, on many subjects. Another plausible explanation for the self-imposed hiatus in English New Testament printing is that in 1531 several of the book traffickers were detained in England and some of them permanently eliminated. It may have taken time for the distribution web to rebuild and reorganise. The other earlier break had come after the first pirate edition, lasting for about three years, until the experiment with the larger format. Here too the gap between printings coincided with disruption of the smuggling network, a setback that could have stalled any immediate plans to issue more Testaments. For part of this period, prior to *Wicked Mammon*, there was really nothing else available for reissue in English except Roye's *A Brefe Dialoge*. Also, the Ruremunds, though undeterred in the long run, may have been discouraged temporarily by Antwerp's law against English Testaments. Yet well before the arrests of Necton and Richard Harman, Hans Ruremund was in London with hundreds to sell. A year after the first printing he still had plenty of inventory. A reasonable conclusion might be that Tyndale's English translation was not an immediate 'best seller' after all. The story of the pirate editions does not leave the impression that England was inundated with vernacular Testaments in the later 1520s. Taking into account that copies were seized and burned at various times and places, considerably fewer than six thousand were in circulation by the end of the decade.

The Ruremunds took the investment risks, not to mention the legal ones, when they printed the Scriptures in English and they necessarily reaped any financial rewards. Scarcely credible, then, is the famous story in Edward Hall's chronicle that sale of an entire press run in 1529 worked to Tyndale's benefit and effectively paid for the printing of his revised edition. When Tunstall and More returned from Cambrai in August via Antwerp, the bishop is supposed to have enquired about buying vernacular Testaments, so they could be destroyed. Enter Augustine Packington, mercer, who claimed to know "Dutche men and straungiers" with English Testaments to sell—inventory obtained from Tyndale himself. Tunstall gladly accepted the merchant's offer to buy up the imprints, whereupon Packington, so the story goes, took the payment directly to Tyndale, now a destitute, debt-ridden refugee, possessing a "hepe" of Testaments for which he had found no other buyer. That they would be burned did not bother him, because he could now settle debts and fund a corrected edition. And so it was that the bishop acquired the imprints, Tyndale had the money, and "when mo newe Testamentes were Imprinted, they came thicke and threfold into England".[121] The perfect irony makes for a good yarn, but nothing more. It asks us to believe that Packington, so willing to aid Tyndale by arranging the sale of his Testaments, had in the meantime allowed him to whither in abject poverty, and that taking the imprints off Tyndale's hands was predicated on Tunstall's offer. Notwithstanding that Tyndale was not in Antwerp but Hamburg at the time, it would be another five years before he produced a revised translation. And for that, according to Joye, he was compensated generously by his printer, Martin de Keyser. Moreover, nothing suggests he was at all involved with any of the pirate printings up to 1534. They were initiatives of the Ruremund press. Unaccounted for, though, is the larger—that is to say octavo—edition supposedly printed at about this time, of which no copy remains. Could Packington have bought the entire inventory and then resold it to Tunstall, perhaps passing along some of his profit to Tyndale? If so, what an altogether fortuitous coincidence that after a three-year interlude the press had just issued another edition and the imprints were there for the taking. Alternatively, following his meeting with Tunstall, might Packington have shown enough money to the Ruremunds for them to hastily set up a printing, all the while ensuring that he and Tyndale would come out ahead when the books were turned over to the bishop?

While so little is certain and no trace remains of this second pirate printing of Tyndale's New Testament, how his own original edition reached England has never been resolved satisfactorily either. On the run from Cologne, Tyndale and Roye are thought to have arrived in Worms sometime in the fall of 1525. Neither of them had been there before, so far as is known. Their sojourn was unplanned. Yet by early in the New Year the translation was completed and printed

---

[121] Hall, *Chronicle*, 762–63. Hall has Constantine later informing More that by purchasing imprints the bishop of London alone sustained the exiles. Fox retells the story in *Acts and Monuments*, 4: 670–71.

in full. The edition is commonly attributed to Peter Schöfer.[122] Did he print it on speculation? Hackett was told that two thousand copies, which must have constituted a huge portion of the Worms press run, had made it no farther than Frankfurt by the autumn of 1526, several months after they were printed. We can not be sure he was correctly informed. If true, though, it is all the less likely that the Christian Brethren organised and financed the publication. Had they been actively involved from the outset, in all likelihood Tyndale would have been directed to Richard Harman and printers in Antwerp. As it turned out, the imprints had to be brought to England from Worms. To whom they belonged when they reached Frankfurt, and who arranged their onward transport, remains unsolved.

As well, unanswered questions persist regarding books printed in English at Strasbourg. It is doubtful that the Brethren funded Roye's *A Brefe Dialoge*. In this instance too, a great many copies remained unsold and available at the Frankfurt mart a year after they had come off the press. Furthermore, it is quite clear that they were still owned by the printer. Hermann Rinck purchased and destroyed them, together with most copies of *Rede Me*, which was also issued many months before. Certainly *A Brefe Dialoge* and perhaps both books had been ready in time for the spring fair at Frankfurt in 1528. It might be expected that a project underwritten by a clandestine organisation of people schooled in commerce would include a plan for distribution, or at least for conveyance to England, but here again the sequence does not suggest one. On the other hand, it is puzzling that Johann Schott should print *Rede Me* at his own expense early in 1528 if he had not been able to dispose of *A Brefe Dialoge*, issued the previous August. William Roye's untold story is likely to remain so, since he was not caught and prosecuted in England. Perhaps, like the other exiles, he spent some time in the Netherlands. An English version of Luther's commentary on Paul's Epistle to Corinthians, which appeared in June 1529, is attributed to him. The false colophon says Hans Luft of Marburg was the

---

[122] Mozley, *William Tyndale*, 66, speculated that two printers worked simultaneously on the Worms edition "and for the last six or seven weeks a third was added" yet conceded "of the printing at Worms we know nothing whatever". E. Arber suggested two printers: Peter Schöfer and Hans van Erfurt. *ENT*, 27.

printer. There is no question, however, that it came from an Antwerp press, either Michiel Hillen van Hoochstraten's or Martin de Keyser's.[123]

With the likely exception of influential apologists such as Eck in Ingolstadt, and celebrity reform theologians in Wittenberg, it remained largely up to an author or translator to approach a publisher or printer with new material. Interested benefactors, including merchants, may have backed some ventures but otherwise a printing house or publisher had to believe there was commercial potential. By the late 1520s, though, Martin de Keyser and other Antwerp printers—Ruremund, Grapheus, and Michiel Hillen van Hoochstraten—probably required little persuading to issue work by Tyndale and the English exiles. And soon, if not already, they would be willing to pay for revised and corrected texts. By extension, once their infamy was established and an attendant consumer interest created, the outlawed authors may have been paid for polemical tracts. Individuals not already connected to some facet of typography, merchants dealing in other wares for example, were not greatly involved at this stage. More likely was some later role in distribution, albeit even then the investment may have been as much emotional as entrepreneurial. If this typically applied to the work of learned polemicists and translators we must suppose, on the other hand, that composers of anonymous libels paid their printers. Local or regional distribution was also up to them. The press was engaged simply to provide a technical service. The same perhaps was true of most first-run vernacular pamphlets authored by ordinary laypersons. The initiative came from people who felt they had something to say and were prepared to incur the costs. A printing house already in receipt of payment might be quite unconcerned with sales and circulation. Virtually any press could, however, reissue a *Flugschrift* that had achieved popular acclaim or, as in Ruremund's case, a vernacular Scripture book, at which point the original motivation of the author or translator would be substantially if not entirely superseded by the prospect of commercial success.

---

[123] Clebsch, "Earliest Translations," 79–86; *STC* 10493. Another English imprint by Hans Luft (sic. Hoochstraten or De Keyser) in 1529 and again in 1530 combined an original prose dialogue with an old Lollard tract against clerical wealth. D.H. Parker suggests it was the work of Roye and Barlowe. *A proper dyaloge betwene a Gentillman and an Husbandman*, ed. D.H. Parker (Toronto, 1996), 22–50. Valkema Blouw, "Early Protestant publications," 105–7, attributes the printing to Martin de Keyser.

Libels aside, controversial English-language imprints in the 1520s consisted not of pamphlets but of longer tracts and Scripture translations. They were issued at Worms, Strasbourg, and above all at Antwerp. Large inventories of some of them remained unsold and available long after publication. Meanwhile, countless German titles were reprinted repeatedly. Again, wholesaling appears to have been essentially the business of printers and publishers, and so too decisions on reissues, pirate editions, and translations of works originally offered by competitors. Publishers and printers, much more so than merchants, underwrote heretical books, just as they did non-heretical ones. Such was the case before Luther and so it remained. Religious controversy did, however, stimulate immeasurably the growth of the printing industry, from which a relatively new and specialised branch of commerce naturally developed. Within the broader mercantile system publishers and typographers exploited opportunities and flourished as never before. The direct result was a proliferation of presses and the ascendancy of formidable sixteenth-century publishing houses. Not all of them survived, but the successful dissemination of vernacular Bible texts and propaganda in the 1520s, which took many parts of Reformation Europe to the confessional stage, would have been difficult without them. Nor could it have been accomplished without the interregional trade networks that were already in place.

The distribution system for illegal English books was not unmasked by spies in Frankfurt or an ambassador in Antwerp, but by interrogations close to home. Even the Calais and Paris connections came to light as the result of searches for a suspect named in the *magna abjurata*. At this critical stage, though, if there ever was an impetus to exploit the advantage and dismantle the network it was overtaken by other developments. Failure of the royal marriage strained Anglo-Habsburg relations and subsequent sabre-rattling led directly to interruption of commerce with the Netherlands. The suffering and disaffection this caused within production and export sectors was then compounded by epidemic and famine. England's king had enough crises to worry about, without taking initiatives against Lollards and Lutherans. Ultimately then, the ordinaries were left to interpret and enforce their own rules. And as a consequence, indicted book traffickers, so long as they recanted their heresies and the state did not intervene, stood an excellent chance of regaining their liberty and resuming their commerce.

Secular courts in the Netherlands, both local and regional, had imperial edicts to enforce. Penalties for issuing and disseminating proscribed titles were clearly spelled out. Implementation was modified, however, by a tradition of judicial discretion rooted in civic and provincial autonomy. Moreover, experience had shown that increasingly extensive censorship risked the inadvertent and counterproductive consequence of silencing allies as well as enemies of Roman Catholicism. And public book fires drew attention to nonconformity, possibly invoking as much curiosity and resentment as fear. While generally stopping short of what the Habsburg placards required, the repression of religious deviance in the Low Counties and in some parts of the Empire created exiles and refugees. Potentially subversive disorder was countered with expulsion of agitators. But intolerance in some locales and sectarian coalescence in others also caused persons to relocate. Their journeys doubtless contributed to even wider dissemination of print. Carrying books from one town or region to the next, émigrés supplemented commercial distribution, especially in Germany and the Netherlands.

Mechanisms for the regulation and control of book production and distribution had not changed significantly. Tactical adjustments by secular authorities in 1529 essentially promised more coercion. Already though, important reform authors and translators had moved to major typographic centres such as Antwerp, Strasbourg, and Basel. Regional cultural integration assisted their relocation, and economic integration ensured wider transmission of their printed works. Jurisdictional boundaries within the regions rendered comprehensive suppression impossible. As crucial as the scholars were the printing houses and publishers. Although the road ahead would be far from easy, by the end of the 1520s they had ostensibly survived the best efforts of princes and bishops to stop them from contributing vitally to the evangelical movement's eventual success.

EPILOGUE

William Tyndale is thought to have spent most of the later 1520s in the southern Low Countries, especially Antwerp. There he was close to printing houses and his anonymous patrons; inconspicuous and relatively safe in a large town accustomed to foreigners. But Fox has him taking ship for Hamburg in late 1528 and staying there for the better part of a year. Tyndale would have had any number of reasons to do this. The controversy over Richard Harman was at its height; Hackett eventually accused him of harbouring the outlaw. Perhaps Tyndale or his benefactors felt he would be safer in Hamburg until the danger abated. Also, through his Lutheran contacts he certainly would know that evangelicals had made a crucial breakthrough there. He may have wanted to observe their success firsthand. March elections had added more Lutherans to the civic government. Some, not surprisingly, also had English connections. Henrich Hesterberch, now part of the municipal council, belonged to the *Englandfahrer* merchant fraternity. The Hesterberchs had been in the London trade for two decades at least. So had one of the new overseers of the town's churches, Lutke Burinck. Another, Henrich Luchtemacher, still divided his time between Hamburg and London, leaving his son in charge of business at the Steelyard when he was not there.[1] On 18 April there had been a town hall disputation between reform theologians and the Catholic clergy and Dominicans, its outcome a clear signal that Hamburg would officially embrace Lutheran doctrine. Georg Richolff had recently returned from Stockholm and was printing the works of Bugenhagen and Luther. Hamburg had also prevailed upon Bugenhagen himself to come in early October. He remained until the following summer, drafting the town's new church order.[2] It may have been in Hamburg, then, that he met and befriended Robert Barnes, who recently had fled England. Later,

---

[1] Postel, *Die Reformation in Hamburg*, 289–91; Reincke, *Hamburg*, 113; *Hanserecesse*, 3rd series, 7: no. 203#20; TNA:PRO C 1/653/44, 1/653/45 and E 122/82/9, 122/83/4.

[2] Postel, *Die Reformation in Hamburg*, 314–17; Beckey, *Die Reformation in Hamburg*, 90–114; 124–43; *VD* B9471; *NB*, nos. 974, 975, 994.

Barnes would be Bugenhagen's guest in Wittenberg. Another English activist, Miles Coverdale, was also in Hamburg in 1529. He and Tyndale stayed at widow Emersen's house until December, when Tyndale returned to Antwerp.[3]

The developments at Hamburg are fairly indicative of Lutheranism's reception in the north. Even in Lübeck popular support for change was building, not least because of a new proliferation of controversial literature. Imprints from Hamburg, Rostock, and Magdeburg were easy to come by. Erfurt and Wittenberg printing houses also contributed publications in the northern dialect.[4] Lübeck printers Hans Arndes and Johann Balhorn were busy in 1527–28 issuing some of Luther's letters as well as Erasmus's *Gesprächsbüchlein* and *Hyperaspistes*, works that were not pro-Lutheran.[5] And trade still took Lübeckers to many ports where the new doctrine had taken hold, placing them among "brokers" of ideas in ports like Riga, Stockholm, and Königsberg, as well as the closer Wendish towns of the Hanse: Hamburg, Rostock, and Stralsund. Regulation of the commerce in books and ideas was ineffective, although Lübeck's magistrates and the cathedral dean forbade people from travelling to nearby evangelical strongholds—Oldesloe in Holstein and Wismar in Mecklenburg—to hear Lutheran sermons. They also tried to persuade Norway's *Reichsrat* to suppress such preaching in Bergen, where Hanse merchants managed the Norwegian fishery, and went so far as to fine one of Lübeck's *Bergenfahrer* for ignoring fast days during a homeward voyage. Nor were provocative outsiders welcome. Melchior Hoffman had been banished long since, and when Robert Barnes visited in 1529 he was ordered to leave.[6] By the end of 1530, though, the old regime's opposition was substantially overcome. Soon Balhorn would be printing Lübeck's new church order composed by Bugenhagen.[7]

Melchior Hoffman, expelled from Livonia, Sweden, and most recently Lübeck, had gone to Kiel and received a letter of protection from Frederick I. With equipment possibly acquired in Lübeck

---

[3] Mozley, *William Tyndale*, 152–53. N.S. Tjernagel says before moving on to Wittenberg, Barnes spent some months in Hamburg assisting Lutheran pastor Johann Aepinus. Barnes, *Reformation Essays*, 12.
[4] *NB*, nos. 955–1015.
[5] *VD* E2456, E3036, D2841, L3778.
[6] Jannasch, *Reformationsgeschichte*, 249–55, 262–63.
[7] *NB*, no. 1085; Beckey, *Die Reformation in Hamburg*, 142–43.

he then set up a printing press. It was a one-man operation; perhaps Richolff had passed along some rudimentary technical knowledge in Stockholm. By this point Hoffman could also count Luther
among those he had alienated. In spring 1528 he began to issue
pamphlets defending himself against Lutheran opponents: Bugenhagen,
Melanchthon, Marquard Schuldorpe, and Nicholas Amsdorf, whose
criticisms of his eschatological views were printed in German at
Hamburg and Rostock. The feuding culminated with a formal disputation at Flensburg in April 1529, pitting Hoffman against the
reform theologians of Holstein. Although his views on the sacraments
were at issue, equally contentious was his criticism of the Lutheran
ministers and Kiel's magistrates. It was they who now turned the
tools of censorship on an outspoken critic. In the aftermath of the
Flensburg disputation Hoffman's printing equipment was confiscated.
The Richolff press issued Bugenhagen's version of the proceedings.[8]
Hoffman went next to Emden in East Friesland, there attracting
numerous followers and consolidating a congregation of sectarian
Anabaptists. Within a year Emden had a printing press.[9] One of the
many Dutch dissenters in East Friesland at the time was David Joris,
who spent part of his exile composing songs in Emden. It is not
known if he ever met Hoffman, but in any case he become increasingly obsessed with apocalyptic judgement, and was imbued with
some of Hoffman's fundamental views by the time he returned to
Delft a few years later, subsequently becoming a leading exponent.
Although Hoffman too moved on, destined to end his days imprisoned at Strasbourg, his influence continued to be felt in the north
for a long time to come. The Emden Melchiorites took their apocalyptic vision into the northern Low Countries, to Leeuwarden and
thence to Amsterdam. Ten were rounded up and eventually executed at The Hague in December 1531. Thereafter, direction of the
Dutch Melchiorite movement was largely in the hands of Amsterdam
artisans.[10]

On his progress from fanatical iconoclast to proto-Anabaptist,
Hoffman courted controversy wherever he went. It was a journey

---

[8] *NB*, nos. 953, 954, 963, 974; *VD* H4215, H4216, H4219; Deppermann, *Melchior Hoffman*, 95–159; Williams, *Radical Reformation*, 388–90; R.C. Bailey, "Melchior Hoffmann: Proto-Anabaptist and Printer in Kiel (1527–1529)," *GJB* (1991), 220–29.
[9] *NB*, no. 1020.
[10] Waite, *David Joris*, 55–59.

ostensibly begun in Livonia, where his early notoriety was unparalleled, except perhaps by Sylvester Tegetmeier's. Tegetmeier, though, had stayed in Riga and ingratiated himself with the town's political elite. He had also married a merchant's daughter, whose dowry included a house once occupied by Third Order Franciscans, the Grey Sisters. Her father, Hermann Mels, purchased it when monastic holdings were dissolved in 1524–25. With few exceptions the ownership of real estate in Riga was restricted to Germans. Those who invested in former Church assets thus had a material interest in the success of religious reforms there. The Livonian towns had indeed freed themselves from the authority of the old bishops. Civic administrations oversaw religious life now. In Riga Tegetmeier was still popular, however in the interest of social and political harmony town officials eschewed more radical innovation and were fairly cautious in their approach to further change.[11] Brießmann was recruited from Königsberg to draft a Livonian church order, a task completed by July 1530.[12]

As Melchior Hoffman and his Lutheran adversaries argued at Flensburg in the spring of 1529 the *Reichstag* convened at Speyer. Among the assembled dignitaries was an elderly senator from Cologne, Sir Hermann Rinck.[13] Cologne's ruling clique remained true to the Habsburg house and resistant to Lutheran reform. Charles was not present, but the loyal Catholic estates constituted a clear majority of representatives. They resolved to uphold the Edict of Worms and void the decision of the 1526 Diet at Speyer that had left religious issues to the individual territorial estates, pending a general Church council or national assembly. A ban on further religious innovation was now introduced. The Diet's closing recess called for all new books to be examined and approved by committees of theologians prior to publication. It also prescribed the death penalty for anyone convicted of adult baptism.[14] Refusing to accept revocation of the 1526 decision, a small group of minority delegates issued their formal protestation on 19 July. The evangelical reform movement thus acquired a new name and the stage was set for subsequent armed

---

[11] Packull, "Sylvester Tegetmeier," 346, 349–50.
[12] *UBRG*, 2: nos. 725, 741; Dietz printed the church order at Rostock. *NB*, no. 1054.
[13] *LH*, no. 111.
[14] *LP*, 4/3: no. 5490; *DCR*, nos. 103–7; Jannasch, *Reformationsgeschichte*, 252.

confrontation between the emperor and the league of Protestant towns and princes.

By the autumn of 1529 the sweating sickness or 'English sweat' (*sudor anglicus*) had cast its grim shadow across northern Germany. The deadly virus came initially to Hamburg, then sweep quickly eastward into the Baltic ports. As many as 30,000 perished in the epidemic, among them Eberhard Queiß, bishop of Pomesania since 1523 and one of the two principal implementers of Lutheran reform in Ducal Prussia.[15] Suffering was not confined to the north. A burgomaster and untold other persons died at Antwerp, even as a procession of the sacrament in late September invoked divine mercy. Civic officials, clerics, and school children carried a thousand lighted torches, according to one chronicle, with many men and women of the commonalty joining in.[16] Only a fortnight later another general procession included holy relics and town regalia. Augmenting prayers for deliverance from the sickness were others for the emperor's prosperity and for victory against God's enemies, the Turks. Reference to heretics was vague and muted. For the time being, their redemption was left to the Almighty.[17]

Ten years had now passed since the university theologians at Louvain and Cologne had condemned Luther's wriitings. As late summer gave way to autumn virtually simultaneous events reflected the new status quo; effectively placing much that had gone before in perspective and pointing to some of the challenges ahead. On 28 September there was a public execution in Cologne. Adolf Clarenbach, learned humanist proponent of Bible-based spirituality, was burned for his supposedly Lutheran views. University theologians had spearheaded the prosecution; Clarenbach spent more than a year in prison before he died. He did not recant. Among the citizenry his loss was widely lamented. Even more predictably, Lutheran sympathisers across Germany quickly memorialised him as a martyr. His death exemplified both the intransigence of hard-core traditionalists and the commitment of some of the reformers: an impasse that would haunt Europe for decades to come. But the evangelical front was far from united.

---

[15] *SRP*, 6: 498. In Lübeck the illness claimed two of the town's secretaries. Jannasch, *Reformationsgeschichte*, 255.

[16] "Chronycke van Nederland," 97.

[17] *AA*, 2: 322–24. "dat God almachtich alsulckdanige persoonen, in dien gavalle, bekeeren, ende inden rechten geloove . . . brengen wille".

With the aim of settling the controversy over Christ's corporal presence in the Eucharist, Landgrave Philip of Hesse had arranged a colloquy at Marburg beginning on the first day of October. It drew together Luther and the Zürich reformer Zwingli to debate Eucharistic doctrine. A dozen other leading theologians participated as well, including Melanchthon, Oecolampadius, and Martin Bucer. Ultimately it did little except accentuate the divisions that had already begun to define sectarian Protestantism.

With the drift toward Lutheranism in northern Germany now clearly beyond his control, the emperor had endeavoured yet again in the autumn of 1529 to assert authority in his patrimonial lands. The October placard amplified all previous decrees pertaining to heretics and their books in the Low Countries. It also implied that to this point enforcement, though not the laws, had been inadequate. So discretionary sentences were no longer acceptable. The Court of Holland's response was to execute the outspoken Dordrecht shoemaker Cornelis Woutersz. Not so moved were magistrates in the towns.[18] Some were sympathetic to evangelicals, and in any case their first responsibility was still the preservation of domestic peace.

The *Reichstag* met at Augsburg in 1530, from April through September. Delegates making their way via Nürnberg would have found for sale there several Lutheran titles printed by Johann Herrgott's widow, Kunigunde. And on Augsburg's northern fringes they easily may have passed pack-wagons bound for Ingolstadt with book consignments, including Lutheran imprints, for Georg Krapff. The emperor attended the Diet, and so did Campaggio. Johann Cochlaeus was there too, now in the employ of Georg of Saxony. Responding to Charles's request for statements on religious questions, Philipp Melanchthon articulated the Lutheran articles of faith—the Augsburg Confession—on 25 June. But the Catholic theologians countered with a 'Confutation' upholding papal supremacy. Eck and Fabri composed it; Cochlaeus added some stylistic improvements.[19] Reconciliation with Germany's Lutherans was out of the question.

As the 1520s drew to a close profound changes were imminent in England, bound up with failed attempts to end the king's marriage. Wolsey would bear the blame. His indictment for præmunire

---

[18] Tracy, *Holland*, 159–60.
[19] Baümer, *Cochlaeus*, 33–36; Spahn, *Cochläus*, 152–65.

came in October 1529. One of the charges brought by his political enemies was that he had supported heresy. Henry still saw himself as an upholder of Catholicism. His quarrel was with the institutional Church at Rome. He was loath to countenance Lutheranism in his kingdom, confessional doctrine that he had no part in formulating. But he was already charting a course that muddied traditional distinctions between spiritual and secular jurisdictions.

England's bishops orchestrated another roundup of heretical books the following spring, and before leaving for Durham Cuthbert Tunstall made one more great fire at Paul's Churchyard.[20] The royal decree followed in June. But the Brethren, as the subsequent spread of Tyndale's works would show, were undeterred. When, in the autumn, Tyndale weighed in on the divorce issue the king vowed much stricter suppression of "Lutheran errors" than was in force in Germany. The imperial ambassador, Eustace Chapuys, did not doubt him. Several London men already had been arrested for distributing *The practyse of Prelates*. That it was supportive of the queen was reason enough to expect that English "Lutherans" were in for a difficult time. But the king was not about to exacerbate his political isolation by antagonising German Protestants—princes or merchants. Indeed, the time for exploring avenues of Anglo-Lutheran co-operation was not far off. Robert Barnes would be invited back to England under royal protection in 1531, following publication of his *Supplicatyon*, a collection of essays emphasising that Lutheranism's central tenets were not incompatible with the king's sovereign authority.[21] So Henry's frustration in the fall of 1530 was directed not at doctrinaire Lutherans but, understandably, at supporters of one particular English exile, William Tyndale. Thomas Cromwell, whose influence in the king's council was now rising, had wanted to recruit Tyndale to defend royal policy on Rome. To that end his agent in Antwerp, future Merchant Adventurers' governor Stephen Vaughan, had secretly contacted the fugitive.[22] Tyndale, though, rejected the offer of a pardon, which in any case was revoked in the wake of *The practyse of Prelates*.

---

[20] Hall, *Chronicle*, 771; *LP*, 4/3: nos. 6401, 6411.

[21] *A supplicatyon made by Robert Barnes doctoure in divinite unto the most excellent and redoubted prince kinge henrye the eyght* was printed in Antwerp by Simon Cock. Barnes, *Reformation Essays*, 96–101; *STC* 1470; Lusardi, "Robert Barnes," 1388–91.

[22] W.C. Richardson, *Stephen Vaughan: Financial Agent of Henry VIII* (Baton Rouge, 1953), 25.

If Henry's disdain for German Lutherans sounds less than genuine, he was nevertheless perfectly at ease resurrecting the weary
cliché that foreigners brought religious discord to his kingdom; that
the emperor's subjects were to blame. Speaking again with Chapuys
in November 1530, he pointed accusingly not to Lollards or English
merchants or fugitives in Antwerp but to "Austrelins" (*Esterlings*) and
the books they carried into the country. He went on to complain
that Danzig was Lutheran despite the best efforts of Sigismund.[23] It
was in fact true that some of Danzig's churches had evangelical
preachers again. However, the rhetoric about *Esterlings* was simply
Henry's way of denying culpability for confusion or religious strife
in England and reminding Charles of his failure to extinguish heterodoxy. As they were intended to, the comments found their way
into Chapuys' diplomatic dispatches. If the king really believed *Esterlings*
and their books were a problem and wanted to do something about
it, he had as his chancellor one of England's most able and committed heretic-hunters. But there was no investigation or prosecution
of Steelyard men now. They were not disseminators of the English-
language propaganda being churned out by exiles, much of which
consisted of translations or adaptations of texts long since available
to German readers. That is not to say that had More come to the
Steelyard again, he might not have found a copy or two of a little
book he abhorred. Simon Fish's *Supplicacyon* had been translated into
German and printed at Nürnberg. Still, from Hanse ports the merchant networks did transmit information about controversy and
change. And the latest tidings from England reached northern Germany
and Scandinavia by the same channels. It is not known how many
vessels from Hanse ports delivered cargoes and news to the London
Steelyard in 1530, but twenty-three English merchantmen docked in
Danzig that summer.[24]

By year's end several of the principal characters that shaped the
initial phase of the northern Reformation had played their final scene.
Sickness had claimed Simon Fish. William Roye had vanished.
Thomas Wolsey, papal legate and principal architect of English foreign policy until his dismissal hoped and schemed against all odds

[23] *Calendar of State Papers—Spain*, 4/1: nos. 460, 481, 492.
[24] Fudge, "Maintaining a presence," 8. Sebastian Franck's translation of Fish,
Klagbrieff oder supplication der armen durfftigen in Engenlandt, was followed by a Latin edition in 1530. *VD* F1211, F1213.

for reinstatement in the king's service, but was arrested for treason on 4 November. Such was the harsh reality of Tudor politics. On the way to London to face trail and almost certainly execution, he died of natural causes at Leicester Abbey on the morning of the 29th. Barely two days later, on the evening of 1 December, Margaret of Austria-Savoy, regent of the Netherlands, passed away peacefully at her residence in Mechelen. England's king, now estranged from both the papacy and the house of Habsburg, is supposed to have uttered that her death was "no great loss for the world".[25] John Hackett attended her state funeral in mid-January. His extant letters reflect an enduring respect for the duchess, in stark contrast to Henry's contempt. Just the same, he was under no illusion about governance of the Low Countries. Margaret's three principal advisors—Lord Hoochstraten, the treasurer Jean de Marnix and audiencer Laurent du Blioul—ruled as they pleased. In Hackett's words, "whatsoeuer they or ii of them may conclude my Lady and al the counsail folowe".[26] For the remaining four years of his own life Hackett stayed on as England's ambassador to the court of Charles's new regent, Mary of Hungary.

Margaret's funeral eulogy, authored by Johannes Fabri, was printed "ex aedibus Quentelianis" in Cologne. Peter Quentell continued to thrive, and to issue books for England's high clergy. Early in 1531 he would finish an edition of a biblical commentary by Haymo, bishop of Halberstadt, commissioned by Tunstall. The work had come to the Cologne printer through his old friend Franz Birckman.[27] Birckman, though, did not see it finished. He too had died in 1530, sometime before 21 June, leaving a remarkable legacy of entrepreneurial success as well as the most telling of clues that he was, after all, the consummate opportunist. Soon his heirs were embroiled in litigation in Antwerp. At issue was the balance Birckman allegedly owed for the printing of seven hundred English New Testaments.[28] Franz's brother Arnold managed the Birckman press in Cologne for

---

[25] *Calendar of State Papers—Spain*, 4/2: no. 584.

[26] *LH*, no. 111. Thereto: nos. 36, 112, 136.

[27] K. Schottenloher, "Widmungsvorreden deutscher Drucker und Verleger des 16. Jahrhunderts," *GJB* (1942/43), 170. Fabri's *Oratio funebris: VD* F222.

[28] S. Corsten, "Unter dem Zeichen der 'Fetten Henne': Franz Birckmann und Nachfolger," *GJB* (1962), 267–72. According to Mozley, *William Tyndale*, 348, the plaintiff was none other than Hans Ruremund. Rouzet, *Dictionnaire*, 19, says he was "un certain John Silverlink".

another decade. Under a second and third generation the firm
flourished and became one of the town's pre-eminent sixteenth-century publishing houses. The connection with England lived on as
well. Already in 1530 Nicolas Prévost issued a Salisbury processional
"imp. iunioris F. byrckman Venundatur Londonij in ed. iunioris F.
byrckman". As his father had done for the better part of three
decades, in the late 1530s Franz the younger imported books into
London. Whether he did so in partnership with other family members is unclear. The "Arnolde Brightman" for whom Henry Harman
kept inventory at Paul's Churchyard was likely the son of Arnold
the elder. In the Birckman catalogue for the 1550s and 1560s are
several reissues of works by John Fisher, including *Assertionis Lutheranae
Confutatio.*[29]

And what of the other printing house that figures so prominently
in this story of prohibited books and their illicit distribution? Sometime
in 1531, in early summer perhaps, Hans Ruremund's brother
Christopher made his fateful crossing to England. Possibly he brought
with him copies of a *Hore beatissime*, newly printed in May. He had
issued it before for Birckman, however this edition, to be sold in
Paul's Churchyard, was his own.[30] Apparently he brought books of
a much different sort to the binder John Rowe. The circumstances
surrounding the arrest and interrogation of the two men are not
known. Certain only is that the laws of Antwerp meant nothing in
England, where More's pursuit of heretics could border on the obses-
sive and where incarcerated suspects sometimes happened to die. No
defenders of jurisdictional privilege or advocates of citizens' rights
came to the printer's rescue, as they had in his homeland some years
before. Nor did anyone else. And so within a short while Christopher
Ruremund's earthly life, like Robert Necton's, came to a miserable
end in a Westminster prison. Far from finished, though, was the
press in Antwerp. It carried on under the direction of Christopher's
wife Catharyn at least until the mid-1540s, thus outliving More,
Fisher, and Tyndale by many years. There were devotional and liturgical books for England, as before, and controversial texts too, above
all the reissues that so vexed Tyndale.[31] Sir Thomas More, having

---

[29] *STC* 16240.5; Schnurmann, *Kommerz*, 71–86; *VD* F1220, F1221, F1231, F1233.
[30] *STC* 15966, 15969 (*NK* 2485, 2490).
[31] *STC* 2825, 2827, 16132, 16149, 16241.5, 16242, 16243. In 1536 Catharyn
Ruremund printed a Latin/English primer for John Gough (*STC* 15992), a com-

refused the Oath of Succession, was under arrest in the Tower of London by the time George Joye corrected and altered the English New Testament reprints. And ignored if not long forgotten was Antwerp's law against them. Their simple colophons evoke the constancy of the printer. There was no attempt at deception: "Here endeth the new Testament diligently ouersene and corrected and prynted now agayne at Antwerpe by me wydowe of Christoffel of Endhouen".

posite that used parts of Joye's *Hortulus Animae*. In the early 1540s came several contentious tracts by Joye, as he sparred with Stephen Gardiner over clerical celibacy. The colophons were falsified, and the author usually resorted to pseudonyms. *STC* 14556, 14826, 14830, 17798, 21804, 26138.

BIBLIOGRAPHY

Manuscript Sources

Belgium
Stadsarchief Antwerpen V235 II Correctieboek 1513–1568; PK914 Gebodboek 1489–1539; PK1561 Gebeurtenissen—Heresie; LZ29 V Poortersboek 1464–1538.

United Kingdom
British Library Cotton. MS Galba B VI, VII, VIII, IX, X; Cotton. MS Nero B II; Cotton. MS Vitellius B II, VI, XXI; Harleian MS 425; Lansdowne MS 170, 171.

Guildhall Library (London) MS 9531/10 Register of Bishop Tunstall 1522–1529/30.

The National Archives: Public Record Office C 1/158/47, 1/410/59, 1/492/44, 1/552/71, 1/586/52 Early Chancery Proceedings; E 122/78/9, 122/79/12, 122/80/2,5, 122/82/9, 122/83/4, 122/99/18, 122/208/2, 122/208/3 Customs Particulars; SP 1/47, 48, 49, 57, 65, 66 State Papers.

Reference and Printed Sources

Aus Antwerpener Notariatsarchiven: Quellen zur deutschen Wirtschaftsgeschichte des 16. Jahrhunderts. ed. J. Strieder. Berlin, 1930. (Wiesbaden, 1962)
Aus der Reformationsgeschichte Niedersachsens. ed. P. Meyer. Hildesheim, 1952.
Barlowe, Jerome and William Roye. *Rede Me and Be Nott Wrothe.* ed. D.H. Parker. Toronto, 1992.
Barnes, Robert. *The Reformation Essays of Dr. Robert Barnes.* ed. N.S. Tjernagel. London, 1963.
Beschlüsse des Rates der Stadt Köln. ed. M. Huiskes and M. Groten, 5 vols. Düsseldorf, 1988–90.
Bibliographia Polonica XV ac XVI ss. ed. T. Wierzbowski, 3 vols. Warsaw, 1889. (Nieuwkoop, 1961)
Bibliographie der Flugschriften des 16. Jahrhunderts. ed. H.-J. Köhler, Teil 1: Das frühe 16. Jahrhundert (1501–1530). Tübingen, 1992.
Bibliotheca Bugenhagiana: Bibliographie der Druckschriften des D. Joh. Bugenhagen. ed. G. Geisenhof. Leipzig, 1908. (Nieuwkoop, 1963)
Bibliotheca reformatoria neerlandica: Geschriften uit den tijd der hervorming in de Nederlanden. ed. S. Cramer and F. Pijper, 10 vols. The Hague, 1903–14.
"Brief Sigismunds I. von Polen an Heinrich VIII. von England." ed. R. Toeppen. *Altpreußische Monatsschrift* 33 (1896): 297–98.
Bronnen tot de Geschiedenis van den Handel met England, Schotland en Ierland. ed. H.J. Smit, 4 vols. The Hague, 1928–1950.
Calendar of Patent Rolls 1494–1509. London, 1916.
Calendar of State Papers—Spain. vols. 1–2. ed. G.A. Bergenroth. London, 1862–66; vols. 3–4/2 ed. Pascual de Gayangos. London, 1873–82; Further Supplement. ed. G. Mattingly. London, 1940.
Calendar of State Papers—Venice. vols. 1–4. ed. R. Brown. London, 1864–73.
Chroniques de Brabant et de Flandre. ed. C. Piot. Brussels, 1879.

Cochlaeus, Johann. *Epistola Johannis Bugenhagii Pomerani ad Anglos. Responsio Johannis Cochlaei.* Cologne, 1526.

Corpus documentorum inquisitionis haereticae pravitatis Neerlandicae. ed. P. Fredericq, 5 vols. The Hague, 1889–1902.

The Correspondence of Erasmus, vol. 7, trans. R.A.B. Mynors. Toronto, 1984.

The Correspondence of Wolfgang Capito, vol. 1, ed. and trans. E Rummel with the assistance of M. Kooistra. Toronto, 2005.

D. Martin Luthers Werke: Kritische Gesamtausgabe. Weimar, 1873–2000.

Documents illustrative of the Continental Reformation. ed. B.J. Kidd. Oxford, 1911. (1967)

Documents sur les imprimeurs libraires cartiers, graveurs fondeurs de lettres, relieurs doreurs de livres, faiseurs de fermoirs enlumineurs parcheminiers et papetiers ayant exercé a Paris de 1450 a 1600. ed. Ph. Renouard. Paris, 1901.

Dürer, Albrecht. *Diary of his Journey to the Netherlands, 1520–21.* ed. J.-A. Goris and G. Marlier. London, 1971.

Ecclesiastical Memorials. vol. 1. ed. J. Strype. Oxford, 1822.

The English Works of John Fisher, Bishop of Rochester. ed. J.E.B. Mayor. Early English Text Society, extra series, 27. London, 1935.

"Extracts from Lincoln Episcopal Visitations in the 15th, 16th, and 17th Centuries." ed. E. Peacock. *Archaeologia* 48 (1885): 249–69.

The First English Printed New Testament translated by William Tyndale. ed. E. Arber. London, 1871.

Fish, Simon. *A Supplicacyon for the Beggers.* ed. F.J. Furnivall, Early English Text Society, extra series, 13. London, 1871.

Flugschriften aus der Bauernkriegszeit. ed. A. Laube and H.W. Seiffert. Berlin, 1975.

Flugschriften gegen die Reformation (1518–1524). ed. A. Laube. Berlin, 1997.

Fox, John. *The Acts and Monuments of John Fox.* ed. G. Townsend, 8 vols. New York, 1965.

Hall, Edward. *The Union of the Two Noble and Illustre Fameles of Lancastre and Yorke.* ed. H. Ellis. London, 1809. (New York, 1965)

Hanserecesse. series 3, ed. D. Schäfer and F. Techen, 9 vols. Leipzig, 1881–1913.

Hanserezesse. series 4, vol. 1. ed. G. Wentz. Weimar, 1941; vol. 2. ed. K. Friedland and G. Wentz. Cologne, 1970.

Inventaire de la Collection Anisson sur l'histoire de l'imprimerie et la librairie. ed. E. Coyecque, 2 vols. Paris, 1900.

Joye, George. *An Apology made by George Joy, to satisfy, if it may be, W. Tindale.* ed. E. Arber. Birmingham, 1882.

"Kleine chronikalische Aufzeichnungen zur Geschichte Preussens im sechszehnten Jahrhundert." ed. M. Töppen. *Altpreußische Monatsschrift* 33 (1896): 393–408.

Letters and Papers Foreign and Domestic of the Reign of Henry VIII. vols. 1–4. ed. J.S. Brewer. London, 1862–67; vols. 5–13. ed. J. Gairdner. London, 1880–93; Addenda, vol. 1/1 and 1/2. London, 1929–32.

Letters and Papers illustrative of the reigns of Richard III and Henry VII. ed. J. Gairdner, 2 vols. London, 1861–63.

The Letters of Sir John Hackett 1526–1534. ed. E.F. Rogers. Morgantown, 1971.

"Mandat des Raths gegen Pasquill- und Lästerschriften 1524." *AGDB* 5 (1880): 86–87.

The Merchant Adventurers of England: Their Laws and Ordinances with Other Documents. ed. W.E. Lingelbach. Philadelphia, 1902. (New York, 1971)

More, Thomas. *The Complete Works of St. Thomas More.* vol. 6. ed. T.M.C. Lawler et al. New Haven, 1981; vol. 7. ed. F. Manley et al. New Haven, 1990; vol. 8. ed. L.A. Schuster et al. New Haven, 1973; vol. 9. ed. J.B. Trapp. New Haven, 1979.

Nederlandsche bibliographie van 1500–1540. ed. W. Nijhoff and M.E. Kronenberg, 6 vols. The Hague, 1923–61.

Niederdeutsche Bibliographie. vol. 1. ed. C. Borchling and B. Claussen. Neumünster, 1931.
"Ordonnantien van het Antwerpsch Magistraat, rakende de godsdienstige geschillen der XVIᵉ eeuw." ed. P. Génard. *Antwerpsch Archievenblad* 2: 308–472.
"Personen te Antwerpen in de XVIᵉ eeuw voor het 'feit van religie' gerechtelijk verfolgt." ed. P. Génard. *Antwerpsch Archievenblad* 7: 114–472.
Post-incunabula and their publishers in the Low Countries. ed. H.D. Vervliet. London, 1978.
Proceedings and Ordinances of the Privy Council. vol. 7. ed. H. Nicolas. London, 1837.
A proper dyaloge betwene a Gentillman and an Husbandman. ed. D.H. Parker. Toronto, 1996.
Quellen zur Geschichte des Europäischen Postwesens 1501–1806. Thurn und Taxis-Studien 9, ed. M. Dallmeier. Kallmünz, 1977.
The Radical Reformation. ed. M.G. Baylor. Cambridge, 1991.
The Reign of Henry VII from Contemporary Sources. ed. A.F. Pollard, 3 vols. London, 1913–14.
Returns of Aliens dwelling in the city and suburbs of London from the reign of Henry VIII to that of James I. vol. 1. ed. R.E.G. Kirk and E.F. Kirk. Aberdeen, 1900.
Scriptores Rerum Prussicarum. vols. 1–5. ed. T. Hirsch, M. Töppen, and E. Strehlke. Leipzig, 1861–74; vol. 6. ed. W. Hubatch and U. Arnold. Frankfurt, 1968.
A Short-Title Catalogue of Books printed in England, Scotland, and Ireland 1485–1640. ed. A.W. Pollard and G.R. Redgrave (London, 1926); 2nd ed. 3 vols. ed. W.A. Jackson and F.S. Ferguson completed by K.F. Pantzer. London, 1976–1991.
Tudor Royal Proclamations. vol. 1. ed. P.L. Hughes and J.F. Larkin. New Haven, 1964.
Tyndale, William. *The Parable of the Wicked Mammon.* Antwerp, 1528.
Urkundenbuch zur Reformationsgeschichte des Herzogthums Preußen. ed. P. Tschackert, 3 vols. Leipzig, 1890.
Verzeichnis der in deutschen Sprachbereich erscheinenen Drucke des XVI. Jahrhunderts. Herausgegeben von der Bayerischen Staatsbibliothek in München in Verbindung mit der Herzog August Bibliothek in Wolfenbüttel. 25 vols. Stuttgart, 1983–2000.

Secondary Literature

Andersen, N.K. "The Reformation in Scandinavia and the Baltic." in *The New Cambridge Modern History.* vol. 2. ed. G.R. Elton. Cambridge, 1958, 134–60.
Armstrong, E. "English purchases of printed books from the Continent 1465–1526." *English Historical Review* 94 (1979): 268–90.
Arnold, U. "Luther und Danzig." *Zeitschrift für Ostforschung* 31 (1972): 94–121.
"Luther und die Reformation im Preußenland." in *Martin Luther und die Reformation in Ostdeutschland und Südosteuropa,* ed. U. Hutter. Sigmaringen, 1991, 27–44.
Arthurson, I. "Espionage and Intelligence from the Wars of the Roses to the Reformation." *Nottingham Medieval Studies* 35 (1991): 134–54.
Aston, M. *Lollards and Reformers: Images and Literacy in Late Medieval Religion.* London, 1984.
Aston. M. and C. Richmond, eds. *Lollardy and the Gentry in the Later Middle Ages.* New York, 1997.
Avis, F.C. *Printers of Fleet Street and St. Paul's Churchyard in the 16th Century.* London, 1964.
"Book smuggling into England during the Sixteenth Century." *Gutenberg-Jahrbuch* (1972): 180–87.
"England's use of Antwerp printers, 1500–1540." *Gutenberg-Jahrbuch* (1973): 234–40.
Bacewiczowa, D. and A. Kawecka-Gryczowa. *Drukarze dawnej Polski od XV do XVIII wieku,* vol. 1/1. Wrocław, 1983.
Bailey, R.C. "Melchior Hoffmann: Proto-Anabaptist and Printer in Kiel (1527–1529)." *Gutenberg-Jahrbuch* (1991): 220–29.

Bang, N.E., ed. *Tabeller over Skibsfart og Varetransport gennem Øresund 1497–1660.* 2 vols. Copenhagen, 1906–32.

Bangs, J.D. "Further adventures of Jan Zevertsz., bookprinter and parchmentmaker of Leiden." *Quærendo* 7 (1977): 128–43.

"Reconsidering Lutheran book trade: the so-called 'Winkelkasboek' of Pieter Claesz. van Balen." *Quærendo* 9 (1979): 227–60.

Bartolomäus, R. "Justus Ludwig Decius: Ein deutscher Kaufmann und polnischer Staatsmann (1485–1545)." *Altpreußische Monatsschift* 35 (1898): 49–111.

Bátori, I., ed. *Städtische Gesellschaft und Reformation.* Stuttgart, 1980.

Bäumer, R. *Johannes Cochlaeus (1479–1552): Leben und Werk im Dienst der katholischen Reform.* Münster, 1980.

Beckey, K. *Die Reformation in Hamburg.* Hamburg, 1929.

Bennett, H.S. *English Books and Readers 1475 to 1557.* 2nd ed. Cambridge, 1969.

Benzing, J. *Buchdruckerlexikon des 16. Jahrhunderts: Deutsches Sprachgebiet.* Frankfurt, 1952. *Buchdrucker des 16. und 17. Jahrhunderts im deutschen Sprachgebiet.* Wiesbaden, 1963.

Bernard, G.W. *War, Taxation and Rebellion in Early Tudor England.* New York, 1986.

Berthoud, G. et al., eds. *Aspects de la propagande religieuse.* Geneva, 1957.

Bieńkowska, B. and H. Chamerska. *Books in Poland: Past and Present,* trans. W. Zalewski and E.R. Payne. Wiesbaden, 1990.

Bietenholz, P.G. *Basle and France in the Sixteenth Century: The Basle Humanists and Printers in Their Contacts with Francophone Culture.* Toronto, 1971.

"Printing and the Basle Reformation, 1517–65." in *The Reformation and the Book,* ed. J.-F. Gilmont and K. Maag. Aldershot, 1998, 235–63.

Biller, P. and A. Hudson, eds. *Heresy and Literacy, c. 1100–c. 1530.* Cambridge, 1994.

Blayney, P.W.M. *The Bookshops in Paul's Cross Churchyard.* London, 1990.

Blockmans, W. *Emperor Charles V 1500–1558,* trans. I. van den Hoven-Vardon. London, 2002.

Blockmans, W. and L. Heerma van Voss. "Urban networks and emerging states in the North Sea and Baltic areas: a maritime culture." in *The North Sea and Culture (1550–1800),* ed. J. Roding and L. Heerma van Voss. Hilversum, 1996, 10–20.

Blockmans, W. and W. Prevenier. *The Promised Lands: The Low Countries under Burgundian Rule, 1369–1530.* Philadelphia, 1999.

Brady, T.A., Jr. "The Reformation of the Common Man, 1521–1524." *The German Reformation,* ed. C.S. Dixon. Oxford, 1999, 94–132.

Bratchel, M.E. "Italian Merchant Organization and Business Relationships in Early Tudor England." in *Merchant Networks in the Early Modern World,* ed. S. Subrahmanyam. Aldershot, 1996, 1–28.

Brecht, M. "'Tosaginge' und 'geloven': Neue Einsichten in die frühe Lutherrezeption in Hamburg." *Archiv für Reformationsgeschichte* 85 (1994): 45–67.

Brigden, S. "Religion and Social Obligation in early sixteenth-century London." *Past and Present* 103 (1984): 67–112.

"Thomas Cromwell and the 'brethren'." in *Law and Government under the Tudors,* ed. C. Cross, D. Loades, J.J. Scarisbrick. Cambridge, 1988, 31–49.

London and the Reformation. Oxford, 1991.

Brooks, P.N., ed. *Reformation Principle and Practice.* London, 1980.

Bruns, F. and H. Weczerka. *Hansische Handelsstrassen.* 3 vols. Cologne, 1967.

Buck, S. *Hans Holbein.* Cologne, 1999.

Bues, A. *Das Herzogtum Kurland und der Norden der polnisch-litauischen Adelsrepublik im 16. und 17. Jahrhundert.* Giessen, 2001.

Buff, A. "Die ältesten Augsburger Censuranordnungen." *Archiv für Geschichte des Deutschen Buchhandels* 5 (1881): 251–52.

Butterworth, C.C. and A.G. Chester. *George Joye.* Philadelphia, 1962.

Caliebe, M. "Die Literatur." in *Handbuch der Geschichte Ost- und Westpreußens: Teil 2/1,* ed. E. Opgenoorth. Lüneburg, 1994, 183–89.

Carlson, E.J., ed. *Religion and the English People 1500–1640*. Kirksville, MO, 1998.
Carus-Wilson, E.M. and O. Coleman, eds. *England's Export Trade, 1275–1547*. Oxford, 1967.
Chester, A.G. "Robert Barnes and the Burning of the Books." *Huntington Library Quarterly* 14 (1951): 211–21.
Chrisman, M.U. "Printing and the Evolution of Lay Culture in Strasbourg 1480–1599." in *The German People and the Reformation*, ed. R. Po-chia Hsia. Ithaca, 1988, 74–100.
Conflicting Visions of Reform: German Lay Propaganda Pamphlets, 1519–1530. Atlantic Highlands, 1996.
"Reformation printing in Strasbourg, 1519–60." in *The Reformation and the Book*, ed. J.-F. Gilmont and K. Maag. Aldershot, 1998, 214–34.
Christianson, C.P. "Paternoster Row and the Tudor Book-trade Community." *The Library*, 6th series, 11 (1989): 352–56.
A Directory of London Stationers and Book Artisans 1300–1500. New York, 1990.
"The Rise of London's Book Trade." in *The Cambridge History of the Book in England*. vol. 3. ed. L. Hellinga and J.B. Trapp. Cambridge, 1999, 128–47.
Cieślak, E. and C. Biernat. *History of Gdańsk*, trans. B. Blaim and G.M. Hyde. Gdańsk, 1988.
Clair, C. *A History of European Printing*. London, 1976.
Clebsch, W.A. "The Earliest Translations of Luther into English." *Harvard Theological Review* 56 (1963): 75–86.
England's Earliest Protestants 1520–1535. New Haven, 1964.
Cole, R.G. "The Reformation in Print: German Pamphlets and Propaganda." *Archiv für Reformationsgeschichte* 66 (1975): 93–102.
"The Reformation Pamphlet and Communication Processes." in *Flugschriften als Massenmedium der Reformationszeit*, ed. H.-J. Köhler. Stuttgart, 1981, 139–61.
Collinson, P. "Cranbrook and the Fletchers: Popular and Unpopular Religion in the Kentish Weald." in *Reformation Principle and Practice*, ed. P.N. Brooks. London, 1980, 171–202.
Coornaert, E. *Les Français et le commerce international à Anvers*. 2 vols. Paris, 1961.
Corsten, S. "Unter dem Zeichen der 'Fetten Henne': Franz Birckmann und Nachfolger." *Gutenberg-Jahrbuch* (1962): 267–72.
Crofts, R. "Books, Reform and Reformation." *Archiv für Reformationsgeschichte* 61 (1980): 21–35.
Cross, C., D. Loades and J.J. Scarisbrick, eds. *Law and Government under the Tudors*. Cambridge, 1988.
D'Alton, C.W. "Charity or Fire? The Argument of Thomas More's 1529 Dyaloge." *Sixteenth Century Journal* 33 (2002): 51–70.
"The Suppression of Lutheran Heretics in England, 1526–1529." *Journal of Ecclesiastical History* 54 (2003): 228–53.
Daniell, D. *William Tyndale: A Biography*. New Haven, 1994.
Davids, K. and J. Lucassen, eds. *A Miracle Mirrored: The Dutch Republic in European Perspective*. Cambridge, 1995.
Davis, J.F. "Lollardy and the Reformation in England." *Archiv für Reformationsgeschichte* 73 (1982): 217–36.
Heresy and the Reformation in the South-East of England, 1520–1559. London, 1983.
De Smedt, O. *De Engelse Natie te Antwerpen in de 16e Eeuw*. 2 vols. Antwerp, 1950.
Den Hollander, A.A. *De Nederlandse Bijbelvertalingen 1522–1545*. Nieuwkoop, 1997.
Deppermann, K. *Melchior Hoffman: Social Unrest and Apocalyptic Visions in the Age of Reformation*, trans. M. Wren, ed. B. Drewery. Edinburgh, 1987.
Dickens, A.G. *Lollards and Protestants in the Diocese of York 1509–1558*. Oxford, 1959.
"The Early Expansion of Protestantism in England 1520–1558." *Archiv für Reformationsgeschichte* 67 (1987): 187–221.
The English Reformation. 2nd ed. Oxford, 1989.

Dietz, A. *Frankfurter Handelsgeschichte*. 3 vols. Frankfurt, 1921.

Dixon, C.S., ed. *The German Reformation*. Oxford, 1999.

Doernberg, E. *Henry VIII and Luther*. Stanford, 1961.

Dowling, M. "Anne Boleyn and Reform." *Journal of Ecclesiastical History* 35 (1984): 30–46.

Droz, E. "Pierre de Vingle, l'imprimeur de Farel." in *Aspects de la propagande religieuse*, ed. G. Berthoud et al. Geneva, 1957, 38–78.

Duff, E.G. *The Printers, Stationers and Bookbinders of Westminster and London from 1476 to 1535*. Cambridge, 1906. (1971)

———. "The Assertio Septem Sacramentorum." *The Library*, 2nd series, 9 (1908): 1–16.

———. "Notes on Stationers from the Lay Subsidy Rolls of 1523–24." *The Library*, 2nd series, 9 (1908): 257–66.

———. *A Century of the English Book Trade*. 2nd ed. Oxford, 1948.

Duffield, G.E. *The Work of William Tyndale*. Philadelphia, 1965.

Duke, A. "Salvation by Coercion." in *Reformation Principle and Practice*, ed. P.N. Brooks. London, 1980, 135–56.

———. *Reformation and Revolt in the Low Countries*. London, 1990.

———. "The Netherlands." in *The Early Reformation in Europe*, ed. A. Pettegree. Cambridge, 1992, 142–65.

Edwards, A.S.G. and C.M. Meale. "The Marketing of Printed Books in Late Medieval England." *The Library*, 6th series, 15 (1993): 95–124.

Edwards, M.U. *Printing, Propaganda, and Martin Luther*. Los Angeles, 1994.

Ehbrecht, W. "Köln—Osnabrück—Stralsund: Rat und Bürgerschaft hansischer Städte zwischen religiöser Erneuerung und Bauernkrieg." in *Kirche und gesellschaftlicher Wandel im deutschen und niederländischen Städten der werdenden Neuzeit*, ed. F. Petri. Cologne, 1980, 23–63.

Ehrenberg, R. *Capital and Finance in the Age of the Renaissance*, trans. H.M. Lucas. London, 1928.

Eisenhardt, U. *Die kaiserliche Aufsicht über Buchdruck, Buchhandel und Presse im Heiligen Römischen Reich Deutscher Nation (1496–1806)*. Karlsruhe, 1970.

Eisenstein, E. *The Printing Press as an Agent of Change: Communications and Cultural Transformations in Early Modern Europe*. 2 vols. Cambridge, MA, 1979.

Erdmann, A. *My Gracious Silence: Women in the Mirror of 16th Century Printing in Western Europe*. Luzern, 1999.

Erler, M. "Wynken de Worde's Will: Legatees and Bequests." *The Library*, 6th series, 10 (1988): 107–21.

Fenske, H., W. Reinhard, E. Schulin, eds. *Historia Integra: Festschrift für Erich Hassinger*. Berlin, 1977.

500 Jahre Buch und Zeitung in Köln: Ausstellung, vor allem aus den Beständen der Universitäts- und Stadtbibliothek, veranstaltet von der Stadt Köln. Cologne, 1965.

Flood, J.L. "The Book in Reformation Germany." in *The Reformation and the Book*, ed. J.-F. Gilmont and K. Maag. Aldershot, 1998, 20–103.

Fox, P. *The Reformation in Poland*. Baltimore, 1924.

Franssen, P.J.A. "Jan van Doesborch (?–1536), printer of English texts." *Quærendo* 16 (1986): 259–80.

Franzen, A. *Bischof und Reformation: Erzbischof Hermann von Wied in Köln vor der Entscheidung zwischen Reform und Reformation*. Münster, 1971.

Freytag, H. "Zur Lebensgeschichte des Hans Nimptsch: Danziger Stadtschreibers und späteren Kammerrates des Herzog Albrecht." *Altpreußische Monatsschrift* 35 (1898): 456–62.

Friedland, K. "Hamburger Englandfahrer 1512–1557." *Zeitschrift des Vereins für Hamburgische Geschichte* 46 (1960): 1–42.

Fuchs, P., ed. *Chronik zur Geschichte der Stadt Köln*. 2 vols. Cologne, 1991.

Fudge, J.D. *Cargoes, Embargoes, and Emissaries: The Commercial and Political Interaction of England and the German Hanse, 1450–1510*, Toronto, 1995.

"Home Ports and Destinations: English Shipping in the Baltic Trade, 1536–1547." *The Northern Mariner* 9 (1999): 13–24.

"Maintaining a presence: Baltic enterprise and the merchants of Lynn during the reign of Henry VIII." in *Britain and the Baltic: Studies in Commercial, Political and Cultural Relations 1500–2000*, ed. P. Salmon and T. Barrow. Sunderland, 2003, 3–19.

Fühner, J.A. *Die Kirchen-und die antireformatorische Religionspolitik Kaiser Karls V. in den siebzehn Provinzen der Niederlande 1515–1555*. Leiden, 2004.

Ganz, P. *Hans Holbein: Die Gemälde*. Basel, 1950.

Geß, F. "Versuchter Nachdruck des Lutherischen Deutschen Neuen Testamentes durch Jacob Thanner in Leipzig. 1524." *Archiv für Geschichte des Deutschen Buchhandels* 12 (1889): 302–3.

"Spuren der Censur in Sachsen um das Jahr 1500." *Archiv für Geschichte des Deutschen Buchhandels* 13 (1890): 245–46.

"Preßpolizei auf der Leipziger Messe 1531." *Archiv für Geschichte des Deutschen Buchhandels* 13 (1890): 250.

Giesecke, M. *Der Buchdruck in der frühen Neuzeit: Eine historische Fallstudie über die Durchsetzung neuer Informations- und Kommunikationstechnologien*. Frankfurt, 1991.

Giesen, J. "Ein Brief des Kölner Ratsherrn Hermann Rinck an Kardinal Wolsey." *Jahrbuch des Kölnischen Geschichtsvereins* 19 (1937): 370–76.

Gilmont, J.-F. and K. Maag, eds. *The Reformation and the Book*. Aldershot, 1998.

Göbell, W. "Das Vordringen der Reformation in Dänemark und in der Herzogtümern unter der Regierung Friedrichs I. 1523–33." in *Schleswig-Holsteinische Kirchengeschichte*. vol. 3. ed. W. Göbell. Neumünster, 1982, 35–86.

Göbell, W., ed. *Schleswig-Holsteinische Kirchengeschichte*. vol. 3. Neumünster, 1982.

Götze, A. *Die Hochdeutschen Drucker der Reformationszeit*. Strassburg, 1905. (Berlin, 1963)

Goris, J.A. *Étude sur les colonies marchandes méridionales à Anvers de 1488 à 1567*. New York, 1925. (1971)

Grane, L. and K. Hørby, eds. *Die dänische Reformation vor ihrem internationalen Hintergrund*. Göttingen, 1990.

Greenberg, C. "John Shirley and the English Book Trade." *The Library*, 6th series, 4 (1982): 369–80.

Greengrass, M. *The French Reformation*. Oxford, 1989.

The European Reformation. London, 1998.

Gregory, B.S. *Salvation at Stake: Christian Martyrdom in Early Modern Europe*. Cambridge, MA, 1999.

Grell, O.P. "The Emergence of Two Cities: The Reformation in Malmø and Copenhagen." in *Die dänische Reformation vor ihrem internationalen Hintergrund*, ed. L. Grane and K. Hørby. Göttingen, 1990, 129–45.

"Scandinavia." in *The Early Reformation in Europe*, ed. A. Pettegree. Cambridge, 1992, 94–119.

Grell, O.P., ed. *The Scandinavian Reformation*. Cambridge, 1995.

Grell, O.P. and B. Scribner, eds. *Tolerance and Intolerance in the European Reformation*. Cambridge, 1996.

Gundermann, I. "Die evangelischen Kirchen im Herzogtum Preußen." in *Handbook der Geschichte Ost- und Westpreußens: Teil 2/1*, ed. E. Opgenoorth. Lüneburg, 1994, 155–60.

"Humanismus und Bildungen beim evangelischen Bevölkerungsteil." in *Handbook der Geschichte Ost- und Westpreußens: Teil 2/1*, ed. E. Opgenoorth. Lüneburg, 1994, 175–82.

Gwyn, P. *The King's Cardinal: The Rise and Fall of Thomas Wolsey*. London, 1990.

Haas, S.W. "Simon Fish, William Tyndale, and Sir Thomas More's 'Lutheran Conspiracy'." *Journal of Ecclesiastical History* 23 (1972): 125–36.

Haigh, C. *English Reformations*, Oxford, 1993.

Hari, R. "Les placards de 1534." in *Aspects de la propagande religieuse*, ed. G. Berthoud et al. Geneva, 1957, 79–142.

Harpsfield, N. *The Life and Death of Sir Thomas Moore*, ed. E.V. Hitchcock and R.W. Chambers. Early English Text Society, original series, 186. London, 1932.

Harreld, D.J. "German Merchants and their Trade in Sixteenth-Century Antwerp." in *International Trade in the Low Countries (14th–16th Centuries)*, ed. P. Stabel, B. Blondé and A. Greve. Louvain/Apeldoorn, 2000, 169–91.

Hase, O. "Studenten-Credit im alten Buchhandel." *Archiv für Geschichte des Deutschen Buchhandels* 10 (1886): 230–31.

Hauschildt, W.-D. "Die Reformation in Hamburg, Lübeck und Eutin." in *Schleswig-Holsteinische Kirchengeschichte.* vol. 3. ed. W. Göbell. Neumünster, 1982, 185–226.

Headley, J.M. "Thomas More and Luther's Revolt." *Archiv für Reformationsgeschichte* 60 (1969): 145–59.

Heerma van Voss, L. "North Sea Culture, 1500–1800." in *The North Sea and Culture (1550–1800)*, ed. J. Roding and L. Heerma van Voss. Hilversum, 1996, 21–40.

Hellinga, L. "Importation of Books Printed on the Continent into England and Scotland before c. 1520." in *Printing the Written Word*, ed. S.L. Hindman. Ithaca, 1991, 205–24.

Hellinga, L. and J.B. Trapp, eds. *The Cambridge History of the Book in England.* vol. 3. Cambridge, 1999.

Higgs, L.M. *Godliness and Governance in Tudor Colchester.* Ann Arbor, 1998.

Higman, F.M. *Censorship and the Sorbonne.* Geneva, 1979.

   Piety and the People: Religious printing in France 1511–1551. Aldershot, 1996.

   "French-speaking regions, 1520–62." in *The Reformation and the Book*, ed. J.-F. Gilmont and K. Maag. Aldershot, 1998, 104–53.

   Lire et Découvrir: La circulation des idées au temps de la Réforme. Geneva, 1998.

Hillerbrand, H.J. "Andreas Bodenstein of Carlstadt, Prodigal Reformer." *Church History* 35 (1966): 379–98.

Hindman, S.L., ed. *Printing the Written Word.* Ithaca, 1991.

Hirsch, R. *Printing, Selling and Reading 1450–1550.* Wiesbaden, 1967.

   "Bulla super impressione librorum, 1515." *Gutenberg-Jahrbuch* (1973): 248–51.

Horst, I.B. *The Radical Brethren: Anabaptism and the English Reformation to 1558.* Nieuwkoop, 1972.

Hume, A. "William Roye's *Brefe Dialoge* (1527): An English Version of a Strassburg Catechism." *Harvard Theological Review* 60 (1967): 307–21.

Hutter, U., ed. *Martin Luther und die Reformation in Ostdeutschland und Südosteuropa.* Sigmaringen, 1991.

Imhof, D., G. Tournoy and F. de Nave, eds. *Antwerp, Dissident Typographical Centre: The Role of Antwerp Printers in the Religious Conflicts in England (16th Century).* Antwerp, 1994.

Jannasch, W. *Reformationsgeschichte Lübecks.* Lübeck, 1958.

Jeannin, P. *Merchants of the Sixteenth Century*, trans. P. Fittinghoff. New York, 1972.

   "The Sea-borne and the Overland Trade Routes of Northern Europe in the XVI and XVII Centuries." *Journal of European Economic History* 11 (1982): 5–59.

Johannesson, K. *The Renaissance of the Goths in Sixteenth-Century Sweden*, trans. J. Larson. Berkeley, 1991.

Johansen, P. "Gedruckte deutsche und undeutsche Messen für Riga." *Zeitschrift für Ostforschung* 8 (1959): 523–32.

Johansen, P. and H. von zur Mühlen. *Deutsch und Undeutsch im mittelalterlichen und frühneuzeitlichen Reval.* Cologne, 1973.

Johnston, A.G. "Printing and the Reformation in the Low Countries." in *The Reformation and the Book*, ed. J.-F. Gilmont and K. Maag. Aldershot, 1998, 154–83.

Johnston, A.G. and J.-F. Gilmont. "Printing and the Reformation in Antwerp." in *The Reformation and the Book*, ed. J.-F. Gilmont and K. Maag. Aldershot, 1998, 188–213.

Jørgensen, N. "Zu welchem Zweck haben die dänischen Reformatoren das

Druckmedium benutzt?" in *Die dänische Reformation vor ihrem internationalen Hintergrund*, ed. L. Grane and K. Hørby. Göttingen, 1990, 223–37.

Jörn, N. *"With money and bloode": Der Londoner Stalhof im Spannungsfeld der englisch—hansischen Beziehungen im 15. und 16. Jahrhundert*. Cologne, 2000.

Karp, H.-J. and A. Triller. "Die Katholische Kirche." in *Handbuch der Geschichte Ost- und Westpreußens: Teil 2/1*, ed. E. Opgenoorth. Lüneburg, 1994, 145–54.

——— "Humanismus und Bildung beim katholischen Bevölkerungsteil," in *Handbuch der Geschichte Ost- und Westpreußens: Teil 2/1*, ed. E. Opgenoorth. Lüneburg, 1994, 175–82.

Kawecka-Gryczowa, A. and J. Tazbir. "The Book and the Reformation in Poland." in *The Reformation and the Book*, ed. J.-F. Gilmont and K. Maag. Aldershot, 1998, 410–31.

Kayser, W. "Hamburger Buchdruck im 16. Jahrhundert: Ergänzungen zu einer Bibliographie." *Zeitschrift des Vereins für Hamburgische Geschichte* 72 (1986): 1–23.

Kick, R. "The Book and the Reformation in the Kingdom of Sweden, 1526–71." in *The Reformation and the Book*, ed. J.-F. Gilmont and K. Maag. Aldershot, 1998, 449–68.

King, J.N. *English Reformation Literature: The Tudor Origins of the Protestant Tradition*. Princeton, 1982.

Kint, A. "The Ideology of Commerce: Antwerp in the Sixteenth Century." in *International Trade In the Low Countries (14th–16th Centuries)*, ed. P. Stabel, B. Blondé and A. Greve. Louvain/Apeldoorn, 2000, 213–22.

Kirchhoff, A. "Franz Birckmann, Buchhändler in Cöln und Antwerpen 1510–1530, und seine Familie." in *Beiträge zur Geschichte des deutschen Buchhandels*. Leipzig, 1851, 88–131. (Osnabrück, 1966)

——— "Kurze Notizen über die Buchführer der ersten Hälfte des XVI. Jahrhunderts." in *Beiträge zur Geschichte des deutschen Buchhandels*. Leipzig, 1851, 132–52. (Osnabrück, 1966)

——— "Johann Herrgott, Buchführer von Nürnberg, und sein tragisches Ende 1527." *Archiv für Geschichte des Deutschen Buchhandels* 1 (1878): 15–55.

——— "Weitere Notizen über Johann Herrgott in Nürnberg." *Archiv für Geschichte des Deutschen Buchhandels* 6 (1881): 252–55.

——— "Buchhändlerische Geschäftspapiere aus den Jahren 1523 bis 1530." *Archiv für Geschichte des Deutschen Buchhandels* 8 (1883): 286–95.

——— "Ein etwas räthselhaftes Document." *Archiv für Geschichte des Deutschen Buchhandels* 10 (1886): 9–26.

Knappert, L. *De Opkomst van het Protestantisme in eene Noord-Nederlandsche Stad: Geschiedenis van de Hervorming binnen Leiden*. Leiden, 1908.

Knecht, R.J. *French Renaissance Monarchy: Francis I and Henry II*. London, 1994.

Koenigsberger, H.G. "The Empire of Charles V in Europe." in *The New Cambridge Modern History*. vol. 2. ed. G.R. Elton. Cambridge, 1958, 301–33.

——— *Monarchies, States Generals and Parliaments: The Netherlands in the Fifteenth and Sixteenth Centuries*. Cambridge, 2001.

Köhler, H.-J., ed. *Flugschriften als Massenmedium der Reformationszeit*. Stuttgart, 1981.

Körber, E.-B. *Öffentlichkeiten der frühen Neuzeit: Teilnehmer, Formen, Institutionen und Entscheidungen öffentlicher Kommunikation im Herzogtum Preußen von 1525 bis 1618*. Berlin, 1998.

Kouri, E.I. "The early Reformation in Sweden and Finland c. 1520–1560." in *The Scandinavian Reformation*, ed. O.P. Grell. Cambridge, 1995, 42–69.

Kouri, E.I. and T. Scott, eds. *Politics and Society in Reformation Europe*. London, 1987.

Kronenberg, M.E. "Notes on English printing in the Low Countries (Early Sixteenth Century)." *Transactions of the Bibliographical Society* 9 (1928): 139–63.

——— "A Printed Letter of the London Hanse Merchants (3 March 1526)." *Oxford Bibliographical Society Publications*, new series, 1 (1947): 25–32.

"Forged Addresses in Low Country Books in the Period of the Reformation." *The Library*, 5th series, 2 (1947): 81–94.

Verboden Boeken en Opstandige Drukkers in de Hervormingstijd. Amsterdam, 1948.

Laantee, K. "The Beginning of the Reformation in Estonia." *Church History* 22 (1953): 269–78.

Latré, G. "The 1535 Coverdale Bible and Its Antwerp Origins." in *The Bible as Book: The Reformation*, ed. O. O'Sullivan. London, 2000, 89–102.

Leroux, N.R. "*In the Christian City of Wittenberg*: Karlstadt's Tract on Images and Begging." *Sixteenth Century Journal* 34 (2003): 73–106.

Lindberg, C. "Karlstadt's *Dialogue* on the Lord's Supper." *Mennonite Quarterly Review* 53 (1979): 35–77.

Lloyd, T.H. *England and the German Hanse, 1157–1611*. Cambridge, 1991.

Loades, D. *Politics, Censorship and the English Reformation*. London, 1991.

"Books and the English Reformation prior to 1558." in *The Reformation and the Book*, ed. J.-F. Gilmont and K. Maag. Aldershot, 1998, 264–91.

Lohmeyer, K. "Geschichte des Buchdrucks und des Buchhandels im Herzogthum Preußen." *Archiv für Geschichte des Deutschen Buchhandels* 18 (1896): 29–140.

Lohse, B. "Humanismus und Reformation in norddeutschen Städten in den 20er und frühen 30er Jahren des 16. Jahrhunderts." in *Die dänische Reformation vor ihrem internationalen Hintergrund*, ed. L. Grane and K. Hørby. Göttingen, 1990, 11–27.

Looz-Corswarem, C. von. "Die Kölner Artikelserie von 1525: Hintergründe und Verlauf des Aufruhrs von 1525 in Köln." in *Kirche und gesellschaftlicher Wandel im deutschen und Niederländischen Städten der werdenden Neuzeit*, ed. F. Petri. Cologne, 1980, 23–63.

Lutton, R. "Connections between Lollards, Townsfolk and Gentry in Tenterden in the Late Fifteenth and Early Sixteenth Centuries." in *Lollardy and Gentry in the later Middle Ages*. ed. M. Aston and C. Richmond. New York, 1997, 199–228.

Lusardi, J.P. "The Career of Robert Barnes." *The Complete Works of St. Thomas More*. vol. 8. ed. L.A. Schuster et al. New Haven, 1973, 1367–1415.

MacCulloch, D. "England." in *The Early Reformation in Europe*, ed. A. Pettegree. Cambridge, 1992, 166–87.

Manley, F. "Circumstances of Composition: Bugenhagen's 'Letter to the English'." in *The Complete Works of St. Thomas More*. vol. 7. ed. F. Manley et al. New Haven, 1990, xvii–xxxvi.

Marc'hadour, G.P. "The Historical Context." in *The Complete Works of St. Thomas More*. vol. 6. ed. T.M.C. Lawler et al. New Haven, 1981, 455–72.

Marius, R.C. "Sources: The Contemporary Scene." in *The Complete Works of St. Thomas More*. vol. 6. ed. T.M.C. Lawler et al. New Haven, 1981, 525–48.

Thomas More. New York, 1984.

Marnef, G. *Antwerp in the Age of Reformation*, trans. J.C. Grayson. Baltimore, 1996.

"Rederijkers en religieuze vernieuwing te Antwerpen in de tweede helfte van de zestiende eeuw." in *Conformisten en Rebellen: Rederijkerscultuur in de Nederlanden (1400–1650)*, ed. B. Ramakers. Amsterdam, 2003, 175–88.

Marshall, P. and A. Ryrie, eds. *The Beginnings of English Protestantism*. Cambridge, 2002.

Martin, J.W. *Religious Radicals in Tudor England*. London, 1989.

McGoldrick, J.E. *Luther's Scottish Connection*. London, 1989.

"Patrick Hamilton, Luther's Scottish Disciple." *Sixteenth Century Journal* 17 (1987): 81–88.

Meyer, C.S. "Henry VIII Burns Luther's Books, 12 May 1521." *Journal of Ecclesiastical History* 9 (1958): 173–87.

"Thomas More and the Wittenberg Lutherans." *Concordia Theological Monthly* 39 (1968): 246–56.

Meyer, F.H. "Papierfabrikation und Papierhandel: Beiträge zu ihrer Geschichte, besonders in Sachsen." *Archiv für Geschichte des Deutschen Buchhandels* 11 (1888): 283–357.

Moeller, B. "Luther in Europe: His Works in Translation." in *Politics and Society in Reformation Europe*, ed. E.I. Kouri and T. Scott. London, 1987, 235–51.

Moger, J.T. "Pamphlets, Preaching and Politics: The Image Controversy in Reformation Wittenberg, Zürich and Strassburg." *Mennonite Quarterly Review* 75 (2001): 325–54.

Monter, W. "Heresy executions in Reformation Europe, 1520–65." in *Tolerance and Intolerance in the European Reformation*, ed. O.P. Grell and B. Scribner. Cambridge, 1996, 48–64.

Moran, J. *Wynkyn de Worde: Father of Fleet Street*, rev. L. Hellinga and M. Erler. London, 2003.

Mozley, J.F. *William Tyndale*. New York, 1937.

Müller, M.G. *Zweite Reformation und städtische Autonomie im Königlichen Preußen: Danzig, Elbing und Thorn in der Epoch der Konfessionalisierung (1557–1660)*. Berlin, 1997.

Musteikis, A. *The Reformation in Lithuania*. New York, 1988.

Needham, P. "The customs rolls as documents for the printed-book trade in England." in *The Cambridge History of the book in England*. vol. 3. ed. L. Hellinga and J.B. Trapp. Cambridge, 1999, 148–62.

Nicholls, D. "France." in *The Early Reformation in Europe*, ed. A. Pettegree. Cambridge, 1992, 120–41.

Opgenoorth, E., ed. *Handbuch der Geschichte Ost- und Westpreußens: Teil 2/1 Von der Teilung bis zum Schwedisch-Polnischen Krieg 1466–1655*. Lüneburg, 1994.

Orme, N. "Martin Coeffin, the First Exeter Publisher." *The Library*, 6th series, 10 (1988): 220–30.

O'Sullivan, O., ed. *The Bible as Book: The Reformation*. London, 2000.

Packull, W.O. "Sylvester Tegetmeier, father of the Livonian Reformation: A Fragment of his Diary." *Journal of Baltic Studies* 16 (1985): 343–356.

Pallmann, H. "Das Erzbischofs Berthold von Mainz ältestes Censuredict." *Archiv für Geschichte des Deutschen Buchhandels* 9 (1884): 238–41.

Pater, C.A. *Karlstadt as the Father of the Baptist Movements: The Emergence of Lay Protestantism*. Toronto, 1984.

Pauli, R. "Die Stahlhofskaufleute und Luthers Schriften." *Hansische Geschichtsblätter* (1871): 155–62.

——. "Das Verfahren wider die Stahlhofskaufleute wegen der Lutherbücher." *Hansische Geschichtsblätter* (1878): 159–72.

Pengerots, V. "Geschichte des Buchdrucks in Lettland bis zum Beginn des 19. Jahrhunderts." *Gutenberg-Jahrbuch* (1935): 213–22.

Petri, F. *Kirche und gesellschaftlicher Wandel in deutschen und niederländischen Städten der werdenden Neuzeit*. Cologne, 1980.

Pettegree, A. *Foreign Protestant Communities in Sixteenth-century London*. Oxford, 1986.

——. "Printing and the Reformation: the English exception." in *The Beginnings of English Protestantism*, ed. P. Marshall and A. Ryrie. Cambridge, 2002, 157–79.

Pettegree, A., ed. *The Early Reformation in Europe*. Cambridge, 1992.

Plaß, H.-P. "Bernd Beseke—Ein Radikaler der Reformationszeit?" *Zeitschrift für Hamburgische Geschichte* 67 (1981): 1–46.

Plomer, H.R. *Abstracts from the Wills of English Printers and Stationers from 1492 to 1630*. London, 1903.

——. "The Importation of Books into England in the Fifteenth and Sixteenth Centuries." *The Library*, 4th series, 4 (1923–4): 146–50.

Plumb, D. "The social and economic status of the later Lollards." in *The World of Rural Dissenters, 1520–1725*, ed. M. Spufford. Cambridge, 1995, 103–31.

——. "A gathered church? Lollards and their Society." in *The World of Rural Dissenters, 1520–1725*, ed. M. Spufford. Cambridge, 1995, 132–63.

Pollard, A.W. "Regulations of the Book Trade in the 16th Century." *The Library*, 3rd series, 7 (1916): 18–43.

Pollard, G. "The Company of Stationers before 1557." *The Library*, 4th series, 18 (1937): 1–38.

"The English Market for Printed Books." *Publishing History* 4 (1978): 7–48.

Porter, H.C. *Reformation and Reaction in Tudor Cambridge.* Cambridge, 1958.

Porter, R. et al., eds. *The Reformation in National Context.* Cambridge, 1994.

Postel, R. *Die Reformation in Hamburg 1517–1528.* Gütersloh, 1986.

———. "Obrigkeitsdenken und Reformation in Hamburg." *Archiv für Reformationsgeschichte* 70 (1979): 169–201.

———. "Reformation und bürgerliche Mitsprache in Hamburg." *Zeitschrift des Vereins für Hamburgische Geschichte* 65 (1979): 1–20.

Poulsen, B. "Wagons and Ships." in *Maritime Topography and the Medieval Town.* Studies in Archaeology and History 4. Copenhagen, 1999, 203–12.

Quednau, H. "Johannes Lohmüller, Stadtsydicus von Riga, ein Träger deutscher Reformation in Nordosteuropa: Mit eine Auswahl aus seinen Schriften." *Archiv für Reformationsgeschichte* 36 (1939): 51–67 and 253–69.

Ramakers, B., ed. *Conformisten en Rebellen: Rederijkerscultuur in de Nederlanden (1400–1650).* Amsterdam, 2003.

Ramsay, G.D. *The City of London in international politics at the accession of Elizabeth Tudor.* Manchester, 1975.

Reed, A.W. "The Regulation of the Book Trade before the Proclamation of 1538." *Transactions of the Bibliographical Society* 15 (1920): 157–84.

Reincke, H. *Hamburg am Vorabend der Reformation.* Hamburg, 1966.

Rex, R. "The English Campaign against Luther in the 1520s." *Transactions of the Royal Historical Society,* 5th series, 39 (1989): 85–106.

Richardson, W.C. *Stephen Vaughan: Financial Agent of Henry VIII.* Baton Rouge, 1953.

Riising, A. "The book and the Reformation in Denmark and Norway, 1523–40." in *The Reformation and the Book,* ed. J.-F. Gilmont and K. Maag. Aldershot, 1998, 432–48.

Ritscher, A. *Reval an der Schwelle der Neuzeit: Teil 1 1510–1535.* Bonn, 1998.

Ritter, F. *Histoire de l'imprimerie Alsacienne aux XVe et XVIe siècles.* Strasbourg, 1955.

———. "Elsässische Buchdrucker im Dienste der Strassburger Sektenbewegungen zur Zeit der Reformation." *Gutenberg-Jahrbuch* (1962): 225–33.

Roberts, S.C. *A History of the Cambridge University Press.* Cambridge, 1921.

Robinson-Hammerstein, H., ed. *The Transmission of Ideas in the Lutheran Reformation.* Dublin, 1989.

Roding, J. and L. Heerma van Voss, eds. *The North Sea and Culture (1550–1800).* Hilversum, 1996.

Rosenfeld, P. *The Provincial Governors from the Minority of Charles V to the Revolt.* Anciens Pays et Assemblées d'États 17. Louvain, 1959.

Rouzet, A. *Dictionnaire des imprimeurs, libraires et éditeurs des XVe et XVIe siècles dans les limites géographiques de la Belgique actuelle.* Nieuwkoop, 1975.

Rupp, G. *Patterns of Reformation.* London, 1969.

Scattergood, J. "Simon Fish's *Supplication for Beggars* and Protestant Polemics." in *Antwerp, Dissident Typographical Centre: The Role of Antwerp Printers in the Religious Conflicts in England (16th Century),* ed. D. Imhof, G. Tournoy and F. de Nave. Antwerp, 1994, 67–73.

Schanz, G. *Englische Handelspolitik gegen Ende des Mittelalters.* 2 vols. Leipzig, 1881.

Scheib, O. *Die Reformationsdiskussionen in der Hansestadt Hamburg 1522–1528.* Münster, 1976.

Schildhauer, J. *Soziale, politische und religiöse Auseinandersetzungen in den Hansestädten Stralsund, Rostock und Wismar im ersten Drittel des 16. Jahrhunderts.* Weimar, 1959.

Schmidt, C. *Auf Felsen gesät: Die Reformation in Polen und Livland.* Göttingen, 2000.

Schmitz, W. "Der Kölner Buchdruck vom 15. bis zum 18. Jahrhundert" and "Daten Buchdruck." in *Chronik zur Geschichte der Stadt Köln.* vol 2. ed. P. Fuchs. Cologne, 1991, 32–39.

Schnurmann, C. *Kommerz und Klüngel: Der Englandhandel Kölner Kaufleute im 16. Jahrhundert.* Göttingen/Zürich, 1991.

Schottenloher, K. *Philipp Ulhart: Ein Augsburger Winkeldrucker und Helfershelfer der 'Schwärmer' und "Widertäufer' (1523–1529).* Historische Forschungen und Quellen 4. Munich, 1921. (Nieuwkoop, 1967)

"Widmungsvorreden deutscher Drucker und Verleger des 16. Jahrhunderts." *Gutenberg-Jahrbuch* (1942/43): 141–76.

Schramm, G. "Danzig, Elbing und Thorn als Beispiele städtische Reformation (1517–1558)." *Historia Integra: Festschrift für Erich Hassinger*, ed. H. Fenske, W. Reinhard, E. Schulin. Berlin, 1977, 125–54.

Schuster, L.A. "Thomas More's Polemical Career, 1523–1533." *The Complete Works of St. Thomas More.* vol. 8. ed. L.A. Schuster et al. New Haven, 1973, 1135–1268.

Schwarz Lausten, M. "The early Reformation in Denmark and Norway 1520–1559." in *The Scandinavian Reformation*, ed. O.P. Grell. Cambridge, 1995, 12–41.

Schwenke, P. "Hans Weinreich und die Anfänge des Buchdrucks in Königsberg." *Altpreußische Monatsschrift* 33 (1896): 67–109.

Scribner, R.W. "Reformation Carnival and the World turned Upside-down." in *Städtische Gesellschaft und Reformation*, ed. I. Bátori. Stuttgart, 1980, 234–64.

For the Sake of the Simple Folk: Popular Propaganda for the German Reformation. Cambridge, 1981.

Popular Culture and Popular Movements in Reformation Germany. London, 1987.

"Oral Culture and the Transmission of Reformation Ideas." in *The Transmission of Ideas in the Lutheran Reformation*, ed. H. Robinson-Hammerstein. Dublin, 1989, 83–104.

Segel, H.B. *Renaissance Culture in Poland.* Ithaca, 1989.

Sessions, W.K. *A Printer's Dozen: The First British Printing Centres to 1557.* York, 1983

Simson, P. *Der Artushof in Danzig und seine Brüderschaften, die Banken.* Danzig, 1900.

Geschichte der Stadt Danzig bis 1626. 3 vols. Danzig, 1918–24. (Aalen, 1967)

Spahn, M. *Johannes Cochläus: Ein Lebensbild aus der Zeit der Kirchenspaltung.* Berlin, 1898. (Nieuwkoop, 1964)

Spliet, H. "Die schwarzen Häupter in ihrem Verhältnis zur deutschen kolonialen Ständegeschichte in Livland." *Zeitschrift für Ostforschung* 3 (1954): 233–27.

Spufford, M. "Literacy, trade and religion in the commercial centres of Europe." in *A Miracle Mirrored: The Dutch Republic in European Perspective*, ed. K. Davids and J. Lucassen. Cambridge, 1995, 229–83.

"The Importance of religion in the sixteenth and seventeenth centuries." in *The World of Rural Dissenters, 1520–1725*, ed. M. Spufford. Cambridge, 1995, 1–102.

Spufford, M., ed. *The World of Rural Dissenters, 1520–1725.* Cambridge, 1995.

Stabel, P., B. Blondé and A. Greve, eds. *International Trade in the Low Countries (14th–16th Centuries).* Louvain/Apeldoorn, 2000.

Steele, R. "Hans Luft of Marburg: A Contribution to the study of William Tyndale." *The Library*, 3rd series, 2 (1911): 113–31.

Stieda, W. "Studien zur Geschichte des Buchdrucks und Buchhandels in Mecklenburg." *Archiv für Geschichte des Deutschen Buchhandels* 17 (1894): 119–326.

Strauss, G. *Nuremberg in the Sixteenth Century.* New York, 1966.

Sturge, C. *Cuthbert Tunstal.* London, 1938.

Subrahmanyam, S., ed. *Merchant Networks in the Early Modern World.* Aldershot, 1996.

Surtz, E. *The Works and Days of John Fisher.* Cambridge, MA, 1967.

Swierk, A. "Hieronymous Vietor (Wietor): Ein Pioneer des polnischen Buchdrucks im 16. Jahrhundert." *Gutenberg-Jahrbuch* (1976): 194–99.

Tazbir, J. "Poland." in *The Reformation in National Context*, ed. R. Porter et al. Cambridge, 1994, 168–80.

Tanner, N.P. *The Church in Late Medieval Norwich, 1370–1532.* Toronto, 1984.

"Penances imposed on Kentish Lollards by Archbishop Warham 1511–12." in *Lollardy and Gentry in the later Middle Ages*, ed. M. Aston and C. Richmond. New York, 1997, 229–49.

Thompson, J.W., ed. *The Frankfort Book Fair*. Chicago, 1911.

Tilley, A. "A Paris Bookseller of the Sixteenth Century—Galliot Du Pré." *The Library*, 2nd series, 9 (1908): 36–65 and 143–72.

Tjernagel, N.S. *Henry VIII and the Lutherans*. St. Louis, 1965.

Tournoy, G. "Humanists, Rulers and Reformers: Relationships between England and the Southern Low Countries in the First Half of the Sixteenth Century." in *Antwerp, Dissident Typographical Centre: The Role of Antwerp Printers in the Religious Conflicts in England (16th Century)*, ed. D. Imhof, G. Tournoy and F. de Nave. Antwerp, 1994, 21–29.

Tracy, J.D. "Heresy Law and Centralization under Mary of Hungary: Conflict between the Council of Holland and the Central Government over the Enforcement of Charles V's Placards." *Archiv für Reformationsgeschichte* 73 (1982): 284–308.
———. *Holland under Habsburg Rule, 1506–1566: The Formation of a Body Politic*. Los Angeles, 1990.

Treptow, O. *John Siberch*, trans. T. Jones. Cambridge, 1970.

Trevor, D. "Thomas More's *Responsio ad Lutherum* and the Fictions of Humanist Polemic." *Sixteenth Century Journal* 32 (2001): 743–64.

Tricard, A. "La propagande évangélique en France: L'imprimeur Simon Du Bois (1525–1534)." in *Aspects de la propagande religieuse*, ed. G. Berthoud et al. Geneva, 1957, 1–37.

Troßbach, W. "Unterschiede und Gemeinsamkeiten bei der Durchsetzung der Reformation in den Hansestädten Wismar, Rostock und Stralsund." *Archiv für Reformationsgeschichte* 88 (1997): 119–65.

Trueman, C.R. *Luther's Legacy: Salvation and English Reformers, 1525–1556*. Oxford, 1994.

Valkema Blouw, P. "Predated Protestant works in Nijhoff-Kronenberg." *Quærendo* 24 (1994): 163–80.
———. "Early Protestant publications in Antwerp, 1526–30: The pseudonyms Adam Anonymus in Bazel and Hans Luft in Marlborow." *Quærendo* 26 (1996): 94–110.

Van Bruaene, A.-L. "Sociabiliteit en competitie: De sociaal-institutionele ontwikkeling van de rederijkerskamers in de Zuidelijke Nederlanden (1400–1650)." in *Conformisten en Rebellen: Rederijkerscultuur in de Nederlanden (1400–1650)*, ed. B. Ramakers. Amsterdam, 2003, 45–63.

Van Dixhoorn, A. "Burgers, branies en bollebozen: De sociaal-institutionele ontwikkeling van de rederijkerskamers in de Noordelijke Nederlanden (1470–1650)." in *Conformisten en Rebellen: Rederijkerscultuur in de Nederlanden (1400–1650)*, ed. B. Ramakers. Amsterdam, 2003, 65–85.

Van der Wee, H. *The Growth of the Antwerp Market and the European Economy*. 3 vols. The Hague, 1963.

Vogel, P.H. "Erstdrucke ausländischer Bibeln von deutschen Druckern des 15. und 16. Jahrhunderts." *Gutenberg-Jahrbuch* (1959): 93–98.

Waite, G. *David Joris and Dutch Anabaptism, 1524–1543*. Waterloo, ON, 1990.
———. *Reformers on Stage: Popular Drama and Religious Propaganda in the Low Countries of Charles V, 1515–1556*. Toronto, 2000.
———. "On the stage and in the streets: Rhetorician drama, social conflict and religious upheaval in Amsterdam (1520–1566)." in *Conformisten en Rebellen: Rederijkerscultuur in de Nederlanden (1400–1650)*, ed. B. Ramakers. Amsterdam, 2003, 163–73.

Ward, J.P. "Religious Diversity and Guild Unity in Early Modern London." in *Religion and the English People 1500–1640*, ed. E.J. Carlson. Kirksville, MO, 1998, 77–97.

Wehrmann, C. "Die Gründung des hanseatischen Hauses zu Antwerpen." *Hansische Geschichtsblätter* (1873): 77–106.

Williams, G.H. *The Radical Reformation*. 3rd ed. Kirksville, MO, 1992.

Winger, H.W. "Regulations relating to the Book Trade in London from 1357 to 1586." *Library Quarterly* 26 (1956): 157–95.

Wunderli, R.M. "Pre-Reformation London Summoners and the Murder of Richard Hunne." *Journal of Ecclesiastical History* 33 (1982): 209–24.

Zorzin, A. "Einige Beobachtungen zu den zwischen 1518 und 1526 im deutschen Sprachbereich veröffentlichten Dialogflugschriften." *Archiv für Reformationsgeschichte* 88 (1997): 77–117.

INDEX OF BOOKS AND PAMPHLETS

INDEX OF PERSONS

GENERAL INDEX

THE NORTHERN WORLD

NORTH EUROPE AND THE BALTIC C. 400-1700 AD
PEOPLES, ECONOMIES AND CULTURES

Editors

BARBARA CRAWFORD (St. Andrews)
DAVID KIRBY (London)
JON-VIDAR SIGURDSSON (Oslo)
INGVILD ØYE (Bergen)
RICHARD W. UNGER (Vancouver)

ISSN: 1569-1462

This series provides an opportunity for the publication of scholarly studies concerning the culture, economy and society of northern lands from the early medieval to the early modern period. The aims and scope are broad and scholarly contributions on a wide range of disciplines are included: all historical subjects, every branch of archaeology, saga studies, language topics including place-names, art history and architecture, sculpture and numismatics.

1. Schutz, H. *Tools, Weapons and Ornaments*. Germanic Material Culture in Pre-Carolingian Central Europe, 400-750. 2002. ISBN 90 04 12298 2
2. Biggs, D., S.D. Michalove and A. Compton Reeves (eds.). *Traditions and Transformations in late Medieval England*. 2002. ISBN 90 04 12341 5
3. Tielhof, M. van. *The 'Mother of all Trades'*. The Baltic Grain Trade in Amsterdam from the Late 16th to the Early 19th Century. 2002. ISBN 90 04 12546 9
4. Looijenga, T. *Texts & Contexts of the Oldest Runic Inscriptions*. 2003. ISBN 90 04 12396 2
5. Grosjean, A. *An Unofficial Alliance*. Scotland and Sweden 1569-1654. 2003. ISBN 90 04 13241 4
6. Tanner, H.J. *Families, Friends and Allies*. Boulogne and Politics in Northern France and England, c. 879–1160. 2004. ISBN 90 04 13243 0
7. Finlay, A. *Fagrskinna, A Catalogue of the Kings of Norway*. A Translation with Introduction and Notes. 2004. ISBN 90 04 13172 8
8. Biggs, D.L., S.D. Michalove and A. Compton Reeves (eds.). *Reputation and Representation in Fifteenth-Century Europe*. 2004. ISBN 90 04 13613 4
9. Etting, V. *Queen Margrete I (1353-1412) and the Founding of the Nordic Union*. 2004. ISBN 90 04 13652 5
10. Lockhart, P.D. *Frederik II and the Protestant Cause*. Denmark's Role in the Wars of Religion, 1559-1596. 2004. ISBN 90 04 13790 4
11. Williams, G. and P. Bibire. *Sagas, Saints and Settlements*. 2004. ISBN 90 04 13807 2
12. Duczko, W. *Viking Rus*. Studies on the Presence of Scandinavians in Eastern Europe. 2004. ISBN 90 04 13874 9

13. Kotilaine, J.T. *Russia's Foreign Trade and Economic Expansion in the Seventeenth Century*. Windows on the World. 2005. ISBN 90 04 13896 X
14. Harreld, D.J. *High Germans in the Low Countries*. German Merchants and Commerce in Golden Age Antwerp. 2004. ISBN 90 04 14104 9
15. Blomkvist, N. *The Discovery of the Baltic*. The Reception of a Catholic World-system in the European North (AD 1075-1225). 2005. ISBN 90 04 14122 7
16. Oram, R.D. (ed.). *The Reign of Alexander II, 1214-49*. 2005. ISBN 90 04 14206 1
17. Boulhosa, P.P. *Icelanders and the Kings of Norway*. Medieval Sagas and Legal Texts. 2005. ISBN 90 04 14516 8
18. Murdoch, S. *Network North*. Scottish Kin, Commercial and Covert Associations in Northern Europe, 1603-1746. 2006. ISBN 90 04 14664 4
19. Cook, B. and G. Williams (eds.). *Coinage and History in the North Sea World, c. AD 500-1250*. Essays in Honour of Marion Archibald. 2006. ISBN 90 04 14777 2
20. Cathcart, A. *Kinship and Clientage*. Highland Clanship 1451-1609. 2006. ISBN-13: 978 90 04 15045 4, ISBN-10: 90 04 15045 5
21. Isoaho, M. *The Image of Aleksandr Nevskiy in Medieval Russia*. Warrior and Saint. 2006. ISBN-13: 978 90 04 15101 7, ISBN-10: 90 04 15101 X
22. Te Brake, W. and W. Klooster (eds.). *Power and the City in the Netherlandic World*. 2006. ISBN-13: 978 90 04 15129 1, ISBN-10: 90 04 15129 X
23. Stewart, L.A.M. *Urban Politics and the British Civil Wars*. Edinburgh, 1617-53. 2006. ISBN-13: 978 90 04 15167 3, ISBN-10: 90 04 15167 2
24. Burgess, G.S. and C. Strijbosch (eds.). *The Brendan Legend*. Texts and Versions. 2006. ISBN-13: 978 90 04 15247 2, ISBN-10: 90 04 15247 4
25. Bellamy, M. *Christian IV and his Navy*. A Political and Administrative History of the Danish Navy 1596-1648. 2006. ISBN-13: 978 90 04 15450 6, ISBN-10: 90 04 15450 7
26. Fonnesberg-Schmidt, I. *The Popes and the Baltic Crusades 1147-1254*. 2007. ISBN-13: 978 90 04 15502 2, ISBN-10: 90 04 15502 3
27. Line, P. *Kingship and State Formation in Sweden 1130-1290*. 2006. ISBN-13: 978 90 04 15578 7, ISBN-10: 90 04 15578 3
28. Fudge, J.D. *Commerce and Print in the Early Reformation*. 2007. ISBN 978 90 04 15662 3
29. Antonsson, H. *St. Magnús of Orkney*. A Scandinavian Martyr-Cult in Context. 2007. ISBN 978 90 04 15580 0
30. Jensen, J.M. *Denmark and the Crusades, 1400-1650*. 2007. ISBN 978 90 04 15579 4